Up the Mainstream

The Rise of Toronto's Alternative Theatres, 1968–1975

In the early 1970s a group of theatre companies in Toronto set out to change the way Canadians thought about theatre. They succeeded. Working out of warehouses and church halls, four companies introduced innovations in staging and presided over a flowering of dramatic writing. Before 1968 there had been no such thing as an alternative theatre movement in Canada; by 1972 the alternative theatres had grown to dominate the landscape of Canada's largest theatre market and were on the brink of attaining national influence.

Denis Johnston provides an engaging history of a vital time in Canada's cultural development. After discussing some of the earlier companies that laid the foundation, he concentrates on the four leading companies of the 'Toronto Movement.'

Each theatre developed a distinct personality. Theatre Passe Muraille, founded in 1968 in Toronto's notorious Rochdale College, brought techniques and plays from 'off-off-Broadway' to curious audiences. In 1970 the Factory Theatre Lab was born, leading Toronto alternative theatre in a new direction. Filled with the nationalist spirit of Expo 67, it was determined to produce only Canadian plays. The plays appeared – first in a trickle, then in growing numbers. With Tarragon Theatre and Toronto Free Theatre came a shift to more mainstream audiences, and both made major contributions to Toronto theatre. Meanwhile, Theatre Passe Muraille was moving towards improvisational playwriting, as in its hugely successful *The Farm Show*.

Denis Johnston traces the story of these companies and others to 1975, when their early growth period was complete and they had taken their place in Canadian theatre. Now the wide-eyed radicals of the 1960s have become the establishment of the 1980s, Johnston says, but they are still fired by the enthusiasm and idealism that fuelled their early success.

DENIS W. JOHNSTON teaches theatre history in the Department of Theatre, University of British Columbia.

DENIS W. JOHNSTON

UP THE MAINSTREAM

The Rise of Toronto's Alternative Theatres, 1968–1975

UNIVERSITY OF TORONTO PRESS
Toronto Buffalo London

© University of Toronto Press 1991
Toronto Buffalo London
Printed in Canada
ISBN 0-8020-5834-5 (cloth)
ISBN 0-8020-6741-7 (paper)

Printed on acid-free paper

Canadian Cataloguing in Publication Data

Johnston, Denis William, 1950–
    Up the mainstream : the rise of Toronto's
    alternative theatres, 1968–1975

    Includes bibliographical references.
    ISBN 0-8020-5834-5 (bound) ISBN 0-8020-6741-7 (pbk.)

    1. Experimental theater – Ontario – Toronto.
    I. Title.

PN2306.T6J6 1991   792'.09713'541   C90-093659-2

Cover illustrations Don Steinhouse and Jim McInnes in *In His Own Write* at Trinity Square, January 1970: Lionel Douglas, photographer; Richard Monette in *Hosanna* at the Tarragon Theatre, 1974: Robert Barnett, photographer, courtesy of the Tarragon Archives, University of Guelph

This book has been published with the help of a grant from the Canadian Federation for the Humanities, using funds provided by the Social Sciences and Humanities Research Council of Canada. Publication has also been assisted by the Province of Ontario, through the Ontario Arts Council, and by the Canada Council, through its block grant program.

Contents

Preface

Since the early 1970s, the most successful new plays first produced by
Toronto's alternative theatres have attracted many productions and a
good deal of scholarly analysis. However, the history of the theatres
themselves, the companies which literally brought these plays into
existence, has remained elusive and fragmentary. A new pattern for
Canadian theatre was established at that time; yet even to people who
now work within that pattern, the origins of their own present-day
theatres are largely unknown. The purpose of this book is to document
the personalities which created these theatres, the forces which shaped
them, and the events which brought them to prominence.

Following Don Rubin and Robert Wallace, both former editors of
Canadian Theatre Review, I have concentrated on the four leading
companies of this 'Toronto Movement': Theatre Passe Muraille, the
Factory Theatre Lab, Tarragon Theatre, and Toronto Free Theatre. It
must be remembered, however, in light of the long records of
achievement of these four 'major' alternative theatres, that they had
other important rivals in their early years. I have therefore included a
chapter on three rival companies founded in the late 1960s, another
chapter on three companies founded in the early 1970s, and another on
the NDWT company, whose long gestation and short life serve as a fitting
end to the whole study. While these secondary companies are all gone
now, and largely forgotten, they were significant in their time and
deserve to have their stories told here.

Since this is the first survey history of this vital movement, I felt that
my primary responsibility was to establish a consensus concerning what
actually happened, a foundation of agreed-upon knowledge on which
other scholars and researchers may build. I did this by first constructing

a consensual story from available archives and printed sources, then interviewing key figures – directors, administrators, and some actors – to test my impressions against theirs. Usually the story as I understood it was endorsed by the people whom I interviewed. In many instances, however, my impressions were enriched and enlivened – sometimes even corrected – by the people who had been there. I will not soon forget Bob Swerdlow's description of Hallowe'en at the Global Village, for example, or David Fox's stories about making new plays with Theatre Passe Muraille. On a few questions there was no consensus: Was Rochdale College a success or a failure? Was *Futz* no more than a tempest in a teapot? Is Tarragon really an alternative theatre? Often the heart of a matter lies at just such points of contention. In unresolvable cases such as these I have tried to present the opposing points of view fairly, although this halo of objectivity may have slipped from time to time.

Besides establishing a consensual history, I felt a responsibility to provide other researchers with a starting point for their own projects. For this reason, I have emphasized information which is not easily obtainable outside Toronto – personal interviews, for example – over information which is more widely available. One result of this decision was that I made very little attempt to analyse the plays which brought these companies to such prominence. This is paradoxical at first glance, since it was primarily the impact of their new plays which made the companies important, and which is the lasting legacy of the Toronto Movement. This study is intended as an historical survey, however, not a literary one. Important plays are discussed insofar as their content and style were significant to the movement, or insofar as they affected the stature of their producing companies within the cultural community. I am pleased to leave dramatic criticism to other scholars who do not have available the materials I had, or perhaps even to myself on another day.

The resulting study is intended to function both as an entertaining story for the casual reader and as a fund of basic information for the scholar and researcher. The company-by-company structure will, I hope, serve both types of reader, with the appended playlist helping to show what was going on in different theatres at a given time. Because it is a scholarly work, I have tried to make it comprehensive; and *although* it is a scholarly work, I have tried to make it clear and accessible to those readers with no theoretical or ideological axe to grind.

I would like to thank the many members of Toronto's cultural community, past and present, who took the time to share their observations with me. These people include Robert Barnett, Paul Bettis, Stan Bevington, Bernie Bomers, Clare Coulter, Dian English, David Ferry, Jim Fisk, David Fox, David Gardner, Jim Garrard, Ken Gass, Mallory Gilbert, Bill Glassco, Jane Glassco, Bill Greenland, Graham Harley, Tom Hendry, Helen Hughes, Shain Jaffe, Urjo Kareda, Martin Kinch, Leon Major, Mavor Moore, Asheleigh Moorhouse, Bob Nasmith, John Palmer, Brian Parker, Peter Peroff, Miles Potter, John Rapsey, Elliott Rose, Alan Rosenthal, James Roy, Booth Savage, Phil Schreibman, Ernest Schwarz, Guy Sprung, Eric Steiner, Robert Swerdlow, Elizabeth Szathmary, Paul Thompson, Keith Turnbull, Edna Widenmaier, and Ralph Zimmerman. Thanks also go to Ken Gass and Keith Turnbull for supplying me with audiotaped reminiscences which they made, and to Dr Neil Carson for his help with the section on Toronto Workshop Productions. Some illustrative material was generously loaned from the private collections of Robert Barnett, Sholem Dolgoy, Jim Garrard, Martin Kinch, Miro Kinch, James Reaney, Elizabeth Szathmary, Henry Tarvainen, Paul Thompson, Hugh Travers, and the Canadian Stage Company. Other photographs are reprinted with the permission of the University of Guelph Theatre Archives and the Arts Department of the Metropolitan Toronto Library.

I would also like to thank the staff of what was the Theatre Department of the Metropolitan Toronto Library, formerly under the direction of Heather McCallum, without whose resources and assistance this work would have been almost impossible. In addition, I received valuable assistance from other archives and special collections: the City of Toronto Archives, the National Archives of Canada, the Provincial Archives of Manitoba, the University of Calgary, the University of Guelph, the University of Toronto, and the University of Victoria.

I owe a special debt to Professor Ann Saddlemyer of the University of Toronto for her advice and encouragement at every stage of this project, as well as to Alan Hughes, Barbara McIntyre, and Barbara and Michael Meiklejohn for sustaining me (more than they know) with their great faith in my work. Another kind of debt is owed to the Social Sciences and Humanities Research Council of Canada for supporting my doctoral studies on which this book is based.

On a personal level, I have been blessed with the support of friends too numerous to list here. I must, however, thank Peter McKinnon and Brian Whitmore for reading and commenting on the manuscript. And special thanks are due to Peter McKinnon and Patricia Fraser, without whose constant encouragement (not to mention their computer!) this work would never have been completed. Finally, thanks are also due to Ken Lewis, my copy-editor at University of Toronto Press, and to Kairiin Bright for her help with the proof-reading.

Abbreviations and acronyms are part of Toronto's theatre community as they are part of the mysteries of any profession. Here are the most common ones I have used:

ACTRA	Association of Canadian Television and Radio Artists
CBC	Canadian Broadcasting Corporation
DDF	Dominion Drama Festival
LIP	Local Initiatives Program
MTC	Manitoba Theatre Centre
NAC	National Arts Centre
OAC	Ontario Arts Council
OFY	Opportunities for Youth
TAP	Toronto Arts Productions
TFT	Toronto Free Theatre
TWP	Toronto Workshop Productions

Themes of self-discovery and self-recognition are as pervasive in the story of these theatre companies as they are in the Canadian drama created within them. I found that, for me personally, writing the history of these companies became a form of self-recognition as well. I would like to dedicate this book to the people who engendered and nurtured these theatres, people whose pursuit of their personal and artistic goals created a new body of work and a new theatrical tradition in Canada. Although I have aimed to write their history as objectively as possible, I must admit that I admire their achievements, and envy them for the mark they have made. I hope they consider my work worthy of their own.

TWP's original production of *Hey, Rube!* (1961) on Fraser Avenue. Note how close the audience is to the action.

Bob Dermer and Trudy Weiss in *Memories for My Brother* at the Canadian Place
Theatre in Stratford, July 1969

Jim Garrard, founder of Theatre Passe Muraille and King of Rochdale College

Memories for My Brother, Part 1 in Toronto (1969), showing the interior of the original Theatre Passe Muraille at Trinity Square. Miro Kinch's pipe-and-scaffold setting was described as a 'jungle gym' by critic Herbert Whittaker. The portly Don Steinhouse (left) was the alternative theatres' leading actor at this time.

Dionysus in 69 at the Studio Lab, 1969–70, the first long-running hit of Toronto's alternative theatres. The central figure is Rita Deverell.

Hair at the Royal Alex, 1970: the counter-culture as mainstream entertainment

The New Directors Group, 1970. Pictured are Martin Kinch, Ken Gass, Henry Tarvainen, and Jim Garrard. Other members of the group were Martin Brenzell, Jack Messinger, John Palmer, and (later) Paul Thompson. This picture appeared in a feature article in the *Globe and Mail* in February 1970, the same month as the opening of the St Lawrence Centre.

Anne Anglin and Louis Thompson in *Out to Breakfast* (1971) directed by John Palmer, one of the first collective creations produced at Theatre Passe Muraille. Louis Thompson was the stage name of Louis Del Grande, one of the alternative theatres' most eclectic talents, better known subsequently for his television show *Seeing Things*.

Paul Thompson in front of the original Theatre Passe Muraille on Trinity
Square, circa 1971

Doukhobors (1971), Paul Thompson's first full-length collective at Theatre Passe Muraille. Thompson described it as 'the world's first non-sexual nude show.'

The Factory Theatre Lab, over the Lonsdale Garage on Dupont Street, at the start of its second season (1971). The poster indicates that George F. Walker was making a rare stage appearance. Ken Gass is second from left, standing with Rosemary Donnelly and their dog, Barney. Eric Steiner is at the rear, standing in the door of the truck.

Creeps at the Tarragon Theatre, October 1971. Robin Cameron (later Robin Craig) as Miss Cerebral Palsy performs for Steve Whistance-Smith (in wheelchair), Victor Sutton, Len Sedun, and Frank Moore. The actor in the Shriner's hat is probably John Candy.

A 'family portrait' from the original production of *The Farm Show*, 1972. From left to right, the actors pictured are Fina MacDonell, Anne Anglin, David Fox, Janet Amos, and Miles Potter.

The exterior of Toronto Free Theatre, reclaimed in 1972 from a derelict gas works at 24 Berkeley Street

Elizabeth (Szathmary) Swerdlow, Pam MacDonald, and the company of *Rats* at the Global Village, 1972. This musical was based on the Swerdlows' experience of taking their hit musical *Justine* to New York.

The Factory Theatre Lab's poster for its 1973 tour to London, England. The dancing beavers were greeted diffidently by the theatre community there.

John Palmer directing *Me?* at Toronto Free Theatre, 1973

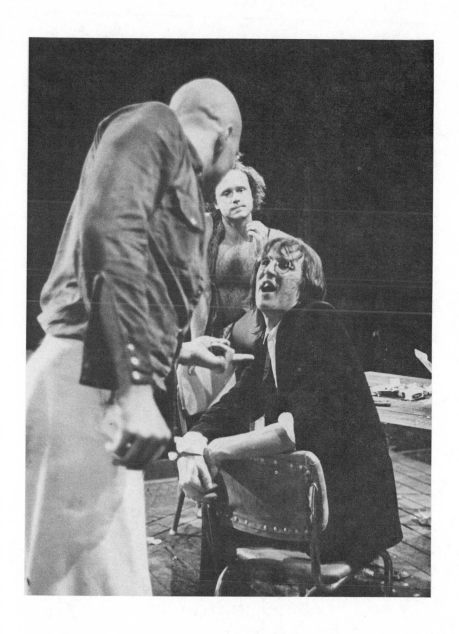

Nick Mancuso, William Webster, and Patrick Brymer in *Clear Light* (1973), a landmark production of Toronto Free Theatre

Tom Hendry (standing), founder of Toronto Free Theatre, with Quebec revolutionary Pierre Vallières during production of *Vallières!* (1973)

James Reaney's Donnelly trilogy at Tarragon Theatre: Richard Carson, Don MacQuarrie, Jerry Franken, and David Ferry in *Sticks and Stones*, 1973. Carson later served as general manager of the NDWT company, and Franken and Ferry starred in its national tour.

Richard Monette in *Hosanna* at Tarragon Theatre, 1974, one of the most celebrated productions of the era

Bill Glassco directing Jim Henshaw and Patricia Hamilton in *Bonjour, Là, Bonjour* at Tarragon Theatre, 1975, one of the last productions before Tarragon's sabbatical

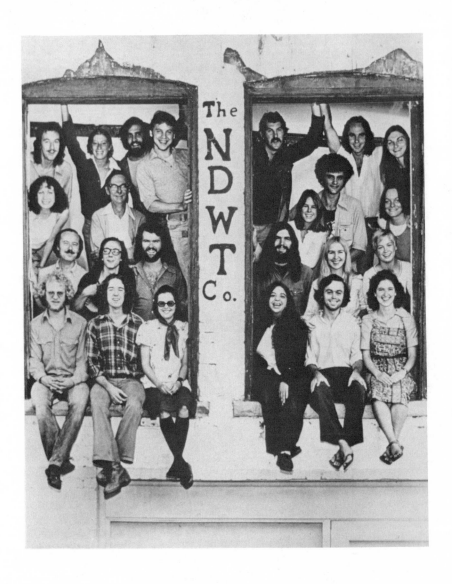

The NDWT company in London, Ontario, 1975, in preparation for the national tour of the Donnelly Trilogy

UP THE MAINSTREAM

1

Before the Flood

When I wrote an article in The Globe and Mail *last May, labelling the productions at the Royal Alexandra and O'Keefe Centre in Toronto as imports, a number of readers seemed surprised that the local scene had changed to the extent that it had in the past decade. Yet the alternate theatre has gained sufficiently in power, support, and interest to establish a whole new perspective on Broadway or British entertainments.*

Herbert Whittaker, September 1972

Over the past two years, Toronto's theatrical sensibilities have reformed themselves around what can best be called the alternative theatres.

The alternative theatre rushes [in] where the commercial theatre fears to tread. The alternative theatre continues a ceaseless flirtation with chaos and ruin. The alternative theatre carries hope for the future.[1]

Urjo Kareda, September 1972

Between 1968 and 1972, a small group of small theatre companies in Toronto completely changed the way Canadians thought about their theatre. Before 1968, before this flood of new theatres and new plays, there was no such thing as an alternative theatre movement in Canada. By 1972, when Whittaker and Kareda (Canada's leading theatre critics at the time) made these comments, the alternative theatres had grown to dominate the theatrical landscape of Canada's largest theatre market, and were on the brink of attaining a national influence. The landscape had changed so quickly that the new theatres had not even acquired an agreed-upon name – underground? alternate? alternative? It had changed so thoroughly that, in the minds of Toronto's own intellectual and artistic community, mainstream theatre became little more than an appendage to the alternative, like a second-run cinema for plays. For example, when the St Lawrence Centre reopened in March 1983 after a $5 million renovation, its drab auditorium and all-purpose stage transformed into a glittering proscenium house, the opening night program justified this splendid mainstream theatre as essential for providing the alternative companies with something they could be alternative *to*. Can you imagine this attitude on Broadway?

The rise of Toronto's alternative theatres was led by four companies (sometimes called the 'major' alternative theatres) which have retained their stature to the present day. The first of these was Theatre Passe Muraille, founded by Jim Garrard in 1968. Passe Muraille was initially an experimental theatre inspired by American models, but under Paul Thompson (who became managing director in 1970) it acquired a nationalistic focus. Passe Muraille was followed by the Factory Theatre Lab, founded by Ken Gass in 1970; then Tarragon Theatre, founded by Bill Glassco in 1971; and finally Toronto Free Theatre, founded by Tom Hendry, Martin Kinch, and John Palmer in 1972. All of these companies created their own small theatres in buildings newly converted from other uses. They were led mainly by directors and administrators who were still in their twenties, along with a few (notably Glassco and Hendry) who were older but who shared the artistic and professional concerns of their younger colleagues. These alternative theatres brought a renewed excitement to theatre in Toronto and, through a series of influential productions and publications, helped to create new patterns for theatre production in Canada.

To define what we mean by alternative theatre in Canada is much more difficult than it is in Britain or the United States. London's 'fringe' and New York's off-Broadway and off-off-Broadway developed in opposition to long-standing institutions of mainstream professional theatre there. In London or New York, the question 'Alternative to what?' can be answered simply and directly; in Toronto, the same question is offered as a subject for debate, or as a sarcastic put-down of the mainstream. Despite a long theatrical tradition in Canada, local professional theatre had only recently gained a firm footing when these alternative companies sprang up seeking institutions to overthrow. The regional theatre network, which had begun with the founding of the Manitoba Theatre Centre in 1958, was still being established in some

Canadian centres, and was surviving only precariously in some others. Strangely, while mainstream professional theatre flourished in Stratford and in Winnipeg in the 1960s, it was moribund in Toronto, so that there was no stable opposition by which Toronto's alternative theatres could be defined. Neither could the alternatives be identified by a dominant style of text or performance, as their repertory and production styles ranged from the wildly experimental to the stolidly traditional. Theatres called 'alternate' or 'alternative' in Toronto can only be defined in terms of a kind of club: the companies' acknowledged membership in a de facto network which grew up between 1968 and 1972. In recent years, the term 'alternate' has become the most popular collective label for these theatres, but 'alternative' was the first one that stuck and therefore the one which I will use.

It is not a misnomer, however. These theatres were, in fact, consciously alternative to something. They were alternative, first of all, to existing forms of professional theatre in Canada, to the highly developed bureaucracy of the Stratford Festival and to the well-heeled respectability of the regional theatres. They were initially influenced by, and took some of their early ideology from, alternative theatre in other countries: Grotowski's and Planchon's alternatives to European state theatre, Brook's and Cheeseman's alternatives to British repertory theatre, Chaikin's and Schechner's alternatives to American commercial theatre. The leaders of Toronto's alternative theatres, like educated people everywhere, were heavily influenced by the American 'counter-culture' of the 1960s, an alternative expression to mainstream mores which found public focus in the civil rights movement and the anti–Vietnam War protests. Canada's aspiring theatre artists were steeped in this liberal/radical sensibility of the 1960s and its anti-establishment catchphrases: Marshall McLuhan's 'global village,' Fritz Perls's 'do your own thing,' Timothy Leary's 'turn on, tune in, drop out.' They possessed the engaging narcissism of the baby boom in young adulthood, a generation indulged by an older one which, having survived the Great Depression and two world wars, was determined that its children should be spared such hardship. These young people received a first-rate education in rapidly expanding universities and professional training schools, but they were impatient for the professional mainstream to accept them as leaders and to adopt their ideas. As much as anything else, the alternative theatres were founded to create professional opportunities for this new generation. As Tom Hendry put it, 'In a way we're behaving like people kept out of golf clubs. We're building our own.'[2]

In their rise to the stature of a new mainstream, Toronto's alternative theatres went through three stages. The first we can call a radical stage (1968–70), in which new alternative companies presented plays and performing styles inspired by American alternative theatre. This stage functioned similarly to Canadian theatre in colonial times, with an aesthetic imported from the coffee-houses of New York rather than the patent theatres of London. The second stage was a nationalist one (1970–72), in which the American models were discarded and indigenous ones created, more or less by trial and error. As they developed, the alternative theatres chose to produce new plays, Canadian plays engendered in their own ranks, which the established theatres did not. During this stage, the new alternative theatres gained enormous critical attention in Toronto and prompted widespread re-evaluation of Toronto's local professional theatre among critics, arts councils, and theatre people themselves. The third stage was a mainstream one (1972–75), in which the dramaturgical and presentational styles developed at the nationalist stage were turned toward finding a broader audience. As each alternative company passed through these stages, it did not remain bound to the attitudes under which it was founded, but rather changed according to these changing trends. As a result, the history of any given alternative company appears baffling unless this changing context is borne in mind. As with all useful generalizations, we shall see, the facts do not always slip neatly into the right categories or between the right dates. However, this pattern is an essential tool for understanding the rise of Toronto's alternative theatres in this period.

In the first stage, the radical theatre stage, new quasi-professional companies such as Theatre Passe Muraille and the Studio Lab presented the best plays of the American counter-culture for a new minority constituency. At this time, the alternative theatres became established as an exciting new voice in Toronto theatre, and the press was entranced by their idealism and daring even when unimpressed by their production standards. This radical stage was soon overtaken by a wave of cultural nationalism which swept Canada in the wake of Expo 67, a wave which also produced regulatory encouragement of Canadian content in publishing, broadcasting, film production, even in investment portfolios. This represented a second-generation expression of post-war nationalism, more strident than that of the first, but embraced gratefully by an older generation which had felt its earlier patriotic outburst dampened by the subsequent expansion of American cultural influence. Encouragement by nationalist critics, along with widespread public interest, helped propel the alternative theatres into a second stage, their nationalist stage, almost as soon as they began.

A vital stimulus at this nationalist stage was a massive injection of public subsidy through two new federal job-creation plans, the Local Initiatives Program (LIP) and Opportunities for Youth (OFY), which flourished between 1971 and 1974. LIP and OFY grants represented a government strategy to reduce unemployment and disaffection among young adults, and could be awarded for any demonstrably worthwhile project. Canada's new theatre artists, largely well educated and unemployed, had little difficulty in obtaining these grants once their leaders had explained their demonstrably worthwhile nationalist goals. These grants were truly revolutionary in the sense that they subverted the established cultural funding procedures which had been in place since the Canada Council was founded, and which had proven slow to respond to the new smaller theatres. As one nationalist critic put it, 'The years of struggle that a regional theatre put in before it worked itself up to the point of receiving $100,000 from the Canada Council were rendered ridiculous by the ease with which a dozen unemployed individuals obtained the same sum in their first year.'[3]

Between 1972 and 1975, the influence of Toronto's alternative theatres spread across the country. Under pressure from the Canada Council, whose policies began to encourage the production of Canadian-written plays, the regional theatres looked to their smaller Toronto cousins to supply proven successes, indigenous plays which might satisfy both the Council's new concerns for literary nationalism and the regional theatres' equally urgent need to maintain box-office figures. Even the *New York Times* noted in 1974 that a popular hit at one of these alternative theatres could 'significantly influence repertory in theaters all across Canada in a season or two.'[4] Playwrights whose works had been returned unread a few years earlier were suddenly in demand, especially if they could demonstrate a broad appeal. At the same time, a small but steady market for their published plays was growing in educational circles, a development which also enhanced the stature of the alternative theatres where the plays had been first produced. The Canadian play, frankly, had become fashionable. With seed money from LIP and OFY grants, branch plants and clones of Toronto's alternative theatres began producing locally written works in disused churches and hastily adapted warehouses all across the country. In addition, the founding of the *Canadian Theatre Review* in 1974 gave these theatres a kind of permanent national lobby, as the successive editors of the

Canadian Theatre Review have clearly preferred alternative and experimental forms of theatre to mainstream ones. The final victory of the alternative theatres has been one of imagery, as they supplanted the regional theatres as the accepted model for founding (and funding) new theatres in Canada. To the Canadian arts bureaucracy of 1972, 'professional theatre' meant something that looked like the Manitoba Theatre Centre. Now it means something that looks like Tarragon.

The Pattern of Canadian Theatre

While the alternative theatres were a wellspring for revitalizing Canadian drama and theatre, it would be foolish to suggest they grew up in a theatrical vacuum. It was in the interest of these companies to depict Canada's theatre as a vast wasteland awaiting its first spring, even though most of their young leaders were trained and encouraged by the country's various theatrical establishments. John Palmer, for instance, described the alternative theatres as 'flickers of light in a dark country,' while Martin Kinch stated (more ambiguously) that 'for many of us Toronto Theatre began with the opening of Theatre Passe Muraille's first production.'[5] Among such leaders, this attitude may have resulted from sheer ignorance of the history of Canadian theatre; but it more probably reflected their desire to rewrite history according to their own priorities in order to minimize the importance of that which came before. By contrast, Herbert Whittaker, with probably the keenest sense of historical perspective among Canadian critics, observed in 1957 that Canada 'has always had the kind of theatre it needs, deserves, and wants.'[6] This remark is as true of the alternative theatres which followed as it was of the earlier theatres to which he referred. At each stage of Canada's development, Canadian theatre has reflected the society's needs, deserts, and wants; and to do so it has undergone a sequence of redefinitions as social and cultural conditions changed.

Evidence of European theatre in Canada usually appears in the earliest records of European garrisons and frontier towns. As far as the word *Canadian* can be used, 'Canadian theatre' before 1920 meant theatre performed for Canadian audiences. The plays, whether written in Canada or elsewhere, were directly imitative of the latest offerings in Paris or London, and the performers usually came from there as well. This was not, as some modern critics would have it, because our forbears were colonial lapdogs. It is because Canada, unlike the United States, was founded as an outpost of an international power. The Union Jacks which draped Canadian playhouses in colonial times were not symbols of foreign oppression, but proud reminders of the great empire of which the audience was a part. Toward the end of the nineteenth century, as railway and steamship networks spread, growing urban centres eagerly competed for visits by international stars such as Henry Irving, Sarah Bernhardt, and countless others. For ambitious cities, as one theatre historian put it, 'to have become a regular stop on the road was a proud achievement';[7] and the many Canadian playhouses built about the turn of the century express this civic pride. The fact that the performers and their plays usually came from outside Canada was no source of shame. On the contrary, when Canada was proud to be the last and longest link in the 'all-red route' of the British Empire, so was its theatre.

'The Road' declined drastically after 1920, decimated by vaudeville and the cinema and finally killed by the Depression. Between the wars, a new image of Canadian theatre arose in the Canadian 'little theatre' movement, which achieved a national expression in the Dominion Drama Festival (DDF) first held in 1933. To the DDF, 'Canadian theatre' meant theatre created by Canadian artists; and although staunchly amateur, many of their leaders promoted the dream of a Canadian professional theatre to be established as soon as conditions would allow. With the new buoyant mood of nationalism which followed World War II this goal was vigorously pursued both by pre-war veterans of the little theatres and by a new generation of aspiring professionals. In the late 1940s, professional companies were founded in several Canadian cities (such as the New Play Society in Toronto and Everyman Theatre in Vancouver), but they all eventually closed due to financial problems and artistic exhaustion. In the 1950s, however, two prototypes for Canadian professional theatre were established by a marriage of business and cultural interests: the Stratford Festival in 1953, and the Manitoba Theatre Centre (MTC) in 1958. Their surprising success enabled a regional theatre network to be established in the next decade, built on the philosophical foundation of the Massey Commission report (published in 1951) and the financial foundation of the Canada Council (created in 1957). Using the MTC model, regional theatres spread from sea to sea during the 1960s, usually with the support of local business interests and local little theatre, to provide mainstage and touring productions for their respective cities and regions.

At the centre of population and of culture in English Canada, Toronto in the 1960s certainly offered the most extensive theatrical menu in the country. In other Canadian cities, when new theatres arose to fulfil changing needs, they tended to replace an outmoded form: the little theatres appeared when the road shows vanished, for example, and were supplanted in turn by professional companies built on amateur foundations. In Toronto, however, with its larger and more diverse population, older forms of theatre persisted alongside the newer ones. American and British touring shows remained a staple of Toronto audiences, not only in its handsome Edwardian playhouse, the Royal Alexandra Theatre, but also in its cavernous opera house, the O'Keefe Centre, which opened in 1960. Amateur theatre also flourished at this time: under the inspiring leadership of Robert Gill, the University of Toronto's Hart House Theatre (opened in 1919) became the most important training centre for Canada's new post-war theatres, while the University Alumnae Dramatic Society (founded in 1918) became a showplace for new intellectual drama from Europe. Post-war professional stock companies abounded, with summer companies such the Red Barn Theatre and the Straw Hat Players in the nearby Muskoka region, and winter companies such as the Crest Theatre in the city. But by the late 1960s, the Crest had closed and other mainstream operations were struggling. In contrast to the splendid record of expansion and achievement in other regional centres, Toronto had yet to establish a viable civic professional theatre company – probably because, with so many other forms of theatre available, including the nearby Stratford and Shaw Festivals, the need for such a company seemed not so pressing as it did elsewhere in Canada. At a time when Toronto's population was expanding, when construction was rampant and optimism high, when other cities boasted new civic companies and new civic playhouses, theatre in Toronto had failed to find a focus for the city's energy and ambition. Because an older generation of theatre people was so well established there, nourished by the growth of CBC radio drama after the war, Toronto also appeared to provide fewer opportunities for aspiring professionals than other cities did. The gloomy conditions in Toronto were even responsible (in part) for the commissioning of a special report on Ontario theatre by the Canada Council and the Province of Ontario Council of the Arts (POCA). This report, published in 1969 as *The Awkward Stage*, concluded that 'Toronto's failure has been more apparent than real,' and that its prevailing image as 'a place where nothing happens disagrees with the facts.'[8] The facts, however, could not lighten the weight of opinion: Toronto in the late 1960s was, by its own collective judgment, a theatrical backwater at the country's metropolitan centre.

By the end of the 1960s, then, conditions in Toronto obviously favoured some new theatrical direction. This was the climate that enabled the new alternative theatres to rise to prominence so quickly. They rejected existing mainstream theatre, but embraced the recently invented infrastructure which supported it. In the process of seeking a mandate, a theatrical need which other theatres were not filling, the leaders of these new companies created a playwright-based one. They redefined 'Canadian theatre' to mean Canadian artists producing Canadian plays, one area in which the regional theatres had not generally been successful. The more politically astute of them recognized that their success depended on persuading critics and cultural agencies of the primacy of this new definition. As Ken Gass put it,

The validity of the Alternate movement stemmed from its two-fold aims: a) Political – a redistribution of economic resources by giving significant funds to groups and individuals who wanted to work in smaller, independent environments, even if this necessitated dismantling the larger organizations, and b) Artistic – the development of new theatrical experiences, particularly in terms of new Canadian plays, which the regional theatre system had markedly discouraged.[9]

What is most surprising is the extent to which the alternative theatres achieved these goals. In the nationalistic climate of the early 1970s, their new playwright-based definition for Canadian theatre allowed them to dismiss a wide range of existing theatre as being simply irrelevant. (The Stratford Festival was a particularly popular target, since so much public money was spent there to glorify a foreign playwright.) Although Toronto's alternative theatres did not begin by producing indigenous drama, it was their timely advocacy of new Canadian plays which brought them such rapid and enduring success.

Toronto's Mainstream in the 1960s: In Search of a Centre

Part of the success of these alternative theatres in the early 1970s was due to the terrible record of failure which clung to Toronto's mainstream theatres in the 1960s. No less than four successive high-profile companies – the Crest Theatre, the Red Barn Theatre, the Canadian Players, and Theatre Toronto – ceased operating between 1964 and 1969. In most instances, financial failure accompanied organizational failure, artistic failure, or failure to find or hold a mainstream audience. As the decade drew to a close, the mainstream ambitions of these companies (and a few others) became increasingly focused on the planned St Lawrence Centre for the Arts, a new civic playhouse and concert hall which finally opened in 1970. In Toronto in the 1960s, the St Lawrence Centre was the Holy Grail of local professional theatre.

The St Lawrence Centre was conceived by civic planners, unlike most Canadian theatres, and has been cursed with civic politics ever since. Inspired by New York's Lincoln Center, the Centre was first proposed in a 1962 municipal report as a massive $25 million cultural complex occupying nine acres of Toronto's downtown core. The next year, a private organization called the Toronto Arts Foundation was created to bring the proposal to fruition. The key element of the Centre was to be a civic playhouse, adopted by the City of Toronto as its official centennial project for Canada's 1967 centenary. As debates raged and cost estimates rose, however, the scope of the enterprise was steadily whittled down to overcome vehement political opposition at City Hall. In fact, the Centre became a political football: it was a major issue in two successive mayoralty campaigns, was subjected to innumerable revisions, and was cancelled entirely at least twice. By 1967, with no agreement in sight, the St Lawrence Centre had become (to many Torontonians) a symbol of the city's short-sighted stinginess in cultural matters, especially when compared to Montreal's glorious Expo. But under general director Mavor Moore, the editor of *The Awkward Stage* and Canada's most ubiquitous man of the theatre, the Foundation finally obtained enough public funding and private donations to build the Centre on a still more modest scale, comprising only an 830-seat theatre and a 480-seat recital hall next to the O'Keefe Centre downtown. Toronto's centennial project finally opened in 1970, three years late, but a jewel in the city's cultural crown nonetheless. By then, the city's mainstream companies had all been trampled jockeying for the hoped-for position of resident company there.

The Crest Theatre, which operated from 1953 to 1966, was the longest-lived of Canada's pre-Canada Council stock companies. It was founded by the brothers Donald and Murray Davis as a means of earning a living in professional theatre in Canada, a goal which had been unattainable for the preceding generation of Canadian theatre artists. In the late 1940s the Davises had trained under Robert Gill at Hart House Theatre in the University of Toronto. In 1948 they founded a summer stock company, the Straw Hat Players, in Ontario's resort region of Muskoka, the first of many summer companies founded in that region after the war. In 1953, spurred on by the miraculous first season of the Stratford Festival, the Davises leased the Crest cinema on Mount Pleasant Road, north of the city core, for a year-round theatre operation. Initially they opened a new production every two weeks, but later runs were longer and could be extended for more popular shows. The Davises succeeded in providing employment not only for themselves, but also for their contemporaries: virtually every significant actor, director, and designer who ever worked in Toronto worked at some point for the Crest. While its repertory was mainly British, it also produced some new Canadian plays by such writers as Robertson Davies and Mavor Moore.[10] In the 1950s the Crest was the flagship of locally produced professional theatre in Toronto; but in the 1960s the company was subjected to increasingly vitriolic criticism, led by drama critic Nathan Cohen of the *Toronto Star*. In 1964 the Canada Council refused to continue funding the Crest due to what it considered lack of managerial and artistic direction. While the Crest carried on for two more seasons, 'out of sheer stubbornness' according to Donald Davis,[11] the Council's public repudiation was the Crest's death-blow.

By the mid-1960s, with the Crest clearly in decline, other companies queued up to provide local professional theatre for a growing audience in Toronto. One of the most respected was the Red Barn Theatre, its name taken from another summer stock operation in Ontario's cottage country. Under the direction of Marigold Charlesworth and Jean Roberts, this summer company expanded into winter operations in Toronto early in 1962, when Charlesworth and Roberts embarked on an adventurous thirteen-week season at the newly renovated Central Library Theatre. This was a 200-seat proscenium house, created from a lecture hall in the city's main library on College Street, which served many groups as an affordable rental space until the library moved in 1977. For three years the Red Barn remained a marginal company there, without influential friends or moneyed backers, although it had one long-running hit in *The Fantasticks* (1963). In 1965 Charlesworth and Roberts were hired to run the Canadian Players, leaving the Red Barn Theatre to continue only in its long-time role as a summer company.

The Canadian Players had been created in 1953 by Tom Patterson and actor Douglas Campbell, two key figures in the birth of the Stratford Festival that year. It was intended to be a classical touring company, an off-season offshoot of the Festival which would provide winter work for some of the Stratford company. Its first touring production, a very spare staging of Shaw's *Saint Joan*, was received enthusiastically wherever it played. In its second season the Canadian Players' tour expanded from its base in southern Ontario, and by 1957 the company was booked solidly for six months across Canada and into the United States. At its height the Canadian Players spread the fame of the Stratford Festival, and Canadian classical theatre in general, throughout North America. By the mid-1960s, however, this group too was in decline. As Herbert Whittaker wrote in 1965, 'the acting itself deteriorated and the purpose of the company seemed to get lost in the struggle to survive. At one point, not so long ago, it found itself employing a largely u.s. cast to play to a largely u.s. audience.'[12] In the spring of 1965, near the end of the Canadian Players' final tour, its interim general manager, Tom Hendry, announced that the company would produce a winter season in Toronto.

The Canadian Players, like the Red Barn before it, presented its 1965–66 season at the Central Library Theatre under the direction of Charlesworth and Roberts. Despite some distinguished productions there (including *The Playboy of the Western World* starring Martha Henry and Douglas Rain), the company was in serious financial trouble by the new year. (Certainly the small capacity of the Central Library Theatre was part of the problem.) As the season drew to a close, the board of the Canadian Players Foundation began negotiating a merger with the equally debt-ridden board of the Crest Theatre Foundation. During the months of negotiations, Charlesworth and Roberts were rendered immobile – the boards of directors could give them no clear idea as to how many plays they should plan for, or in what theatre, or even if they would still be in charge. By the time the terms of the merger were settled, neither board had an artistic team or even a venue, just a lot of debt. As a result, in Canada's centennial year Toronto had no mainstream theatre company as well as no civic playhouse.

The board of the amalgamated Canadian Crest Players Foundation, under the leadership of advertising executive William Graham, attempted to re-establish a mainstream professional company under the name Theatre Toronto. Seeking (as one board member said) a 'prophet who was going to lead us out of the dramatic desert,'[13] it hired Clifford Williams from Britain's Royal Shakespeare Company and sold a remarkable eleven thousand subscriptions for a brief four-play season which began in January 1968 at the beautifully refurbished Royal Alexandra Theatre. But although Williams gained international attention with his English-language première of Hochhuth's *Soldiers*, Toronto's cultural community perceived him as a carpetbagger earning an exorbitant salary. The Toronto audience, moreover, was unhappy with productions it thought were preoccupied with homosexuality and sadism. Subscriptions dropped by almost 50 per cent for Theatre Toronto's second season. It opened in January 1969 with Marlowe's *Edward II*, a play bound to offend what Williams called Toronto's 'flowered-hat brigade,'[14] in which Stratford favourite William Hutt, as Edward, was killed nightly in an obscene fashion with a red-hot poker. A few days after the opening, and under increasing pressure, Williams tendered his resignation, and the board accepted it with alacrity and relief. That spring, the company was closed honourably in a nominal coalition with the St Lawrence Centre for the Arts, which was still under construction.

The composition of a resident theatre company at the St Lawrence Centre was as volatile an issue in cultural politics as the building itself was in civic politics. When the Centre was first proposed in 1962, the Crest company seemed an obvious candidate to be resident there. Its long-time location on Mount Pleasant Road was distinctly out-of-the-way, and Nathan Cohen (for one) believed that the whole St Lawrence project was 'the out-growth of an attempt by the Crest theatre to find itself a downtown home.'[15] (Indeed, the first chairman of the Toronto Arts Foundation, businessman John Lockwood, was also then chairman of the Crest Theatre Foundation.) The Crest's ambitions in this area probably caused the attacks on it to escalate, as Donald Davis has speculated:

I have always believed that the Crest inadvertently found itself in a political situation. The proposed St. Lawrence Centre was already a drawing-board reality. Some of Toronto's cultural mafia thought the Crest was the logical incumbent for the new theatre. Needless to say, the Crest thought so too. Others of this mafia did not and made certain that it would not happen.[16]

The hope of occupying the new civic theatre seems also to have motivated the Canadian Players to move to Toronto in 1965 and to produce plays on a scale the company really could not afford. The same hope was axiomatic to the founding of Theatre Toronto in 1967. It may also have influenced the city's one alternative company of the time, Toronto Workshop Productions, in moving to a more central location and a more conventional production schedule at the end of that year. Finally, however, Mavor Moore and his director of theatre Leon Major, a veteran of Hart House Theatre and the Crest, decided to create a new resident company for the Centre rather than to adopt an existing one.

To those with long experience in amateur and pre-professional theatre in Toronto, the creation of a permanent local professional company in the new civic arts centre was the triumphant culmination of decades of struggle. This triumph was short-lived, however, as the St Lawrence Centre soon found itself a battleground for civic and cultural politics once again. Shortly after it opened in February 1970, Moore left the Centre for other projects and was succeeded by Major. Their brief first season consisted mostly of new Canadian plays and new Canadian translations of seldom-performed European plays. In effect, this was alternative programming for a mainstream audience, and proved to be a critical and popular disaster. Besieged by bad reviews, poor box-office, and a new spasm of fiscal outrage at City Hall, Major retreated to the kind of mixed programming which was typical of other regional theatres: proven Broadway and West End successes, sprinkled with some classics and occasionally a new Canadian play. Having hastily retreated from the vanguard of Toronto theatre, Major's Centre, cast unwillingly as a symbol of establishment theatre and as the unworthy beneficiary of wrongheaded cultural funding policies, was harried remorselessly by the vocal leaders of Toronto's new alternative theatres. In 1971, moreover, the city altered the administrative structure of the Centre, reducing the stature of the Toronto Arts Foundation (later Toronto Arts Productions) to that of merely the facility's principal tenant.

Nominally Toronto's civic theatre company, TAF/TAP had difficulty establishing a mandate there. Its programming was bounded on all sides by popular touring shows at the O'Keefe and the Royal Alex, by classics at the nearby Shaw and Stratford festivals, and (after 1970) by new Canadian drama in Toronto's alternative theatres. The record suggests, however, that this mainstream institution, often under fire itself, consistently supported new Canadian talent and new Canadian plays, and sometimes suffered by that support. Major himself remained artistic director until 1980, enduring criticism that would have wilted a weaker man, while the city's theatrical focus shifted from the St Lawrence Centre to the new alternatives.

Alternative Theatre in the 1960s: George Luscombe and Toronto Workshop Productions

Canada had a strong tradition of alternative theatre in the 1930s, consisting of leftist and agitprop theatre produced by local workers' theatre clubs in many Canadian cities. These organizations were parallel to, and drew inspiration from, workers' theatre groups in Europe and the United States. The first such group in Canada was the Workers' Experimental Theatre (WET) in Toronto, a branch of Toronto's Progressive Arts Club, whose first recorded performance took place in May 1932.[17] WET's greatest success was the original full-length drama *Eight Men Speak*, first performed in December 1933, an agitprop play based on the alleged attempt on the life of Canadian communist leader Tim Buck in his jail cell in Kingston. This group, reformed as 'Theatre of Action' two years later, mounted ten major productions from 1936 to 1940, most of them American-written. Canada's alternative theatre of the 1930s even infiltrated the mainstream of the day when the Progressive Arts Club of Vancouver won the BC regional final of the 1936 Dominion Drama Festival with a stirring production of Clifford Odets' *Waiting for Lefty*. At the DDF finals in Ottawa, so the story goes, the entire black-tie audience (including Governor-General Tweedsmuir!) leapt to its feet at the play's climax, shouting for the downtrodden taxi-drivers to strike.[18] For all the widespread impact of left-wing arts clubs in the 1930s, however, World War II effectively ended such activity, and the prosperity which followed the war did not encourage its resumption. The tradition of alternative theatre in Canada was severed, to be reinvented in a different way by George Luscombe in the 1960s.

Luscombe, born in Toronto in 1926 and trained as a commercial artist, had his first contact with theatre through a youth club associated with the left-wing CCF party.[19] In 1948 he toured Ontario with a short-lived group called the 'People's Repertory Theatre' – not, as it may sound, a left-wing theatre. In 1950 Luscombe left for England to gain more experience, which he did in great variety, from pantomime to a touring 'fit-up' company in Wales. At the end of 1952, he was accepted into Joan Littlewood's Theatre Workshop, which was just then moving into its new home at the Theatre Royal, Stratford East, London. Luscombe remained a member of Littlewood's company for three years.

Littlewood, of course, became famous as the director of and dramaturgical force behind a number of important plays of the new British drama, including *The Hostage* (1958), and *Oh What a Lovely War* (1963). Her pre-war work in England had included some agitprop experiments, and her dedicated leftist politics shone through even her classical productions, as Luscombe's did later. But Littlewood did not, during Luscombe's years with the Theatre Workshop, use improvisational methods to develop scripts as both she and Luscombe were to do in their best-known work. Rather, Littlewood's methods of movement and improvisation were hurriedly applied to more traditional scripts at this time, as the company resorted to biweekly stock to keep its Stratford East home afloat. Later, after Luscombe had left, the Theatre Workshop gained wider fame through its long-running transfers to the West End.[20]

While Luscombe was in England, a number of new opportunities had arisen for the professional actor in Canada – CBC television started producing in 1952, the Stratford Festival in 1953, the Crest and the Canadian Players in 1954. Luscombe heard of these hopeful new developments, and he came back to Canada in 1956 determined to make his living as an actor. He was tired of the poverty and the communal living which Littlewood's 'group theatre' imposed on its members. However, he was also steeped in the ideals of the Theatre Workshop, and so was soon involved in similar projects in Toronto. The quintessential story about George Luscombe's dedication to theatre comes from his attending a meeting in Toronto held (probably) in 1957. As writer and critic Antony Ferry reported, it was 'a kind of action meeting where everyone lamented the lack of good theatre in Toronto. Good ideas were aired, money was never mentioned, and there was a painful pause.'[21] Luscombe suddenly stood up and said, 'If it's worth while, I'm ready to give ten years.' He gave closer to thirty.

While Luscombe eked out a living as an actor, Tony Ferry persisted in his goal of founding a 'group theatre' in Toronto. Ferry initiated a play-reading circle in 1958; and in 1959 he obtained free workshop space for the 'Theatre Centre' (as he called it) in the basement of a printing shop at 47 Fraser Avenue, located in a drab industrial area on Toronto's west side. Ferry also persuaded the Welsh classical actor Powys Thomas, a regular performer at the Stratford Festival, to join the group as artistic director. The Theatre Centre was to have two main activities: a company built around the nine actors already working with the group, and a dramatic school which would help finance the enterprise. The school would begin full operation that summer, it was announced, with instructors including Ferry, Thomas, Luscombe, voice specialist Esme Crampton, and actress Joan Maroney, Ferry's wife, a Canadian who had trained in England.[22] When Thomas left the Theatre Centre a few months later, to head the English-language section of the new National Theatre School, Luscombe became artistic director. Under the name Workshop Productions, Luscombe's group made its public debut in December 1959 in a double-bill of Chekhov's *The Boor* and García Lorca's *Don Perlimplin*, a program which played for only a week. Another double-bill, Chekhov's *The Marriage Proposal* and Len Peterson's *Burlap Bags* (adapted from Peterson's earlier radio play of the same name), followed in May 1960. *Burlap Bags* received excellent reviews; and Mavor Moore, writing in the Toronto *Telegram*, identified Workshop Productions' North American context when he called it 'the furthest off of all off-Broadway theatre.'[23]

Luscombe's next production, *Hey, Rube!*, catapulted his company into the front rank of Toronto theatres. It was the company's first original play, developed from improvisation classes, about a group of down-at-the-heels circus performers. During the long rehearsal period, Luscombe's group received an eviction notice – their landlords had found a paying tenant – and their circus play acquired added significance as the story of another group of homeless performers. Tony Ferry created a script from the group's improvisations, mainly strengthening the story line, and *Hey, Rube!* opened in February 1961. Houses were small to begin with, but word-of-mouth advertising and excellent reviews soon brought capacity crowds to the company's tiny 100-seat arena theatre. Nathan Cohen, for one, described the production as 'an exhilarating adventure among the theatre arts,' and one which 'stands head and shoulders above most drama productions shown in Toronto, or likely to be shown, this season.'[24] *Hey, Rube!* finally closed after five weeks, having played to almost two thousand people. After the final performance, the eighteen actors and technicians received envelopes containing their share of the profits for the run – $37.83 each. Counting evenings spent scavenging lumber and building bleachers, Ferry estimated, six months' work and nine thousand man-hours went into the experiment.[25] But its mark on Toronto theatre was indelible, and it had provided a vital first success for the fledgling company.

After *Hey, Rube!* Luscombe was widely recognized as (in Herbert Whittaker's words) 'the most dedicated and original creative talent working in our theatre';[26] and his basement stage among the factories became an important landmark for serious theatre-goers in Toronto. Luscombe's reputation inevitably attracted some new young talent, as did his group's professed interest in new Canadian plays. A key addition at this time was Jack Winter (b. 1936), who adapted the group's next play, ... *And They'll Make Peace* (1961), from the *Lysistrata* of Aristophanes. Winter, a Montreal-born poet and teacher, served as Luscombe's dramaturge and resident playwright for over ten years in all. In 1962 Winter worked with Luscombe and his actors on a Pirandello adaptation, *The Evil Eye*, and the following year wrote an adaptation of

Büchner's *Woyzeck*. Nathan Cohen led the critical praise for the Luscombe/Winter *Woyzeck* as 'truly a passionate work of art.'[27] Incidentally, in 1965 Winter wrote a new adaptation of *Woyzeck* on short notice when another playwright, Jack Brundage, withdrew the version on which he and Luscombe had been collaborating. Four years later Brundage, under his pen-name John Herbert, gained enduring fame when his play *Fortune and Men's Eyes* became a long-running hit off-Broadway. Herbert's own adaptation of *Woyzeck*, which he finally produced in 1969, had a great impact on the career of Ken Gass and the founding of the Factory Theatre Lab, as we shall see in chapter 3.

From 1961 through 1967, Workshop Productions (renamed Toronto Workshop Productions in 1964) mounted about two new shows per year on Fraser Avenue. The plays included *Before Compiegne* (1963), *The Mechanic* (1964), and *The Golem of Venice* (1967), each of these written by Winter, and each revised and restaged several times. The company also performed a great deal outside Toronto, beginning in 1961 with a six-month tour of Ontario. TWP played at Stratford for four consecutive summers (1964–67), performing in a tent in the civic park adjacent to the Festival Theatre. It played at several universities (including Waterloo, Queen's, and York) during this same period – in fact, one plan of Luscombe's was for his group to be a resident professional company within a university, an idea that was very much in the air at the time. TWP was the only Toronto company to be invited to perform at Expo 67; indeed, in the summer of 1967 it was practically the only surviving resident theatre in Toronto, as the city's mainstream companies were either dormant or dead.

In the same period, Luscombe's company made several gestures toward establishing itself as an ongoing institution – one cannot live on good reviews alone, and not all of them were good. In 1963 it received its first operating grant from the Canada Council, and at the same time was reconstituted as an Equity company. In 1964 it remounted *Before Compiegne* to open the Colonnade Theatre on Bloor Street, a new 200-seat arena theatre which was expected to serve as a downtown showcase for TWP's more popular shows. Unfortunately, the Colonnade never established a clear identity in the community, and served instead as a rental house for all kinds of small companies in Toronto. Luscombe, by then recognized as a leading innovator with arena stages, sat on design committees not only for the Colonnade but also for York University's 650-seat Burton Auditorium (opened in 1965) and for the St Lawrence Centre. In each of these cases, arena stages were built which

Luscombe hoped would provide a permanent home for his company. In each case his hopes were not fulfilled, however, and the arena configuration proved awkward for other groups which inherited the spaces. Meanwhile, the company's love-hate relationship with its basement home on Fraser Avenue ripened into hate, as its bad location and small capacity continually caused problems for a company which always lived from hand to mouth. Finally, under the leadership of June Faulkner (who joined the company in 1963 and served as general manager from 1967 through 1979), TWP leased a new theatre space downtown at 12 Alexander Street, in a former automobile showroom near Yonge and College streets. The company moved into it in December 1967, built a 300-seat arena theatre there in only a month, and previewed a new play, *Gentlemen Be Seated*, on New Year's Eve. As June Faulkner pointed out, in reference to the St Lawrence Centre, this was *one* centennial project that opened on time.

At his new downtown location, Luscombe found himself grappling with mainstream problems just as Littlewood had fifteen years earlier at Stratford East. Although TWP drew about $50,000 in annual subsidy by 1968, it also required a lot more revenue to sustain its new home. For the first time, Luscombe sold subscriptions for a fixed season, and opened a new play every month. Critical reaction varied a great deal from one show to the next, with particular praise for *The Good Soldier Schweik* (1969), in a new adaptation by Michael John Nimchuk, and for *Mr. Bones* (1969), Luscombe's reworking of *Gentlemen Be Seated*, a show about race relations in the United States presented in a minstrel-show format. In March 1970 came one of Luscombe's most successful shows ever, *Chicago 70*, a presentational docudrama about the famous conspiracy trial which arose from the riots outside the 1968 Democratic National Convention. As topical as yesterday's newspaper, *Chicago 70* quickly joined *Hair* and *Dionysus in 69* as Toronto's long-running locally produced hits. After almost three months on Alexander Street, *Chicago 70* transferred to New York for a further three weeks off-Broadway.

The move to Alexander Street was not without its costs, however; indeed, the high price of success is a recurring theme in the story of Toronto's alternative theatres. Throughout the 1960s Luscombe had provided an ongoing antithesis to theatre institutions in Toronto; by the end of the decade he had become an institution himself. As with Littlewood at Stratford East, the exigencies of supporting TWP's home seemed to blunt its sense of purpose. These problems were not due to the change in venue; rather, the change in venue was symptomatic of other changes wrought by the growth of the company. Jack Winter, who left TWP in 1967, made these observations three years after the move:

I found the group ideal in TWP was dissolving from within. We weren't going anywhere. We were becoming rigidified in all the wrong areas and I found that we were all sitting down and confirming our prejudices endlessly. And I think George is still doing that to some extent. I was working in a theatre that was not accomplishing its self-stated goals.[28]

However, added Winter, 'there is no one in the business now worth working for except George' – an opinion echoed by many actors who have passed through TWP. And Winter himself returned to write several shows with Luscombe in the 1970s.

Luscombe describes himself as a survivor, and TWP has proven to be a survivor too. It survived a fire which gutted the Alexander Street theatre in 1974. It survived further eviction crises in 1977 and 1981, when the property barely escaped demolition at the hands of private developers. It even survived further successes, the greatest of which was *Ten Lost Years* (1974), an ensemble play based on the reminiscences of Canadians who lived through the Depression. *Ten Lost Years* was TWP's biggest box-office success ever, with national and international tours, and renewed the company's stature in Toronto. In 1984, with the help of the provincial government, TWP finally gained control of its own building; and in 1986 Luscombe stepped aside as artistic director, appointing as his successor a like-minded young director named Robert Rooney. But two years later, Luscombe and Rooney were discharged by a new business-oriented board of directors who wished to make a deal with property developers. Luscombe and a 'Committee of Concern' from the theatre community began battling once again for TWP's very existence and, just as importantly, its sense of purpose. In the commercial climate of today's theatre, it seems unlikely that the company will survive this latest crisis.

I have not included TWP in the main body of this book because it was not really one of the 'major' alternative theatres, yet it is too important to include with the others in chapter 7. Nor, in a sense, did TWP contribute to the explosion of new theatres after 1968 because it was already fully grown by then. Although its production style had some influence on individual artists of the subsequent alternative theatres (notably Paul Thompson and James Reaney), Luscombe's TWP was a precedent rather than a model, an inspiration mainly in the sense of being a durable company founded and maintained on anti-mainstream principles. Despite many characteristics in common with Toronto's later alternative theatres, TWP was not born of the same sensibility, nor was it part of the same network. While the best of the new young directors respected Luscombe and appreciated him, they did not want to work with him: it is significant, for instance, that Garrard and his confrères did not invite Luscombe to join their New Directors Group, nor to take part in their Festival of Underground Theatre in 1970. Luscombe remained a separate force in Toronto theatre, a maverick. As critic Alan Filewod observes, 'TWP prepared the way for the alternative theatre in Canada but had little effect on its development.'[29]

With the many claims of 'firsts' put forth by the major alternative theatres in the early 1970s, it is worth reviewing some of the precedents set by TWP in the previous decade. It was the first alternative theatre to use actors to develop scripts, and the first to promote new Canadian plays. It was the first to set itself in opposition to the Stratford establishment, and to perform as a 'fringe' attraction to the Festival. It offered other struggling theatre groups, notably Toronto Dance Theatre and the Museum Children's Theatre, a congenial and central rental space on Alexander Street. It represented Canadian alternative theatre abroad at the 1969 Venice Biennale and again in 1976 on a European tour of *Ten Lost Years*. While mainstream theatre in Toronto suffered through a series of expensive failures in the late 1960s, TWP showed that there were alternative ways of creating local professional theatre. Indeed, several of the smaller alternative theatres were spin-offs of TWP, such as Open Circle and Redlight Theatre, as some of the brightest of Luscombe's performers founded their own companies in the 1970s. The four 'major' alternative companies, however, were led by people too independent ever to work for George Luscombe.

Critics in the 1960s and 1970s: Spreading the Word

Toronto's alternative theatres were buoyed in their rise by the attention they received from the country's best and most influential critics, who at that time were fixtures in Toronto's daily press. The most senior of these was Herbert Whittaker (b. 1910), the lead critic of the Toronto *Globe and Mail* from 1949 to 1975. Whittaker trained as a stage designer in his native Montreal, and as a young man toiled as a clerk in a railway station by day and as a designer in Montreal's amateur theatres by night.[30] His familiarity with the local theatre scene led to an offer to write some reviews for the Montreal *Gazette*, where he became lead critic in 1945. Four years later he moved to Toronto to accept a similar position at the *Globe and Mail*. He continued to be a theatre practitioner in Toronto as well – for example, he won the award for best director in the 1951 Dominion Drama Festival, and designed an Inuit setting for the Canadian Players' production of *King Lear* in 1961, probably that company's most memorable production.

What Herbert Whittaker brought to his criticism was a thorough knowledge of making theatre in Canada. As a designer in Montreal between the wars, he shared his generation's fervent wish to create locally based professional theatre in Canada. As a director and critic following World War II, he observed the achievements and the mistakes of companies attempting to realize that wish. During his long tenure at the *Globe*, Whittaker became known for his lifelong devotion to the professional arts in Canada, while becoming something of a cultural institution himself. His critical reputation was that of a gentleman who could express his most searing commentary in the (apparently) gentlest of rebukes. Nowadays, the complaint levelled against Whittaker is that he was *too* nice, *too* encouraging, and that standards suffered as a result. But Canadian theatre needed this kind of encouragement in Whittaker's day, his concern for building professional opportunities and his tolerance for unusual styles. Post-war professional theatre in Canada needed a publicist and a lobbyist as well as a critic, and it had them all in Herbert Whittaker.

Whittaker's celebrated rival at the *Toronto Star* was Nathan Cohen (1923–71), lead critic there from 1959 until his death in 1971. Cohen's background was in journalism rather than theatre: before coming to Toronto in 1945, he had already courted controversy with abrasive articles for his student newspaper at Mount Allison University and a union-run newspaper in his native Nova Scotia. In Toronto, Cohen wrote for several left-wing publications, started his own magazine called *The Critic*, and became one of Canada's leading media personalities on *Fighting Words*, a popular CBC radio and television panel show of which he was moderator. While he was not trained in the arts, his knowledge of theatre and entertainment was truly encyclopaedic. Already known as a keen and acerbic commentator on the arts when he joined the *Star* in 1959, Cohen became one of the leading theatre critics in North America in the 1960s – Canada's only real critic, Cohen himself was fond of saying.

Nathan Cohen cut a formidable figure in Toronto theatre in the

1960s, brandishing his public esteem along with his ever-present cane. For all his reputation for uncompromising standards, however, Cohen prided himself on going to shows in the smallest, meanest theatres in search of excellence. His rave review of *Hey, Rube!*, for instance, mentioned in passing that there were only seven other people in the audience. Cohen seemed to enjoy finding and championing a hard-working underdog, and finding and debunking a complacent success. For Toronto's alternative theatres, underdogs on the rise, it would be cruel but true to say that Cohen's death came at just the right time. They benefited from his initial encouragement without ever really having to face up to his standards.

Cohen's young successor at the *Star*, Urjo Kareda (b. 1944), became the most articulate spokesman for Toronto's alternative theatres and their new Canadian drama. Indeed, it is no coincidence that their rise to mainstream stature occurred during Kareda's short (1971–75) critical reign. Born in Estonia, Kareda came to Canada at age five and quickly developed a passion for film, theatre, and especially opera. While studying English literature at the University of Toronto, he wrote film and theatre reviews for the *Varsity*, and free-lance articles on entertainment for the *Globe and Mail*. He completed his MA in 1967, then accepted a federal government fellowship to pursue doctoral studies at Cambridge. There he worked on a thesis (never completed) on Chekhov and the Theatre of the Absurd. While in England Kareda continued his work in journalism, contributing a regular 'London Letter' to the *Toronto Star* and reviewing local plays while home for the summer. In 1970 he became the *Star*'s film reviewer, and in 1971 (after Cohen's death) the lead theatre critic. Later he served as literary manager of the Stratford Festival (1975–80), and as director of script development for CBC Radio Drama. Finally, completing a kind of career circle, Kareda succeeded Bill Glassco as artistic director of Tarragon Theatre in 1982.

During Kareda's four years as lead critic for the *Star*, the four major alternative theatres became the most important and influential theatres in Toronto. Kareda has described his own role in this as being merely the fortunate observer of a vital movement:

I was remarkably lucky to be a drama critic in Toronto at the time so much new theatre was emerging. It was an exhilarating time and I was enormously excited by what I saw. I liked and admired many of the personalities and the work associated with that period and I tried to write about it in a way that reflected that admiration.[31]

In this assessment, Kareda is being unduly modest. His literate, passionate reviews had an enormous impact on theatre in Toronto. Unlike Whittaker and Cohen, Kareda was a contemporary of the younger leaders of Toronto's new theatres. He was steeped in the same post-Expo nationalism, yet had an international heritage and education. His knowledgeability and his articulateness were above reproach. Writing for the largest newspaper in Canada's largest anglophone market, Kareda was, at the very least, a morale-booster for the small theatres. However, the theatre leaders themselves recognize that he was also a factor in their rise to prominence. 'When he wrote about new shows, he communicated his excitement,' says Paul Thompson; 'he made theatre an event.'[32] Kareda loved all kinds of theatre, from improvisation to grand opera; but he was particularly fond of the paradoxes of theatrical naturalism, which he described in Toronto as 'an almost forgotten dramatic style.'[33] He also seems to have been particularly attuned to Bill Glassco's aesthetic sense; so that when Tarragon struck the right note, Kareda's praise was eloquent and unreserved.

There were other critics, of course, at this time. Perhaps the most noteworthy was Brian Boru (pen-name of free-lance designer and critic Brian Arnott), who wrote for *That's Showbusiness*, a biweekly trade newspaper on entertainment which was published from 1971 to 1976. Boru's critical stance was diametrically opposed to Kareda's: he despised naturalism as a regressive form of art, and so his reviews (particularly those of Tarragon Theatre) make an intriguing contrast with Kareda's. Another important critic was Don Rubin, first as a back-up to Cohen in the late 1960s and later as founding editor of the *Canadian Theatre Review*. Rubin, like Cohen, seemed to encourage the *idea* behind new work, even when he did not like the work itself. The critics at the other Toronto dailies, the *Telegram* and the *Toronto Sun*, had little impact on the arts during the period in question. For a consistent view of the rise of Toronto's alternative theatres, this book will rely on the three major critics of the time – Whittaker, Cohen, and Kareda. Unlike later critics, these three perceived themselves as part of the process of establishing theatre in their community, not merely as journalists providing a consumers' guide to local live entertainment. As Martin Kinch put it, they accepted 'a wider responsibility to create the cultural climate' in Toronto.[34] It is significant that the pall which settled over the alternative theatres after 1975 coincided with Kareda's departure and Whittaker's retirement. Subsequent critics never gained the respect of the theatre community as Whittaker, Cohen, and Kareda did.

The comments by Whittaker and Kareda which introduce this chapter were written at an important watershed in the rise of Toronto's alternative theatres. The movement had begun in the late 1960s when American counter-cultural values were at their zenith, with alternative lifestyles publicly flaunted at Toronto's notorious 'free university' of Rochdale College and in the 'hippie' district of Yorkville. Theatre Passe Muraille's production of *Futz* in 1969 and the Festival of Underground Theatre in 1970 were the most important landmarks of this stage. After this festival, Toronto's alternative theatre turned from general social concerns toward more specifically theatrical ones: in 1971, Passe Muraille's *Vampyr* brought stylish production values to the alternative theatre, while Factory Theatre Lab's *Creeps* brought national attention to the promotion of indigenous plays.

The watershed of 1972 is marked by three almost simultaneous events. First, in May, David French's *Leaving Home* opened at Tarragon Theatre, an 'old-fashioned, naturalistic drama' as Kareda described it.[35] *Leaving Home* found a mainstream audience and brought Toronto's alternative theatres into the consciousness, and the repertory, of the larger regional theatres. Next, in June, Toronto Free Theatre opened on the strength of a $100,000 LIP grant, bringing mainstream administrative models and the first substantial public funding to Toronto's alternative theatre. And finally, in August, Theatre Passe Muraille produced *The Farm Show*, its quintessential collective creation. *The Farm Show* established Passe Muraille's new direction under Paul Thompson and led to the dissemination of the Passe Muraille collective as the most distinctive performing style of the new Canadian theatre. After 1972, on the other side of the watershed, the four major alternative theatres exerted a national influence and became an established institution in their own right. In the years which followed, their energies were poured into solidifying and building on the stature which they had attained.

2
Theatre Passe Muraille to 1970

[Theatre Passe Muraille] has become the focal point for Toronto's burgeoning studio and non-establishment theatre movement.[1]

Nathan Cohen, January 1971

Theatre Passe Muraille was the first and most important company in the explosion of new theatres in Toronto in the late 1960s, and has been a hub for new theatre activity ever since. The early history of Passe Muraille has been all but obliterated by the subsequent success of Paul Thompson and the series of 'collective creations' which he brought to life in the 1970s. Thompson's influence is eclectic and wide-ranging. His encouragement ('nagging' might be a better word) is literally responsible for the first plays of such writers as John Gray and Linda Griffiths, and for the establishment of such companies as the Blyth Festival and Newfoundland's Codco. Thompson is now so strongly identified with Theatre Passe Muraille that even theatre professionals in Toronto think that he founded it. In fact, Theatre Passe Muraille was already an established force in experimental theatre in Toronto when Paul Thompson joined the company in 1969. The following year, with its previous leaders drifting off and the company in disarray, Thompson assumed the title of Managing Director and kept the theatre from disintegrating.

The story of Theatre Passe Muraille is really the story of two successive companies linked by a transitional period. The first company, founded by Jim Garrard in 1968, began with improvisational workshops at Rochdale College, at that time the most important centre of radical culture in Canada. Garrard's company attracted very little notice for almost a year, until his production of *Futz* in 1969 resulted in obscenity charges and sensational publicity. This notoriety, in turn, attracted a number of new young theatre artists to the company. Between 1969 and 1972 (between *Futz* and *The Farm Show*), Passe Muraille was led by a dynamic co-operative rather than by a single director, a co-operative in which the regular actors took a much stronger decision-making role than is normally found in any theatre company, alternative or mainstream. In this transitional period, artistic leadership of Passe Muraille gradually shifted from Garrard, through Martin Kinch and (to a lesser extent) John Palmer, until it finally fell to Thompson more or less by default. That the company survived and then flourished under Thompson is mainly due to his tenacious commitment to its widening role as an advocate for Canadian themes. Under Thompson, then, Theatre Passe Muraille became one of the leading nationalist theatres in Canada. In the beginning, however, under Garrard, it was the foremost among several companies which introduced the plays and techniques of American alternative theatre to Toronto.

Indeed, alternative theatre in Toronto began, not as the nationalistic expression which it later became, but as an imitation of radical theatre in the United States. American culture, spread through a profusion of print and electronic media in the 1960s, influenced young Canadian theatre artists both politically and aesthetically. Radical politics and radical aesthetics both protested the unquestioning acceptance of a cultural *status quo*. Political militancy in America in the early 1960s was focused first in the civil rights movement, then in the rising wave of protest over the Vietnam War. Thousands of American draft dodgers and military deserters were welcomed by liberal society in Toronto, and many young Canadians joined in the anti-war protests on both sides of the border. The climax of confrontation between establishment and anti-establishment ideologies came in 1968, when police battled demonstrators outside the Democratic National Convention in Chicago. In the public's mind, this political radicalism was confused with the 'hippie' subculture with which it had some high-profile trappings in common, notably recreational drugs, sexual licence, and long hair. In fact, however, these similarities were superficial: while the hippies were smoking marijuana and listening to music, political activists were trying to turn society upside down.

Militancy in theatre, not surprisingly, grew at the same time as militancy in society at large. In theatre, however, the chief enemy was accepted public aesthetics instead of accepted public ethics. In North America, knowledge of new European intellectual dramatists such as Beckett and Ionesco was disseminated through a proliferation of university drama courses and of new academic criticism in the 1960s. Theatre intellectuals, disdainful of a Broadway in decline, took as their alternative model the Polish Theatre Lab of Jerzy Grotowski, whose book *Towards a Poor Theatre* (1968) became the theatre iconoclast's bible. Highly physical performing styles similar to Grotowski's were also developed by the Living Theatre and the Open Theatre in New York, and were widely promoted by the radical aesthetics of the quarterly *Tulane Drama Review* (later *The Drama Review*). On the textual side, new American playwrights found a platform in New York's off-off-Broadway coffee-houses such as Joe Cino's Caffe Cino and Ellen Stewart's Cafe La Mama. Although off-off-Broadway also had its intellectual overtones, the need to find and hold an audience (even in small Greenwich Village basements) meant that the temptations of commercial theatre were never very far out of mind. While a few resolutely radical artists persisted in anti-commercial ghettos of performance art or guerrilla theatre, off-off-Broadway soon found itself defining success in terms of off-Broadway, then in terms of Broadway. The symbolic death and ascension of off-off-Broadway came in 1967, the year in which Joe Cino committed suicide and in which the La Mama Experimental Theatre Club attained international fame by taking two of its plays to England, *Tom Paine* and *Futz*, both directed by Tom O'Horgan. The next year, the two La Mama productions were presented off-Broadway, while O'Horgan broke into Broadway's charmed circle with his phenomenally successful production of *Hair*.

In less than a decade, then, New York's alternative theatre had risen to become part of the mainstream. In Canada, the rise of the alternative theatres was to be even more rapid and more enduring. The importance of Garrard's Theatre Passe Muraille in this rise was to create a stature and an expectation for alternative theatre in Toronto which were essential to the success of the whole movement.

Rochdale College to *Futz*, 1968–69

Theatre Passe Muraille, created by Jim Garrard in 1968, was modelled on radical theatre which could be found in New York and London but not in Toronto. Garrard (b. 1939) grew up in Ontario, in the vicinity of Oshawa and St Catharines. Since he could not afford to go to university, he attended teachers' college and worked as the principal of a small elementary school near Welland. He began taking correspondence and summer courses from Queen's University, and soon left teaching to complete a BA at Queen's in English, drama, and philosophy. Under the inspiring leadership of Fred Euringer, then head of the Drama Department at Queen's, Garrard found himself involved in some forty productions in his three years there (1963–66) and made up his mind to become a professional director. He applied to the London Academy of Music and Dramatic Art (LAMDA) and was accepted for its two-year acting program beginning in 1966.

As a theatre student at the centre of the theatrical world, Garrard attended a wider variety of performances than he would have thought possible in Canada, from France's experimental Panic Circus to Olivier's *Othello*. But the greatest impression on Garrard was made by the La Mama Experimental Theatre Club, which he saw perform their counter-culture hit *Tom Paine* during their tour to London in 1967. As Garrard recalls,

It was completely different from anything I'd ever seen, a true ensemble piece. It had brilliant direction from Tom O'Horgan, a very fascinating style of play, lots of musical instruments, the use of bodies to create settings ... Later I saw *Futz* at the Mercury Theatre Club by the same company with basically the same cast. I was really struck by this idea that a lot of really young energetic actors could get together and work together through the kind of ensemble techniques we admired at the time, and put on these shows which were very very different. So I came back to Canada with the view in mind to starting a theatre like La Mama, or like what's later been called an alternative theatre or an underground theatre.[2]

Garrard returned to Canada in February 1968, anxious to put these new ideas into practice:

I wound up in Toronto pretty much because I knew the city best and I did want to work in a large city. I checked out all the usual places for acting jobs and directing work – Stratford, the National Theatre School – but no one had anything available. Charlotte Holmes, the theatre contact at the Ontario Arts Council, suggested that I try to affiliate with a college if I could and she told me about Rochdale. It sounded fairly interesting and it gave me both a place to live and a place to work.[3]

Mention Rochdale College in Toronto today, and people will still roll their eyes and shudder. By the mid-1970s, Rochdale College had become a symbol of all that was bad with the pursuit of personal freedom in the 1960s, a filthy high-rise tenement housing indigent runaways, wilting hippies, and malevolent drug profiteers. But Rochdale began with the best intentions of its era, as an expression of an unprecedented faith in the combined power of technology and idealism. This faith reached its zenith between 1967 and 1970, between the manned moon launches and the Kent State shootings in the United States, between Expo 67 and the October Crisis in Canada. In this period, Rochdale College became a centre for radical thought in North America, a sanctuary for draft dodgers, a laboratory for radical education, and a meeting place for writers and artists of all kinds. The decline of Rochdale as a viable educational institution began even before it opened. As its first registrar, Jack Dimond, said, 'Once the decision was made to let anyone move in who wanted to, Rochdale was doomed.'[4] The principles of personal freedom upon which it was founded were difficult to administer, and easy to take advantage of. (In hippie terms, for instance, it was considered immoral to evict people who couldn't pay their rent.) Strangely, however, the 'Rochdale Experiment' achieved its goals to an extent which public opinion never appreciated: for the people who lived there, Rochdale provided a unique and practical education far beyond the scope of any university.

Rochdale College was planned as a high-rise student residence by Campus Co-operative Residences Incorporated, a member-owned company created in 1937 to provide low-cost rental housing for Toronto students. By 1957, when teenager Howard Adelman became president, Campus Co-op owned six houses in a declining neighbourhood adjacent to the University of Toronto. Under his mercurial leadership, the Co-op's holdings expanded to thirty houses, an on-campus credit union, and assets of almost a half-million dollars by the mid-1960s.[5] In 1963 Adelman began lobbying for his Rochdale project, which was in effect a practical embodiment of his theories on student housing. Rochdale was intended to be just the first of a series of newly designed student residences built by private enterprise, with public financing, in several Canadian cities. Each residence, Rochdale included, would incorporate several different styles of student accommodation. Conceptually, it was as if Adelman had taken all those old brick Co-op houses and stacked them on top of each other, with the high-rise design yielding a far lower cost per bed than any existing form of student housing.

One of Adelman's critical manoeuvres in the creation of Rochdale

College was acquiring legal status for it as an educational institution. This was not only a brilliant stroke of expedience, it also launched Rochdale's tradition as a thorn in the side of the WASP establishment of the University of Toronto. In 1963, the university's great benefactor Vincent Massey had created a modern incarnation of his own Oxford school days by building Massey College for the university. Housing the male (only) graduate students who were expected to be Canada's next intellectual elite, it was an architecturally superb low-density building with a genteel air, complete with maid service for student residents and bar for members only. What infuriated Adelman was that, although Massey College conducted no classes and granted no degrees, this bourgeois vision of the Groves of Academe had been legally declared an educational institution, so that it could benefit from tax relief for which his proletarian Co-op houses were ineligible. Before he settled on the name 'Rochdale College' (after the English town where the co-operative movement had begun in 1844), Adelman even toyed with the idea of naming his project 'Ferguson College,' to poke fun at the Massey-Ferguson farm machinery empire on which the Massey family fortune was based. With Massey College cited as precedent, the Rochdale project was granted legal college status through a special act of the Ontario legislature. Indeed, with university populations expanding so rapidly in the 1960s, the university's administration eagerly welcomed this student initiative to help alleviate terrible shortages in student housing. Rochdale's legal status as a college was also crucial to its capital financing. First, as a student residence, it was eligible for federal government mortgages totalling 90 per cent of its $5.4 million cost. Then, as an educational institution, it was eligible for sales tax rebates on building materials, which covered much of the remaining 10 per cent.[6]

Excavations were already under way at the corner of Bloor and Huron streets when the direction of the Rochdale project was abruptly changed by Campus Co-op's Education Committee. Until 1967 this committee was an incidental service arranging for in-house films and lectures in the Co-op's houses. But under the spiritual leadership of Dennis Lee, a young lecturer at Victoria College and later a celebrated poet and editor, the Education Committee became the tail wagging a five million dollar dog. Lee and a group of similarly idealistic educators used the democratic structure of the Co-op to change the Rochdale project from a housing experiment to an educational one. Its college status, initiated as merely a fiscal expedient, became instead a philosophical watchword. After a diligent door-to-door campaign to lobby Co-op members, a general meeting of the Co-op in March 1967 ratified the Education Committee's vision of Rochdale College as an institution of alternative higher education, sort of a Summerhill for young adults. Thus was created Canada's first free university.

For the 1967–68 academic year, six Co-op houses were designated as 'Rochdale College' while construction continued on the new building. Lee quit his position at Victoria College to become a full-time educational planner for Rochdale, his salary paid initially through the federal government's Company of Young Canadians program. There he exhausted himself nurturing and promoting the Rochdale concept, while creating a prototype curriculum in preparation for the opening of the Rochdale building the following year. In theory as well as in practice, Rochdale's curriculum was a grass-roots response to the interests and abilities of its members. Seminars were offered on a wide range of topics, including phenomenology, Eastern thought, and contemporary social problems, while workshops were held in silkscreening, film, music, and drama. The drama workshops, co-ordinated by Lee's wife Donna, were held in a church basement on Huron Street, where about a dozen people met for weekly improvisational work led by the Lees' friend Tony Parr, a professional actor. Although sometimes treated as a 'frill' in less expansive times, drama was central to educational theory in the 1960s, not only as a performing art but also as a tool for social interaction and public re-education. It is not surprising, then, that when Jim Garrard appeared at the Rochdale office in 1968 to ask if he could start a drama workshop, after the original one had run its course, Dennis Lee told him simply to put a sign up.

Garrard's workshops began in April 1968 in a coach-house owned by Adelman's brother on Avenue Road. Meanwhile, Garrard prepared a twelve-page brief for Rochdale's governing council outlining his plans for a far-reaching drama project for the college. He had coined the name 'Theatre Passe Muraille' while studying in England, when his wife had read him a French story about a character with the power to pass through walls as thick as the Great Wall of China. To Garrard, this was a striking metaphor for the kind of alternative theatre he wished to create, and which he now proposed to the Rochdale council. 'Theatre Without Walls,' he wrote, 'a theatre free of distinctions between actor and spectator, between "inside" and "outside" the theatre, between drama as one art form, music as another and dancing as yet another.'[7] Tailoring his proposal to the goals of Rochdale, Garrard stressed experimentation, social research, and the relationship of theatre to its immediate society and beyond. There were to be three components to the Rochdale Drama Project: a Community Theatre, an Educational Unit, and a Performing Unit. The objective of the Community Theatre, he wrote, was 'to avoid the kind of isolation that generally accompanies high-rise living and to bring about the kind of contact that community should provide,' while that of the Educational Unit was 'to make theatre relevant for society.' In contrast to these rather vague objectives, the goals and activities for the Performing Unit were described very specifically. It was to be a permanent resident company composed of a managing director, nine actors, and two technicians, assisted by three researchers with expertise in music, design, and educational liaison. The actors, by working exclusively within the group, were to develop a relationship of trust and understanding enabling them 'to perform not just as superb technicians, but as human beings involved in an event.' In addition, Garrard proposed a collapsible, transportable 'plastic theatre' for Rochdale's second-floor terrace, with a working area of at least sixty feet by forty feet, providing 'seating and stage facilities flexible enough to provide as extensive a range of dramatic relationships between the audience and the players as there are natural relationships between people.' The style of the company would stress adaptability, flexibility, idealism, experimentation, and ensemble performance, disdaining 'theatre as architecture' in favour of 'the *experience* that ought to be and can be the theatre.' The cost of the first year's operation would be $128,500.

One interpretation of Garrard's brief is that it represents an early exercise in alternative theatre grantsmanship, with the nebulous goals of the Community Theatre and the Educational Unit designed to win approval from the Rochdale council for Garrard's ambitions for a professional company. Such an interpretation is unduly cynical: in fact, Garrard was attempting, like other educational and social visionaries at Rochdale College, to put his theories into practice in this highly sympathetic social laboratory. The distinctions among the three components of Theatre Passe Muraille were artificial, wrote Garrard, and 'employed only for the sake of convenience. They cannot exist in fact, for theatre as produced entertainment and theatre as education cannot be distinguished.' Similarly, as theatre and society were inseparable concepts to Garrard, so were theatrical experiment and social experiment. His later preoccupation with the escalating problems of Rochdale College, and his resulting drift away from Passe Muraille, were entirely consistent with this philosophy.

Amid a great deal of media coverage, the Rochdale building opened in September 1968, with several floors still not ready for occupancy. The college listed Garrard as a full-time resource person (the Rochdale equivalent of a faculty member) and allowed him half his rent on a large two-bedroom apartment in exchange for his services. In addition, the multicoloured college catalogue (the Rochdale equivalent of a university calendar) described the structure of Rochdale's new drama project:

There are two aspects to theatre at Rochdale, one of which is presently functioning because the minimum requirements for its existence are a place and the interests of a group of people; this is the Community Theatre. The other aspect, professional theatre and educational research, is at present in an embryonic state while fundraising and organizing are carried out.

The Community Theatre: using the whole building and as many of Rochdale's members as are interested. Al Morgan is available to help groups to use theatre as a recreational activity, a means of expressing and developing the sense of community, or for any other reason. Workshops, seminars, guerrilla theatre, magic, animals, circuses, games all are possible if anyone wants them. Al is also interested in playwriting workshops and directing small productions. Watch the bulletin board or the newsletter for more information.

The Professional Theatre: Jim Gerrard [sic] hopes to establish a professional theatre ensemble within the Rochdale environment, providing entertainment for everyone, resource people and other help for the Community Theatre, and research into possible uses of drama in education and community work.

With the opening of the new building, Garrard's improvisational workshops moved from Avenue Road to the spacious living-room of his eighteenth-floor 'Zeus Suite' at Rochdale. Led by Garrard and Al Morgan, an American draft resister, these workshops consisted mainly of theatre games and sensitivity training: psychological exercises, trust exercises, birth exercises, and so on. A charismatic leader, Garrard's messianic style was accentuated by his remarkable resemblance to popular images of Jesus Christ: tall and gaunt, with penetrating eyes, long brown hair and beard, and a soft-spoken intensity. 'I didn't like it at all later,' he recalls now; 'I didn't like that whole messianic approach, it seemed manipulative and it seemed cheap. But at the time, it was very useful and it sometimes had very beautiful results.' A playwrights' workshop also functioned that fall, with performances taking place in Rochdale's basement parking garage once or twice a week. Morgan put up $5000 of his own funds as seed money for the company, and the

Ontario Arts Council contributed $4000 for an educational project. Considering the financial projections for Rochdale, Garrard might have reasonably expected more support from the college itself, as his original brief requested; but Rochdale's cash flow very quickly became a permanent crisis, and Garrard's other fundraising efforts for his theatre came to nought. And when it became apparent that Garrard's goals did not involve politically activist theatre, Morgan withdrew his remaining funds and left the company.

Meanwhile, Garrard's improvisational workshops began to coalesce into rehearsals for a production of *Tom Paine*, the play which had so impressed him in London. During the rehearsal period, he negotiated with a British agency for the performance rights to the play, unaware that the playwright, Paul Foster, had sold the North American rights to a New York producer. When this producer learned of their rehearsals, Rochdale's *Tom Paine* was threatened with legal action. The irony of the situation was not lost on Garrard:

It was quite odd. This play is all about Tom Paine and liberty and freedom. I phoned the playwright and I said, 'What's going on here? We've got a bunch of people up here who want to do your production, we're doing a beautiful production, and we're getting lawyers' letters saying we've got to close it down. Is this consistent with the play that you've written?'

He'd never met me before, but he said, 'Jim, I'm an American, and all Americans are tainted.' And that was the end of his contribution.

Due to its precarious legal situation, the Rochdale *Tom Paine* was given only one 'private' performance, in the building's underground parking garage in December 1968. As Garrard recalls the performance,

We used probably sixteen or twenty [parking] bays. We painted those black, we brought in 220 power, and it was played completely on the flat. People sat on the floor, and we used a couple of bays as the stage. So it was three-quarters round, there was a concrete back wall to it, and we had in that little space up to 25 actors.

One of the La Mama techniques was to use bodies to construct scenery ... it was good, it was cheap ... they were all in leotards anyway, and they'd just put on a cloak or put on a hat. It was very simple, like child-play really ... like exuberant kids dressing up.

Although it was produced and performed by people with very little theatrical experience, Garrard remembers *Tom Paine* as 'one of the best productions I've ever been associated with' and 'the perfect kind of monument to the times.' In the sunset glow of 1960s optimism, the naïvety and technical weaknesses which might be seen in this production were overshadowed by the revolutionary nature of the material and the clandestine atmosphere of its performance. In later years, this single performance acquired a mythic importance in Toronto's alternative theatre scene. As critic Don Rubin recalled in 1978,

I remember trying to find my way one rainy night through the incensed halls of Rochdale College to see a production of Paul Foster's off-Broadway hit, *Tom Paine*. When I finally found the space, I was told by Jim Garrard, the director of the piece and the founder of the group that would eventually call itself Passe Muraille (Beyond the Walls), that they were having trouble getting production rights to the script. This, for all intents and purposes, on opening night. Nevertheless, the show went on, Tom Paine spoke out for human freedom and the modern phase of theatrical growth in Toronto was officially ushered in.[8]

The libertarian content and radical style of this production, within the revolutionary context of Rochdale College, attracted a group of like-minded theatre professionals to work with Garrard. Frank Masi, another American draft resister, had come to Rochdale with his actress wife, Judith. He quickly proved himself a brilliantly innovative designer who also possessed outstanding technical skills. Masi's fascination with large-scale effects, while never given full rein in the small theatre spaces of Toronto's underground theatres, later found expression in his work with the horse-drawn Caravan Theatre of British Columbia, and with theme parks and touring rock-and-roll shows. Frank Masi designed *Tom Paine* and several subsequent productions under Garrard's direction, and Judith Masi acted in them. Another addition to the Passe Muraille team was Ron Terrill, a 24-year-old native of Belleville, Ontario, who had earlier worked as an administrator for Toronto Workshop Productions and as production co-ordinator for a new company called Trio Productions. Terrill came to see this *Tom Paine* and stayed on to become the first general manager of Theatre Passe Muraille. He was also a prime mover of the Festival of Underground Theatre in August 1970, another event of mythic importance in the rise of Toronto's alternative theatres.

Naturally, the early closing of *Tom Paine* was a disappointment to everyone involved, and rehearsals began almost immediately for a new production. This time, Garrard chose Rochelle Owens' *Futz*, the second of the La Mama plays he had seen in London. Workshops and rehearsals continued in his Zeus Suite, and performance rights were obtained without complications. However, the company's original operating funds had all been spent, and Rochdale's governing council by early 1969 was too busy contending with police harassment, public disapproval, and terrible administrative and fiscal emergencies to be able to help with production costs. Fortunately, Terrill persuaded his former employers at Trio Productions to attend a rehearsal of *Futz* with an eye to financing the show. It was a bizarre first meeting. With half the cast missing (which was hardly unprecedented), the ragtag group was rehearsing in the vault of an unoccupied bank on Rochdale's ground floor, with one of the world's most flamboyant rock bands helping to fill in the gaps. As Garrard recalls,

All of the Mothers of Invention except for Frank Zappa were visiting the city ... Penny Gawn, who was in the cast of *Futz*, had found them in the [Rochdale health-food] restaurant, chatted with them, and they came in. They had actually had experience in these funny theatre games that we were doing, so they came in. They were making these fences, rolling around on the floor, Cy was there with his pig – it was a pretty surreal production. It's a surreal play.

Trio Productions was a one-year-old company consisting of publicist-producer Bill Marshall (who later founded Toronto's 'Festival of Festivals') along with lawyers Arthur Pennington and Miles O'Reilly. A Scotsman by birth, Marshall had already made a great impact and quite a bit of money in Toronto theatre by importing (ironically) an indigenous play, John Herbert's off-Broadway hit *Fortune and Men's Eyes*, which had performed in Toronto and Montreal for almost four months in the winter of 1967–68. Pennington and O'Reilly had both participated in student productions while attending the University of Toronto, and later joined a very active amateur theatre group at their Unitarian church, of which Terrill was also a member. With this group, dubbed the Uniplayers, Pennington and O'Reilly produced an evening of absurdist plays at the Colonnade Theatre in March 1968, with Marshall as one of the directors.[9] That August the three of them formed Trio Productions, announced a season, and began selling subscriptions. Their concept for Trio was not nationalistic, altruistic, or political: it was to produce new modishly controversial plays for profit, plays which were proven money-makers in the metropolitan centres of New York or London but which had not yet been seen in Toronto. (No doubt they drew some encouragement from the troubles at Theatre Toronto, where play selections tended to be controversial but not modish.) Trio's season began ambitiously in September 1968, with three productions opening within a week in three Toronto theatres: *Black Comedy* at TWP, *Staircase* at the Colonnade, and *Marat/Sade* in the church hall on Trinity Square, the same hall which (ironically again) became home to both Theatre Toronto and Theatre Passe Muraille within a year. Perhaps Trio overestimated the eagerness of Toronto audiences to see these well-known plays, or perhaps the three productions spread their audience too thinly, or perhaps their standards were just not professional enough. In any event, the productions received mediocre reviews, and box-office receipts fell far short of the company's requirements. Financially under siege, Trio retrenched. By the time they came to see the *Futz* rehearsal, the producing partners had not opened a show in almost six months.

In retrospect, this chaotic rehearsal in an abandoned vault seems a poor inducement for Trio to throw its slender resources into a counter-culture ensemble play. The partners, however, were not in a position to be too fastidious. Having lost a lot of money on their own productions, they were nonetheless committed to providing two more plays for their subscribers. They had solved half of this problem by relinquishing Trio's production rights to *The Killing of Sister George* to Theatre Toronto in exchange for tickets for Trio's subscribers. *Sister George* finally opened at the Royal Alexandra Theatre in March 1969, the last production ever for Theatre Toronto. In terms of audience expectation, the Royal Alex and Theatre Passe Muraille were at opposite ends of a spectrum; but Trio had badly misjudged theatrical fashions once already, so that Marshall chose to cover all bases this time. He told the press that Trio chose to back *Futz* because 'that's the kind of play we want to do – a real troublemaker of a play – because other people here aren't doing anything like it.'[10] While this may be true, it is also true that backing *Futz* would cost far less than mounting their own professional production; and if the show caught the public's imagination there might be some profit to be made, which was not the case with the *Sister George* deal. While the rehearsal they watched was something of a shambles, the volatile subject matter and reputation of the play might also attract a lot of attention, while potential losses could not be too great. It seemed, at worst, a marginal risk.

Of course, Trio wasn't about to bring its subscribers to an underground parking garage at Rochdale College. Instead, the company rented the nearby Central Library Theatre, a 200-seat proscenium theatre at St George and College streets. The Central Library had housed such mainstream operations as the Red Barn and the Canadian Players, and Marshall himself had done well there with *Fortune and Men's Eyes*. As opening night approached, and Passe Muraille's work still bore little resemblance to rehearsals as they understood the term, the Trio partners became increasingly worried about the show's ability to draw an audience. Putting on a brave face, however, they sold the show on the basis of its unconventionality and its young cast. As Marshall told the press on the day that *Futz* opened, 'It's a madhouse. These kids never seem to come to rehearsal on time and when they do show up they're reading their lines off little scraps of paper. But you know, the dress rehearsal looked more organized than any dress rehearsal we've ever had before.' Still, the producers were walking a fine line, and they knew it, in hoping the production would be risqué enough to attract public attention, but still respectable enough for a mainstream audience. As Garrard recalls, Trio nearly withdrew *Futz* the night before it opened, demanding cuts which he as a high-principled young artist at first refused to make. 'Finally we struck an agreement,' recalls Garrard. 'I said we'd cut these four pieces, and they agreed they'd go the distance with us ... They then turned around and made the fuss themselves by sending out press releases saying this play is full of nudity and obscenity and you've got to get down here.'

It seems incredible, now, the uproar that this production caused. On a reading, *Futz* seems devoid of offence. Indeed, like much avant-garde drama, it is scrupulously moral. In Owens' play, first produced in a workshop in Minneapolis in 1965, a farmer named Cyrus Futz lives quietly in sin with his pet sow Amanda in some Ozark-like part of rural America. The hypocritical moral stance of his neighbours is contrasted to the pure uncomplicated love of Cy and Amanda, whose noisy offstage lovemaking was a highlight of the group theatrical effects which O'Horgan created in his New York production. In keeping with the 'new morality' of the 1960s, the sexual repression of young people by outmoded and unbending mores is the villain of the piece. In one subplot, a young man runs mad when he stumbles across Cy and Amanda making love, kills the flirtatious object of his own desires, and is hanged for his crime. In another, the town slut, jealous of Amanda, eventually brings about the death of both Cy and his beloved pig. From its previous productions in Minneapolis, New York, and London, *Futz* had already acquired a reputation for its bestiality and nudity, even though the bestiality was entirely offstage, and the nudity consisted only of a brief glimpse of the bared breast of one young actress as she offered to suckle her condemned son in a symbolic act of maternal grief. In his inflammatory pre-show publicity, Marshall offered to challenge the taboos of Toronto the Good – 'We want to see what you can put on in Toronto,' he said – and the *Toronto Star* co-operated with the titillating headline 'Futz brings nudity, bestiality to Toronto stage' on the day the play opened. For its part, Toronto's morality squad seemed uninterested. Said a police spokesman, 'If all it's got to show is a couple of bare mammary glands, I don't think we'd even bother with it.' Pennington and O'Reilly also invited to the opening night performance crown counsel Peter Rickaby, who, in a *cause célèbre* of Toronto's cultural community in 1965, had been both complainant and prosecutor in the obscenity conviction of gallery-owner Dorothy Cameron. At the Central Library Theatre that night, when a plainclothes police officer asked Rickaby if he thought obscenity charges ought to be laid, the counsel replied, 'It would be laughed out of court.'[11]

But despite the moral nature of its content and the marginal nature of its impropriety, *Futz* was 'busted.' The stage manager, who later quit the show to avoid prosecution, telephoned the performers on the day the *Star* article appeared to warn them of possible police action. After their opening night performance, the actors left the theatre by a fire escape to avoid meeting any officers of the law. Charges were laid following their second performance, and the next day the police issued summonses to everyone involved in the production: director, producers, performers, stage crew, even the hat-check boy at the Central Library. And so it was for every performance: summonses were issued all round, every day, since each new performance constituted a new alleged offence. The daily summons ritual turned into a media circus, with press and television coverage. The air was soon heavy with both types of revolutionary rhetoric, passive resistance ('We need to be reminded to do our own thing and to leave others to do theirs') and active defiance ('If they arrest us – unless they deny us bail – we will keep performing').[12] Ticket sales soared due to the production's sudden celebrity, and the producers added extra performances to the weekly schedule. A bewildered Rochelle Owens was brought to Toronto to keep the publicity mills churning, and offered this cosmopolitan perspective: 'This couldn't happen in New York. All this prurient sex. It's very corny.'[13] Those who were not outraged by public displays of lewd activity on one hand, or by the arbitrary suppression of free speech on the other, were embarrassed by the provincialism of the whole uproar. As an article in the Toronto *Telegram* put it, 'The press, the police, and those responsible for the production have this much in common: they have all become excited by a trace of smut.'[14]

Futz closed as scheduled after three weeks, since another group had booked the Central Library Theatre. The possibility of transferring the show to another venue was discussed, but not pursued: Passe Muraille had no money to produce it themselves, the Trio producers were knee-deep in summonses, and a sobering awareness of the potential personal consequences of a conviction under the Criminal Code, under which the police had chosen to lay charges, had crept over everyone involved. By the time the case reached Provincial Court in June 1969, charges had been dropped against everyone except Garrard and the three producers. After a two-day trial, all four defendants were found guilty of staging an indecent performance. An appeal was made to a higher court, and in April 1970 the defendants were acquitted of all charges. The Crown chose not to appeal this decision. Incidentally, the Trio partners kept their promise to Garrard just as they had kept their promise to their subscribers: he was never asked to contribute toward the legal costs.

The *Futz* affair and its attendant media coverage brought tremendous public attention to alternative theatre in Toronto, and galvanized the theatre community. At this distance, however, it is hard to determine why the participants were charged, why the director and producers were convicted, and why these convictions were later overturned. In the first place, it seems that the charges arose because, for Toronto in 1969, the performance *was* obscene – not the play that Rochelle Owens wrote, but the whole La Mama-inspired Passe Muraille version. The show at the Central Library was actually entitled *An Evening with Futz*. While the second act consisted of Owens' simple parable, the first act was a multi-media 'happening'-style collage, developed in Garrard's improvisational rehearsals, which was designed to prepare the audience for the play. 'I've always hated sitting in the dark in the theatre,' he says. 'I'm always trying to find ways to make the theatre more social.' With *Futz*, this began when the doors opened, and audience members found they had to pick their way to their seats through cast members lying in the aisles. After the cast did some warm-up exercises, they interrogated the audience about their preconceived notions of such matters as bestiality and the play's reputation. Jokes and skits on sexual matters were intermingled with slides of related images, such as Disney's 'Three Little Pigs' and a porcine posterior. A tape recorder played the Beatles' 'Why Don't We Do It in the Road.' One reviewer described the first act as 'an extended series of obscene songs and dreary old jokes ("Do you smoke after sex?" asks one actor. "I don't know," says another, "I've never looked.")[15] By all accounts this first act was handled quite badly: the exercises were interesting enough, but the interrogations were inept and the songs and jokes were puerile. Garrard himself disliked the first act so thoroughly that he usually stayed in the lobby, unable to watch.

The first *Futz* trial took place in June 1969, with front-page press coverage. The prosecution called only two witnesses, two morality squad officers, who testified that they found the play both obscene and offensive. Their testimony centred on the *Futz* proper of the second act, citing the naked breast, a simulated sexual encounter among two men and a prostitute, and Cy's noisy offstage lovemaking with Amanda. The defence, conducted by well-known trial lawyer Julian Porter, countered with a number of experts who discussed the artistic and moral values of the play. (Perhaps the most trenchant observation came from witness Nathan Cohen, who called Rochelle Owens 'a playwright of high moral and ethical ambitions, but of no talent.')[16] In addition, a cross-section of liberal society, including two clergymen, testified that they found the performance neither obscene nor offensive. In all, thirteen defence witnesses unanimously swore that Trio's production of *Futz* was consistent with community standards and with prevailing theatre practice in Toronto and elsewhere.

The trial judge, P.J. Bolsby, had a reputation as a maverick, a man who was not well educated in the law but who cared passionately about it, and who sometimes showed old-fashioned impatience with know-it-all lawyers.[17] The first day, during a recess, Judge Bolsby read through a transcript which police officers had made of Garrard's first-act 'happening,' and he returned to the courtroom furious at the gratuitous coarse language which he found there. Although he conceded he had heard such language informally at Ontario magistrates' meetings, Bolsby was certain that four-letter words had no place in the theatre. Angrily, he quoted from this transcript a hoary old joke about Little Red Riding Hood which, he said, was 'hopelessly vulgar, irrelevant, distasteful, and objectionable':[18]

LRRH: My, what great big teeth you have, grandma.
WOLF: All the better to eat you with.
LRRH: Eat, eat, eat. Doesn't anyone fuck any more?

Despite assurances to the contrary by the parade of defence witnesses, the judge refused to believe that this was common schoolyard talk, or that it was quite inoffensive in its context. 'There's freedom of expression,' he fumed, 'but does it have to be done in the language of the barnyard or the barroom? Do we have to have vulgarisms hurled down our throat because of freedom of expression?'[19] After this initial flare-up, there was no doubt of the judge's opinion. During the defence's examinations and summation, he frequently interjected his concerns over coarse language, and he complained to the prosecutor that no expert witnesses had been called to refute those of the defence. He even seemed perplexed by the obvious sincerity of the defence witnesses.

In his verdict, the judge dismissed all the expert testimony as legally irrelevant, since the Criminal Code defined obscenity according to an optimum community standard and not an expert one. Indeed, he expressed misgivings about expert opinion which we may have all felt at one time or another: 'I do pay respect to their special knowledge. But if left to my own devices, I could not see in it what they say is there.'[20] Having reserved for himself the responsibility of interpreting community standards, the judge declared one matter as certain:

People of this country do not wish the private intimacies between man and woman portrayed for the public view, any more than the people of this country want to peer into the bedrooms of the nation.

There remains, as I sense it, a desire to retain an overall climate of decency in which we may live as social creatures and raise and develop and educate children. This does not mean knowledge and information should be suppressed. But we do not have absolute license and we do not seek to acquire licentiousness.[21]

The four defendants were found guilty and fined a total of $1300.

This decision wiped the smile off the face of liberal society. The daily press, for instance, fretted publicly not only over the issue of free speech but also over Toronto's reputation as a Grundy among the world's major cities. The *Toronto Star* cast its lead editorial in the form of a theatre review, ostensibly of a play-within-a-play entitled 'The Damnation of Futz,' and recommended the whole brouhaha as 'a fine piece of theatre that is both amusing and rich with insight into our contemporary moral condition':

What the Damnation of Futz lacks in originality it makes up for with a Chaplinesque, deadpan humor that is nicely sustained from start to finish. Only occasionally are there lapses into slapstick comedy, as when a defence witness says that *Futz* can't be all that bad when a local moviehouse is showing an even racier epic called Can Heironymous Merkin Ever Forget Mercy Humppe and Find True Happiness?

Like Batman and Robin at the mere mention of crime in Gotham city, the police scribble down an approximation of the movie title and race off to defend Virtue in Toronto. Sure enough, the movie is as obscene as they said it was – at least, the police think so – and the operators and distributing companies are promptly issued with summonses. It looks like a clean sweep for Virtue until we come to the punchline; Heironymous Merkin had already been approved for viewing by the Ontario Board of Censors. What happens now? If the distributors are just as responsible as the exhibitors, must the police also lay charges against the censor? The comic possibilities are endless.

The editorial concluded with a skilful evisceration of the legal concept of obscenity, particularly as applied to *Futz*:

What remains to be shown is how anyone can be corrupted by a book, a movie or a play who wasn't corrupt before. In the case of a four-letter word, for example, only two things are possible: Either the listener hasn't heard the word before – in which case it is meaningless to him – or he knows it – in which case he is already corrupt. Even with something as demonstrably outlandish as Futz, would anyone believe that depraved theatre-goers are suddenly going to start flocking to the countryside? That no pig will be safe in its sty?

Ridiculous, yes. But no more ridiculous than the idea that a judge, censor, minister, or detective can presume to know the meaning of obscenity or to know the 'prevailing opinion' about something as intimate as personal morality. Who knows? Perhaps closing down theatres is more obscene than anything that goes on inside them. Whatever the case, Toronto's new comedy deserves to be laughed out of town.[22]

In general, the press portrayed the defendants as victims of an over-zealous police force and an old-fashioned judge, anticipating the famous 'Chicago Seven' conspiracy trial which took place later that year. Newspapers depicted the police witnesses as oafish philistines reading haltingly from their notebooks, and gleefully reported the judge's incredulity at the intellectual morals patiently drawn by such liberal critics as Nathan Cohen and Robert Fulford. While the press's image-making in this case is defensible, it is surely simplistic. The conviction of the 'Futz Four' reflected, not the misuse of power in the hands of a few misguided prudes, but rather a genuine concern over the breakneck speed at which society was careening toward God-knows-where. The recent and rapid growth of Toronto had brought it a new stature as the metropolitan centre of Canada, but with this stature came such troublesome phenomena as strip clubs, drug busts, and social revolutionaries. The social forces which spawned Rochdale College and Theatre Passe Muraille deliberately challenged everything about the existing order; and the existing order was beginning to fight back. What made the trial so funny was that, because of the nature of the law and our traditions of free speech, it had to be fought on the basis of naked nipples and four-letter words. But for both revolutionary and reactionary elements in the dispute, the real issue was clear: 'Society isn't really the way the play depicts it,'[23] complained the judge, and the fact that he had neither read nor seen the play makes this observation no less vital in summarizing his point of view.

Similarly, for Theatre Passe Muraille the moral parable of *Futz* was the parable of Rochdale and of the wrath of society in crushing the ideals of radical social change. As Garrard puts it,

What really bothered people was the idea that this guy slept with his pig, and the idea that we were saying something about the society we lived in. In Rochelle Owens' play everybody wanted to kill Cy Futz, they *do* kill him; and the only thing he does [wrong] is he's in love with his pig Amanda. He lives quietly by himself, minding his own business on his farm, and everybody in society wanted to kill him.

We felt we were in a similar position. It's true. Everyone wanted to kill Rochdale, and they eventually did. They used all the powers of the police, the courts, everything ... Rochdale was a beautiful place. For all the violence that was there, there was also incredible gentleness and getting along together and fair-mindedness. It was a very, very beautiful place.

While this analogy may have been true for the bulk of Rochdale's residents, it was not true for Rochdale's public image. Increasingly, the image of all 1960s social movements had become dominated by politicized troublemakers who provoked confrontations with authority. Unlike Cy Futz, the leaders of the counter-culture did not live quietly apart and mind their own business. Rochdale attracted radical thinkers to the biggest city near American culture but out of reach of its laws, to the centre of that city, where they pursued their goals stridently and persistently. They did not wish to be left quietly alone; they wished to change the very nature of society. Social reformers of the late 1960s did not just reject the prevailing order; they wished to take it over. And the forces in society which existed to preserve this order fought back as if their very lives depended on it, which they did. In an aesthetic rather than a political arena, Garrard's theatre was also confrontational. In its content, presentational style, even in its published goals, Theatre Passe Muraille was dedicated to breaking down barriers between artists and audience, between people and people. It is significant that Garrard's experiments provoked no official reaction so long as they were confined to his Zeus Suite or to Rochdale's basement parking garage: as 'barnyard language' is inoffensive in a barnyard, as the counter-culture is no threat until it aspires to become the culture, so *Futz* would probably have attracted no notice in a workshop setting. But Trio Productions professed to bring confrontational theatre to Toronto, and rented one of the city's few conventional theatre spaces to do it. 'This is for the public,' argued Judge Bolsby, 'not a group of intellectuals.'[24] And ultimately, this was the obscenity of which *Futz* was found guilty.

In general, the institution of theatre serves its constituency, and the constituency supports its theatre. In Toronto, those segments of society concerned about new forms of expression rallied to the cause of *Futz*, but the theatre community was not one of them. Before the trial, Nathan Cohen expressed his dismay over this lack of interest or sympathy; indeed, he said, 'some groups have gone to considerable trouble to disassociate themselves from any possible connection with Trio Productions, Theatre Passe Muraille, or the production of plays which might incur police displeasure.'[25] Unlike Cohen, these groups did not perceive this kind of censorship as a threat to their freedom of artistic expression, because the Rochdale Drama Project and its constituency were qualitatively different from theatre and society as they understood these terms. As Garrard puts it, 'The existing theatrical community didn't regard us at that time as legitimate and serious theatre practitioners.' However, conditions had changed by the time of the second *Futz* trial the next year. In the interim, society had assimilated radical culture and radical theatre in a safe, palatable form: while the biggest theatrical news of 1969 had been the *Futz* bust, the biggest news of 1970 was the record-breaking year-long run at the Royal Alex of *Hair*, the musical that had brought rock music, hippies, and nudity to the Broadway stage. But, as Cohen rightly observed, its phenomenal popularity was more attributable to slick packaging of 'zeitgeist entertainment' than to any real challenge to the status quo. 'It appears to embody,' wrote Cohen, 'all the trends and impulses of the late 1960s among disaffected youth. In point of fact, when you find society applauding and embracing a show that claims to be savaging it, you can be certain that its real revolutionary menace is non-existent.'[26]

Despite their relatively light fines, the Trio partners were forced to appeal the verdict because two of them were lawyers: along with other possible consequences, conviction under the Criminal Code could be grounds for disbarment. At the second trial, held in March 1970, the success of *Hair* in Toronto became an important factor in their acquittal. The prosecution presented a lacklustre case, calling only the same two police officers as witnesses. This time, however, the defence was able to argue successfully that any society which could accept *Hair* as mainstream entertainment could also accept *Futz*. In terms of nudity and coarse language, this is unquestionably true. In terms of intent, however, the Toronto production of *Hair* might be described as the opposite of Cohen's acerbic comment about Rochelle Owens: it was a display of tremendous talent, with virtually no moral or ethical ambitions. Nonetheless, since bare breasts and four-letter words were once again the only grounds on which the court could deliberate, the defence's argument was irrefutable, and the prosecution's case seemed very old-fashioned indeed. The defence even invited appeal judge William Lyon to attend a performance of *Hair* to help him gauge community standards. This he agreed to do only after tickets were also provided for a number of court officials, and for his wife! Where Bolsby had been passionately concerned, Lyon was imperturbable; and indeed, there was no longer anything to be perturbed about. In the year since *Futz* had opened, Rochdale College had continued to sink in the mire of its own quixotic ideals, and Theatre Passe Muraille had retreated from the vanguard of social concern to perform largely conventional plays in unconventional spaces rather than the other way around. The 1960s were over. Society, no longer under attack, could afford to be magnanimous. Quoting the Supreme Court's guideline that 'tolerance is to be preferred to proscription,' Lyon ruled that *Futz* served no base purpose, and that to remove sex from the play would seriously impair its dramatic impact. He delivered a cold slap to the police witnesses by recommending that policemen be more aware of public acceptance of standards of taste and morality, and he acquitted the four defendants. The artistic community gloated unbecomingly over this belated victory. Cohen, for one, suggested that 'the police may be effectively deterred, through Judge Lyon's decision, from laying charges of obscenity against theatrical presentations.'²⁷ But events surrounding *Clear Light* in 1973 and *I Love You, Baby Blue* in 1975 proved him wrong, as we shall see.

In the year following *Futz*, Jim Garrard's attentions were increasingly drawn away from Theatre Passe Muraille and toward the doomed struggle to save Rochdale College. 'As the problems became more mundane,' he recalls, 'we looked for more romantic solutions.' Garrard spearheaded Rochdale's fundraising drive, which gained national notoriety for selling degrees by mail. He also became King of Rochdale after suggesting (in a dull committee meeting) that monarchy was a more efficient form of government than democracy. He would wear his royal robes to public events at Rochdale, to the delight of the press and his entourage, and loyal subjects would kiss his ring. Finally, after his acquittal with the Trio producers in April 1970, an exhausted Garrard accepted a position as artist-in-residence at Simon Fraser University in British Columbia. Bill Marshall got a job as public relations officer to Toronto's mayor, David Crombie. Lawyers Pennington and O'Reilly returned to their practices, never again to dabble in professional theatre. Society, at least that powerful minority who patronize the Royal Alex, had made peace with the counter-culture, or so they thought. But the *real* counter-culture, not the up-tempo squeaky-clean hippies of *Hair*, but the dwindling faithful who still believed in the urgency of fundamental social change, lived out the lingering death of 1960s idealism among the cockroaches and the heavy drug dealers that flourished in what was once the Rochdale Experiment. Trussed up in legal and fiscal entanglements, the building was taken over in 1973 by its mortgagee, the Central Mortgage and Housing Corporation, and sold to Metro Toronto in 1976. After its last bedraggled tenants were evicted in 1975, the building stood vacant for some time, then was renovated to provide government-assisted housing for senior and handicapped citizens. It finally reopened for that purpose in 1980, although the Rochdale name was gone. For those with long memories, the building still stands (as one commentator wrote) as 'Toronto's perpetual monument to the fickleness of social concern.'²⁸ Passe Muraille's association with Rochdale gradually faded – first the physical connection, then the financial – but the spiritual affiliation lingered for many years.

Trinity Square to FUT, 1969–70

In its first year of operation, Theatre Passe Muraille had mounted only one production for the public, but with that production had made the biggest news of Toronto's theatrical year. It had imported radical theatre from the metropolitan centres of New York and London to culturally ambitious Toronto. It had provided a new generation of theatre professionals with a focus, a celebrity, and a reputation. Moreover, it had provided Garrard with a living laboratory for experimenting in ensemble theatre techniques, and provided a group of actors with experience in these techniques. But the novelty of locally produced avant-garde theatre could only briefly and thinly veil the inadequacies of the company as a durable operation. Besides problems of underfunding, it did not have a stable working place or a pool of professional talent; nor had it cultivated any kind of constituency beyond the walls of Rochdale, despite the public curiosity which enabled *Futz* to draw large houses at the Central Library. In the end, the most important benefit of the *Futz* controversy was that it brought the company a new permanent home, in the parish hall of the Church of the Holy Trinity on downtown Toronto's Trinity Square. This new home, in turn, fundamentally affected the development of the company.

Completed in 1847, the Church of the Holy Trinity was a posthumous gift from an Anglican minister's wife in England, who had reportedly been impressed with Bishop Strachan's preaching tour there. She made an anonymous donation of £5000 for the building of a church in the diocese of Toronto. Her only conditions were that the church should be dedicated to the Holy Trinity and that the pews should be 'free and unappropriated forever': that is, in keeping with Anglican reforms in England, anyone could sit anywhere at no charge. When Bishop Strachan chose the city of Toronto as the site for this new church, the Hon. John Simcoe Macaulay, the son of Lord Simcoe's personal physician, donated a plot of land from his family estate off Yonge Street north of Queen. It is one of those delightful ironies of history that Theatre Passe Muraille should have thus benefited from the social conscience of these pillars of the 'Family Compact,' the ruling class of early Toronto, whom the company took so thoroughly to task in its celebrated production of *1837* at Trinity Square. In any case, the church's reformist beginnings and downtown location fostered a tradition of social concern which has endured to the present day.

When the *Futz* controversy broke out in March 1969, Holy Trinity's rector, Jim Fisk, publicly supported the moral values of the play, and later testified in its defence. Fisk was so offended by this official suppression of free speech that he offered Trio Productions his parish hall at 11 Trinity Square, so that the run could be extended. This hall had long served Holy Trinity's interest in education, social concern, and live theatre. Built in 1888 at the southeast corner of the square, it housed a parochial school and Sunday school until 1930, a hostel for unemployed men during the Depression, and a lodge for servicemen during World War II. It was leased by a local radio station for live drama broadcasts from the late 1940s to the late 1950s; but with the arrival of the dynamic Fisk (rector 1962–76), the auditorium and its small offices were once again turned over to social programs. As urban churches took on more active social roles in the 1960s, Fisk and the Church of the Holy Trinity, with its liberal tradition already deeply ingrained, became central to the rapidly expanding street activity in downtown Toronto. Theatre was already a recognized part of Holy Trinity's ministry, with a celebrated 'Christmas Story' performed annually from 1937, and an Easter play performed most years as well. In the 1960s the parish hall housed the office of a Religion and Theatre Council and was often rented for independent theatre productions as well, such as Trio's *Marat/Sade* in the fall of 1968. For the remainder of the 1968–69 season it had served as headquarters for Theatre Toronto, the demise of which made the hall available once more. It was offered to Theatre Passe Muraille for only $500 per month.

Garrard went to look at 11 Trinity Square and was enthralled. The large open room with its high ceiling was, in effect, a non-transportable embodiment of the flexible performing space he had envisioned for Rochdale's second-floor terrace. It was about forty feet by sixty feet, with two small offices at one end and a meeting room above the offices. The auditorium had an ample crawl space above the ceiling, and it was sufficiently old and made-over that a few more screws and drill-holes wouldn't be noticed. Although demolished in 1974, this building still has a reputation as having been the finest performing space in the city, an excellent 'empty space' in Peter Brook's terms, with superb acoustics. Not only was this an ideal performing space for the young Theatre Passe Muraille, it was also in an ideal location: adjacent to the bustling cosmopolitan activity of the Yonge Street strip, but only a short walk from the mainstream opulence of the Royal Alex, the O'Keefe Centre, and the yet-unfinished St Lawrence Centre. Despite Rochdale's growing financial difficulties, its governing council (of which Garrard was by then a member) agreed to pay for Passe Muraille's monthly rent on Trinity Square, maintaining the kind of defiant vestigial idealism which was incomprehensible to financial institutions awaiting late mortgage payments.

Theatre Passe Muraille took up residence at Trinity Square on 1 May 1969. Its first public event there, described in the press as a 'huge free-form happening,' was a benefit dance on June 23 that raised over $2500 for the *Futz* defence fund. Performances began the next weekend, as part of a street festival sponsored by Holy Trinity Church, with a visiting university group from Ann Arbor, Michigan. The American group, named 'A Company,' was led by an expatriate Newfoundlander, Chris Brookes, who later returned to his home province and founded the Mummers Troupe. 'A Company' remained in residence at Trinity Square for the summer, producing three original plays (*Portrait, Itch,* and *Nightmare with Hat,* all by company member Jeff Levy) as well as Beckett's *Endgame* and Sam Shepard's *Forensic and the Navigators.* There was, as Garrard recalls, some friction between the two companies: 'They thought we were too sloppy, and we thought they were too humourless.' This friction was aggravated when Brookes's group blithely cut a hole in the floor of the hall for one of their productions.

That summer, the parish hall functioned under the name 'Theatre 11.' It became home to a tremendous amount of local theatre activity, as well as to the Michigan company. A number of independent small-budget productions inaugurated the Passe Muraille tradition of sharing its theatrical resources and expertise with fledgling artists and companies. Garrard summarized this activity in a report to the Ontario Arts Council at the end of the summer:

Our major production efforts were *Balls* (Paul Foster), *Home Free* (Lanford Wilson), and *An Evening with The Maids* (Jean Genet). Other productions were *The Marriage Proposal* (Chekhov), *New Step* (Leonard Cohen), *Escurial* (Michel de Ghelderode). In addition, we were responsible for the production of several plays by persons involved in our theatre drop-in centre at Trinity Square. These included *Santa Claus* (E.E. Cummings), *The Babies* (Anna Lippman), *Project x* (Philip Hopcraft), *The Laundromat Special* (group) and four weeks of rehearsal for *The Beard* (Michael McClure).[29]

One highlight of the summer was the performance in *Home Free* of Trish Nelligan, a young actress from London, Ontario, who under the name Kate Nelligan later starred in West End and Broadway plays and in major commercial films. Another highlight was Garrard's environmental version of *The Maids,* entitled *An Evening with The Maids,* with (as in *An Evening with Futz*) the play forming only part of the show. For this production, Theatre 11 was transformed into a sleazy dockside bar in Marseilles, where patrons gathered at midnight to watch a transvestite performance of Genet's play. Male waiters wore gold-lamé jock straps, Nelligan circulated as a French floozie, and Phil Schreibman (who had composed songs for Garrard's productions of *Tom Paine* and *Futz*) improvised a cohesive musical score at his piano beneath the stage. That summer, Passe Muraille also became a busy 'drop-in' centre, as Garrard explained in the same report:

For a number of reasons, mostly financial, we saw fit to open our doors to anyone who showed interest, good intentions, and could fit in with the existing group. By the end of July we had over 40 people working more or less regularly on theatre things at Trinity. Many of these people were untrained. Only twelve were being paid ... Here were a group of people, of very diverse theatrical experience, many of whom would normally be more properly found on the audience side of things, joining together to solve theatrical problems for themselves.

For the social educator in Garrard, all this activity was very satisfying. For the theatre professional, it was not.

Garrard's report, written as a financial appeal to the provincial arts council, outlined his company's past and projected activities exactly one year after that first prospectus for his 'Theatre without Walls.' While gratified by the summer's activity, Garrard felt it had retarded Passe Muraille's growth as a professional company. For the 1969–70 season, he planned to curtail the group's community and educational activities in favour of more intense artistic explorations and more productions arising from them. 'This does not reflect a dissatisfaction with our accomplishments during the past year,' he wrote. 'But we are looking for excellence. And a much leaner operation is necessary.' In retrospect, Garrard's projections for the coming year seem curiously Rochdale-centred, as if he had not recognized the impact that Trinity Square had already had on the company. He said that he expected Passe Muraille's relationship with its community to 'take a new form, rather than disappear outside of performance,' but he apparently did not realize the extent to which this had already occurred. The new location had brought Theatre Passe Muraille out of its college setting and into the community at large. There, already, it was part of broader and more pragmatic expressions of social concern than the intellectually based Rochdale experiment. In its journey from the Zeus Suite through the

Central Library Theatre to Trinity Square, the company had passed from a theoretical exercise among intellectuals and social reformers, through a confrontation with institutionalized society, to gain a recognized place in Toronto's street scene among the hawkers and the street musicians. At Trinity Square, Passe Muraille became more than just a theatre, and more than just a place to hang out: as actor Booth Savage put it, 'You didn't go there to see plays, so much as to find out what was going on.'[30]

Like other key figures at Rochdale, Garrard was a conceptualist in search of a laboratory; however, Passe Muraille was becoming less of a theoretical expression and more of a practical one. With his attentions divided, the problems of mounting plays devolved to three new directors who were drawn by the accessibility and sudden fame of Passe Muraille at Trinity Square. One of Garrard's goals in the fall of 1969 was to strengthen the talent pool of the company: to this end, he recruited a number of new actors through the referral service of the Canadian Theatre Centre and approached the 26-year-old Martin Kinch, then a theatre consultant with the Central Ontario Drama League, to help him direct the productions. Kinch in turn, having just completed a summer season with his own experimental company at Stratford, brought along his tempestuous partner John Palmer. Shortly thereafter Kinch invited another friend, Paul Thompson, to join the company as stage manager and technical director. These three directors gradually became a kind of artistic triumvirate leading Theatre Passe Muraille. Whereas Thompson, less experienced and less well known than the other two, initially had little artistic input into the company, Kinch and Palmer had an immediate impact. While Garrard's more cerebral approach to theatre continued as a subordinate theme, the experienced showmanship and mainstream ambitions of Kinch and Palmer brought Passe Muraille the popular successes which sustained it in this long transitional period. In addition, their enduring rivalry began a spirited internal competition in which Thompson was soon a participant.

Martin Kinch (b. 1943) was born in London, England, and came to Canada with his family about five years later. As a youngster he was actively involved in theatre both in high school and at the London (Ontario) Little Theatre, of which his mother was an active member. He continued this involvement at the University of Western Ontario, where he took an honours degree in English literature. There, in 1965, Kinch won a prize for directing Genet's *Deathwatch* as UWO's entry in the Canadian Universities Drama League competition held that spring in

Montreal, where he first met Carleton University student John Palmer. That summer, Kinch directed Genet's *The Balcony* for fellow student Keith Turnbull's summer season in downtown London, while acting in two other productions. (This operation is described in more detail in chapter 9.) The next summer, after graduation, Kinch again acted and directed with Turnbull in the all-Canadian 'Summer Theatre 66' in London, which by a circuitous route led to the creation of James Reaney's Donnelly trilogy and the establishment of Turnbull's NDWT company in the next decade. UWO was a hothouse of talent in the mid-1960s; in fact, students Kinch, Turnbull, and Paul Thompson all shared an apartment there one winter.

After his stint with Summer Theatre 66, Kinch took a job as an insurance adjuster in Toronto, but he found working outside of theatre very unsatisfying. The next summer he applied to a new program for young directors being instituted by the Youth and Recreation Branch of Ontario's Department of Education. This scheme, the brainchild of George Merten in the Youth and Recreation Branch, also received considerable support from Charlotte Holmes of the Ontario Arts Council and Tom Hendry of the Canadian Theatre Centre, two people who were to figure prominently in the rise of Toronto's alternative theatres only a couple of years later. This program, entitled Directors Training in Britain, was intended to transform Ontario's loosely affiliated amateur theatres into a network of regional repertory companies, by training the young directors necessary to lead them. Successful applicants, selected by a panel of experts in Toronto, would be sent to Britain to apprentice with an established professional company there. After a year abroad, these promising young directors would return to Canada to be employed in Ontario's community theatres for the ensuing two years. Both Martin Kinch and John Palmer applied for and were accepted into the program, along with two others (Richard Howard and Collin Gorrie). Palmer went to the Citizens' Theatre in Glasgow in the fall of 1967, and Kinch went to Birmingham Repertory Theatre.

In Birmingham, Kinch was put in charge of a new series of experimental late-night productions. For this series he directed Beckett's *Endgame*, van Itallie's *War*, Olwen Wymark's *Lunchtime Concert*, and an act of *Daily News from the Whole World* by Rae Davis, with whom he had worked in London, Ontario. Meanwhile his wife, Miro Kinch, who also had a great deal of experience in community and university theatre back home, attended the School of Theatre Design at Birmingham's College of Art. Here the Kinches became great friends with Palmer, who would

telephone and visit regularly from Glasgow. Another Canadian studying in England that year was Jim Garrard, who met both Kinch and
Palmer there.

Following his year in Britain, Kinch was hired by the Central Ontario
Drama League as an itinerant director with its member clubs. His
productions during the winter of 1968–69 included *Inherit the Wind* in
Oshawa and Pirandello's *Right You Are* in Etobicoke. This was the same
season that Theatre Passe Muraille produced *Tom Paine* and *Futz*, and
experimental theatre was in the air. In June 1969, at the time of the first
Futz trial, Kinch directed *Plague ... So Far* at Toronto's Central YMCA, a
collective creation based on Defoe's *A Journal of the Plague Year* but with
many twentieth-century allusions. It was a production which Garrard
saw and admired. Immediately following this play, Martin and Miro
Kinch joined Palmer in Stratford to open a storefront theatre operation
with him.

John Palmer (b. 1943) was born in Sydney, Nova Scotia, but grew up in
Ottawa. Like Kinch he began acting while in his teens, at school and at
the Ottawa Little Theatre. After a year of pre-med studies at Queen's
University, Palmer enrolled in English literature at Carleton University.
There, along with other future professionals such as Tim Bond, Larry
Kardish, and Saul Rubinek, he worked with Carleton's Sock and Buskin
drama club, which produced mainly the members' own original plays. At
the Ottawa Little Theatre, Palmer had found himself impatient with
conventional dramatic exposition; at university he was able to explore
his anti-realistic leanings as a writer and director, at a time when the
ideas of European absurdist drama were just becoming widely known in
North America. In the 1965 university drama festival in Montreal,
where he met Kinch, Palmer's own *Visions of an Unseemly Youth* won an
award for best original play. When this festival was held in Toronto the
following year, Palmer's production of *Goebbels Gobbledygook* by Larry
Kardish won awards for best production, best direction, and best
original play. It was also remounted that spring at the Colonnade
Theatre in Toronto, and was invited to a drama festival at Yale
University.[31]

While Kinch was working in insurance in Toronto, Palmer was
already establishing himself as a prominent angry young man in
Canadian theatre. Upon graduating in 1966, and having decided on a
career in theatre, Palmer wrote to a number of Canadian professional
companies offering his services in any capacity whatever. A few of them
wrote back to decline his overtures, but most simply ignored him. This

treatment infuriated Palmer, who felt he was being denied the opportunity to work in his own country, in his chosen field, by foreigners. 'The reason I couldn't get a job was that I was Canadian,' he says. 'The theatres were run by Brits, and they were bringing over more Brits ... I thought, well, this has got to change. To a certain extent, that was fundamental to my whole career up to 1979.'[32]

To Palmer, gaining a career in Canadian theatre was as much a political act as an artistic one, and he took it as a personal mission to help create professional opportunities for himself and his contemporaries. Though not an aggressive man by nature, Palmer adopted a proselytizing role – as he describes it, 'a combination of Saint Joan and Moses, to go to people and say, "You've got to do this."' As actress Gale Garnett put it, at the time Toronto Free Theatre was founded, 'John Palmer, though outspoken and aggressive in print, will hide in the closet rather than talk to strangers, and, when the strangers have gone, will emerge from said closet and ask you in all seriousness why people find him aloof.'[33] Palmer would court publicity by saying provocative things to the press, yet would be privately embarrassed to see them in print. In one such instance, he told Herbert Whittaker that 'Canada needs me,' and was mortified when the *Globe and Mail* used this phrase in its headline. Palmer was uncompromising in his demands for Canadian theatres to produce Canadian plays, to the point of damaging his own success with these theatres. For example, when Toronto Arts Productions went out on a limb to produce Palmer's *Memories for My Brother, Part II*, he accused Leon Major of putting a 'token [Canadian] playwright on the main bill.'[34] Whether this attitude represented self-promotion or self-destruction is hard to say, but Palmer undoubtedly made a habit of biting the hands that fed him. In the early 1970s, he was the quintessential *enfant terrible* of Canadian alternative theatre, and was lionized by the Toronto press. Whittaker even dubbed him Toronto theatre's 'man of the year' for 1971.[35] For all these reasons, Palmer's work has seldom been considered separately from the manic persona he projects; and eventually, as with Shaw's Saint Joan, even those who benefited most from his foolhardy victories wished he would keep quiet, or go home.

Unable to find theatrical employment in 1966, Palmer and his Carleton friends formed their own company to produce plays at Le Hibou, Ottawa's celebrated coffee-house, where the proprietor would schedule their productions between musical bookings.[36] The company rehearsed in an unheated upstairs room and mounted an eclectic season on the small club's tiny stage, producing *The Seagull, Woyzeck, The Knack, Entertaining Mr. Sloane,* and *The Duchess of Malfi,* with each play normally running three nights per week for three weeks. At the end of their season in Ottawa, Palmer, with his unerring instinct for putting his head in the lion's mouth, decided to take his little company to Stratford to offer an alternative to the mammoth Festival. 'If we're going to change the country,' he reasoned, 'we've got to go to Stratford.' A sympathetic university professor, whose wife acted with the Le Hibou company, loaned the group $1000 and a station wagon. They drove to Stratford, rented a house, located another celebrated coffee-house, the Black Swan, and persuaded owner Harry Finlay to let them perform between musical bookings as they had in Ottawa.

Palmer's company was renamed the 'New Vic Theatre' for its summer in Stratford in 1967. Its repertory consisted of two plays by Palmer, *Visions of an Unseemly Youth* and *Confessions of a Necrophile, or Never Laugh When a Hearse Goes By,* and a one-man show for Saul Rubinek, *Diary of a Madman,* adapted from Gogol. A fourth play, *Occasional Seasoning* by Larry Kardish, was announced, but was not produced until Palmer returned to Stratford with the Canadian Place Theatre two years later. The remarkable thing about the New Vic company was that even though its audiences were ludicrously small (often less than five in number), it attracted the attention of some highly influential people in Canadian theatre. Perhaps Canadian theatre was looking for inspiration from its youth, as much of Western society was in the late 1960s. Keith Turnbull remembers such high-profile artists as John Hirsch and Martha Henry driving down to London to see his Summer Theatre 66; similarly, one night at the Black Swan, Palmer was shocked to discover that Nathan Cohen and his family were the *only* audience members for a performance of *Diary of a Madman.* When the play finished, Palmer leapt onto the stage and offered another play to the surprised Cohens, in effect a command performance. While Cohen found little to recommend the productions, he admired the group's chutzpah – 'there is the nucleus here of something theatrically alive and perhaps eloquent,' he wrote, 'an organization which might deserve a future.'[37] Later that summer, Shaw Festival founder Brian Doherty invited the New Vic company to perform on a Shaw Festival off-day at Niagara-on-the-Lake. Ever the iconoclast, Palmer staged his two plays on the set of *Major Barbara* – but only after all the furniture had been hung on the walls or piled in front of the doors. Other incidents at that time also illustrate Palmer's profound ambivalence toward mainstream theatre, particularly as represented by the Stratford Festival. He barred British star Alan Bates from a New Vic performance when the actor arrived late; and he once stormed into Jean Gascon's office and *demanded* to direct a production on the Festival stage, before being unceremoniously shown the door. Indeed, Palmer's biggest disappointment from founding two alternative theatres in Stratford was that the Festival's management took so little notice of him: 'I could have been co-opted very easily,' he recalls somewhat wistfully. This desire to destroy the mainstream, and the simultaneous desire to become the mainstream, is a recurring theme in the rise of Toronto's alternative theatres. Nowhere is this theme more clearly illustrated than in the career of John Palmer.

After his summer at the Black Swan, Palmer (like Kinch) auditioned for the Directors Training in Britain program and was apprenticed to the Glasgow Citizens' Theatre for its 1967–68 season. There he was put in charge of the company's experimental stage, called the Close Theatre Club, where his productions included plays by Ionesco and Jules Feiffer. While Palmer believes that he learned a great deal about the technique, craft, and organizational qualities a director requires, neither he nor Kinch was very impressed with the quality of British theatre they saw, either in the regional theatres or in London. Palmer recalls that this experience made him all the more determined to work at the highest levels in Canada, 'because you came back realizing you were as good as anybody else.' He returned to Canada in the fall of 1968, after a summer travelling in Europe with Rubinek; and while Kinch toiled for a variety of drama clubs in the central Ontario region, Palmer went to Woodstock, Ontario, as director of the Little Theatre there.

Under Palmer, the Woodstock Little Theatre became a centre for disaffected young people and for his own brand of theatrical iconoclasm. In his own mind, Palmer had finally identified the Canadian Little Theatre tradition as the true enemy to his professional aspirations, since the model of the Dominion Drama Festival was fundamental to a system which encompassed both the regional theatres and the Stratford Festival. In particular, he perceived the DDF's annual competition as abject colonialism, perpetuating a style of British theatre outmoded even in Britain since *Look Back in Anger*. Typically, however, instead of ignoring the 'old guard,' Palmer attacked it with all his energy and talent. His striking production of *Tango* by Slavomir Mrozek (whom he later met in Stratford) was judged the best of the 1969 Ontario regional festivals; and, to the delight of the Woodstock Little Theatre, it was chosen to represent Ontario in the DDF's final competition in Kelowna,

BC. There Palmer's production created a controversy which attracted national press coverage and scandalized the upper reaches of the DDF. On the night that *Tango* was performed, the high-society audience arrived at the theatre to find huge lengths of plastic tubing draped over the front steps, banner-waving youths shouting slogans from the roof, and an odd assortment of junk heaped in the lobby. Inside the auditorium, every single seat was already occupied – by an inflated plastic garbage bag. On stage, televisions tuned randomly to local stations were pointed at arriving audience members, already confused about how to take their seats. The production itself was also wildly unconventional: as the Canadian Press reported, 'The three hours of just about every modern theatrical idea in the book included flashing lights, a gogo band and a brief topless appearance by Elaine Reed, her back to a dwindling audience in the 900-seat Kelowna Community Theatre.'[38] The next morning, Palmer recalls, he was summoned to be chastised by the formidable Pauline McGibbon, former president of the DDF and later lieutenant-governor of Ontario. Back in Woodstock, the Little Theatre which had revelled in Palmer's regional victory with *Tango* was embarrassed by the fuss it had caused at the final festival. As a result, and by mutual agreement, Palmer did not return to Woodstock for a second season.

After the debacle in Kelowna, Palmer returned to Toronto to see his friend Martin Kinch. In Britain, the two young directors found they held similar views on both theatre aesthetics and theatre politics. Now, with the model of the Edinburgh Festival in their minds, they decided to make another assault on the Stratford establishment, to create a 'fringe' to the Stratford Festival by producing original Canadian works in an unconventional theatre space, as Palmer had done two years earlier. They rented a vacant dry goods store diagonally opposite the Stratford Festival's Avon Theatre, and installed a simple thrust stage with seating for about sixty. They called their company Canadian Place Theatre, after off-off-Broadway's American Place Theatre,[39] and recruited actors from Palmer's Carleton and Woodstock groups, from Kinch's work in central Ontario, and from local enthusiasts they found in Stratford. It was summer, and it seemed like everyone was falling in love. Company members lived communally in a rented house and were paid seven dollars per week, irregularly. The group usually had dinner at the Black Swan, where Harry Finlay's daily communal meal for summertime gypsies had become a tradition. They held marathon work sessions to put their theatre in readiness; and, if frustrated, they could smash abandoned coke bottles against a 'bouncing wall' in the second-floor rehearsal hall as a kind of primal therapy. Their season opened in July with *Occasional Seasoning* by Larry Kardish and *The Dance* by Terry Cox. In August the repertory was changed to two plays by Palmer, *Memories for My Brother* and *Anthem*.[40] This last play, purportedly inspired by Proust, used lengthy recorded autobiographies of the performers to accompany mimed actions. It also contained some nudity, which prompted threats of closure from the local police, a telephone call to the Festival's literary manager, Tom Hendry, requesting his support, and a meeting of the triumvirate that was to found Toronto Free Theatre less than three years later. Hendry, already disenchanted with the Festival, preferred the company of these free-spirited youngsters to that of the Stratford establishment. Hendry and Palmer also shared as playwrights the dream of a Canadian theatre devoted to Canadian plays.

Like the New Vic operation two years earlier, the Canadian Place Theatre attracted much more in the way of critical attention than it did in the way of audiences. Toronto theatre that season had been greatly influenced by American experimental theatre, most notably Theatre Passe Muraille's *Futz*; now the idea of producing experimental Canadian plays was both timely and newsworthy. The Toronto press, moreover, as it had already shown, seemed very forgiving of theatrical weaknesses for the sake of theatrical novelty. For example, Don Rubin's review of *Occasional Seasoning* in the *Toronto Star* dismissed the script as 'embarrassing and incoherent blather,' and described the acting as bad, the staging worse, and the lighting effects worst of all. Yet this same review concluded with extravagant praise for the nationalistic principles of the company:

Yet, for all this negativism, I have the distinct feeling that Canadian Place Theatre may yet make a real contribution to Canadian playwriting. Its people are serious and its intentions honorable. Such a combination offers real possibility and possibility – at a time when so many young writers are looking toward the theatre as perhaps [a] place for future endeavor – is something that just must be encouraged.[41]

In fact, critical opinion of the Canadian Place Theatre that summer was unanimous: praiseworthy goals, poor production standards. Nonetheless, CPT was a highly significant company in the ensuing rise of Toronto's alternative theatres. First, as already mentioned, it brought together the artistic triumvirate which was later to found Toronto Free

Theatre. More importantly, it was vital as an early promoter of new Canadian drama, and was perhaps the first company to draw critical encouragement for this nationalist concept. Finally, and most significantly at the time, it led to Kinch and Palmer's association with Theatre Passe Muraille, and their resulting impact on that company and the whole alternative theatre scene in Toronto. Canadian Place Theatre was the vehicle which established Kinch and Palmer as two of the brightest young leaders in Canadian theatre. When they arrived at Passe Muraille in September 1969, their renown in this area was exceeded only by Garrard's.

At the end of their summer in Stratford, Kinch and Palmer returned to Toronto. Through his production of *Plague ... So Far* that June, Kinch had become reacquainted with Garrard, whom he had first met in England. Garrard had great respect for Kinch as a director, and desperately needed help with his twin roles of Artistic Director of Passe Muraille and King of Rochdale College. Kinch brought along Palmer, despite the fact that they had not been getting along well recently; their relationship has always been a stormy one, both personally and professionally, and the closing party of the Canadian Place Theatre had ended in a fistfight. Kinch also brought the efficient Edna Widenmaier from the Canadian Place company, who soon became secretary to Kinch, to Garrard, and to the New Directors Group they formed that winter. Passe Muraille's first production in the fall of 1969 was supposed to be *Tom Paine*, the performance rights now secured. While Kinch conducted most of the rehearsals, he felt sometimes at a loss trying to interpret the word of Garrard, whom the actors treated as a departed god.[42] Perhaps these difficulties slowed down the rehearsal process, for Passe Muraille's season opened instead with Palmer's new production of *Memories for My Brother, Part I* in early November, after which Palmer left for Ottawa on one of his periodic writing retreats. *Tom Paine* followed in the same month, with essentially the same cast. Both productions were designed by Miro Kinch, whose later work at Toronto Free Theatre did so much to provide a distinctive 'look' to that company.

While these two productions at the end of 1969 re-established Passe Muraille as a producing company, they were received indifferently by the press and public alike. For Palmer's *Memories*, Miro Kinch's steel-pipe-and-scaffold setting prompted a memorable headline for Whittaker's review: 'Nude Memories swing about jungle gym.' As usual, Whittaker's criticism tended to be gentle and encouraging ('Palmer writes sensitively, poetically, and entertainingly, although not always at the same time'). Nathan Cohen, on the other hand, pulled no punches: he found Palmer's writing 'fat with ambition, [but] skeleton-thin in technique,' and the acting and directing marred by obvious inexperience.[43] Whether these critics liked a particular show or not, however, and whether they knew it or not, they contributed enormously to the credibility of Passe Muraille simply because they took its work *seriously*, at a time when much of the theatrical community in Toronto did not. In his lengthy review of *Tom Paine*, for example, Cohen demanded that Theatre Passe Muraille show him the same kind of professionalism, within its own aesthetic, which he also expected of larger more established theatres:

What the production needs above all else, if it is to have any impact, is a surging vitality. That is entirely absent. The images are pedestrian ... and the interpretation of them is without depth or discipline.

Being an ensemble means more than taking an ensemble stance. It means having a basic craft and bringing a common point of view to the exercise of that craft. The actors have neither craft nor grace. They speak the words as if they hated the very thought of communication through language.

Like Rochdale College, where it originated and to which it is still affiliated, Theatre Passe Muraille has a laudable desire to break free of traditional and sterile practices. It wants to be relevant in form and content, to stir theatre-goers to new perceptions and considerations. Such intentions are honorable. But it will have to do infinitely better if it is to establish a real place for itself and exert any influence.[44]

In December 1969, following these two productions, another severe crisis struck Theatre Passe Muraille. Its latest administrative director had left – there had been five to this point – and its cheques began to bounce. Fortunately Shain Jaffe appeared on the scene, a young former businessman who had recently fled from the United States to avoid military service. Jaffe set up some accounting procedures and taught Edna Widenmaier and Paul Thompson how to maintain them. (Later, Jaffe helped the Factory Theatre Lab in a similar way, and in 1972 became the first general manager of Toronto Free Theatre.) Responding to this financial crisis, Garrard resigned as artistic director so that he could devote himself full-time to fundraising for both Theatre Passe Muraille and Rochdale College, and he named Kinch as his successor. At this point rehearsals had already begun for Kinch's next production, *Richard III*. (These rehearsals are still remembered by people who saw them for the stunning theatrical effect of actress Bernice Gai Hune's clinging to Richard's shoulder to portray his hump.) To save the company from bankruptcy, Kinch cancelled this production and reduced the size of the acting company from about fifteen to six. The weekly salaries of fifty dollars were also cut off until new revenue could be generated. An emergency grant from the Ontario Arts Council (through Charlotte Holmes) kept Passe Muraille alive for the time being, but Kinch still knew that the company would collapse very soon unless he could come up with a show that would sell a lot of tickets. He finally decided on a double-bill of two short plays, *Sweet Eros* by Terence McNally and *In His Own Write* by John Lennon, Victor Spinetti, and Adrienne Kennedy based on Lennon's prose works. Difficulties in meeting production costs delayed the opening until the end of January 1970. When the double-bill finally opened, however, reviews were excellent and audiences filled the theatre.

No doubt part of this success was due to the tantalizing, sexy nudity which was central to *Sweet Eros*. In the play, a story of a shy young man who kidnaps the object of his infatuation, actress Margaret Keith was tied to a chair facing upstage, while her abductor undressed her scene by scene. At the play's climax she was completely naked. In an ironic way, this play fulfilled Passe Muraille's expressed goal of bringing new audiences to the theatre: the front rows at Trinity Square tended to fill up early with the 'raincoat crowd,' lone men who usually took their entertainment at the nearby Yonge Street strip clubs and movie arcades. Box-office for the double-bill was also boosted by John Lennon and Yoko Ono's famous 'bed-in' for peace, which had taken place in Montreal the preceding summer, and by new rumours of the Beatles' impending break-up. *Sweet Eros* and *In His Own Write* ran for seven weeks at Trinity Square, then were performed at York University and Brock University. Thus, this double-bill was not only Passe Muraille's first popular success since *Futz*, and one which saved the company from early collapse, but it was also the first touring product of the new alternative theatres. Indeed, after Passe Muraille lost its Trinity Square home four years later, the company survived and prospered by touring.

Despite the popularity of *Sweet Eros* and *In His Own Write,* this show was merely a reprieve for the company's financial problems, not a permanent solution. Passe Muraille's next major production, John Osborne's *A Bond Honoured* (adapted from Lope de Vega), was a fiasco, and returned the company to the same brink of ruin from which it had just been delivered. Like any good co-operative in the 1960s, everyone at

Passe Muraille changed jobs from time to time, no matter how ill-suited an individual might be to some of the tasks. *A Bond Honoured* was directed by Asheleigh Moorhouse, a stalwart Passe Muraille actor since *Futz*, who also put up the money for production expenses. The cast included three of the best actors Toronto's alternative theatre ever produced – Clare Coulter, Booth Savage, and the mercurial Don Steinhouse – and three of the worst, reputedly, in Martin Kinch, Shain Jaffe, and Paul Thompson. A turgid flop in its original production at Britain's National Theatre, *A Bond Honoured* at Passe Muraille was despised by everyone: critics, audiences, even the actors themselves. Booth Savage hated the production so much that one night he put a sign on the door advising customers that the show was cancelled; usually fewer than ten would show up anyway. In his review of *A Bond Honoured*, Whittaker gave the company a generous benefit of the doubt (although he may have been joking) by suggesting that the play's comic effect was intentional: Moorhouse's greatest ally in turning this 'Spanish tragedy into a kindergarten comedy,' he wrote, was Martin Kinch in the leading role, 'whose performance as Leonido would be shockingly bad if it were not so very funny.' Cohen's review a few days later was more blunt, and seems to have taken an incidental swipe at Whittaker's indulgence:

Conceivably, the production is meant to satirize the excesses of Renaissance melodrama and Osbornian vehemence. But this attributes to the director and his players a sense of design and intelligence unwarranted by their observable actions. Like the play, the show is both a tragedy and a farce, but for all the wrong causes.[45]

Booth Savage remembers Cohen shouting with rage as he left the show, and banging the wall with his ever-present cane.

The Passe Muraille season concluded with two Canadian plays which were no more successful than *A Bond Honoured*, either with critics or with audiences. The first was *Notes from Quebec*, adapted by Paul Thompson from Jean-Claude Germain's play *Diguidi, Diguidi, Ha! Ha! Ha!*. The production is significant now only because it was the first play Thompson directed at Theatre Passe Muraille. It was also the play in which Clare Coulter, the daughter of playwright John Coulter, a classical actress by training and inclination, discovered her commitment to small audiences in small theatres:

When I first started out, I used to have all my sights trained on big audiences and big theatres. But I adjusted from that after coming to Passe Muraille. I can trace my transition back to a show we did when no one was coming to the theatre. We had this little play with just three people and it got to be 8:30 and there were only two people in the audience. I thought to myself, we have a couple of minutes to put into our heads that we are going to enjoy playing to two people. I worked so hard at that idea during those two minutes that at the end of those two minutes, four people walked in and I felt crowded out.[46]

Notes from Quebec was followed in May 1970 by David Helwig's *The Hanging of William O'Donnell*, directed by Garrard in his last production before leaving for British Columbia. Helwig's play was supposedly inspired by the Donnelly massacre of 1880, although it was not a precursor to Reaney's Donnelly trilogy in any sense. The slovenly standards of this production were the subject of a brutal review by a discouraged Nathan Cohen.[47] The only saving grace of the show, apparently, was its evocative setting of rough timber. This was yet another example of the generous support given by Rochdale College, although the support was unintentional this time as the timbers had been spirited away from Rochdale's seventeenth-floor terrace. A third new play planned by Garrard, a collective creation about the *Futz* furore to be entitled *The Metropolitan Police Dossier*, never reached the stage. Garrard himself was exhausted and depressed at this time, and his attentions were diverted by the demands of other projects.

In the late spring of 1970, Theatre Passe Muraille underwent another series of tremors in its organization and leadership. Martin Kinch was hired as an assistant director at the Stratford Festival, where Miro Kinch was also employed in the production area. Before leaving Toronto, Kinch turned the operation of the company over to Paul Thompson, who had joined Passe Muraille as stage manager and technical director after the second *Tom Paine*. Thompson, who had already taken on some additional administrative and artistic responsibilities, believed that this was to be just a caretaking period while Kinch was out of town. But the spring's failures had taken their toll on Kinch, and he privately believed that the company could not survive much longer. Without Thompson, it may not have. However, Passe Muraille was once again saved from collapse, not only by Thompson's stubborn leadership, but also by two external events in the summer of 1970 which breathed life into an alternative theatre scene which was already flagging. The first event, which had gradual and far-reaching effects, was the founding of the Factory Theatre Lab by Ken Gass. The Factory's all-Canadian programming policy focused on an issue toward which Theatre Passe Muraille had been drifting already, particularly through the nationalistic concerns of Palmer and Thompson. The Factory also provided a new outlet for some workers (including Edna Widenmaier) who felt that Passe Muraille's oligarchy had not rewarded them with sufficient artistic opportunities. The second event, the effects of which were immediate and dramatic, was the Festival of Underground Theatre.

The FUT festival, as it is often redundantly termed, was the brainchild of the New Directors Group, an association that emerged the preceding winter from the smoke-filled rooms of Rochdale College, where (by this time) Garrard, Kinch, and Thompson all lived. Although the NDG had no money and no real status, it provided a means of mutual support for its members and a forum for exchanging ideas about the art and the business of theatre. Membership was strictly by invitation. Besides Gass, Kinch, Palmer, and Garrard (at age thirty its eldest member), the New Directors Group consisted of three University of Toronto graduates: Martin Brenzell, Jack Messinger, and Henry Tarvainen. Brenzell, considered the most accomplished director in the group, had previously directed at the Cafe La Mama in New York, and was then in charge of the theatre program at McMaster University. His career was tragically cut short when he was drowned in Israel in 1972. Messinger was primarily an actor rather than a director, and only belonged to the group because he was a good friend of Brenzell. In fact, Messinger was eventually drummed out of the NDG in a tongue-in-cheek ceremony. Finally Tarvainen, also a Rochdale resident, had trained under Leon Major at Hart House, and had moved over to the St Lawrence Centre to become Major's assistant there. Although Tarvainen's career has been highlighted by many fine shows, his disastrous production of John Palmer's *Memories for My Brother, Part II* on the mainstage of the St Lawrence Centre in 1971 was to become one of the most important turning points in the story of Toronto's alternative theatres. Besides Brenzell, Kinch was considered the most talented director of the group, while Garrard was considered the theorist and ideological leader. Later, Paul Thompson was added to the NDG roster when he became known as a director as well as a technician.

One early project of the New Directors Group, in January 1970, was an exchange of directing techniques, with each director conducting a two-hour workshop using Brenzell's McMaster students. The main activity of the NDG, however, was just to get together regularly to talk about theatre. The young directors' meetings, often held in popular beer parlours, were relaxed and social, their discussions made the more discursive and giddy by the marijuana always available at Rochdale. Most of their schemes, fortunately, never saw the light of day, such as the idea of sending black wreaths to critics they didn't like, or of disrupting an opening at the Stratford Festival by chaining themselves to the central pillars of that famous thrust stage. Nevertheless, the recognition of common goals and the sharing of common dreams were vitally important to these young men striving to fulfil their early aspirations and promise. As Tarvainen put it, shortly after the group was established, 'More and more the spirit of the New Directors Group is an unlimited faith in each other's work and integrity. And if one person wants to do a play they will get the support and encouragement and financial aid and cooperation they need.'[48] The strong egos in this group were never completely submerged, and psychological gamesmanship was a part of their interaction. For example, Kinch recalls Garrard proclaiming that there were two-and-a-half geniuses in the New Directors Group, but refusing to say who they were. Nevertheless, with such a mixture of headstrong individuals, the members themselves were pleasantly surprised at how well they were able to get along. 'The fact that we survived more than two meetings was extraordinary,' Tarvainen added. 'If anyone had said these specific individuals could get together in one group, sharing ideas on a friendship basis, I just wouldn't have believed it.'

In retrospect, as with the Canadian Place Theatre and Theatre Passe Muraille itself, the media attention paid to the New Directors Group seems out of proportion to its accomplishments at that time. For example, the group was featured in a magazine supplement to the *Globe and Mail* in an article which bore the headline 'Can these directors come up with an answer?' Pictured were the shaggy-haired Kinch, Gass, Tarvainen, and Garrard, all clad in black and looking dour. In private they were a fun-loving lot, but their public image was a very serious one.

The most significant legacy of this group (as a group) was the Festival of Underground Theatre, which ran from 19 August to 6 September 1970. The idea was first brought up by Henry Tarvainen, who felt that the St Lawrence Centre might react favourably to such a project. With the failure of the Centre's first mainstage season, and with terrible attendance for community programs at the adjacent Town Hall, the time was indeed right. Bruce Lawson, program director of the Town Hall, needed some kind of high-profile success to justify his programming there; and, as fate would have it, Passe Muraille's former general manager, Ron Terrill, was now working as Lawson's assistant. Planning for the FUT festival began very late, considering the magnitude of the project. First the NDG approached Charlotte Holmes of the Ontario Arts Council, who had already proved sympathetic to alternative theatre by finding emergency operating funds for Passe Muraille the preceding autumn. The OAC's initial contribution of $1000 for a feasibility study set the wheels in motion for the festival. Ken Gass, who was opening his Factory Theatre Lab at about the same time, moved into the Town Hall offices to write this study, and Jim Garrard embarked on a fundraising campaign. Perhaps dour young leadership was what the OAC was seeking, for Gass's study brought an additional grant of $15,000, which became the keystone of the festival's financing. (Smaller grants were also obtained from the City of Toronto and the Canada Council, who were less enthusiastic about the idea.) The OAC grant, however, was contingent on the festival being affiliated with a more solidly established arts organization, especially to oversee the financial management of the project. This condition, of course, was perfectly acceptable to both the NDG and the Town Hall. Through this arrangement, the St Lawrence Centre became the major grantor to the FUT festival, although it did not intend to be. Affiliation with the mainstream St Lawrence Centre introduced these young directors to concepts of cash flow and deficit financing, which they'd never heard of before. Ron Terrill became FUT's full-time administrator, Frank Masi was brought aboard as technical director, and Ken Gass took over most of the responsibilities for programming, although he had plenty of advice from his fellow NDG members.

As far as the New Directors Group was concerned, the main purpose of the FUT festival was to provide a platform for their own work. Indeed, the central element in the programming was that each director guaranteed to bring a piece of work to the mainstage, although not everyone finally did. Under the banner of Theatre Passe Muraille, Paul Thompson presented *Ubu Raw*, an adaptation of Jarry's famous avant-garde play, with Don Steinhouse as King Ubu and featuring a ten-foot green phallus on wheels. Martin Kinch brought a collective creation entitled *Separate Cell*, inspired by the writings of psychologist R.D. Laing, which he had developed collectively (and hurriedly) between other projects at Stratford. Ken Gass's new Factory Theatre Lab presented a program of four short plays, three of them directed by Gass himself. John Palmer, absent for several months from the Toronto scene, brought a production of Ibsen's *A Doll's House* from Ottawa. (Ever the iconoclast, Palmer wanted to produce something totally bourgeois for this festival of counter-culture work.) Other Canadian productions on the mainstage were Louis Capson's *Dead Sun Rise* presented by his Creation 2 company, Jean-Claude Germain's *Si Aurore m'était contée deux fois* presented by his Théâtre du Même Nom from Montreal, and a play-in-progress presented by John Juliani's Savage God company from Vancouver.

While showcasing the New Directors Group was central to its programming, another goal of the FUT festival was to bring important alternative theatre from elsewhere. To this end, the FUT organizers brought two internationally renowned alternative performing groups. The first was Peter Schumann's Bread and Puppet Theatre from New York, whose huge puppets led the opening day parade from Queen's Park south to the St Lawrence Centre. The next night, Schumann's group performed their anti-American satire *The Difficult Life of Uncle Fatso.* Closing the mainstage festival more than two weeks later was Jerome Savary's Théâtre de la Grande Panique from Paris (also known as the Panic Circus), with their lively Tarzan take-off entitled *The Colonial Fairy Tale.* Other out-of-town groups were invited to perform, such as the feminist company Burning City Women from New York, and still others just heard about the festival and turned up on the Town Hall's doorstep. Meanwhile, fringe and after-hours activities at the Global Village Theatre encompassed a great variety of music, dance, and theatre performances, including a comedy group called Swamp Fox from Buffalo and the transvestite Revolting Theatre from New York. One of the highlights of the festival took place when Martin Brenzell, who had promised to bring an evening of off-off-Broadway plays from McMaster, cancelled on only a few days' notice. In the spirit of improvisation and fun which pervaded the festival, a 'FUT Extravaganza' took Brenzell's spot in the mainstage schedule. With Ron Terrill acting as emcee and Savary's Panic Circus as animateurs, a kind of counter-culture variety show was presented, much to everyone's delight. Popular excerpts were brought over from the Global Village, serious actors did comic turns, and the audience even got into the act with egg races at intermission. Two days later, the festival came to an idyllic close with a Sunday afternoon picnic on the Toronto Islands.

For the members of the New Directors Group, the FUT festival was an unqualified success. They had produced an eclectic range of experimental performances in Toronto's new civic cultural centre. They had invited some of their international heroes (such as Schumann and

Savary) to perform, and had come to know them personally. They had attracted a good-sized audience, and maintained that audience's interest over an extended period of time. Although they had decided not to bother inviting the critics (since each show was performed only twice), they had received quite a lot of press coverage, particularly from the *Toronto Star*. These young directors also encountered to their surprise what was to become a familiar revelation: that conditions in Europe or New York were no more conducive to making theatre than those in Toronto. Savary, for instance, said he found North America a more receptive place for experimental theatre than was France, where his actors were expected to support themselves with outside jobs.[49] While Nathan Cohen lamented the 'painful superiority of those visiting performers to the domestic breed, most of all the host groups from Toronto,'[50] he did not allow for the fact that the local productions were all premières, with the high risk of failure that always attends new work, while the visiting performers brought plays which they had proven successful elsewhere. The long-term effect of the 1970 FUT festival was similar to that of *Futz* the year before. It created a common bond among the people responsible for its success, and galvanized an alternative theatre community which still remembers that excitement. For instance, many of Ken Gass's subsequent major projects, such as his *Works* series at the Factory Lab and the Toronto Theatre Festival of 1981, have been attempts to rekindle the excitement of the FUT festival.

With the success of the festival, there were of course some discussions about making it an annual event. One reason that this never came to pass was that the New Directors Group stopped functioning as a group, and the career paths of its members never converged again as they had at that time. A second reason is that, having incurred a deficit of about $15,000 on the project (on a $40,000 budget), the St Lawrence Centre was not anxious to sponsor another one. Accounting and approval procedures at the Centre were a bit disorganized that summer, and the FUT organizers were able to requisition cheques against the Centre's line of credit. As a result, all the performing groups were paid at the time of their performance, and the magnitude of the deficit was not discovered until weeks later. This was a particular blessing for the impoverished Theatre Passe Muraille and Factory Theatre Lab: in fact, it was money from the FUT festival which kept these companies from folding before they were able to bring in some box-office money the next winter. The St Lawrence Centre management was furious, of course, when they realized what had happened. However, the FUT deficit was tiny compared with the Centre's overall deficit and growing maintenance costs, which soon brought on another round of political struggles with City Hall. There were dark rumours in some quarters that Ron Terrill, who left the country soon after the FUT festival closed, was to blame for the shortfall; but at this distance, it seems that the deficit resulted from the young directors' indifference to the financial problems of what they perceived to be a fabulously wealthy, publicly funded theatre. Besides, they thought, it had been good value for the money.

The FUT festival marked the end of Passe Muraille's interest in American radical theatre, and the beginning of its reconstitution as a nationalist theatre. During the transitional phase between Garrard's era and Thompson's, as we shall see in chapter 4, the company increasingly concentrated on Canadian-written plays. Partly this was a function of the change in leadership. Garrard left for British Columbia even before the FUT festival opened, and his fascination with the La Mama style was declining in any case. He was no longer to be a direct influence on Passe Muraille, although he remained something of an *éminence grise* in Toronto's alternative theatre for many years. Palmer was already dedicated to producing more Canadian-written plays, and Thompson's play selections too were becoming less European and more Canadian. Like Palmer and Thompson, Kinch was moving away from scripted plays and toward improvisational playmaking, which in Canada is a form of Canadian playwriting as well. Besides this shifting of individual goals, moreover, Passe Muraille found itself at the forefront of a new concern for Canadian drama in the years following the FUT festival. In 1971 the success of *Creeps* at the Factory Lab and the nationalistic demands of two conferences on Canadian playwriting made literary nationalism the most widely debated issue in Canadian theatre.

3

The Factory Theatre Lab

In theatre, fashion is everything and the great sin is being demonstrably passé or unaccountably ahead of one's time. The idea of Canadian work in Canadian theatres is an idea whose time has apparently come.[1]

Tom Hendry, January 1972

The Factory Theatre Lab was the first of Toronto's alternative theatres to make an issue of Canadian content. The company initially grew out of Ken Gass's desire to lead a group of his own. Ironically, his original vision was highly derivative of American off-off-Broadway theatres such as the Cafe La Mama. At the time he started the Factory, however, Gass realized that the public profile of his new company would be greatly enhanced by having an identifiable programming policy. Therefore, he announced that the Factory would produce only Canadian plays. This policy was not unprecedented: similar ones could be found in Keith Turnbull's summer theatre operation in London (Ontario) in 1966, in the Dominion Drama Festival in 1967, and at the Canadian Place Theatre in Stratford in 1969. In the regional theatres too, indigenous drama had proven occasionally popular, although it was still considered something of a curiosity. In cosmopolitan Toronto, while less prominent and less adventurous companies used imported plays exclusively, some leading companies included Canadian plays as part of a mixed international repertoire, notably the Crest Theatre, Theatre Toronto, Toronto Workshop Productions, and the University Alumnae Dramatic Society. However, when the St Lawrence Centre's all-Canadian première season in 1970 proved such a debacle, the voice of the Canadian playwright in

Canadian mainstream theatre seemed to grow weaker.[2] The founding of the Factory Theatre Lab later that year, scarcely noticed until the success of *Creeps* in February 1971, was a vital link in the development of new Canadian drama, eventually bringing the Canadian play to the forefront of the 'Toronto movement.'

More than any other alternative theatre, the Factory was in a constant state of chaos, and continually on the brink of collapse. While partly due to poor organization, the chaos at the Factory stemmed mainly from the high sense of purpose brought to the company by its founder, Ken Gass. The process by which the Factory became 'the home of the Canadian playwright' (promising in the bargain to read and comment on all manuscripts it received) was indicative of the way the company was to operate. Gass would propose a policy or a project for the simple reason that it was a commendable idea; then all the talent and energy at the Factory would be plunged into a terrible struggle to make it happen. His reckless pursuit of high-principled theatrical ideas initiated a number of events which brought public prominence to Toronto's alternative theatres: the Festival of Underground Theatre of 1970, the Factory's *Works* festival of 1972, the Factory's tour to England in 1973, and the *Winter Offensive* uproar in 1977. Cooler heads would never have tackled such projects, and both the Factory and Gass himself would be exhausted by them. Through such events, however, Gass became a major catalyst in creating an established underground theatre 'scene' in Toronto which transcended the obsessions of particular artists or companies. He was recognized as a leader of incorruptible (even naïve) vision, and the Factory was driven by the purity of his causes.

With the chaos at the Factory came opportunity. Curious volunteers who wandered into the Dupont Street theatre would often be assigned tasks on which the very existence of the company depended: raising money, reading manuscripts, conducting workshops, directing plays. In this way, the Factory helped launch the careers of such directors as Paul Bettis and Eric Steiner, such administrators as Shain Jaffe and Ralph Zimmerman, such playwrights as George F. Walker and Michael Hollingsworth, and many others. Indeed, Gass's reputation as an artist in his own right has never equalled his reputation as a creator of artistic opportunities for others. Similarly, the Factory's artistic accomplishments were often subordinated to its concerns for serving new Canadian plays. The Factory consistently produced new scripts before they had been adequately polished, and under constraints of time and money which did not allow them to be presented to their best advantage.

Whether this process was truly serving the Canadian playwright was a question which led directly to the founding of Tarragon Theatre, created with a similar programming policy. Later, when Tarragon scored a number of popular and critical successes in mainly a realistic style, the Factory tended to choose anti-realistic plays which grew less accessible to a broad audience as time went on.

In the altruism of Gass and the Factory, one finds an element of self-denial that approaches self-destruction. Plays would be too arcane and too thinly produced to appeal to a broad segment of the theatre-going public. Sometimes a production would be mounted, not because the script was worthwhile, but because Gass felt the playwright would benefit from such encouragement. The development of artists was given precedence over the cultivation of audiences; yet the artists themselves would eventually gravitate toward other companies which could provide better pay and much better working conditions. Popular successes came less frequently to the Factory, and were seldom exploited as fully as they might have been. Gass was insistent in rejecting any pattern for the Factory which resembled a formula for success, in favour of continued experiment and exploration. In the mid-1970s, as audiences and funding agencies came to expect some kind of recognizable mandate, this insistence further weakened the Factory's identity and stature – ironically, since the Factory had pioneered the concept of an identifiable programming policy. For all these reasons, the Factory Theatre Lab was in obvious decline by 1975, at a time when other alternative theatres were also suffering from creative exhaustion. The whole of the Factory – energizing, experimental, catalytic, high-principled – is much greater than the sum of its parts. Strangely, the impact which the Factory has had on Canadian theatre may be seen in the works of other companies more easily than in its own. As one of its most severe critics wrote in 1981, 'Every alternate theatre in town owes something to the Factory.'[3]

Background to 1970

Ken Gass (b. 1945) grew up in Abbotsford, British Columbia, and studied theatre and creative writing at the University of British Columbia. His early theatre experience included acting in children's plays for Holiday Theatre in Vancouver. He received his BA in 1967 and took courses toward an MA in directing the following year. In the spring of 1968 Gass came to Toronto, partly to get away from Vancouver and partly to find work, since there was a shortage of teachers in Toronto.

After obtaining a teaching certificate from the University of Toronto's College of Education, Gass began teaching English at Parkdale Collegiate in September 1968, and taught night school as well. In both positions, he used his teaching situations to produce avant-garde plays, such as *Interview* from the Open Theatre's celebrated *America Hurrah*. At the end of the 1968–69 school year, Gass gave up his Parkdale position and began to write theatre reviews and features for the *Summer Varsity*, a weekly summer edition of the University of Toronto's student newspaper. In July 1969 he went to the Garret Theatre on Yonge Street to review *The World of Woyzeck* and to interview its adaptor/director, John Herbert.[4]

Then forty-two years old, Jack Brundage, better known by his professional name of John Herbert, was Canada's best-known playwright, as one critic said 'for lack of any serious competition as much as anything else.'[5] At about age twenty, Brundage had spent six months in a reformatory, an experience which became the basis for his hit play *Fortune and Men's Eyes*.[6] Initially championed by Nathan Cohen, this play was given a workshop performance at the Stratford Festival in 1965 and was finally produced off-Broadway in 1967, where it ran for almost a year. Virtually overnight, *Fortune and Men's Eyes* became the admired example of a Canadian play with international acclaim, and a symbol of achievement for indigenous playwrights. In May 1967, with royalties earned from the play, Herbert established his Garret Theatre in a second-storey studio at 529 Yonge Street, to be 'an actors' and writers' studio where the emphasis will be on indigenous talent.'[7] There he lived, taught workshops in acting and playwriting, and mounted productions in his 35-seat theatre. Herbert's *The World of Woyzeck*, adapted from Büchner's play, opened at the Garret in May 1969, where it performed on weekends for almost six months.[8]

When he met Herbert, Gass was impressed with his quiet intensity, his gypsy lifestyle, and the way in which theatre functioned as an extension of himself. While *The World of Woyzeck* (like all Garret productions) played to extremely small houses, Gass gave it an excellent review. 'In retrospect,' he recalls, 'I'm sure I overrated the production';[9] but in *Woyzeck* he saw one of his favourite plays being presented with great earnestness and commitment. He was also fascinated by the fact that a production by Canada's foremost playwright should be so thoroughly ignored.

In the fall of 1969, Gass spent much of his time at the Garret, taking and giving workshops there while continuing to teach night-school classes to make ends meet, and soon he was functioning as Herbert's assistant. At the same time, several other aspiring professionals began taking classes at the Garret, people who were to be instrumental in founding the Factory Theatre Lab. Three of them had been colleagues of Gass at Parkdale Collegiate: Ivan Burgess, whose first play was being workshopped by Herbert, and actors Peter Kunder and Frank Trotz. Another was Marcella Lustig, a founding member of the later 'second-wave' companies Open Circle Theatre and Redlight Theatre. Finally, there was Shain Jaffe, at the time an ex-businessman and an aspiring playwright, who was later to become the first general manager of Toronto Free Theatre. That winter, Gass also became involved at Theatre Passe Muraille, initially intending to produce a theatre periodical there with the help of Jaffe, later conducting workshops and directing some modest productions. This was the connection that brought Jaffe to the rescue of Passe Muraille's bookkeeping problems in the winter of 1969–70, and brought Gass into the New Directors Group and (ultimately) the FUT festival.

Meanwhile, Herbert's work on Ivan Burgess' *Horseshoe House*, a play about racial tensions in a Toronto rooming-house, had reached an impasse under Herbert's rambling rehearsal methods. Gass offered to produce the play himself under the Garret banner. With Herbert planning to move to England, it was also agreed that Gass would assume control of Herbert's theatre. While Herbert vacillated over the exact timing of this changeover, Gass and his friends began planning for a new era for the Garret. By the time *Horseshoe House* opened there in February 1970, with very little publicity and very small houses, Herbert had proclaimed Gass as his successor. The changeover in leadership was finally precipitated when Herbert received notice of a substantial rent increase for the Garret, effective mid-April 1970, and he decided to give up his Yonge Street studio. Gass and Frank Trotz obtained a bank loan of $3500 on the basis of their teaching certificates, and leased a warehouse on Dupont Street for occupancy May 1. They also arranged for temporary storage of the Garret's properties at Theatre Passe Muraille for the two-week interim period. Meanwhile, during an extension of *Horseshoe House* which Gass had arranged at the Central Library Theatre, a schism split the Garret. A number of Herbert's most devoted followers objected to Gass's new authority, and the future of the Garret was hotly debated in some emotional group meetings. At first, Gass recalls, Herbert decided that the Garret's name should be carried on; however, he changed his mind a few weeks later when Gass refused to consider producing a Tennessee Williams play because of Gass's new policy of presenting only Canadian drama. Ironically, it appears that Herbert had sown the seeds of this policy the summer before, when he told Gass he wanted 'to deliver Canadian babies,' to rescue 'the dozens of good, homeless Canadian scripts.'

Gass's new theatre space at 374 Dupont was a second-storey warehouse above an auto-body shop, an open area some 110 feet long by 40 feet wide. At one time it had been a candle factory, which had no doubt contributed to the thick soot which covered all the interior surfaces. There was a great spirit and sense of adventure among Gass, Trotz, their friends from the Garret, and some of Gass's night-school students, who set about cleaning, painting, caulking, and otherwise readying their new theatre for operation. With the help of Brian Meeson, a drama consultant with the Toronto Board of Education, the Factory was given $200 to run a playwriting contest for local high-school students. Acting classes began by mid-May, and the high-school workshops by the end of the month, even while work continued to make the theatre habitable: Gass recalls climbing up on the roof to recaulk the skylights while they dripped water on those first workshops. The Factory's first major production opened in July, a double-bill of two new plays entitled *An Act of Violence* (by Stan Ross) and *We Three, You and I* (by Bill Greenland). These were followed in August with four short plays for the Festival of Underground Theatre. Despite the Factory's precarious finances, Gass insisted the actors in these productions be paid a token amount, to establish a principle of professionalism within the company. Meanwhile, in order to meet the monthly theatre rental and loan payments, workshops in acting, movement, directing, and creative drama were given virtually every day and every evening.

In these formative months, there were two qualities which Gass brought to the Factory which enabled it to find a place in Toronto theatre. One was his decision to produce only Canadian plays. As Gass later said, 'The idea of doing only Canadian plays was an accident. It was simply that I had been working with some new playwrights, and I sensed there was a need for this.' This policy, as he explained in 1974,

seemed an extravagantly foolish ideology for the time. The policy, however, did not stem from any passionate nationalism. Rather, it was a simple and arbitrary way of escaping the Canadian theatrical rut of following fashion. Regional playhouses were (and, largely, still are) shaping their seasons to reflect the fashions of Broadway and the West End, and young directors like myself in

Studio or University companies were modelling our work after 'Tulane Drama Review' descriptions of Off-Off-Broadway and Eastern Europe. By limiting the Factory to only new Canadian plays, we were forced to abandon the security blanket of our colonial upbringing. We found ourselves in a vacuum, without roots, and, indeed, without playwrights. The plays soon surfaced, happily, many of them bouncing to life after years of neglect. We also discovered to our surprise that the country was indeed ready for a surge of nationalism in many fields and that we were on the crest of a timely wave.[10]

His second vital contribution was, as Gass put it, 'a high tolerance for other people.' Even more than at Theatre Passe Muraille, the Factory's open-door structure attracted all sorts of willing workers, some of whom later made highly successful careers in theatre and some of whom did not. Said Gass, 'People began to take the Factory seriously because it was open ... Certainly it wouldn't have survived if it had simply been my domain or a place for me to direct my shows.' Anyone could join in, anyone could help, and there was no real pecking order to watch out for. In both these policies, Gass showed the kind of instinctive vision for which he came to be admired. In addition, the Factory's scrambling approach to script development soon proved more successful than that of the St Lawrence Centre, where Canadian programming had been so disappointing in its opening spring season in 1970. As Gass put it, 'Here was a grassroots situation with enormous energy, and not much else, doing an enormous body of work and striking a chord of response. So the Factory was the kind of place that people gravitated towards.'

Production at the Factory, 1970–75

However articulate and laudable its goals, the Factory started without much fanfare. That first double-bill opened at the end of July 1970, running Thursdays through Sundays for only two weeks. Despite the modest scale of the production, its brief run, and its small houses, it still attracted a review from Nathan Cohen and a lengthy feature in the *Summer Varsity* (written by Gass's editor from the previous summer). Stan Ross's *An Act of Violence* was based loosely on incidents at Sir George Williams University in Montreal, where racial tensions and student protests culminated in the burning of its computer centre in February 1969. The play was staged environmentally, its set dominated by rough strands of barbed wire reaching from the ceiling to the floor. Nathan Cohen described the play as 'a farrago of ludicrous sloganizing, nitwit characterization, and structural shapelessness.'[11] The second one-act was more successful, Bill Greenland's *We Three, You and I*, a memorable two-hander about a matron soliciting charitable donations through the blatant exploitation of a little girl in a wheelchair. The action of this play is introduced as a charity appeal before the 'real' play begins, a sleight-of-hand which has often fooled audiences and caused unpredictable reactions: in charity-conscious Britain, for instance, Gass's 1973 production of *We Three, You and I* created a near-riot, with some audience members demanding a discussion of the play and others calling the police. Originally produced at the University of British Columbia as a combined project of directing and creative writing students, this play became something of a signature piece for Gass, who has produced it several times.[12]

For the Festival of Underground Theatre in late August, the Factory presented a program of four short plays, all by Toronto playwrights: *Light*, by Ken Gass, *Close Friends* by John Herbert, REM by Larry Mollin, and *The New Woman* by Harvey Markowitz. REM was an 'ensemble creation' directed by Mollin, and the other three plays were directed by Gass. While the Factory's presentations received mixed reviews, Gass's efforts on behalf of the FUT festival established his new theatre as a significant member of this brash new theatrical community.

The autumn of 1970 saw the first influx of new talent into the Factory. Maruti Achanta, originally from Bombay, began conducting some of the company's workshops, thus taking some of the load off Gass, and directed the Factory's first full-length production to open the season. Bill Glassco also joined the Factory at this time, working for Gass for the season before he founded the Tarragon Theatre in 1971. Glassco started with dramaturgical tasks at the Factory, reading manuscripts and directing playwrights' workshops, and he also undertook some modest fundraising. Other new people included Shain Jaffe, who set up some accounting procedures while continuing to do similar work at Theatre Passe Muraille; Sandra Gathercole, who worked as publicist for almost two years on a volunteer basis; Joyce Penner, who directed some playreadings and helped with administration; Rosemary Donnelly, an actress whom Gass later married; and her friend Jacquelyn Jay, an aspiring actress who also helped with administration. Autumn also saw the departure of Factory co-founder Frank Trotz, frustrated at not being cast in productions despite his hard work and personal sacrifices for the company. This was to be a continuing problem at the Factory, as Gass later recalled: 'What was beginning to happen already was that the needs of the individual actors who were associated with the Factory were different from the needs of the theatre, and the theatre had to put the playwrights first ... "Who does the Factory serve?" was a recurring question.'

By September 1970, the Factory was subsisting on proceeds from workshops and from the Festival of Underground Theatre, although Gass himself was so broke that he lived in the theatre for a time. In October a series of weekly playwrights' workshops, initially organized by Glassco, began once more with the winners of the high-school playwriting contest, and continued with the more promising manuscripts received by the company. In the Factory's usual manner, this weekly workshop commitment often caused a scramble for scripts and for readers, but it also began to produce palpable results: playwrights like George Walker were encouraged, and plays like Harvey Markowitz's *Branch Plant* were developed for later production. While the Factory's dramaturgical process had obvious weaknesses, it was a notable advance at this time to offer *any* kind of process for script development, as Frank Trotz pointed out:

Okay, so the audiences for the readings are made up of relatives, students and so on. But the important thing is that writers have an opportunity of seeing their work on a stage without having to battle for a full-scale production. The Factory professionals have an opportunity to help the writers analyze their mistakes. Sure we lack good Canadian plays. But there is just as much playwriting potential in this country as anywhere else. The trouble is that it has never been allowed to develop through active experience in the theatre.[13]

Such theatre people as Tom Hendry and Herbert Whittaker began to take an interest in the Factory process because of its singular effort to nurture new Canadian scripts. These workshops also marked Bill Glassco's first involvement with new plays, for which he later became so celebrated as a shaping influence.

By the time its first full-length production opened in November 1970, the Factory had been operating for six months. In his program notes for this occasion, Gass published a rallying cry for his fellow alternative theatres to lead in the production of new Canadian plays. It was an idea which was to catch fire in Toronto in the ensuing two years:

We started with an insistent need. The need for a laboratory in which to develop original material and a showcase in which to present our products. The

FACTORY is presenting only original Canadian works. However, I do not feel unusually nationalistic; I am simply trying to relate to the world around me. Also I am bored with imitating the latest East European or Off-Broadway successes.

The major theatres of the country – notably The St. Lawrence Centre, The Vancouver Playhouse and Stratford – have reneged on their commitment to Canadian plays. This is particularly regrettable now, for Canada is at a point in history where she is begging for a cultural identity. As the American Dream dissolves itself into absurdity and ex-patriots rush to this virgin country, Canadians are less insistent on the u.s. or British stamp of approval before accepting their own artists, even though such playwrights as Herschel Hardin, John Herbert, Beverley Simons, Doug Bankson and Joseph Addison still are having their works produced in the u.s. before they achieve acceptance here.

Playwrights must stop depending on our large regional playhouses to promote their work. As in politics, only a guerilla action will precipitate a cultural revolution. However different Toronto and New York may be, the coffee house and garage theatres of Off-Off-Broadway which proliferated a vibrant whole sub-culture to contrast the staid commercialism of Broadway still offer us our best model. Rather than rail against the inflexibility of large concrete playhouses or the museum theatres of universities, we must build our theatre culture and let the others prove themselves irrelevant. Let's not wait for the government; let's do it!

Maruti Achanta had planned to direct Beverley Simons' *Crabdance* for this first production, but the performance rights were refused. Instead he chose *A Bedtime Story* by Frank McEnaney, the story of a precarious young marriage upset by a malevolent third party. This play had been circulated among several directors and critics in Toronto, and had attracted a great deal of interest but no productions until the Factory came along. A sign of the Factory's increased stature in Toronto theatre was that *A Bedtime Story* received lengthy reviews in all three daily newspapers. Another sign was the increased box-office returns, although Gass recalls that these were bolstered by vigorous sales by the playwright's mother. Although critics expressed reservations about the quality of the production, they felt that McEnaney was a significant new writer with an instinct for the stage. While McEnaney did not prove as successful as some of the Factory's other playwrights, he later served as writer on Passe Muraille's collective creation *Them Donnellys,* and his play *To Covet Honour* (about the assassination of President Kennedy) was given a mainstage production by Theatre Aquarius in Hamilton in 1978. More importantly for the Factory, *A Bedtime Story* proved Gass's contention that there existed worthwhile Canadian scripts which under present conditions were not being produced.

The next major production at the Factory was in February 1971, a double-bill of *Snails* by UBC student Michael Mirolla and *Creeps* by David Freeman. While Gass's production of *Snails* was reviewed in disdainful terms (when it was mentioned at all),[14] Bill Glassco's production of *Creeps* received lavish critical praise. Freeman's play, a lacerating character study of a group of cerebral palsy victims employed in a sheltered workshop, quickly attracted overflow houses and national press coverage. *Creeps* not only established the Factory as a major force in Canadian theatre, it also became an admired example of a successful Canadian play, just as *Fortune and Men's Eyes* had four years earlier. Despite its signal success, however, the run of *Creeps* was extended only from three weeks to four. Popular demand was a problem for which the Factory was unprepared: another new script was in rehearsal, and it finally went on as scheduled. Gass's inclination to consider the playwright before the audience was, in Glassco's mind, detrimental to both; and Glassco's desire to improve both the script and the production of *Creeps,* in order to reach the widest possible audience, became the final impetus for his founding Tarragon Theatre.

Inevitably, *Creeps* was followed by two less successful productions, both earnest plays about Canadian political and economic self-determination. The first, *Two Countries* by Joseph Addison, depicted a threatened u.s. invasion of Canada in retaliation for Canada's nationalization of some American-based industries. It was the most blatantly anti-American expression of the Factory's nationalist sentiments. The second, *Branch Plant,* by Harvey Markowitz, directed by Bill Glassco, was a dramatization of the controversial closure of the British-owned Dunlop plant in Toronto the previous year. Former Dunlop employees had attended Glassco's workshops on the script; but critics complained that while the play was faithful to the issues involved, its characters were neither credible nor interesting. 'There was excellent material here for a debate,' said one, 'but not for a drama.'[15] That *Branch Plant* opened on May 1 was appropriate for two reasons: international workers celebrated May Day, and the Factory celebrated its first anniversary. Gass's program notes on this occasion addressed the significance of his company's survival:

On May 1, 1970, our lease on the FACTORY space began. We moved in without even a hammer and began sifting through the layers of dirt and garbage.

Somehow in this earthy space, we hoped to build a repertoire of new Canadian plays.

With the failure of the St. Lawrence Centre's first season of original plays, we encountered many skeptics over our firm 'Canadian only' policy. Our playwrights have not let us down, however; this policy has proved a solid backbone for the theatre. At first we had difficulty finding good scripts; now we have difficulty scheduling productions of all the good scripts available and cannot run our productions long enough. Gradually we are defeating our playwrights' greatest enemy: Canada's psychological distaste for her own art and artists.

At this time it was becoming obvious that Bill Glassco would be leaving the Factory, taking with him most of the cast and crew of *Creeps*. Simultaneously, however, there was another influx of new people who became central to the Factory's success in the years to follow. One was Eric Steiner, age twenty-four, a Toronto native who directed many of the Factory's most successful productions. After studying theatre at Emerson College in Boston, Steiner had spent the 1970–71 season working backstage in London and New York before returning to Toronto. Another was Paul Bettis, age thirty, British-born actor and director and later founder of the experimental Theatre Second Floor. An Oxford graduate, Bettis had originally come to Canada in the mid-1960s to teach English at the University of Victoria; he then taught theatre at Simon Fraser University alongside such well-known directors as John Juliani and Michael Bawtree. Later, Bettis joined Bawtree's short-lived studio company at the National Arts Centre in Ottawa, and came to Toronto early in 1971 when that company was dissolved. Both Steiner and Bettis found a much greater vitality to Toronto theatre than they had known before, a vitality that made them want to stay in Toronto to work. A third important addition was George F. Walker, age twenty-three, a young writer working as a taxi driver, who had spotted a Factory leaflet asking for submissions of new plays. Backed by Gass's faith in their abilities, Steiner, Bettis, and Walker were immediately embroiled in all sorts of projects. In particular, the development of George Walker as a major Canadian and international playwright became the most persuasive evidence for Gass's reputed vision and his nose for talent.

In the office, administrative leadership fell to Ralph Zimmerman, age twenty-five, a business graduate of York University. While taking Mavor Moore's new course in the history of Canadian theatre, Zimmerman met a Factory volunteer who encouraged him to come down to the theatre to help. In the 1971–72 season Zimmerman took an MBA at York in arts administration, but spent much of his time working at the Factory. By March he had become the administrative head of the company, which he remained until 1976. While his training at York primarily addressed operations the scale of the Stratford Festival or the National Ballet, Zimmerman enjoyed the challenge of 'guerrilla administration' at the Factory. It was an almost daily responsibility of his to decide which creditors to pay, and which to put off even longer. Zimmerman's post-Factory career was determined, quite offhandedly, by John Palmer, who came to help with the unsolicited manuscripts which continued to pile up after Glassco's departure. (On the verge of his most productive season ever in Toronto, Palmer left the Factory for the new Toronto Free Theatre the following January, but retained his affiliation with both companies for several years.) It was Palmer's suggestion that the Factory's playwrights needed an agent, and that Zimmerman should be it. In response, Zimmerman founded his Great North Agency in the spring of 1972, with Palmer as his first client. Great North operated out of the Factory for several years, and is still a major broker for Canadian writers, actors, and directors.

In June 1971, the Factory scored its second major success (after *Creeps*) with *Esker Mike and His Wife, Agiluk* by Vancouver writer Herschel Hardin. For a fledgling theatre, the second success is perhaps even more important than the first; this was certainly true of both the Factory and Tarragon. Like *A Bedtime Story*, it also exemplified Gass's contention that there were good Canadian scripts going begging: *Esker Mike* had been published in *The Drama Review* in 1969, but had never been produced anywhere. Gass contacted the surprised playwright in Vancouver, and obtained grants from the Canada Council and from the Cultural Exchange Program of the Ontario Department of Education for Hardin and director Maruti Achanta to visit Aklavik in the Northwest Territories, where the play is set. Critics praised Hardin's 'stark, engrossing tragedy' and Achanta's austere direction.[16] As with *Creeps*, the run of *Esker Mike* was not extended past four weeks, since other scripts were awaiting production. However, unlike *Creeps*, *Esker Mike* remained identified with the Factory. It was revived at Dupont Street in 1972, on the Factory's tour to England in 1973, and with Gass's subsequent company, Canadian Rep Theatre, in 1986.

The summer of 1971 saw a variety of activity at the Factory. In June, while *Esker Mike* was still running, the company's new brainstrust made its debut in a program of short plays in late-night weekend performances. One of them was Sheldon Rosen's first play, *The Love Mouse*, directed by Eric Steiner. Another was George Walker's first play, *The Prince of Naples*, directed by Paul Bettis.[17] Walker's play was presented as an open rehearsal, as Urjo Kareda described it, 'with actors still carrying scripts, the furniture arranged at random, and the director shouting instructions to his cast.'[18] However, even then Kareda remarked on Walker's crackling dialogue and unusual use of language. In July came Ken Gass's production of *The Red Revolutionary*, his own adaptation of Charles Mair's interminable nineteenth-century verse drama *Tecumseh*. As with many of his later plays, Gass's use of historical analogy here was awkward in places: as one reviewer put it, 'while his desire to draw parallels is admirable, the material Gass is using just doesn't seem up to the strain.'[19] Nonetheless, after its Factory run, the entire production of *The Red Revolutionary* was loaded into two vans and a Volkswagen and driven to Vancouver, where Gass presented it to his academic supervisors at UBC as his long-deferred directing project required for his Masters degree.[20] Meanwhile, back at the Factory, performances continued in August with new Canadian plays by two other companies: Louis Capson's Creation 2 group presented his *I Love You Billy Striker*, and Dennis Hayes's 'Performing Group' (from St Francis Xavier University in Nova Scotia) presented his *The Death of Artaud*. Both plays were favourably reviewed.[21]

The Factory's zealous promotion of new Canadian plays could not have come at a more propitious time. The company's surprising success with these plays became an important argument at two seminal conferences in Canadian playwriting, both held in the summer of 1971. The first conference was convened by the new Canada Council Theatre Arts Officer, David Gardner, a native of Toronto who (like so many professionals of his generation) had trained under Robert Gill at Hart House Theatre. Gardner had acted with the Crest Theatre and the Stratford Festival in the 1950s, and worked as a producer and director with the CBC in the 1960s. In 1969 he became artistic director of the Vancouver Playhouse, succeeding Joy Coghill following popular but controversial productions of two plays by George Ryga, *The Ecstasy of Rita Joe* (1967) and *Grass and Wild Strawberries* (1969). One of Gardner's first tasks with the Playhouse was to restage its production of *Rita Joe* in June 1969 at the National Arts Centre in Ottawa. Deeply affected by this experience, Gardner wished to produce more new Canadian drama, and commissioned another Ryga script for the 1970–71 season. This play, finally titled *Captives of the Faceless Drummer*, was rich in parallels to

Canada's October Crisis of 1970; and the production was first deferred
and then cancelled due to the reluctance of the board of directors of the
Playhouse to court further controversy. Gardner, who had already
accepted his new position with the Canada Council, left Vancouver
convinced that regional theatre boards were not sensitive to the need for
developing Canadian playwrights. On his arrival in Ottawa, moreover,
Council head Peter Dwyer asked Gardner to try to help the new small
theatres in Toronto, which did not fit into existing categories for Council
operating grants. It was in this spirit of change that Gardner organized a
conference on Canadian playwriting at Stanley House, the Council's
rural retreat on the Gaspé Peninsula, 19–23 July 1971.

The report on the Gaspé conference, put together by playwright and
Canadian Theatre Centre head Jack Gray, noted that the position of the
playwright in Canadian theatre was an abnormal one. In other cultures,
said the report, 'really successful theatres demand new work and in fact
depend on it for their existence.'[22] In Canada, however, the leading
theatres depended on remounted plays from other countries. The most
contentious of the nineteen recommendations of this report was that
government subsidy for any Canadian theatre should be made contingent on that theatre producing at least 50 per cent Canadian-written
plays. Predictably, leaders of the regional theatres bristled at the
suggestion of any kind of quota, even when they agreed with the
principle involved. Those most opposed to this quota rightly perceived
the pressure as emanating from, in effect, a special-interest lobby of
Canadian playwrights.[23] Nonetheless, with a similar quota in effect for
Canadian radio and television, the playwrights had found a sturdy
platform from which to demand greater opportunity to practise their
craft in their own country.

A second playwrights' conference was held in Niagara-on-the-Lake on
14 and 15 August, organized by lawyer, playwright, and Shaw Festival
founder, Brian Doherty. Doherty's long experience in Canadian theatre
enabled him to put the question of indigenous playwriting in some kind
of historical context: 'Now that we have the theatres, the performers, the
technicians,' he wrote, 'I will not accept the idea that we cannot produce
native writers to match them.'[24] While only twelve delegates had attended
the conference at Stanley House, there were thirty-seven at the Niagara
one, mostly playwrights once again. The second conference served mainly
to disseminate the ideas from the so-called 'Gaspé Manifesto,' and to
discuss the promotion of Canadian plays in practical terms. Its resulting
report stated the playwrights' position with clarity and wit:

As far as the playwright is concerned ... the issue is fairly clear. It is one of opportunity to write in the first place. Once the play has been written he needs opportunities to have the work produced.

And once his work is produced, the playwright wants an opportunity to be exploited, as imaginatively and widely as possible, even to the point of becoming rich, or famous, or both.

The report concluded that fundamental change was imminent:

It was the feeling of the meeting that this gathering, and that held in the Gaspe, were hopeful signs after many years of building and equipping theatres throughout Canada, and of training artistic and technical personnel, that now in the seventies [it] would finally be possible to pay attention to what was to go into these theatres ... Change was upon us, and we could be sure that it would be the most exciting development we had yet had in the theatre in Canada.

The Niagara report specifically mentioned the Factory Theatre Lab and Theatre Passe Muraille as companies which produced exclusively Canadian work and thrived by it.[25] Not surprisingly, this high-profile support increased the flow of nationalist rhetoric emanating from the Factory and its supporters. John Palmer, for instance, attacked the established Canadian theatres as 'sick with lack of self-respect' for ignoring Canadian playwrights.[26] Meanwhile Gass, in an article previewing the Factory's second season, made much of the Factory's role as a leader in this area:

A year ago, our 'Canadian-only' policy at Factory Theatre Lab was viewed with much skepticism. Today it is foremost in this country's theatre fashion, as other theatres are adopting similar policies and even the most conservative theatres are making serious efforts to include some original Canadian work among their repertoire of British and American standards ... While in the first year we were freely picking neglected masterpieces off the ground, today we are entering a climate of healthy competition.[27]

In its first sixteen months, the Factory had done ten major productions and about thirty playwrights' workshops, on a total budget of about $20,000. It had also found an audience (a small but significant one) for both types of endeavour. Despite its professional pretensions and ambitions, the Factory's administration was still entirely volunteer, and its artists were paid only token amounts. The workload was perilously high and the resources perilously low. With recognition beginning to accrue to the company, however, this was no time to stop for reflection, nor was it in the Factory's nature to do so. As Gass put it, 'If we had really stopped to think about it, we probably wouldn't have done it, or done half of what we did; but we just tended to constantly barge ahead.' And so they did again, in the fall of 1971, announcing an ambitious season of ten more productions. Talent again rushed in to fill the vacuum, while organizational chaos reigned. But still, there was a sense that it was all working. As Zimmerman recalls, the company was 'fuelled by intelligence and energy and the sense of a terrific battle ... If you believed in it, you did it.'[28] With the new Tarragon Theatre situated just two blocks away, and at first struggling to find its style and its audience, the Factory's 1971–72 season was also fuelled by rivalry. This was to be the Factory's finest season, created by a volatile mix of new talent, youthful energy, and the sudden and unexpected availability of large sums of money.

The Factory's second season, 1971–72, was its most memorable. With Tarragon and Toronto Free Theatre starting up the same year, the Factory's success led the surge of the alternative theatres in establishing a new shape to theatre in Toronto. Its season opened in October with *The Jingo Ring* by Raymond Canale, directed by Paul Bettis, an allegory of greed and corruption set in a Mexican village. While Herbert Whittaker praised the Factory for its service to Canadian theatre, he found the dialogue hard to listen to and the characters boring ('stupid peons, speaking especially stupid peonese'). Urjo Kareda, replacing the late Nathan Cohen at the *Star*, lambasted this 'fantastically pretentious production' in all respects and did not even review the Factory's next show.[29] He therefore missed George F. Walker's first full-length play, *Ambush at Tether's End* (directed by Gass), a dark absurdist comedy in which friends of a suicide victim are bullied by notes he has left for them. While Whittaker had some reservations with Gass's production, particularly with Paul Bettis in one of the leads, he concluded that 'the play does nothing to deflect the Factory Lab's winning streak.'[30]

The Factory's third play of the season was a collaboration of two of the brightest stars of Toronto's new theatre: *A Touch of God in the Golden Age*, written by John Palmer and directed by Martin Kinch. *A Touch of God* is a long and demanding play about two men coming to grips with themselves and their relationship to each other on a lonely Christmas Eve. Whittaker, who did not stay to the end, described it as a 'lengthy personal statement by a man who may not have much talent as an editor, but, thank heaven, has some as a dramatist.' Kareda was more pointed, calling the play 'a two-character, three-act (and three-hour) talkathon' which was 'fundamentally undramatic, with neither structure nor development.'[31] It was not an opinion shared by the alternative theatre community, many of whom remember this production as one of the finest of its era. Tom Hendry, for one, predicted that Palmer's play would have as strong an effect on Canadian playwriting in the 1970s as *Look Back in Anger* had had on new British drama after 1956.[32] (Hendry's enthusiasm may have been coloured by the fact that, by this time, Kinch and Palmer were his new partners at Toronto Free Theatre.) That *A Touch of God* had no such effect was due not only to its poor reviews (unlike *Look Back in Anger*), but also to its lack of appeal to a general audience. In an obvious marketing blunder, the Factory opened this unremittingly dark play just three days before Christmas, presumably because of the play's Christmas setting. Disappointed by the extremely small audiences, Gass literally tried to give the tickets away, and found he could not. It was a sobering incident on the eve of ventures in free theatre in Toronto.

In January 1972, the Factory received its first LIP grant, of $30,000. The grant was earmarked for financing three productions, with two performances per week to be given for free and admission charged for the others. However, the company managed to stretch this capital to support four productions by soliciting kickbacks from their newly salaried actors and staff. Gass recalls that the standard weekly salary was ninety-five dollars, less a 'donation' of thirty dollars. This money was used to pay for the extra production, and also to pay for other employees (such as Zimmerman) who were ineligible for LIP employment. There were two precedents here which became common practice as alternative theatres began to tap into government arts and employment funding, but which were strictly forbidden by the granting agencies: the unapproved reapportioning of funds (even for the best of reasons) and the expectation of kickbacks from employees. Indeed, this grant was nearly cancelled because of the Factory's inability to keep LIP funds separate from its overall operations or to provide any acceptable accounting for its cash flow. As Zimmerman recalls, this major grant came at precisely the time when the initial energy which started the Factory was beginning to expire. Without doubt, it supported the most concentrated period of popular success of the Factory's first decade.

The first of the LIP-financed productions was Larry Fineberg's *Stonehenge Trilogy*, directed by Eric Steiner, which opened in January

1972. The Montreal-born Fineberg had been working in both Broadway and off-off-Broadway theatre since graduating from Emerson College, where he and Steiner had been friends. Indeed, it was at Steiner's encouragement that Fineberg submitted his play to the Factory and came to Toronto for its production. Critically, this collection of three one-act plays drew equivocal responses, but the scheduling of free performances helped attract a new audience to the Factory. *Stonehenge Trilogy* was followed in February by *Brussels Sprouts*, a play by John Palmer's friend from Ottawa, Larry Kardish. A nostalgia play about two young men travelling in Europe in the 1960s, whose friendship is threatened when they share a hotel room with a pretty girl, *Brussels Sprouts* was greeted with enthusiastic notices and sell-out houses. Kareda attributed the play's effectiveness to its naturalism,[33] a style which the Factory was to reject in subsequent years, and which was to become Kareda's most prominent critical theme. With the Factory labouring under a financial crisis a year later, *Brussels Sprouts* was revived for profitable runs at the National Arts Centre in Ottawa and the Central Library Theatre in Toronto. In April came *Sacktown Rag* by George F. Walker, who was by then the Factory's dramaturge and resident playwright. *Sacktown Rag* is more important now than it was then, as it shows Walker weaning himself from absurdist models and indulging in a sprawling theatricality which may be found in many of his subsequent plays. Although critics did not appreciate Walker's new cartoon style of comedy, Kareda's review provides a vivid glimpse of the kind of eccentric behaviour commonplace in Toronto's new theatres at the time:

Factory Theatre Lab openings often tend to be exciting for extra-dramatic reasons ... last night, there was the girl who sat at the edge of the stage and during the first act worked out her Tarot cards to the accompaniment of her own thundering cough. It was only when she was removed at the intermission that it became clear that she wasn't part of the play, thus disappointing a number of people who had already worked out her symbolic role.[34]

The Factory's euphoric success continued in May with its most popular production to date, Louis Del Grande's *Maybe We Could Get Some Bach*. *Bach* was a nostalgic comedy about two youngsters trying to break into show business in New York, set in the late 1950s when, as a program note said, 'there was nowhere to go but up, and everybody was sure of getting there.' Eric Steiner, the play's director, had a happy knack for incorporating the seedy environment of the Factory into the design style of his productions. For *Bach* he installed a pretty rainbow-painted proscenium arch hung with red velvet curtains and a garish, glowing juke-box which belched out recordings of Bill Haley, Ethel Merman, and Teresa Brewer. The effect, recalls Steiner, was of a demented Broadway comedy, as the insistent use of a rickety turntable and mangy sequinned curtains provoked howls of laughter from the audience. In retrospect, it seems odd that a nationalist theatre like the Factory should have scored such a triumphant success with an American comedy by an American expatriate.[35] If John Palmer was Toronto theatre's man of the year for 1971, however, Louis Del Grande surely deserved the title in 1972, directing, writing, and acting in some of the year's most popular successes and most challenging experiments.[36] (Del Grande's mainstream instinct and offbeat comic flair were also evident in his later creation *Seeing Things*, one of Canada's most acclaimed television series.) Perhaps the most curious aspect of the Factory's string of successes is that they were predominantly nostalgia plays: as Whittaker said of *Brussels Sprouts*, 'it is a shock to see such a young theatre indulging in nostalgia so soon.'[37] But these plays touched a nerve in the Factory's baby-boom audience, who perhaps could feel their careless youth slipping away already.

The season ended on a false note, with James Nichol's rural tragedy *The Book of Solomon Spring*, directed by David Gustafson. To the Factory's credit, it had once more staged a Canadian play which had been published but never produced.[38] However, Gustafson's direction seemed to emphasize the play's shortcomings and, as Gass put it, the production was too straightforward a failure for the Factory to be satisfied with: 'If one did fail, one should fail in a very interesting and adventurous way, because of something one believed in.' While Kareda dismissed *Solomon Spring* as a television-style melodrama, Whittaker moderated his criticism out of respect for the Factory's 'splendid season ... of notable service to the Canadian Drama';[39] indeed, his review began with, in effect, an unpaid advertisement for the Factory's membership drive for the next season. Once again the Factory Lab could look back on a year crammed with activity: eight major productions, about twenty workshop productions, and several one-act plays. That summer, Gass won a Canada Council grant to study in England for two months, which (typically) he managed to live on for more than a year. The company was left in the hands of an established management team in his absence: Zimmerman as business manager, Steiner as associate artistic director, Bettis now dramaturge, and Walker, the resident playwright, already working on a new script.

The Factory's 1972–73 season, its third, began with Victoria writer Lawrence Russell's *Foul Play*, a set of five surrealistic playlets linked, as Kareda said, by 'brief, unrelated monologues of almost unrelieved nastiness.'[40] This was September 1972, a watershed for Toronto's alternative theatres, the month that Passe Muraille's *The Farm Show* came to the city, the month that Tarragon's *Leaving Home* was remounted for a Montreal transfer, and the month that Kareda saluted the new small theatres with his important article 'Alternative theatre offers hope for the future.' Thus, even though Kareda found both the script and Timothy Bond's production of *Foul Play* undistinguished, his outlook remained buoyant: 'When you can really feel a measure of improvement even in failed evenings, it is an affirmation that Toronto's theatrical life remains in the ascendant.' For the Factory, *Foul Play* represented a decisive break with the realistic successes of its previous season. In effect, it also inaugurated the stylistic rivalry between the Factory and Tarragon Theatre, which had found its audience and its realistic production style with *Leaving Home*.

In October 1972 the Factory presented a revival of *Esker Mike and His Wife, Agiluk*, this time directed by Eric Steiner. While Kareda praised the 'strong, original' script and Steiner's 'stunning' production, Whittaker found that the revival lacked the drive of the first production despite some improved production values.[41] Another interesting contrast in their two reviews was that Kareda commended the Factory Lab for remounting *Esker Mike* in the absence of any larger theatre's interest in it, while Whittaker worried about the implications this revival might carry for the company's dedication to new work. 'Does it mean that the mainstream of new Canadian drama has dried up,' he asked, 'when the Factory Lab returns to a script it first explored 16 months ago?' As if to answer the question, Gass next embarked on the maddest of his mad projects, the *Works* festival, the first of a series of catastrophes which brought the Factory Lab to the brink of collapse in the following year.

The *Works* festival, which opened in early December, was a program of thirteen short plays in two evenings, with the two bills alternating during the run. In it, Gass attempted to disturb the pattern of production into which the Factory was settling, and to establish an ongoing festival of new plays as (one feels) a dramaturgical heir to the already legendary Festival of Underground Theatre. The 'works' themselves were by twelve playwrights, including Hrant Alianak and Larry Fineberg, staged by twelve directors, including Gass, Steiner, Palmer, Bettis, Bond, Gustafson, Alianak, and Herbert Whittaker. In his program notes, Gass described *Works* as a deliberate departure from the trend toward 'larger, more cinemascopic productions' in what was once Toronto's underground theatre scene:

WORKS, to me, is the most ideal kind of Factory production. It is a project embedded with chaos and confusion and is really too large for our resources. But it is ideal in that it is totally eclectic and that around one event so many actors, directors, playwrights and technicians with so many diverse viewpoints can work together. I would like to think that this eclectic ideal applies to the Factory as a whole, and that it can be expanded for larger projects in the future.

Some critics, however, were not impressed with these good intentions. Urjo Kareda, for instance, suggested that thirteen of the world's greatest short plays could not survive this kind of project, let alone the 'numbing abominations' presented here. He also questioned whether the event, exceeding four hours each evening, truly served the plays and playwrights. 'What one finally responds to is not to individual plays,' he wrote, 'but to the marathon process of watching them.' What Gass found so exciting, Kareda found tedious, self-indulgent, even demeaning:

What he [Gass] has forgotten, it seems, is that for an audience the project is an absolute killer – particularly for an audience which is required to spend the whole endless evening on the ground, and not even in one place, but to scamper, as the acting areas shift, from corner to corner, like lemmings in search of their cliff.[42]

Kareda's attitudes here toward serving the playwright and the audience are obviously congruent with those which led Bill Glassco to leave the Factory. While it would be unfair to describe Kareda as biased toward any particular company, it is true that his criticism showed much more sympathy with the aims and achievements of Tarragon Theatre than it did with those of the Factory. Indeed, Tarragon's often immaculate productions and Kareda's often brilliant criticism were theatrical forces which fed on each other over the ensuing three years.

The immediate effect of the *Works* festival was to trigger a dispute with the Canadian Actors Equity Association which nearly closed the Factory. Equity regulations, devised for American stock and Canadian regional theatres, were often inappropriate to the very different conditions in the new small theatres in Toronto. Even by alternative theatre standards, moreover, *Works* was a bizarre undertaking: for example, actors for

Steiner's production of *A Day with Peggy*, a sentimental schoolgirl comedy from the 1920s, were not required to attend rehearsals, to learn their lines, or even to turn up for performances if they didn't want to. Conditions like these, obviously, were not accounted for in the Equity rulebook. Gass had tried to negotiate contractual concessions from Equity, but could obtain none beyond a 'studio' classification for which the Equity minimum was sixty-five dollars per week. Instead, the Factory offered each of the thirty-five actors involved fifty dollars for the entire project, signing *pro forma* contracts with Equity members which both sides agreed would not be honoured. Generally, Equity was aware that such violations were commonplace, but, as Gass said, played a charade of 'let's pretend that you don't know what you know we know.'[43] Finally, perhaps inevitably, a complaint was lodged with Equity from a source which could not be ignored or mollified.[44] Equity demanded that the Factory honour its contracts, which, even if only the twelve Equity actors were paid the required difference, would cost the company more than $2500 in back wages. When Gass refused, choosing instead to take a moral stand on the issue, Equity forced its members to quit *Works*, placed the Factory on its list of managements in default, and removed its authorizing certificate from the Factory's lobby. Gass responded with a long letter to Equity objecting to the association's hypocrisy in now enforcing rules it had formerly let pass, and in destroying a co-operative forward-looking effort with its inflexibility. He also demanded that, if Equity genuinely wished to serve its members, it find new ways of accommodating the new smaller theatres, and join with them in tackling the major problems facing Canadian theatre. Finally, from his nationalist trench, Gass attacked Equity for catering to 'a theatre industry that is predicated upon American and British tastes,' and for stifling the future of Canadian theatre 'through irrelevant, inapplicable rules and bureaucracies.' In an accompanying press release, Gass accused Equity (rather unfairly) of being 'simply an American-based union that is not responding to the exigencies of the Canadian theatre context.'

Gass's stand on the issue made for very good rhetoric, but very bad politics. Certainly he had caught Actors Equity in blatant hypocrisies, and certainly Equity was not serving Canadian theatre to the extent that Gass was. But Gass's own inflexibility in asserting his moral rectitude suggests a sophisticated self-martyring process at work, a theme which he explored brilliantly in his later play *The Boy Bishop* (1976). With the dispute remaining unresolved, Canada Manpower could not allow itself to support an employer which violated collective agreements, and the

Factory's anticipated LIP grant of $40,000 was lost in the process. Administrative salaries at the Factory were stopped as of 20 December 1972, the day Equity's sanctions were imposed, and the Factory remained on the brink of extinction for several months.

In this period, the company survived solely on income from two productions with non-Equity casts. The first was Michael Hollingsworth's *Strawberry Fields* directed by Paul Bettis, the most successful script from the *Works* festival. Originally entitled *Fields*, the play deals with a gruesome encounter among three drug-dazed stragglers amid the morning-after debris from a rock festival. (Indeed Hollingsworth, a former rock musician, wrote the play after attending the Strawberry Fields rock festival at Mosport, Ontario, in 1970.) While Kareda admired the play's 'violent, horrifying vision,' Whittaker was clearly offended by the material: 'It is a work not so much played by its trio of actors ... as masturbated,' he wrote.[45] The following autumn, Whittaker's even greater revulsion at Hollingsworth's next play, *Clear Light* at Toronto Free Theatre, marked the end of his tolerance for sex and violence in new Canadian plays, and helped trigger the alternative theatres' first encounter with the morality squad since *Futz*.

The Factory's second non-Equity production at this time was a revival of *Brussels Sprouts* directed by Martin Kinch, which had already been booked by the National Arts Centre before the *Works* controversy began. Although observers agreed that this production was weaker than the original, the performing fee from the NAC and box-office revenues from an ensuing run at Toronto's Central Library Theatre kept the Factory Lab afloat. Meanwhile, Gass declared to his colleagues that the Factory was no longer 'the home of the Canadian playwright' (a slogan which by then appeared on the company's stationery) since it was financially unable to produce new work. At one point Gass threatened to close the company if $20,000 were not raised by a certain deadline, which was met with only ten minutes to spare. Gass was willing to shut down the Factory, but desperately wanted to produce George Walker's new play, *Bagdad Saloon*, as a final statement of his theatre. He even threatened to quit theatre entirely if money were not found to mount the play properly. Although Gass's colleagues did not especially like the script, they rallied behind it because of his insistence on its value, and because of their loyalty to Gass as leader. Actors Equity even smoothed the way for an emergency grant from the Ontario Arts Council to settle the *Works* dispute, while $5000 was obtained from Labatt's brewery and Eric Steiner's father put up the Equity bond.

'From a certain point on,' says Steiner, 'the best shows at the Factory were as much about the theatre itself as about anything else.' That point is surely Steiner's production of *Bagdad Saloon*, a play which reflected the continuing frustration of those most deeply committed to the Factory's ideals. As Gass wrote in his introduction to the published play, there were two images which remained in the forefront of the Factory's thinking: 'First the realization that the Canadian cultural field was a desert, a place of shifting fashions, lacking in roots or traditions. Second, a sense of inertia, a recognition of the impossibility of change, and the literal banging of one's head against the wall.'[46] Although peopled with Arabs and Americans, *Bagdad Saloon* was 'as Canadian as moose meat,' said Gass, in showing the indiscriminate adoption of American mythic heroes by a society which had failed to develop its own. Company members genuinely expected this to be the Factory's last production, which resulted in a funereal edge to the show. (It ended, for example, with a recording of the cynical torch song 'Is That All There Is?') Rumours of the company's death also lent a eulogistic tone to the reviews. Kareda in particular, noting the opportunities the Factory had provided for Walker, described *Bagdad Saloon* as 'an almost definitive example of how a young writer, provided with freedom and the resources of actual production, can develop and mature.'[47]

But the theatre community, not yet as fragmented as it became later in the decade, would not let the Factory die. A number of theatre organizations, mindful of the Factory's great contributions to the development of Canadian drama, issued a press release in support of the beleaguered company. The release expressed 'concern and support for the Factory Theatre Lab at this time of crisis for that important organization' and urged provincial and federal arts councils to comply with the 'modest emergency funding' requested by the Factory Lab.[48] It was signed by the Shaw Festival, Stratford Festival, Toronto Arts Foundation, Tarragon Theatre, Theatre Passe Muraille, Toronto Free Theatre, Global Village Theatre, Toronto Dance Theatre, Canadian Artists Representation, and the Toronto Drama Bench. Enough support was gathered to enable the Factory to keep running, and Gass again left for England to write and to chart new directions for himself and for his theatre. As it turned out, however, *Bagdad Saloon* was the last major production mounted in the Factory's Dupont Street home. When the Factory was founded in 1970, it had originally registered with the city as a drama school, not as a public performing space. Flammable materials were always present, fire exits were not up to code, and with the additional hazards of the auto body shop beneath it, the Factory was frankly a firetrap. In the fall of 1973, city inspectors finally barred further performances in the Factory Theatre, although it remained in use for rehearsal and administrative purposes for the year following *Bagdad Saloon.*

In the summer of 1973, the Factory was once again a centre of frantic activity. First, there was the very theatrical wedding of Ken Gass and Rosemary Donnelly: the bride was given in marriage by their dog Barney, and the homily was read by George Walker. Gass and Zimmerman were also invited to Banff that summer to give a course in festival management; and while the course did not proceed as planned, their encounter with young Alberta playwright Gary Engler led to the establishment of the short-lived Factory Theatre West in Calgary. But the main focus of activity was a planned festival of Canadian theatre in London, England, a project hatched by Gass on his last trip there. Funding was obtained from a new government source, Canada's Department of External Affairs, in the amount of $42,000. Originally, Gass had intended to involve Toronto's other three major alternative theatres – Passe Muraille, Tarragon, and Toronto Free – but these companies were not interested in the project or were otherwise engaged. The local contact for the tour was Daryl Sharp, former executive director of Playwrights Co-op, then living in London. The company was the strongest the Factory had ever assembled, including Factory regulars such as Dean Hawes and Patricia Carroll Brown, top actors from other alternative theatres such as David Fox and Brenda Donohue, even a mainstream actor in Joy Coghill, late of the Vancouver Playhouse and the National Theatre School. Mainstage performances were scheduled for the Bush Theatre, a well-established London fringe theatre above a pub, with Steiner's productions of *Bagdad Saloon* and *Esker Mike and His Wife, Agiluk* to be performed in repertory for three weeks. A fringe festival, much of which was put together after the company's arrival in England, was scheduled for several other venues. Fringe activities included lunchtime one-act plays, screenings of some Canadian films, and concerts of electronic music by John Mills-Cockell, a Toronto musician then based in London.

The London tour was a coup in one sense: since it was funded by External Affairs, the Factory could claim to be the official representative of Canadian theatre in Europe. However, as with the *Works* festival, this public victory was won at a debilitating cost. The tour was planned in a great rush and, like most of the Factory's major undertakings, became an organizational shambles. The tone was set on the company's arrival at the Bush Theatre. After struggling through traffic jams and police cordons caused by a bomb scare at adjacent BBC studios, the Canadians climbed the stairs to find a theatre much smaller and more barren than they had expected. It did not even have a dressing-room. There, they found a lone technician passed out on the floor, whose dog was relieving himself on the company's groundcloth. Some scenery and costumes went missing in transit; and because the blueprints of the Bush Theatre had been misread, the sets literally would not fit in the room. There was no effective advance publicity, little press coverage, and small audiences. In addition, the local theatre community greatly resented the seemingly extravagant salaries the Canadians were earning, from government coffers, to parachute their plays into the London fringe. Publicly then, in terms of the Factory's stature back home, the London festival was a great success; privately, however, it was yet another disaster in a series of disasters, as Steiner recalls: 'It wasn't that we were badly received, it's that we weren't received at all ... There are other people who will say it was all worth doing, but I think it exhausted the company. It was dispiriting. These were productions that everyone [in the company] believed in, and there was just no interest.'

After the London tour, Gass took several months off in Europe, while Zimmerman coped with the city building inspectors at Dupont Street. The Factory resumed production in January 1974 in rented premises in the Bathurst Street United Church complex, which later housed the Studio Lab and NDWT. Its productions there were *Ms. America* by Leon Rooke, directed by Tim Bond; *Spaces,* written and directed by Dennis Hayes; and a George Walker double-bill, *The Prince of Naples* and *Demerit,* directed by Gass on his return. In May 1974, exactly four years after its founding, the Factory moved to new quarters, another converted warehouse at 207 Adelaide Street East which had previously housed the Second City comedy group. The Factory's first production there was Walker's jungle-movie parody *Beyond Mozambique,* one of his best plays but one which was not well received at the time.

There was a mood of discouragement throughout the company, and its driving forces were drifting away. Bettis had left in a dispute over *Ms. America,* and Steiner's reluctance to work in the chaotic conditions of the Factory was growing, along with his popularity with other companies as a free-lance director. Gass was disappointed that there was so little public interest in the Factory's productions after the London tour, particularly in his own work as a director. Even *Beyond Mozambique* proved divisive, despite Steiner's thoughtful and polished production and the presence of two of Canada's foremost mainstream actors (Donald Davis and Frances Hyland) in the leading roles. While reviews generally admired the acting and the strong black-and-white visual style of this production, the script was heavily criticized. Retrospective opinion, however, is that the virtues of the play were somehow obscured by Steiner's strong production concept, an opinion reinforced by Walker's happier mounting of the play four years later. Walker himself was so discouraged that he quit theatre for a time, travelling and working on a novel. The public's lack of interest in the Factory apparently reflected a diminished inclination to forgive organizational and artistic shortcomings for the sake of experiment and vitality. Such forgiveness, it seems, had been granted in expectation of improvements in those areas, not as a permanent dispensation. Even the Factory's long-time admirer Brian Boru, the articulate critic for *That's Showbusiness*, expressed his impatience at the Factory's potential so long unfulfilled:

The results of the Factory's spreading itself so thin artistically were apparent in the Walker double bill. After four years of production, the Factory's presentational style is still badly underdeveloped. The staging of the Walker plays was only marginally in advance of a play-reading-with-movement ...

The Factory is showing signs of attrition throughout. In an interview in the Canadian Theatre Review, Ken Gass was recently quoted as saying that 'running a theatre is an exhausting, dreary occupation.' The time has come for the Factory to review its product line; then re-tool, retrench, and revive its faith in the Canadian stage.[49]

But there were to be fewer reckless projects, and little of the compelling activity which had swirled about the Factory for so long.

Plagued with this gloom, the Factory's fifth season was, in Gass's terms, 'perhaps our least memorable.' It opened in October 1974 with *Sudden Death Overtime* by the Factory West's Gary Engler, a play about a family fixation on ice hockey. It was chosen largely because Zimmerman felt it had commercial potential. However, all critics agreed that the play was a bad one, and it fared no better in its production at Theatre Calgary later that season. Late in November came *Hurray for Johnny Canuck*, written and directed by Ken Gass, with cartoon-like designs by Eric Steiner. On one level, the play was a serious attempt to examine Canadian mythmaking at a time in history when American influence was unusually slight: during World War II, imported comic books had been banned as non-essential items, and the resulting Canadian comics which filled this void were the source for Gass's play. The parallel between the Canadian comic-book heroes, which sprang up when American ones were arbitrarily excluded, and the growth of Canadian drama, which had largely occurred when foreign plays were arbitrarily excluded, was an intriguing one. The play, unfortunately, did not explore this parallel in any depth, and ultimately Gass's script had very little to say. As Kareda put it, 'As a children's play, it has a lot to recommend it ... as anything beyond a kiddie romp, it is bosh.'[50] However, *Johnny Canuck* has proved an enduringly popular script for young audiences and young performers, and has been produced many times across the country.

The 1974–75 season finished without further noteworthy theatrical highlights. In April 1975, however, the Factory presented another *Works* festival, which is of historical interest at least. More than two years after its prototype had nearly closed the Factory, the second *Works* demonstrated the company's loss of spirit in the interim. This time, there were only six one-act plays on three programs, with each program running for a week. Two of the plays had previously been performed at Vancouver's New Play Centre, two had recently been workshopped at the Factory, and the other two were not new plays.[51] On the positive side, the *Works* festival was re-established as a Factory tradition which has continued for many years. As an event in itself, however, *Works II* was only a pale imitation of the first *Works*. In view of the Factory's record, it is sad to read of Gass promoting this as a 'more considered venture,' and of Kareda (in his last months at the *Toronto Star*) trying to whip up some enthusiasm for such a relatively tame project:

In what's some of the best news to come out of the alternate theatres lately, the Factory Theatre Lab seems to be getting some pep back.

Things have seemed somewhat somnolent since they moved into their new home ... but now they've come up with a program – called Works II, featuring at least six new plays within three weeks – as frenzied, energetic and adventurous as the Factory of old.[52]

This was a very bleak period for Toronto's alternative theatres.

The Factory after 1975

The Factory Theatre Lab was never the same cultural force after the *Works* festival of 1972. Before this point, Gass's Factory was the dramaturgical conscience of Canada's nationalist theatre, championing the Canadian playwright as a neglected stepchild come of age and demanding its due. After this point, Gass's ambivalence toward mainstream measures of success prevented the Factory from broadening its audience base as the other major alternative theatres did. The early success of these companies, including the Factory, meant that continued popular success was expected of them, both by their public and by the theatres themselves. In Gass's opinion, this expectation (which he labelled 'the hit syndrome') damaged 'the most vital part of the alternate theatres, their unconventional programming and their restless search for something indigenous and unique.'[53] Because of its sincere inability to reconcile its iconoclastic beginnings with its new need for popular success, the Factory was the most obvious victim of the malaise which settled over all the alternative theatres at mid-decade. The chaotic conditions continued there as they always had; but without the fervid sense of purpose which previously fuelled the Factory, its struggles seemed pointless where they had once seemed visionary, debilitating rather than energizing. The pointlessness reached its nadir with *Winter Offensive* in November 1977, Gass's play about social amorality set in war criminal Adolf Eichmann's villa in 1944. The gratuitous sex and violence in this play shocked the theatre community. Outraged critics even suggested that the Factory's public funding ought to be cut off; and although Gass vigorously defended the artist's right to free speech, the ensuing debate clearly exhausted and discouraged him still further. He announced his resignation in April 1978, and helped effect the transition to artistic director Bob White and managing director Dian English in the 1978–79 season. During the next decade, under their leadership, the Factory slowly caught up with the other major alternative theatres in capturing a share of the mainstream audience, particularly with new plays from George F. Walker.

For Gass himself, however, there was one last artistic triumph before the Factory Lab moved on under other leaders: his production of *The Boy Bishop* in April 1976. Set in New France, Gass's play depicts a corrupt regime which, to distract an increasingly restive populace, inaugurates a 'Boy Bishop' ceremony, a society-wide inversion of roles as practised in medieval Europe. But in Gass' play, the boy selected is an insightful misfit who turns the burlesque of a revolution into a genuine one, albeit bizarre. This large-scale production, clearly beyond the resources of the Factory, loomed as another of Gass's foolhardy projects. Steiner adamantly refused to direct it, and Zimmerman left the Factory (to work full-time at his Great North Agency) rather than stand in Gass's way. In many respects, writing the play was a personal catharsis for Gass: as he pointed out, *The Boy Bishop* really has nothing to do with New France, but a great deal to do with the reckless pursuit of ideals which was typical of his whole career.[54] As the opening date approached, rumours circulated that the play was an exposé of the Toronto theatre scene. While this was not literally true, the theatre community flocked to see the play, and was indeed touched by it. Paradoxically, despite the personal nature of the allegory, the achievement of *The Boy Bishop* transcended the aroma of self-indulgence which clung to some of Gass's ostensibly selfless crusades, and finally gave him the directorial success which had been so elusive. Gass himself was easily identifiable with the idealistic Boy who said, 'This is *my* New Order. I made it, and so far it's served everyone but me.'[55] Toronto's theatre community seemed gratified that Gass had finally created an artistic opportunity which served himself as well.

More than a year later, the uproar over the long-awaited *Winter Offensive* carried out the self-immolation of which Gass had written in *The Boy Bishop*. The exhaustion and discouragement which led Gass to leave the Factory, however, were not the product of this single debacle, but may be found in his writings for several years previously. In a newspaper entitled *Theatre Notebook*, published by the Factory Lab in October 1975, Gass reflected on having fulfilled his five-year commitment to his theatre, and on his apprehension at 'the possibility of losing another five years of my life' at this task. 'For me running the Factory has been one of the most loathsome, irritating, mind-destroying jobs imaginable,' he wrote.[56] He explained that the essence of his theatre had always been misunderstood, since there had always been a discrepancy between the accomplishments most recognized by its public and those most prized by its artists. He rejected the demands of the 'hit syndrome' and wrote of his theatre with a nostalgia that prefigured his own departure:

The only thing I have insisted upon at the Factory is that it remain eclectic and not settle into formula programming. While we are now reasonably stable economically, I am concerned that we continue to challenge ourselves in every way. If that leads to more chaos, the risk must be taken; without continuous change, we die. If we find ourselves becoming comfortable, we must take the responsible move and self-destruct. I believe the work at the Factory has been genuinely important, but we certainly don't need to leave any monuments behind us.

It is clear to me that the miracles of the future will happen much less quickly than the miracles of 1970 to 1973. I think the general and professional public must see beyond the pleasant surface of show-to-show production and join us in a long-term quest for something beyond our reach. For without some visionary impossibility to lead one beyond the day to day chaos, the artistic directorship of the Factory certainly has no allure.

4

Theatre Passe Muraille after 1970

Certainly Passe Muraille has brought us to new understandings of what drama can mean. We all owe Paul Thompson a great deal more than we can ever acknowledge.[1]

Urjo Kareda, January 1974

In the early 1970s, Theatre Passe Muraille moved toward a nationalist expression and mainstream success while somehow managing to remain faithful to its radical roots. The navigator of this delicate artistic course was Paul Thompson, who became sole head of Passe Muraille after Martin Kinch and John Palmer left to help create Toronto Free Theatre early in 1972. Up to this point, as technical director, managing director, and de facto comptroller, Thompson had been responsible for the financial survival of the company; after this point, he assumed sole responsibility for its artistic policies as well. Between the Festival of Underground Theatre in 1970 and *The Farm Show* in 1972, the repertory and performing style of Theatre Passe Muraille varied wildly. In this transitional period, the company survived due to the artistic contributions of many diverse talents, while Thompson himself was developing the play-creation methods which were to become Passe Muraille's dominant style and his own distinctive trademark. After 1972, Passe Muraille became an unequivocally nationalist company, its performing style crystallized by that of *The Farm Show*.

One of Thompson's most consistent goals was to attract audiences who were not habitual theatre-goers. While all alternative theatres professed to serve the theatrically disenfranchised, experimental theatre in practice had a very narrow appeal. 'I'd like to make theatre as popular as bowling,' said Jim Garrard;[2] yet he and other young directors did nothing to seek out the bowling public, whose idea of theatre was still the touring shows at the O'Keefe Centre or the Royal Alex. While Thompson seemed less radical than his contemporaries, his pragmatism went much further: it even challenged how plays were made, and for whom. In seeking to woo audiences unaccustomed to theatre, Thompson gravitated toward new content and a new form.

This form, an actor-centred co-operative approach to playwriting, became known as the collective creation. Thompson did not invent the collective; indeed, it is easy to cite Peter Cheeseman's documentary methods and George Luscombe's vigorous stage imagery as influences, or to credit earlier collectives created by Kinch and Palmer. However, Thompson's collectives had two characteristics which made them unmistakably different. First, they took ordinary (even banal) Canadians as their central figures. Then, from *The Farm Show* onward, they were initially performed for their real-life models (or present-day equivalents). At their most compelling, the collectives' resulting affinity with their second-person audience produced an electric atmosphere which deeply affected the performers as well. For example, actor Bob Bainborough recalls the remarkable reception given to *Paper Wheat*, an offspring of Thompson's collectives, in its first performance in rural Saskatchewan:

The community hall of Sintaluta was packed. There must have been 350 people crowded into a hall designed for 150 or so. They sat through three hours of scenes and went crazy at the end. I have never experienced a moment like that curtain call. The hall was cheering and yelling and clapping and standing – all hell had broken loose. It was the most gratifying and exciting moment I have ever experienced. It was indescribable.[3]

Among Canada's acting fraternity, the hysterical circumstances surrounding most of these collectives are legendary. To act in a Thompson collective could happen to anyone once. To return to such a difficult, frustrating form again and again, however, required a tremendous degree of commitment from Thompson's actors, commitment no doubt made possible only by the kind of unique impact which Bainborough describes. Playwright John Gray, who cut his theatrical teeth on a number of Passe Muraille collectives in the mid-1970s, makes these observations about the actors' frustrations working in Thompson's shows:

Rehearsals tended to go on for months, and took place in shabby, often unheated buildings. I remember demoralized, exhausted, terrified actors in their winter coats improvising scene after scene, speech after speech, frantically groping for a story, a theme, any handhold at all, while Thompson performed the role of cheerleader, group psychologist and ideologist, firmly believing in the creative potential of anarchy, resolutely refusing to come to conclusions until the last possible moment. Months of waltzing on the edge of the abyss can unhinge anyone, and at times it was sheer bedlam. Finally the show was thrown together in a blind panic a few days before opening. On opening night there were scene lists taped to the back of scenery and, even as the house lights dimmed, pairs of perspiring actors could be seen gathering in corners, frantically working on bits of dialogue that they would be performing before a paying audience in a matter of moments.

I don't think there was a single actor who didn't finish a production swearing never, never to work with Thompson again, but they always did. As soon as they went on to other things, actors discovered just how uncreative and suffocating the Canadian theatrical scene can be. Compared not to God, but to the competition, Thompson became a shining knight of vision and integrity, and in fact his excruciating process developed an exceptionally creative generation ...[4]

As well as through their content, Thompson's collectives reached out to new audiences through their nonlinear structure and their presentational style. As Thompson put it, describing *The Farm Show*, 'There is no "story" or "plot" as such. The form of the play is more like a Canadian Sunday School or Christmas Concert where one person does a recitation, another sings a song, a third acts out a skit, etc.'[5] Non-theatre-going Canadians seemed more comfortable with this structure, and with a more direct form of address than theatre's conventional fourth wall. John Gray consciously chose this style for his two-man play *Billy Bishop Goes to War*, which he and Eric Peterson developed using collective techniques they had learned at Passe Muraille. As Gray wrote,

One choice we made: *Billy Bishop* would take its narrative form from a phenomenon I noticed while playing the barn circuit of Southwestern Ontario. Playing on stages where you had to kick the cowpies aside while crossing the boards, I noticed that Canadians don't much like listening in on other people's conversations. They think it's impolite. This plays havoc with the basic convention of theatre itself, so what do you do? Well, you drop the fourth wall and you simply talk to the audience. They tend to relax a bit because they are in an arena whose aesthetics they understand: the arena of the storyteller.[6]

Thompson believed that Canadians habitually failed to recognize their own accomplishments. His collectives celebrated Canadian heroes, which he uncovered either in ordinary people around him or in neglected incidents from history. His nationalism, as fervent as the Factory's, was aimed at the Canadian audience rather than the Canadian playwright. Through their confluence of audience, subject matter, structure, and style, the best of his collectives retained their magic even when removed from the original second-person audience. Through them, as *Paper Wheat* director Guy Sprung put it, Canadian audiences 'desperate for the cross-fertilization of ideas and experiences' were able to affirm their own national identity in the activities and attitudes of Canadians in other regions.[7] While the Factory Theatre Lab became the home of the Canadian playwright, Theatre Passe Muraille's collectives became a second focus of the alternative theatre's nationalist stage, the home of a new dramaturgical and performance style. In the five years following *The Farm Show,* Passe Muraille was probably the most influential company in Canada. As its style spread across the country, actors creating their own plays from local materials became a common feature of Canadian theatre.

FUT to *The Farm Show,* 1970–72

Paul Thompson (b. 1940) was born in Prince Edward Island and raised in rural western Ontario, where his father was a veterinarian. While studying French at the University of Western Ontario, Thompson competed in intercollegiate wrestling and began taking part in college musicals as a respite from his lonely training regimen. Soon he gave up competition to devote more time to productions. After graduating in 1963, Thompson won a scholarship from the French government to study at the Sorbonne in Paris; there he attended up to twenty plays per month to better attune his ear to spoken French. While he found production standards in Paris were uneven, he was struck by the way the French used theatre 'to explore ideas, or to defend this cause, or to get you to think in a certain way or react in a certain way.'[8] In the spring of 1964, the celebrated populist director Roger Planchon brought his company from Lyons to Paris to present a season of four plays. Enthralled, Thompson inquired about working for Planchon and was told he would be welcome as a 'stagiaire,' an unpaid apprentice director permitted to watch rehearsals. After a year in Canada completing what he calls 'the fastest MA in history' at the University of Toronto,

Thompson joined Planchon's company in Lyons in 1965, supporting himself by playing walk-on roles and by giving private lessons in English. His summers were spent back in London, Ontario, with Keith Turnbull's summer theatre. For Turnbull's landmark 1966 season, Thompson directed the French medieval play *The Farce of Poor John* (performed on a pageant wagon), co-directed a play with Martin Kinch, and served as technical director for the whole operation. On the advice of some Canadian actors he met in Europe, Thompson also applied for Canada Council support for his second year with Planchon. This support freed him from tutoring and allowed him to travel to see theatre in Germany, Czechoslovakia, and Italy. Thompson concluded his career in France at the 1967 Avignon Festival, appearing there in Planchon's production of *Tartuffe*. At that time he had opportunities to stay in France, teaching and acting, but he wanted to return to Canada. 'If you're going to do something, you have to do it where you come from,' he reasoned. 'I am not a Frenchman, no matter how much I enjoyed the meals and talking politics passionately.'[9] So he came back to Ontario, hoping to apply the techniques and attitudes he had learned in European theatre to create a new kind of theatre in Canada.

Through Tom Hendry at the Canadian Theatre Centre, Thompson was engaged to direct a community theatre group in Sault Ste Marie in the fall of 1967. However, he found that his middle-class charges were not particularly interested in making plays about working-class heroes. In the spring, on the strength of his work with Planchon, he was hired as an assistant director at Stratford, where he worked on Jean Gascon's production of *Tartuffe*, among others. In the Festival's workshop program, Thompson found himself working with new writers and a nucleus of enthusiastic, experienced actors eager to stretch themselves artistically. He directed an adaptation of Michael Ondaatje's *The Man with Seven Toes*, and another of Molière's *Don Juan*. There he also met actress Anne Anglin, whom he married in 1970, and who was to become one of the most admired actors at Theatre Passe Muraille.

During the winter of 1968–69, Thompson worked with 'Instant Theatre' in Montreal, a precursor to the regional Centaur Theatre, which had begun in 1965 as a lunchtime theatre in the basement of Place Ville Marie. With Instant Theatre he directed Beckett's *Endgame*, Elaine May's *Not Enough Rope*, and Paul Foster's *The Recluse*. He also created a mixed-media play with a Czech actress who had fled from the 1968 invasion of her homeland.[10] Returning to Stratford for the summer of 1969, Thompson was given much more responsibility as an assistant director, particularly in rehearsals for a remount of *Tartuffe*. At the same time he became increasingly certain that the Festival was not the kind of theatre he wanted to do. In retrospect, Thompson also feels that working at the Festival prevented him from progressing toward what became the backbone of his work, making plays based on his own and his audience's heritage. 'When I was in Stratford,' he said, 'it was like I had to deny the fact that I came from 30 miles away. All the time I was there I visited my roots only once, and it was like going to the ends of the world, longer than the journey from Lyons to Toronto.'[11] Disaffected with the Festival, Thompson and Anglin became two of Stratford's biggest boosters of the Canadian Place Theatre, the storefront operation run by his university friend Martin Kinch.

Thompson returned to Montreal in the fall of 1969 but, at Kinch's invitation, visited Passe Muraille to see both Palmer's remounted *Memories for My Brother, Part I* and the Kinch/Garrard production of *Tom Paine*. Kinch was in the process of taking over as the company's artistic director; and knowing Thompson's technical work from his summer seasons in London, Kinch asked him to join Passe Muraille in that capacity. Thompson accepted, because he saw great potential for both the company and its Trinity Square home. He started as stage manager on Kinch's cancelled *Richard III* and the *Sweet Eros* double-bill. That season, with Garrard distracted, with Kinch directing with several groups, and with Palmer away writing in Ottawa, Thompson actually staged more productions than anyone else did at Passe Muraille. His productions included a lunchtime improvised play called *Charlie in So Many Ways* in March 1970, the poorly attended *Notes from Quebec* in May, and *Ubu Raw* for the Festival of Underground Theatre in August. By this time Thompson had also learned enough about bookkeeping from Shain Jaffe to take over the business end of the company. With Kinch's departure for Stratford that summer, Thompson was left in charge of Theatre Passe Muraille, taking the title of Managing Director, as he puts it, 'as a trust for a number of talents who had the right to work out of there.' He retained both the title and the trust long after the other talents had gone on to other things.

The 1970–71 season was the first of two extremely successful ones under Passe Muraille's informal group leadership. One key to this success was the great number of opportunities available to the company's diverse talents. The season opened in October 1970 with Wedekind's *Spring's Awakening*, directed by Martin Kinch, one of the few non-Canadian plays produced at Passe Muraille after Thompson joined the company. Nathan Cohen described Kinch's production as 'a sturdy interpretation, rich in substance and insight,'[12] but these compliments did not appear in print until after its short and poorly attended run was over. At the same time, the playlets *Six of a Kind* were given a short late-night run. These were written and directed by Louis Del Grande, then working under the stage name Louis Thompson, a former spear-carrier at Stratford and a new addition to Passe Muraille's artistic collective. *Six of a Kind* marked the professional debut of young Brenda Donohue, one of the first star performers of the alternative theatres, and middle-aged Doris Petrie, who gained prominence two years later in the landmark Canadian film *Wedding in White*. In November 1970, Del Grande staged *I Had It but It's All Gone Now* by Richard DeCanio, a picaresque satire on American society featuring Saul Rubinek and Bembo Davies. Over the Christmas season, Anne Anglin and Clare Coulter produced their own puppet show for children, *Noah*, after which Paul Thompson staged another work for family audiences, his own adaptation of Saint-Exupéry's *The Little Prince*. Evening performances resumed in January 1971 with *Out to Breakfast*, an experimental collective creation in which John Palmer first chose four of his favourite actors (Anglin, Del Grande, Rubinek, and Davies), and then asked them to select their own characters. The resulting play contained a preacher, a model, a Maoist milkman, and Adolf Hitler. While critical reaction to *Out to Breakfast* was extremely poor, the production was greatly admired by some people, notably Thompson himself, who kept it running despite small audiences.

At this point, early in 1971, the company had not produced a box-office success since the *Sweet Eros* double-bill a year earlier. Once again, the promise of Theatre Passe Muraille as a fusion of experiment and entertainment was waning, and it appeared the company might succumb to financial pressures. But once again, Martin Kinch produced an offbeat popular hit, which was soon followed by equally popular productions by Thompson and Palmer. The first was *Vampyr*, created by Kinch, Shain Jaffe, and musician Phil Schreibman. Together they devised a scenario from which the actors improvised the text, at one point rehearsing continuously for twenty-four hours. Influenced by Britain's Hammer films, Kinch sought to explore themes which frightened him personally, in particular the soul-draining capacity of the central character (played by Booth Savage). Like this character, sexuality in *Vampyr* was both attractive and terrifying, as were other legacies of 1960s liberalism which the play evoked: the proliferation of soft-core pornography, the romanticizing of terrorism, and the discomfiting mixture of hedonism and mysticism that could be found at Rochdale College (where Kinch was living). Its campy gothic mood heightened by Schreibman's music and Paul Williams' powerful setting, *Vampyr* became the first of Kinch's obsessive productions which earned him the nickname 'Mr. Sex-and-Violence.' Reviews were excellent, and audience line-ups were common through its six-week run.

Passe Muraille's next production, Paul Thompson's collective creation *Doukhobors*, was in effect the obverse of *Vampyr*. Distressed by the negative tone of Kinch's sexual imagery, Thompson wanted to use the current vogue for onstage nudity in a more positive way. The result was, as he said, 'the first non-sexual nude show.'[13] Unlike the company's preceding collectives, *Doukhobors* was a chronicle play that required some research – not just character analysis and background reading, but enough basic information about the topic to get the play on stage. While Thompson's later collectives were more clearly divided between the sociological and the historical, *Doukhobors* straddled that boundary uncomfortably. Indeed, it finally had much more to do with the hippie movement of the 1960s than with an immigrant sect seeking religious freedom. More importantly, Thompson himself seemed dissatisfied with the research, which he was to approach more carefully in the future. He betrayed this dissatisfaction in 1973 in his introduction to the published play:

We created an impressionistic approach to the Doukhobors. It was what we knew about them. We chose the title *Doukhobors* instead of *The Doukhobors* because we didn't feel that we knew enough to say 'This is what the Doukhobors are all about.' It became: 'Doukhobors – what we know about them as people living in Ontario.'[14]

Like *Vampyr, Doukhobors* received excellent reviews and overflow houses; and like *In His Own Write* it was toured to some Ontario universities (Brock, Trent, and Laurentian) following its run at Trinity Square. As Thompson recalls, this period at Passe Muraille was marked by an intense but productive artistic rivalry among the young directors there. 'There were popularity shoot-outs – or outshoots – where we'd each be going along in our work and then suddenly one of us would have a really popular show.'[15] When this happened, he recalls, the balance of authority would inevitably swing toward the director who was bringing in the audiences.

Passe Muraille's productions of the next season, 1971–72, completed the transition of leadership which had begun with the arrival of Kinch, Palmer, and Thompson in the fall of 1969. The season encompassed formal experiments, another popular hit, and a solidification of Thompson's approach to the content and method of collective creation. It opened in October with the collective *Free Ride*, about cross-country hitch-hiking which had become common among young Canadians in the years following Expo 67. For this production, having learned his lesson from *Doukhobors*, Thompson and actor Larry Mollin researched the topic by hitch-hiking across Canada the previous summer. *Free Ride* was followed in November with the rock musical *Charles Manson a.k.a. Jesus Christ* by Fabian Jennings and Allan Rae, brilliantly directed by John Palmer, the third tumultuous success of the 'popularity shoot-outs.' This production featured Paul Williams' three-storey scaffold set, which accommodated the audience as well as some of the action, and a mesmerizing performance by Peter Jobin in the title role. As with *Vampyr* and *Doukhobors*, audience line-ups were the rule.

In January 1972, Garrard returned from British Columbia with a new show derived from his recent theatrical experimentation. Garrard had become extremely depressed before leaving Toronto in the summer of 1970. At Simon Fraser University, he was further discouraged by what he judged an arid educational environment, particularly after the fertile grassroots democracy of Rochdale College. Garrard's devotion to the Rochdale experiment was founded on a profound love of personal freedom; yet at the point of leaving Passe Muraille, he realized that his own work in theatre had done nothing for the personal freedom of the actor. In the theatre business, the actor is the fulcrum upon which any production turns, yet the actor is usually reduced to simply doing as he is told – by the playwright, by the director, by the management, even by the stage crew. Under a messianic leader such as Garrard, the actor's personal freedom is at its weakest. When he arrived in British Columbia, Garrard recalls, although he was stuck in his messianic directing style, he no longer believed in its value, nor in the value of any of the group theatre he had created in Toronto. 'When I got to SFU,' he recalls, 'I didn't have any tools, but what I had was a blank canvas.'[16]

At SFU Garrard began working with a young writer named Frank Powley. Powley had studied a form of improvisation called 'rule play' under Paul Bettis, who had taught at SFU a few years earlier. Together, Garrard and Powley developed rule play improvisation into a performance concept which they called 'survival theatre.' Garrard disliked the quick spontaneity common to other forms of improvisational performance ('Theatresports' is a recent example) because he felt it encouraged superficiality. Survival theatre was designed to elicit more thoughtful responses. Like the concepts of theatre games and Bettis' rule play, survival theatre involved improvisation by rule. The difference was that there was only one rule: without hurting anyone physically, the actor's objective was 'to survive in theatrical terms.' Putting this phrase into practice became the sole focus of survival theatre performances. For example, Garrard recalls a thirty-six-hour performance in British Columbia which climaxed in the stunning effect of an actress cutting off her waist-length hair. While Garrard found that audiences (and particularly other actors in the audience) were often angered at these performances, he felt that survival theatre greatly enhanced the actor's personal freedom. 'If everyone succeeded brilliantly within the rules, then a lot of people would want to see it,' he says, 'and it would be fabulous freedom, freedom for the performer.'

A grant was obtained from the Educational and Cultural Exchange Program of Ontario's Department of Education to bring Garrard and Powley to Theatre Passe Muraille. There they would present their 'survival theatre' show *The Black Queen Is Going to Eat You All Up*. Powley was listed as 'playwright,' although the meaning of the term here is obscure: there was no script, and the content of the play was expected to change every performance. A few of the performers came from British Columbia with Garrard and Powley, while others were veterans of Garrard's earlier productions at Passe Muraille. In rehearsals, which were open to the public, the actors struggled with their new burden of freedom. On opening night, another group of actors, led by Frank Masi and calling themselves the Royal Canadian Mounted Theatre, even took over the stage for a time from *The Black Queen*'s designated performers. Audience members who wished to see the production again could do so without paying; and, indeed, some people returned several times. It was, to Garrard, 'a fabulous, fascinating show.' Reviews, however, were uniformly negative, from Whittaker's benign indulgence ('not everybody who likes theatre games is going to be good at them') to Kareda's articulate vitriol ('a cast almost unparalleled for their ineptitude for improvisation').[17] While the alternative theatre community was intrigued with the experiment, *The Black Queen* had no mainstream appeal and quickly vanished from the public mind. However, it has remained something of a touchstone to veterans of those early years at Passe Muraille, and was a very important production in this transitional period for the company. Garrard himself returned to British Columbia after *The Black Queen* and remained relatively inactive in theatre for several years.

Passe Muraille's last three productions of the 1971–72 season represent a completion of this transitional period, and a further preparation for Thompson's later collectives. In February came the collective creation *Bethune!*, directed by Peter Boretski, an earnest stage biography of the Canadian hero of China's communist revolution. From *Bethune!* Thompson may have learned to avoid (as Kareda called it) the 'Hollywood Reverential'[18] tone in his later portraits of Canadian heroes. In April came *Tantrums*, a set of four surrealistic playlets by newcomer Hrant Alianak, directed by Louis Del Grande. In the next few years, Alianak became the leading experimental playwright in Toronto. He was born in Egypt in 1950, immigrated to Canada in 1967, and eventually settled in Toronto, where he began acting in amateur theatre and was 'discovered' by Del Grande. Through the 1972–73 season, he staged three of his short plays (*Western, The Violinist and the Flower Girl*, and *Brandy*) for late-night audiences at Passe Muraille, as well as *Mathematics* for the ill-fated *Works* festival at the Factory Lab. His B-movie imagery and tongue-in-cheek sentimentality have made Alianak a favourite writer in the circles in which he works. However, his lack of wider popular appeal has remained a puzzling disappointment to Thompson (among others), who had hoped Alianak would fulfil Passe Muraille's need for urban avant-garde hits after Kinch and Palmer left. *Tantrums* received a glowing review from Kareda,[19] but was too intellectual or too obscure to attract a broad audience.

Completing the season in May was Carol Bolt's *Buffalo Jump*, another chronicle play developed collectively by Thompson. This play, about the 'On to Ottawa Trek' of unemployed workers in 1935, was originally produced as *Next Year Country* at the Globe Theatre, Regina, and was brought to Passe Muraille from Toronto Workshop Productions when Bolt and TWP's Luscombe could not resolve a disagreement over future rights to the revised script. Whittaker liked the production, admiring in particular the 'visual distinction' given to the play by St Catharines artist John Boyle.[20] Boyle, a friend of Thompson from his summer theatre days in London, Ontario, created pop-art sketches of objects and people important to the march on Ottawa, which were used as settings for the production. Despite *Buffalo Jump*'s good intentions, however, Kareda found the play formless, shallow, and wearying. 'The dewy sentimentality of poverty and hardship in Buffalo Jump,' he wrote, 'seems awfully easy and maybe even a little cheap.'[21] Thompson avoided this kind of sentimentality in his later collectives, using restraint rather than abandon at times of high emotion.

Buffalo Jump was less significant as a production than it was as a benchmark in Thompson's development as a director. It represented a major step forward in his awareness of visual style, which became such an asset in *The Farm Show, 1837,* and other productions. It also represented a further step toward emphasizing a central hero in his historical plays, in this case 'Red Evans,' a portmanteau name derived from two real leaders of the trek. Buffalo Jump was also the first of Thompson's collectives in which he worked with a playwright in the rehearsal process. 'I'm not anti-writers,' he said later, 'they can help as much as anyone else.'[22] But unlike the Factory Lab, Thompson's Passe Muraille would never make the writer the pivotal artist in its collaborations. Instead, Thompson insisted on the artistic primacy of the actor in the playmaking process – sometimes over the objections of the actors themselves! In *Buffalo Jump* Thompson began to rely more heavily on the improvisational skills of his actors. When the play was first brought to his attention, Thompson found the ideas in it more exciting than the script itself. So, as he said,

we reinvented the play. We had the actors improvise scenes, and Carol wrote from the improvisations while I tried to key in on what the actors were bringing in and utilize that energy. Somewhere in there I moved away from my Platonic conceptualization of theatre toward the notion of starting with just an impulse or a theme and drawing the rest of the material out of the actors and building a play from that.[23]

While this method was similar to that used in *Vampyr* and other earlier Passe Muraille collectives, in Thompson's hands it became a more actor-centred process than it was with other directors. In addition, *Buffalo Jump* began Thompson's consistent use of playwrights on his historical collective projects, a use which was expanded and refined in his second decade of directing. In his later work with actress-playwright Linda Griffiths, culminating in such plays as *Maggie and Pierre* (1979) and *Jessica* (1982; rev. 1986), the improvisations were performed by the playwright herself rehearsing under Thompson's direction.

The Black Queen and *Buffalo Jump* were watershed productions at Theatre Passe Muraille, because they marked the final division between the company's radical aesthetic beginnings under Garrard (molded into popular success by Kinch and Palmer) and the more pragmatic pursuit of new audiences which interested Thompson. Within the context of Toronto's alternative theatre scene, this break also occurred at a time when the original impetus of the New Directors Group and the FUT festival was being transmuted into the four dominant companies, each with a distinct personality. The NDG's fitful alliance of disparate personal and artistic goals had always been a marriage of convenience, with strong egos never quite submerged in common cause. During the earliest stages of these theatres, recalls John Palmer, 'you could ally yourself with anybody because the enemy was so powerful.'²⁴ By early 1972, however, the alternative theatres had gained a foothold in Toronto and were beginning to affect the way people thought about theatre in Canada. With this new stature and stability came an urge to be independent, to differentiate one's own company from others with similar attributes. The Passe Muraille logo of this time, four perpendicular arrows pointing radially outward, was intended to reflect the artistic diversity of the company; but in retrospect, it also seems to symbolize the different directions these four companies were to take. Tarragon's direction, for one, was effectively stated by Kareda in his review of *The Black Queen*: 'It may be time to put in a meek word for form and content, two dramatic values which appear to many to be hopelessly archaic and reactionary.' These values were to earn extravagant praise for *Leaving Home* a few months later, a production which exemplified the literary values of the 'Toronto movement.' Although Thompson too disliked *The Black Queen*, its concepts of freedom for the performer and of structuring improvisational rehearsals by rule rather than by narrative informed Passe Muraille's playmaking methods from *Buffalo Jump* onward. At the same time Kinch and Palmer, whose previous successes drew on both the avant-garde intellectualism of early Passe Muraille and the nationalist/iconoclast stance of Canadian Place Theatre and the Factory Lab, now moved to Toronto Free Theatre. There the alternative theatre acquired some of the mainstream values and connections of its instigator, Tom Hendry. With Garrard no longer a factor in Toronto's alternative theatre, the four directions were the Tarragon, the Factory, the Free, and Thompson's version of Passe Muraille.

While the quality of avant-garde experiment never completely left Passe Muraille, it was certainly overshadowed by the imagery of small-town Canadian heroes in Thompson's subsequent collectives. Not wishing to pursue Thompson's socio-political interests, three of Passe Muraille's veteran performers – Booth Savage, Geza Kovacs, and Phil Schreibman – founded Supernova Productions to continue the formal experiments of *The Black Queen*. Over the ensuing five years, productions such as *The Joke Show* (1974), *The Great Theatre of Oklahoma (1976)*, and *The Ballad of Jack O'Diamonds* (1975; rev. 1977 as *Jack of Diamonds*) were mounted within improvisational frameworks, to pursue Supernova's goal of breaking down the barrier between the stage actor and the stage musician. But the public's interest in formal experiment was largely spent by this time. While Supernova's work attracted the interest of other people who had started out in the early alternative theatres, its constituency was too small to have any impact on an alternative stage increasingly attuned to the exigencies of mainstream success. Meanwhile, with the departure of the other key leaders in Passe Muraille's artistic co-operative, Thompson inherited the unchallenged authority to steer the company in whatever direction he chose. At this propitious time, he chose a project which changed the image and nature of Theatre Passe Muraille, and which ultimately brought national attention to his company and to his method of making plays. This project was *The Farm Show*.

The Farm Show to Baby Blue, 1972–75

The Farm Show originated with just an idea, the idea of doing a play about the kind of Ontario farming community in which Thompson had been raised. In the spring of 1972, Thompson was commuting from Trinity Square to Brock University in St Catharines, where he was teaching theatre and organizing a festival of original plays. At the same time, British director Peter Cheeseman, who had gained an international reputation for his documentary methods in creating community-based drama, was conducting workshops as a guest of Theatre Ontario, a new provincial arts organization which grew out of Ontario's regional amateur networks. Two of Cheeseman's workshops were held at Theatre Passe Muraille in Toronto and at Brock University. These workshops no doubt enlivened the discussions which Thompson was having with fellow Brock lecturer Ted Johns, later a mainstay of Thompson's collectives, about creating a play about rural Ontario where they had both grown up. Johns had relatives in the farming community of Clinton who would be willing to lend them a vacant farmhouse and barn for the summer. There Thompson would be able to create a show about this community. Although Passe Muraille did not have the funds to underwrite such a project, Thompson decided to use his own earnings from Brock, and set about assembling his cast.

The actors he chose were not longstanding affiliates of Passe Muraille, but rather a new group of actors who were to become the nucleus of Thompson's subsequent collectives. The most experienced one was Anne Anglin, Thompson's wife, a youthful veteran of the Stratford Festival, various regional theatres, and lately Trinity Square. Another was Miles Potter, a recent arrival from the United States, who had been producing some children's theatre in Toronto and had appeared in *Buffalo Jump*. Another was Janet Amos, who had originally been cast in *Doukhobors* but had dropped out of it. Less significant to the future of Passe Muraille were Alan Jones, who had appeared in both *Doukhobors* and *Buffalo Jump*, and his girlfriend Fina MacDonell, an actress whom Thompson had met in Winnipeg while researching *Free Ride*. Finally, a vital addition to the group was David Fox, a native of northern Ontario who had been teaching high school and working in community theatre in Brantford for nine years. When Fox decided to give up teaching for professional theatre, he came to Toronto and called Theatre Passe Muraille, which he thought was still being run by his university friend Martin Kinch. Thompson remembered Fox as an excellent student actor at Western, and was quick to offer him the 'professional' opportunity of his summer project in Clinton. The actors would be paid thirty-five dollars per week plus accommodation, although Anglin and Amos were Equity members and had to complete *pro forma* guest artist contracts.

By this time, Thompson had gained confidence in his collective methods. He believed that the structure and content of the new play would be most effective if it evolved out of the cast's research and rehearsal, rather than being imposed by the director. Although he told his actors that he had no preconceived notions about what form the show was going to take, most of them believed that this was merely a directorial posture. As Miles Potter later said, incredulously, 'We assumed he was lying, but he wasn't. He really didn't know what he was going to do.'[25]

But he did know how he was going to start. By the time the actors arrived in Clinton, Thompson had already spoken to many of the farmers in the vicinity. Each day, he sent his actors out to meet and talk with specific neighbours. Each day, the actors would report back to the whole group, with initial rehearsals taking the form of improvisations on their day's findings. Unlike Cheeseman's reverence for factual reproduction, however, *The Farm Show* evolved from an artistic rather than a literal truth, mixing real characters and stories with imagined ones. As Thompson later said, 'I don't think it's documentary theatre; I think it's folk theatre because in many cases we're not interested in fact. If an emotional, exciting lie makes better theatre and gets the point of the scene across better, then I'm more interested in the lie than the fact. We're primarily interested in making exciting plays.'[26]

The actors did not take kindly to Thompson's insistence on individual research. Amos found interviewing strangers embarrassing for both parties. Potter was livid after his miserable first day of farm work, which eventually was re-enacted in a hilarious 'haying' scene. Jones so hated the physical labour, and Thompson's insistence that it be continued, that he finally announced he would leave the show after its first performance, which he did. In addition, the process of creating a play from found materials was unfamiliar to many of the cast, and difficult for all of them. Despite such problems, however, moments of theatrical magic began to pop up during rehearsals. Ray Bird, the farmer who had loaned Thompson the house and barn, recalled that the power of their playmaking was so strong that even the cast seemed slightly afraid of it as their first performance approached.[27]

The Farm Show was first performed in Bird's barn on Sunday afternoon, 13 August 1972. There were no lights, no sets, and no seating except for stacked hay bales. An audience of fifty or sixty was expected, but about two hundred turned up. The impact of the show was startling. The cast's uncanny mimicry and heartfelt insights were given and taken in a spirit of honest affection between two communities which a few weeks earlier had been completely alien to each other. The unique power of *The Farm Show* was that it was not only about a farming community, but also about strangers being brought together in a life-long way – the farmers, the actors, and the farmers with the actors. Appropriately, a nearby small-town newspaper printed a moving report of this first performance:

With songs, poems, skits, interpretive exercises, and monologues, the three actors and three actresses from Toronto bewitched their audience ... As a matter of fact, those in the audience who were from the area recognized most of their neighbours in the scenes. Howls of laughter and groans of embarrassment burst continually from the straw bleachers.

And somehow the actors managed, while laying open the characters of the community for all to see, not to offend anybody (they hope) and not to bear false witness to the personalities of any of their new-found friends.[28]

After three weeks of further rehearsal, *The Farm Show* opened at Trinity

Square with Thompson replacing Jones in the cast. It received excellent reviews, led by Kareda's unqualified praise: 'In *The Farm Show*, Thompson and his actors have helped us to know, understand and love a community of people beyond our sphere of familiarity. As artists, they can have no higher ambitions.'[29]

Theatre Passe Muraille, at this time, was in the best position of any alternative theatre to capitalize on its occasional runaway hits. Its Trinity Square home was by far the largest and most flexible of Toronto's new small theatres, and its university touring connections had been loosely established since *Sweet Eros* and *In His Own Write*. During the two preceding transitional years, Thompson had found that one or two substantial box-office successes could support his theatre for a whole year, at least under the tight-fisted financial control which he maintained. Passe Muraille did not join the rush for LIP funds at this time. Thompson felt that the program was upsetting a fragile ecology in Toronto's small theatre scene, and he suspected (rightly, in many cases) that it would create problems of bureaucracy and dependency beyond its value to a company. Instead, at first by necessity and later by choice, Thompson paid his actors a very small weekly stipend plus a percentage of box-office receipts. Equity actors would sign *pro forma* contracts, as at the Factory Lab; but without the Factory's near-fatal attraction to huge projects, Passe Muraille found negotiated illegalities easier to manage. The actors benefited from the regular work, from good wages on the hit shows, and from Thompson's habitual husbandry such as arranging for billeting of actors on tour. Popular success meant more to Passe Muraille than just a financial lifeline, however. In Thompson's view, it also legitimized his theatre's cultural identity, particularly with audiences unfamiliar with theatre or with Theatre Passe Muraille. It was not in Thompson's nature to close a show merely to move on to other projects, as Gass would: as he told the cast of *The Farm Show*, 'You'll get tired of it before the audience does.'[30] Indeed, *The Farm Show* was revived for several new tours in succeeding years, with some cast changes, finishing with a tour of England in 1979. More significantly, the pattern of *The Farm Show*, that of seeking to discover the essence of a community and then to reflect it back to that community, became the leitmotiv of Thompson's work for several years, as he sought to celebrate his Canadianism and to capture the imagination of a new public.

While Thompson had found a rural theme for his own work, he recognized that Passe Muraille needed an urban side as well. 'These things go in fashions,' he recalls. 'It was clear even then that the fashion for self-celebration in a rustic way was going to be limited.'[31] Accordingly, he attempted to provide opportunities for theatrical experimentation at Trinity Square, to compensate for the loss of Kinch and Palmer, while his own rural explorations continued. The productions which Thompson encouraged in this period spanned at least as broad a range of themes and styles as in Passe Muraille's preceding years. At Trinity Square, *The Farm Show* was followed by Louis Del Grande's production of *Dog in the Manger*, his own zany adaptation of a Lope de Vega comedy of misplaced love. Del Grande's manic sense of humour was rivalled by that of Ken Campbell, an Englishman who conceived and directed Passe Muraille's next production, *Pilk's Madhouse*. This was a comic revue ostensibly presenting the works of expatriate Canadian playwright Henry Pilk, who was in fact the product of Campbell's own eccentric imagination. Thompson's quick acceptance of Campbell, whom he had first met at the closing party of *Buffalo Jump*, reflected his eagerness to incorporate contrasting leaders into the structure of Passe Muraille. Indeed, Campbell had already acquired a reputation in England for his comic touring shows, and these connections brought an invitation for *Pilk's Madhouse* to perform at London's Royal Court Theatre in December 1972. When Campbell's show left for London, another urban-oriented show moved into Trinity Square, *The Separate Condition* by Barbara Nye, directed by the iconoclastic John Juliani of Vancouver's 'Savage God' group. *The Separate Condition* was a bizarre collection of four related monologues, with overtones of transsexuality. It received very poor reviews. Like *The Black Queen*, this was a show which Thompson would never have staged himself, but which reflected his belief that diversity was essential if Passe Muraille was to live up to its mandate.

While these last two plays were performing at Trinity Square, Thompson was preparing for his next production, *1837*, a play chronicling the popular uprising in Toronto in that year. He had been considering another play on a similar theme, *William Lyon Mackenzie* by Herschel Hardin; but he found the script unwieldy, and he was relieved when Toronto writer Rick Salutin approached him with an idea for a new collective creation. Salutin's diary of rehearsals, published as a preface to a subsequent version of *1837*, reveals the high artistic risks which accompanied Thompson's methods. Salutin describes the pall of panic and despair which settled over the production only nine days before it opened:

Awful. Just awful. I can't say how bad. There is nothing there. And they will not

work, will not give. The Family Compact is a horror; we haven't dared touch it for five days ... We are at a dead halt – no, we are careening backwards. There is no giving, no expansiveness – and no script to fall back on!
    Christ, I said to Paul, is it this way every time?
    I don't know, he sighed. I can't remember. I guess so.
    How do you stand it?
    I must forget. If I remembered I would never do it again.[32]

Their comments demonstrate how difficult the process of collective creation is, even for a show that works. With a cast that included three veterans of *The Farm Show* (Amos, Fox, and Potter), *1837* opened at Trinity Square in January 1973, and was again an enormous success. After extensive revisions the next year, to emphasize the rebellion's rural roots rather than its more famous climax in the streets of Toronto, *1837: The Farmers' Revolt* was toured and later remounted several times just as *The Farm Show* had been. As portrayed by Eric Peterson, who became another pivotal performer in Thompson's collectives, the character of Mackenzie blossomed as the charismatic hero of the piece. Subsequently, the exploration of an individual rather than a collective hero became a competing theme in Thompson's collectives.

The eventful season of 1972–73 finished without another success on this scale, but with further wide-ranging activity. In March alone there were three new productions. The first was Philip Hopcraft's *The Master* directed by Jim Garrard, who had recently returned to Toronto. Garrard had effectively given up theatre at this time and did not wish to direct the show, but he could not persuade Hopcraft that the production would be better served by a different director. Hopcraft, finally horrified at the onstage results, had his name removed from the program at the last minute, and did not write for the theatre again. At the same time, a group called Children's Pantomime Theatre, led by Miles Potter, gave daytime performances of two original scripts, *The Moon Princess* and *The Musicians of Bremen*. It was Potter's fourth holiday children's production at Passe Muraille since he arrived a year before. Also opening in March was a less ambitious Thompson collective, *Pauline*, a stage biography of Canadian Indian poet and lecturer Pauline Johnson. Carol Bolt served as playwright, as she had on *Buffalo Jump*; Anne Anglin played the title role, with Janet Amos and Factory Lab co-founder Peter Kunder playing all the others. Critics generally found the material in *Pauline* too thin for an evening's entertainment. Kareda added the intriguing observation that Passe Muraille's collective methods seemed more suitable to sketches of communities than of individuals.[33]

In April 1973, *The Farm Show* was given a triumphant remounting at Trinity Square, followed by a tour of southern Ontario. This tour was particularly important because Passe Muraille's hall had been slated for demolition to make way for the new Eaton Centre. The tour established a small-town circuit which became Passe Muraille's bread-and-butter for several years, sustaining the company with consistently large audiences and continued artistic credibility at a time when the loss of 11 Trinity Square might well have proved a mortal blow. To Thompson, this outreach to new audiences was a political act as well as an artistic or a commercial one. 'Democratization for the arts is a cliché until we feel something for the people who don't go to the theatre,' he said. 'Then we come to them. This tour is about how culture has been grabbed off by the city people with leisure.'[34] *The Farm Show* tour concentrated on small communities which were bypassed by other touring groups (Orangeville, Listowel, Wingham, and so on), playing in auction barns, old opera houses, meeting halls, and high-school gyms. The tour finished with a performance symbolic of the ambitions of Toronto's alternative theatres: on the Festival Stage in Stratford, where as Thompson drily noted, 'We're sponsored by a local drama group – the Stratford Festival.'[35] That August *The Farm Show* also played at the National Arts Centre in Ottawa, and the following spring it toured Saskatchewan. Michael Ondaatje's film documentary *The Clinton Special*, first televised in 1974, spread the fame of *The Farm Show* still further, as did the play's publication in 1976.

In the summer of 1973, between tours of *The Farm Show*, Thompson and his actors spent two months in the community of Cobalt, Ontario, creating a play called *Under the Greywacke*. Once the centre of northern Ontario's mining industry, Cobalt by then was a dying single-resource town. The 'greywacke,' a layer of conglomerate rock under which silver ore is found, symbolized to Passe Muraille the dreams of a hoped-for new strike which would save the town from its long decay. As with *The Farm Show*, the company attempted to provide a broad picture of the community through a collage of skits, songs, and personality sketches based on their own research. As with *The Farm Show*, they also attempted to become a part of this community, and succeeded to some extent: actress Jacquie Presley even finished second in a Miss Cobalt contest! Thompson obtained a disused movie house for the performances in Cobalt, which were received enthusiastically by the local populace. Despite adhering to the formula of *The Farm Show*, he insisted that this show was quite different simply because 'the people are different. *Under the Greywacke* is about drinking, tall stories and the gambling instinct. Cobalt, which has a population of 2,200 now, is a ghost town that refuses to die.'[36] *Under the Greywacke* also proved to be different from *The Farm Show* in that it had very little popular appeal beyond its original second-person audience, although the reasons for this are unclear. Perhaps the picture of a dying community living on illusions was too discouraging a premise, or perhaps *Under the Greywacke* lived too obviously in the shadow of *The Farm Show*. Certainly the location chosen for its Toronto run, the cavernous and uncomfortable Church of the Holy Trinity, did not help the performers make contact with either their material or their audience. Reviews were positive without being enthusiastic. The most significant judgment was by Thompson himself, who chose neither to rework the show nor to tour it.

After *The Farm Show*, almost all Passe Muraille's most significant productions were developed outside of Toronto. Nonetheless, the sheer volume of its local activity kept the company in the forefront of Toronto's alternative theatre scene. In the fall of 1973, the impending demolition of its Trinity Square home seems to have intensified the already frantic pace of production there. After *Under the Greywacke* came Hrant Alianak's first full-length play, *Noah's Kiosk*, a gothic send-up of movies about the American South after the Civil War. *Noah's Kiosk* received poor reviews and poor houses, and Alianak himself (who also directed) deemed it a failure.[37] Also in October, in the smaller space upstairs, Louis Del Grande staged his one-act *So Who's Goldberg* for late-night audiences. A gently ironic character study about a homosexual pianist and a man he has picked up for the evening, *Goldberg* had previously been given a workshop production at New York's Lincoln Center, and received excellent reviews in Toronto. Also scheduled was a revue entitled *Crime and Punishment*, the first Toronto appearance of a group of actors who would later call themselves Codco. This group's irreverent comedy was to give Passe Muraille some of its most popular shows in Toronto at mid-decade, while Thompson continued to cultivate audiences elsewhere with his 'rustic self-celebration.'

While these performances were taking place at Trinity Square, Thompson was preparing a new collective creation, *Them Donnellys*, with writer Frank McEnaney. Intended to build on the small-town audience gained with *The Farm Show*, *Them Donnellys* opened in the soon-to-be-restored Victoria Playhouse in Petrolia, Ontario, in November 1973. It then toured along the network established the previous spring for *The Farm Show* tour, ending with three performances at Stratford's Festival Theatre. With an explosion of interest in Canadian themes, 1973–74 was the year of the Donnellys in Ontario theatre: James Reaney's *Sticks and Stones* opened at Tarragon Theatre at the same time as *Them Donnellys* in Petrolia, Peter Colley's play *The Donnellys* was a huge success at Theatre London later that season, and yet another Donnelly play was created at Trent University in Peterborough. By this time, Tarragon had overtaken the Factory Lab as the leading producer of new Canadian scripts, while Passe Muraille had become widely admired for the energy of its performance style and the immediacy of its themes. It was inevitable (but probably irrelevant, as Kareda said), with *Them Donnellys* and *Sticks and Stones* opening almost simultaneously, that these two treatments of the Donnelly legend should invite comparisons. Kareda praised them both, although his enthusiasm for Reaney's seemed more unbridled. Brian Boru, in *That's Showbusiness*, much preferred the Passe Muraille version, although his disdain for Tarragon's conservative approach was no secret by then (as we shall see in the next chapter).[38] Perhaps the most even-handed comparison comes from Thompson himself, who points out that the two different plays had had entirely different styles and purposes:

We came out of country and western. We wanted the Donnellys to be as contemporary as the kind of guys I grew up with who tore down the gravel roads in borrowed cars with cases of beer in the back ... It was built out of the idea that country and western music could make you kind of wild, or mad; and we wanted to have that audience understand that redneck sensibility that could get to the point of taking the law into your own hands ...

It was folk theatre ... One [Reaney's] was a much more carefully constructed art form, and one was more of a folk version.[39]

Meanwhile, back in Toronto, the demolition of Trinity Square drew ever nearer. Thompson not only continued to encourage diverse activity there, but he also established other playing spaces elsewhere in the city. He rented office and rehearsal space behind a tavern on Breadalbane Street, near Toronto Workshop Productions, and opened Theatre Passe Muraille East in a church hall at Dundas and Sherbourne. The first production there, in November 1973, was a Theatre Convention and Festival of Two-Minute Plays organized by Frank Powley (of *The Black Queen*) for his ad hoc organization GNATCAN (The Grand National Academy of Theatre of Canada). Kareda found that, while Powley's conception was 'inspired' and the design 'cheerily lunatic,' the execution was 'lumpish and boring.'[40] In December at Trinity Square came Larry Fineberg's *All the Ghosts*, directed by Louis Del Grande, a downbeat play about a retired psychiatrist and the young couple she has taken in as summer boarders. The most significant aspect of this production was the appearance of Jane Mallet, a veteran comedienne and one of the city's most admired actors. Thus Mallet became one of the first of the older generation of mainstream actors to work with one of Toronto's alternative theatres, anticipating the more highly publicized appearance of Donald Davis and Frances Hyland in the Factory Lab's *Beyond Mozambique* later that season. By this time, the success of the alternative theatres, particularly of Glassco's Tarragon, had made an indelible mark on mainstream theatre in Toronto. Established actors began to seek new challenges with these companies just as younger ones did.

The Trinity Square era came to an end in January 1974, when Passe Muraille was finally evicted and its hall demolished to make way for the Eaton Centre. For this occasion, a whimsical farewell show called *Toronto Pixie Caper* was devised by Ken Campbell. It was intended as a theatre fair, with various attractions distributed around the hall for an audience of browsers. Among other attractions, Anne Anglin drew 'psychic portraits' of customers, Phil Schreibman played piano and sang, and Booth Savage offered his own oral history of the company. It was not exactly a dramatic performance, and not exactly a success, but it was greeted with nostalgic indulgence by the company's many admirers. As Kareda wrote in his review,

Passe Muraille, in addition to occasionally very terrible (but rarely indifferent) work, has given us a wealth of exciting, revelatory, transforming theatre ... I honestly don't dare to start listing my favourites for fear that I'll forget some particular gem. But I can remember so clearly how exciting my first Theatre Passe Muraille production was, and I know how happily I'll remember this lovely place.[41]

The loss of Trinity Square occurred exactly two years after the defection of Kinch and Palmer. Like that previous setback, it could have killed a company with a less resilient leader than Thompson. In Toronto, his determination to broaden the base of his company to compensate for this loss led to two new experimental productions, one an intriguing failure and the other a roaring success.

The first was *Adventures of an Immigrant*, a collective creation in which Thompson (with Rick Salutin) attempted to adapt the formula of *The Farm Show* to the growing ethnic community of Toronto. 'Theatre Passe Muraille has literally become a theatre without walls,' said Thompson of the loss of Trinity Square. 'But instead of being a calamity, maybe it's a godsend in disguise to help bring theatre to Joe Lunch Pail.'[42] The first sign of problems ahead for this show was that he could not persuade any ethnic actors to perform in it. In fact, David Fox recalls being rebuffed by rising alternative theatre star Nick Mancuso, who said that only a WASP do-gooder would take on such a project with so little hope of economic reward. As a result, the cast consisted mainly of experienced collective performers, including Amos, Anglin, Fox, and Peterson. As usual, they researched their topic by interviews and by involving themselves in the community: Anglin even worked in a garment factory for a time, and wrote a song about it for the show. Performances began in an Italian community club, and subsequently moved to other ethnic halls. One performance was even given on a chartered streetcar. The diligent cast would make up signs as titles for each scene, in Brechtian fashion, and learn key phrases phonetically in whatever language was appropriate. In theory this was the perfect adaptation of Thompson's second-person theatre to ethnic Toronto. In practice, however, the second-person audience would not come to see it, and the play could not succeed without them. The highly literate Kareda, himself once an immigrant child with no English, admired the idea of the show and was saddened by its failure: 'Last night's performance, gentle and mild as it was, nevertheless fell rather flat because of a missing ingredient – the Italian immigrants themselves ... Without them, the performers seemed – probably without meaning to – slightly patronizing.'[43] It appears that the European ethnic communities were offended at commentary, however well-meaning, from outsiders. Unlike the shows in Clinton and Cobalt, theatre here was not an attractive novelty, nor was the intended audience won over by the cast's disarming efforts to understand their way of life. Perhaps language was the critical cultural barrier: an ethnic audience *did* support Open Circle's *The Primary English Class* in 1977, a runaway success which used the language barrier both as a central metaphor and as a running gag.

The other experiment at this time was *Cod on a Stick*, as great a success as *The Immigrant Show* was a failure, by the group which later called itself Codco. In the fall of 1973, when Thompson was casting for *Them Donnellys*, several young Newfoundland actors auditioned for him. 'Their auditions were fantastic,' Thompson recalled, 'but I couldn't use them. Their accents just weren't southern Ontario.'[44] Struck with their 'totally unique sense of humour and a sense of chemistry,' he diverted $300 from another budget and gave it to them with this advice: 'Create your own show that's a send-up of Mainlanders' attitudes to your native culture.'[45] Their revue, *Cod on a Stick,* opened in November 1973 at Passe Muraille East. It proved so popular that it was remounted in the new year, then toured Newfoundland under CBC sponsorship. Codco returned to Toronto several times to perform new revues, including *Sickness, Death and Beyond the Grave* in 1974, *Would You Like to Smell My Pocket Crumbs* in 1976, and *Laugh Your Guts Out with Total Strangers* later in 1976. As peripatetic and likeable as Passe Muraille itself, Codco's performers were embraced for their fresh and ingenuous irreverence at a time when such qualities were notably absent from Toronto theatre.

The remaining productions of the 1973–74 season were indicative of Thompson's continued pursuit of three goals for Passe Muraille: his own nationalist rural work, his encouragement of certain experimental urban work, and expansion of the company's touring connections. The touring expanded into western Canada with a Saskatchewan tour of *The Farm Show* in the spring of 1974, a visit during which Thompson met the actors at Saskatoon's 25th Street Theatre. This new connection led to a number of western collectives by both companies, notably *The West Show* (1975) and *Far As the Eye Can See* (1977) by Passe Muraille and *If You're So Good Why Are You in Saskatoon?* (1975) and *Paper Wheat* (1977) by the 25th Street group. The connection also led to a new infusion of actors and writers to the extended family of Theatre Passe Muraille, notably Linda Griffiths and Layne Coleman who were acting with the 25th Street company at the time. In Toronto, urban experiments continued with Shakespeare's *The Tempest,* directed by Cheryl Cashman in the unfriendly confines of the Church of the Holy Trinity, and *Rail Tales,* three thematically related one-act plays directed by Hrant Alianak at Passe Muraille East. Thompson's rural reflections were seen in Ted Johns's one-man show *Naked on the North Shore,* based on stories Johns had gathered while teaching in northern Quebec in the late 1960s. This was Thompson's first attempt to improvise a show with a single actor, a technique which later proved so successful with Griffiths. *Naked on the North Shore,* Johns's first play, had two runs at Passe Muraille East that spring, and was subsequently revived for several tours. Also that spring, Thompson, Salutin, and a small group of actors created the new version of *1837: The Farmers' Revolt,* most of them living in Ray Bird's farmhouse while rehearsals took place in nearby Blyth. In the summer of 1974, Thompson was commissioned to produce yet another community portrait, *Oil,* for the town of Petrolia, the centre of Canada's petroleum industry in the nineteenth century. The grand Victoria Playhouse was not as good an environment for Thompson's brand of improvised drama as were the auction barns of Ontario's agricultural belt. The mood of the audience, moreover, seemed to be one of self-congratulation rather than of self-recognition, as Herbert Whittaker reported: 'Oil is a play for them, about them and there is a town full of neighbours to share it with. So when the first night audience rose to its feet it was only partially a tribute to the Passe Muraille actors; it was very much a tribute to the townspeople's ancestors and friends.'[46] As with *Under the Greywacke* the previous summer, the most damning criticism was Thompson's: *Oil* was never played outside Petrolia. However, the company also performed *1837: The Farmers' Revolt* there before taking it on tour once again.

For the 1974–75 season, Thompson formalized the kind of encouragement he had been giving to new talents and experimental projects with a new program he called 'Seed Shows.' As he was quick to point out, such encouragement had been part of Passe Muraille since it first occupied Trinity Square, but the provision of facilities had seldom been accompanied by any funds. For the coming season, however, $1000 was to be set aside for each of twelve theatrical projects. In an interview, Thompson explained his rationale for the program:

Well, you can't justify it in terms of audience, because some of the projects will be popular and some of them won't. And it won't necessarily be the popular ones that will be the most important. It's just absolutely necessary for us to continue discovering forms and giving people with ideas a chance to explore and display their ideas. Theatre Passe Muraille has always been a place that welcomes new ideas and really survives on the continuation of new ideas.[47]

As he predicted, the Seed Show program created some significant new shows for Passe Muraille. One was *Alligator Pie*, a revue based on Dennis Lee's delightful children's verse, collectively devised by director Janet Amos and actors Clare Coulter, Geza Kovacs, and Miles Potter. *Alligator Pie* has been frequently remounted for holiday productions, and has been produced in many other cities as well. Another significant seed show was Clarke Rogers' production of *Almighty Voice*, a collective creation about Saskatchewan's martyred Indian outlaw of the 1890s.[48] This was the first show at Passe Muraille for Rogers, an *enfant terrible* of regional theatre who had quit Theatre Calgary in 1972 in a highly publicized row. Rogers' western tour of *Almighty Voice* helped lay further groundwork for Passe Muraille's Prairie connections, which became increasingly important from mid-decade onward. Rogers himself became director of Passe Muraille's script development program in 1978, and succeeded Thompson as artistic director in 1982. A third seed show that season was *Follies of Conviction*, written and directed by York University graduate James Roy, a mock-historical melodrama about the attempted censorship of a burlesque show in Toronto in 1912. Although the play itself was not memorable, Roy extended Passe Muraille's growing network the following summer by founding a permanent summer company in Blyth (at Thompson's suggestion) called the Blyth Festival. In subsequent years, productions transferred in both directions between Blyth and Passe Muraille, and the connection was maintained when Janet Amos succeeded Roy as artistic director in 1979. Finally, Thompson himself took advantage of his Seed Show program to produce a new collective called *Canadian Heroes Series 1: Gabriel Dumont*. Although it was given only four performances, this play is significant with respect to Thompson's interest in Canadian heroes in general, and in the Métis leader Dumont in particular (a character which appeared in his later collectives *The West Show* and *Spirit of '85*). Moreover, Thompson by this time was able to tap an astonishing range of talent for this project, including actors Fox, Johns, Peterson, and Potter, co-director John Gray, set designer Brian Arnott, and painter John Boyle.

Besides these seed shows, Passe Muraille's productions in the fall of 1974 consisted mainly of remounted versions of past successes. The revised *1837: The Farmers' Revolt* finally reached Toronto in September 1974, finding an appropriately historical venue at the Enoch Turner Schoolhouse near King and Parliament streets. *Them Donnellys* opened at the Church of the Holy Trinity the following month, rekindling the rivalry with Reaney's trilogy, as *The St. Nicholas Hotel* was in rehearsal at Tarragon at that time. Both *1837* and *Them Donnellys* were greeted as honoured travellers by the critics, although the latter production was hampered by the difficult acoustics of the Holy Trinity sanctuary. Also in October, Codco opened a new revue at the Bathurst Street Theatre entitled *Sickness, Death and Beyond the Grave*. This was an even greater success than *Cod on a Stick*, establishing Codco as a favourite with Toronto audiences, and the corpulent Andy Jones (who had toured with Ken Campbell in Europe) as its comic talent with the most engagingly questionable taste.

Early in 1975 came Thompson's most controversial success, *I Love You, Baby Blue*. For a long time Thompson had wanted to find a way of adapting *The Farm Show*'s second-person appeal to a show for and about the people of Toronto. *Adventures of an Immigrant* was one such attempt, but it failed. A successful idea finally arrived from an odd source. In 1972 a brash new independent television station, CITY-TV, began showing soft-core porn movies on Fridays at midnight. Within six months, these 'Baby Blue Movies,' as they were billed, were being watched by an estimated 280,000 viewers each week, an astonishing 60 per cent of the television audience at that hour. The widespread interest in these movies gave Thompson his thematic key for creating a show in which Torontonians would watch themselves: as he put it, 'we took the techniques of *The Farm Show* and tried to apply them to the sexual fascination of the big city.'[49] For once, Thompson was not able to draw on his nucleus of actors who had created *The Farm Show* and *1837*, for Fox, Potter, and the others did not want to take part in a show in which they would have to take off their clothes. (Times had surely changed since *Doukhobors*!) As Thompson explained, 'The point is that it was a hard show for everybody to do. Taking your clothes off in public is hard. Before I started, I approached some of the regular actors at the theatre but they couldn't feel comfortable with the idea – however much they were prepared to put themselves on the line in other ways for other plays.' Undaunted, as usual, Thompson gathered together a cast largely inexperienced in his methods, sent them out to do research on sexual mores in Toronto, and began improvisational rehearsals in his Breadalbane Street studio. Anticipating a difficult rehearsal period and a potential popular hit, he asked for a longer-than-normal commitment from his cast.

Baby Blue was not a grim strip show for the trench-coated clientele of Yonge Street, nor even a leering revue like *Oh! Calcutta!* Although filled with humour, it was a serious attempt to examine the nature of sexuality in Toronto, from singles bars to massage parlours to people just sitting home alone watching television. However, it was (as a censor might put it) completely concerned with sex. Since it contained frequent nudity and coarse language, controversy was anticipated when *Baby Blue* opened at the Bathurst Street United Church in January 1975. In his review, Kareda expressed his concern that 'there is less tenderness here than in any Paul Thompson show I've ever seen, and for that reason alone, this is the most depressing.'[50] The church's congregation fretted over a sex show performing in their rented sanctuary, and the police fretted over some of the explicit language. However, the public response was tremendous. *I Love You, Baby Blue* ran for over three months, proving highly remunerative to the company as well as to the actors (who, as was Thompson's practice, worked for a share of the box-office). For the first time in any of his collectives, Thompson's artistic motives came into question, as Passe Muraille's surplus soared along with ticket sales. One view of Thompson's success with *Baby Blue* was that, in creating a play concerning (in part) the exploitation of sex for profit, Thompson himself was exploiting sex for profit. Even the cast recognized that aspect of the show. As *Baby Blue* actress Terry Schonblum put it, 'The show was very raw, and titillating and sexy, and sometimes that's hard to admit. Lots of people came for tits and ass. It was truly the best show in town for that.'[51] Thompson's defence was that he intended to touch the public consciousness of Toronto, and that the show's profitability merely indicated the achievement of this goal. 'It was really hard to tell people – although I think it was true – that the money was a side effect,' he said. 'It just happens that there is money to be made with any show that fascinates the public to the extent that *Baby Blue* did.'

Another side effect was the reappearance of Toronto's morality squad, absent from its theatres since *Clear Light* in 1973, and absent from Passe Muraille since *Futz* in 1969. In an interview in *Canadian Theatre Review*, Thompson reviewed the police involvement in *Baby Blue*, from its opening to the eventual arrest of himself and his cast. Shortly after the play opened in January 1975, representatives of the morality squad visited the theatre, expressed their concerns over certain aspects of the show, and asked to see a script. This being a Thompson collective, of course, there wasn't one. However, the police were able to meet amicably with the company and to describe scenes in which they found the dialogue too explicit. For the morality squad, articulate explanations of social and aesthetic purpose were not part of their daily routine: as Thompson put it, 'primarily the squad deals with the owners of dirty book stores and body rub places and so I gather they weren't used to this kind of treatment.' Some of the cast objected on principle to censoring their material. But the pragmatic Thompson felt that 'we were getting to say what we wanted and that it was silly to argue over three or four "fucks".' The textual changes were made, the police went away satisfied, and the obscenity issue vanished for almost three months. But the police came back with a vengeance and the issue exploded just before the show was to close. As Thompson described it,

At some point during this time a provincial election was called and one of the campaign promises called for a clean-up of Yonge Street and an end to the kind of free sexuality that had been allowed to start in Toronto. We were arrested on a

Friday night, two days before we were to close anyway, and the [Premier] Bill Davis stand against explicit promiscuity hit the papers on Saturday. So it seems very likely that it was politically motivated. All the actors, the stage manager, and myself as director and producer were charged with 'performing an immoral stage performance.'

It was a quandary for Passe Muraille. They wanted to close the show, but they felt compelled to keep it open on principle. The artistic community, long starved for a good libertarian issue, flocked to support (in effect) a show that was over. The night after the arrests, Thompson held a public meeting instead of a performance. It was decided to give three reprise performances the following weekend; and to satisfy the moral indignation of his many supporters, Thompson enlarged a crowd scene to include a number of aldermen, arts officials, ministers, and theatre folk. He even signed them to contracts, at their insistence, so that they would also be subject to arrest. The shows sold out, of course, and the presence of the media added to the circus atmosphere. Although the police did not show up for these closing festivities, they had helped to create yet another triumph in community involvement for Paul Thompson. As Thompson himself said, *I Love You, Baby Blue* was a true theatrical event at a time when it was becoming harder and harder to create a sense of event in Toronto theatre.

By contrast, the obscenity trial the following November was a dull affair. As Thompson recalled, 'The prosecution played a tape of the show and had a policewoman attest to what she saw and what she thought it meant. We were heavily backed by the city and the establishment and after half a day the prosecution could see that their approach wasn't working – that their case was weak – and they withdrew it.' In the six years since the *Futz* arrests, then, Passe Muraille had become part of the mainstream culture of Toronto. The *Baby Blue* trial did not function as the *Futz* one had, opening the door to previously forbidden territory. Rather, as Thompson himself noted, it proved merely 'an articulation of a social situation which already existed. The challenge was whether we were right in saying that it existed.' One intriguing echo of the *Futz* case was the spectre of the underground becoming the mainstream, more in regard to CITY-TV and the Yonge Street strip than to Theatre Passe Muraille. Although *Baby Blue* was not offensive by Toronto's alternative theatre standards, its widespread popularity brought it the same official disapproval as had these other more prominent threats to mainstream propriety. As Thompson said,

We weren't doing anything on stage that hadn't been done before or saying words that hadn't been said before. But unlike the limited runs of what were, in some cases, more extreme productions by other underground theatres, we were playing it to six hundred people at every performance with no let-up in sight. That soon adds up to a significant number of people, significant in the sense that it was becoming part of the public domain. What is permitted within a closed or cloistered situation (i.e., if you don't bother us, we won't bother you) is not permitted, it seems, if a lot of people get to hear about it.

One last side effect of *Baby Blue*, like *Futz*, was the acquisition of a new home for the homeless Theatre Passe Muraille. As with all of Thompson's collectives, *Baby Blue*'s actors were paid a small weekly stipend plus a percentage of the box-office. As Thompson recalls, the cast felt embarrassed by the amount of money they were making on this hugely popular show. He therefore capitalized on their embarrassment by persuading them to take a lower percentage of the gate, so that a building fund could be started. By the time *Baby Blue* closed, this fund had reached $30,000, and Thompson was looking for a building on which to spend it. Charles Pachter, a well-known Toronto artist and a friend of Thompson, was then heavily involved in real estate in the artistic neighbourhood of Queen Street West. Pachter found an abandoned warehouse on Ryerson Street, near Queen and Bathurst, which he felt would suit Passe Muraille. He also discovered that its present owner was interested in demolishing the building for new development, but he forestalled that plan by persuading the city government of its historic value. Passe Muraille purchased its new home for $100,000 late in 1975; a decade later, estimates of its resale value ranged up to a million dollars. Because of its equity in the building, Passe Muraille has been able to carry a deficit which would be alarming for other small theatres. The company still lives from hand to mouth. But as a property owner, its financial situation is reminiscent of that familiar line from *The Farm Show*, 'A farmer lives poor and dies rich.' Unique in so many ways, Theatre Passe Muraille was for many years the only theatre group in Toronto to own the building in which it performed.

Passe Muraille after 1975

Although the success of *I Love You, Baby Blue* did not stop the decline of Theatre Passe Muraille's direct impact in Toronto, its indirect impact has remained enormous. Its Ryerson Street home has continued to provide an inexpensive and credible performing venue for later arrivals on the alternative theatre scene, including such groups as Buddies in Bad Times, The Clichettes, The Hummer Sisters, Necessary Angel, Triple Action Theatre, and Michael Hollingsworth's Videocabaret. It has introduced significant new Canadian plays to Toronto, many by members of Passe Muraille's extended family, such as Hrant Alianak's *The Blues*, Jim Garrard's *Cold Comfort*, John Gray's *18 Wheels*, and Linda Griffiths' *Maggie and Pierre*. Passe Muraille's outreach campaign continued through its connections with 25th Street House, the Blyth Festival, and Codco, through new plays created in Alberta and the Northwest Territories, through continued touring in Canada and beyond, and through the distribution of Passe Muraille veterans through all levels of Canadian theatre.

Thompson continued to work in his favourite form, the collective creation, with mixed results. New shows included *The Horsburgh Scandal* (1976), *The Olympics Show* (1976), *Shakespeare for Fun and Profit* (1977), which related grassroots theatre to the Stratford Festival, and *Les Maudits Anglais* (1977), in which his anglophone actors performed in French to audiences in Quebec. He also continued to court mainstream success, although he usually sought to discover new audiences rather than to cater to existing ones. These two impulses came together in Linda Griffiths' *Maggie and Pierre*, which began in Passe Muraille's tiny second stage on Ryerson Street, and eventually went on to play at the Royal Alex, in New York, and on several highly acclaimed tours. This was a play which literally would never have been born without Thompson as midwife. As Griffiths recalled, 'The original idea was Paul Thompson's … In rehearsal [for *Les Maudits Anglais*], I began fooling around with a Pierre Trudeau character and one day Thompson said, "That's it. That's your one-person show. You play both of them." I thought he was out of his mind. A year later, we began rehearsal.'[52]

Developed in 'jam sessions' with Thompson, *Maggie and Pierre* enabled him to pursue one implication of his collective work to its logical conclusion: to improvise a play with actor and writer embodied in a single person. With this play, Thompson also managed to touch the Canadian consciousness to an extent he had not achieved since *The Farm Show*. 'One of Thompson's favourite memories,' writes Paul Wilson, in a review of Thompson's career, 'is of overhearing a man who had evidently not seen the show himself explain to some friends outside Toronto's Royal Alexandra Theatre what *Maggie and Pierre* was all about. Once again, he felt he had managed to connect with something in the national imagination.'[53]

Theatre Passe Muraille is one of the longest-lived of all Toronto theatres, currently second only to Toronto Workshop Productions. It survived through three distinct stages of alternative theatre in Toronto (radical, nationalist, and mainstream), and it still embodies elements of each. Under Paul Thompson, however, the nationalist theme was the dominant one. First of all, Passe Muraille sought to produce new Canadian works, be they scripts or collectives, adaptations or originals. Secondly it sought to illustrate Canadian themes, often through the depiction of some of Canada's many regions and subcultures. It sought to extend Thompson's principles of self-recognition and self-celebration into all parts of the country, reporting back to Toronto with news of its cultural explorations. In the 1970s, moreover, the style of the Passe Muraille collective was the most recognizable style of indigenous Canadian theatre. In this nationalist stage, the Factory Lab may have been the home of the Canadian playwright, but Theatre Passe Muraille was the fountainhead of a new style of Canadian performance.

5

Tarragon Theatre

As they approach a season of well-earned self-examination and renewal, Bill Glassco and his exceptional colleagues deserve all our gratitude. For everyone who loves theatre in this city and this country, they have changed our lives. We'll await them at the next wave.[1]

Urjo Kareda, May 1975

Whether measured in terms of administrative stability, audience development, or dramaturgical influence, Bill Glassco's Tarragon Theatre must be considered the most consistently successful of Toronto's alternative theatres. Despite this success, however, or perhaps because of it, this company also provokes the most widely divergent comments from Toronto's theatre community. Tarragon's conservative approach to dramaturgy and production is despised by those who most admired Garrard's environmental or free-form experiments, Thompson's collectives, or the challenges to public taste served up by Gass, Kinch, and others. Critical opinion has been similarly divided: one commentator described Tarragon as 'the heart and soul of the alternative theatre movement in this country,' while another has dismissed it as 'fully mainstream' and not really an alternative theatre at all.[2] Even the Tarragon's one attribute which seems beyond criticism, its programming of new Canadian scripts later supplemented by neglected classics, has been compared to the 'consistently formulaic offerings' of Toronto's mainstream theatres.[3]

The common theme in such criticisms is that Tarragon gained its success by playing safe. There is an element of truth in this charge.

Whereas both Garrard's 'survival theatre' and Thompson's collective creations at Theatre Passe Muraille stripped the actors of their usual support systems to push them toward new theatrical awareness, Tarragon Theatre used all these systems to maximize a production's potential for pleasing its audience. Tarragon also avoided the sensationalism which brought notoriety to other alternative theatres. Unlike Garrard, Bill Glassco had no interest in changing the nature of rehearsal and performance. Unlike Gass, he would not compromise the theatrical effectiveness of one production for the sake of more numerous productions. Unlike Thompson, he had no wish to redefine the traditional tasks of director, playwright, and actor, nor did he seek out a new audience. Rather, he used traditional theatre practices to try to change the habits of an existing one. As Glassco recalls, 'I wouldn't say we were in reaction against a theatre company so much as against the audience in Toronto. We wanted to shake up the audience, and make them realize there was something else.'4

At other alternative theatres, artistic goals were intertwined with social or aesthetic experiments. At Tarragon they were not, which denied the company some of the excitement of unpredictability which could be found elsewhere. Because of Tarragon's undeniably conservative aesthetics, some commentators have ascribed its success to a single foolproof formula: established playwrights churning out 'kitchen-sink' realism acceptable to middle-class audiences. This argument is very unfair, however, as it ignores the conditions under which that success was achieved. First of all, there exists no reliable formula for theatrical success: indeed, in 1971 it was an almost unprecedented gamble to open a new small theatre dedicated to developing new Canadian plays. Second, even the best-known Tarragon playwrights (French, Freeman, Tremblay, and Reaney) were not then the pillars of modern Canadian drama that they are today. Rather, they *became* established due in part to Tarragon's productions. And finally, the plays did not adhere to a uniform style. While French's plays were resolutely naturalistic, and helped build Tarragon's reputation for realism, Freeman's were only equivocally so, and Tremblay's and Reaney's not at all.

In retrospect, perhaps Tarragon's most surprising achievement is that it accomplished precisely what it set out to. It developed new Canadian playwrights by giving their scripts the best productions possible. It found an audience for these new plays, it cultivated that audience through meticulous public relations, and it built upon that audience through consistently solid production values. Finally, the popular success of several of Tarragon's plays brought regional theatres across the country to recognize the potential of new Canadian drama on their larger stages. Tarragon had perhaps the most modest goals of any of Toronto's alternative theatres, expressed without revolutionary rhetoric or self-serving hyperbole. Perhaps the attainability of these goals made them more durable, and thus more subversive. As revolutionary attitudes of the 1960s receded in the ensuing decade, Tarragon's conservative approach to plays and production remained intact, its artistic and administrative stability inviolate, and its reputation as a breeding ground for new Canadian scripts unequalled among its rivals.

Background to 1971

The son of a prominent Canadian business executive, Bill Glassco was born in Quebec City in 1935, raised in Toronto's posh Forest Hill district, and educated at prestigious private schools. At university he studied English literature, receiving an AB from Princeton in 1957 and an MA from Oxford in 1959. Returning to Canada, he began teaching at the University of Toronto while studying for his doctorate in English. However, he soon found that he hated lecturing and lost interest in academic life. It seemed irrelevant to his own interests and to the social concerns of the time:

Princeton in the '50s had been a heady, golden experience, and when I went on to Oxford, that was even more gorgeous. I developed a false idea of the university and when I came back to Toronto I was ruined and disenchanted ... I found that teaching English didn't humanize people. It was the whole scholarly apparatus that finally got me, when I realized that I was reading volumes and volumes of criticism instead of the actual texts.

I became disgusted with myself, with my colleagues and with my students, all of whom were doing the same thing. I was shrivelling up inside, feeling like an old man at 30.[5]

As he became less satisfied with academic life, Glassco gravitated toward the theatre, which had fascinated him since childhood. He remembers producing basement shows with his neighbourhood friends as a child, and acting in school plays from Upper Canada College to Princeton. But as he grew very tall and slender, self-consciousness overtook his acting ambitions, and for several years his involvement in theatre consisted only of attending plays and of writing songs for college musicals. In 1963, however, through family connections, he was asked to serve on the board of the Crest Theatre, which he continued to do until that company was dissolved three years later. In 1964, along with director Bob Hamlin and fellow academic Dennis Lee, Glassco helped organize a company called the 'Muddy York Theatre Club,' which presented a summer season at the University Alumnae Dramatic Society's Coach House Theatre. The plays they chose were Wilder's *The Matchmaker*, Chekhov's *The Seagull*, and an original play by Lee entitled *How the Beast Was Took*, which did not reach the stage.[6] Finally in 1966 Glassco directed his first production, Pinter's *A Night Out*, with student actors in a student lounge at Victoria College. On the basis of its success, he was then invited to direct the Jacobean comedy *A Chaste Maid in Cheapside* at St Michael's College, also in the University of Toronto.

By this time Glassco had completed his doctorate, but had no interest in continuing to teach English literature. Another opportunity arose through a friend from his Oxford years, Michael Bawtree, who had been working under Michael Langham at the Stratford Festival. Bawtree introduced Glassco to Langham as a potential asset to his next theatrical venture. Langham was leaving Stratford to head a new professional theatre in La Jolla, California, and it was agreed that Glassco would serve as his academic liaison with the university there. Details were ironed out during a trip to La Jolla in December 1966, and Glassco obtained a leave-of-absence from Victoria College for the 1967–68 academic year. But when the state of California cancelled its anticipated funding, the project was postponed, and Glassco found himself without any prospects for the coming year. Meanwhile, Glassco's student producer at St Michael's College asked him to act as unofficial host for the brief lecture visit of Robert W. Corrigan, the founding editor of the *Tulane Drama Review*, who had recently moved to New York University to start a new theatre program there. Desperate for advice on how to start a directing career at age thirty-one with virtually no experience, Glassco broached the subject with Corrigan, who suggested he come to NYU to study at his new School of the Arts. Corrigan's colleague Richard Schechner, whose celebrated production of *Dionysus in 69* later emerged from this school, had met Glassco in La Jolla and was equally enthusiastic about the idea. Glassco would teach in the academic portion of their program, which was not their primary interest anyway, while participating in acting and directing workshops alongside his students. He was more than just an expediency for the School of the Arts, however: a faculty member was even sent up to Toronto to see Glassco's next directing effort, James Saunders' *A Scent of Flowers* at the Central Library Theatre.

For someone who had always taken a cerebral approach to the theatre, Glassco found his 1967–68 year at NYU a revelation, a cornucopia for the emotionally undernourished. 'I was at NYU the whole time,' he recalls, 'and I was just going crazy. It was like having the adolescence I'd never had ... getting in touch with my emotions and feelings and getting all the bullshit out of my head.' He credits actress-teacher Olympia Dukakis for showing him how much he needed to unlock himself emotionally, and director-teacher Peter Kass for persuading him to trust his instinct over his intellect. Glassco enjoys telling the story of his first directing project at NYU, for which he chose the second act of Ben Jonson's *Catiline*. Over drinks, after a presentation of several such projects, Kass gave animated and detailed critiques on all the other student directors' work, but ignored Glassco's completely. Finally, Glassco asked Kass what he thought of the *Catiline* piece:

He said, 'Oh, that thing with all the fancy clothes? I didn't understand, I don't know what was happening.' I said, 'Couldn't you hear?' ... He said, 'Oh, I could hear what they were saying all right, [but] I didn't know what the fuck was going on.'

Schechner advised Glassco to take just two of Kass's acting students and to keep working with them until he had something worth showing. Glassco chose a modern American play, *Mrs. Dally Has a Lover* by William Hanley, and spent much of his rehearsal time in quiet exploratory conversation with his cast. From his work on this play, Glassco recalls, 'I learned the value of actors talking to each other, and trusting each other. I think that's the cornerstone of my work, and I learned it there. I learned that I could do it as well as anybody.'

Returning to Toronto for the summer of 1968, Glassco and his friend Brian Meeson formed a company of NYU and Toronto students to play at 11 Trinity Square. Meeson, a teacher who had also worked extensively with the Alumnae theatre, directed Hanley's *Slow Dance on the Killing Ground* and Turgenev's *A Month in the Country*. Glassco directed *The Winter's Tale* which, ironically, opened during a July heat wave. As he recalls, the production was 'truly awful,' and the critics agreed. On this occasion Urjo Kareda, whose enthusiasm for Glassco's later work became so important to the success of Tarragon Theatre, placed the blame squarely on the director. 'It is mainly director Glassco's calamity,' he wrote. 'I cannot imagine attempting to do The Winter's Tale with no hope of achieving credibility when the actors speak. It would be like staging King Lear with pygmies.'[7]

After his summer at Trinity Square, Glassco returned to NYU. However, he did not enjoy his second year's training as he had the first, because he found himself impatient to begin a professional career. Again at a crossroads, he applied to be an assistant director for the 1969 Stratford Festival. The Festival's associate director John Hirsch interviewed him, but advised him to go elsewhere and direct rather than aspire to be an assistant. Glassco sent letters of application to all sorts of theatre companies, amateur and professional, in southern Ontario and beyond. The only reply he received was from a summer stock company in Kingston, called the St Lawrence Summer Playhouse, whose American artistic director was impressed with Glassco's NYU training and felt it would be politic to engage a Canadian director. There Glassco staged Molière's *The Miser* and Bill Manhoff's *The Owl and the Pussycat*. He expected to enjoy working on a classic comedy more than on a commercial one. Surprisingly, though, he found *The Owl and the Pussycat* more satisfying because it gave him greater scope for developing the kind of interpersonal directing style that he had first explored with *Mrs. Dally*. That fall Glassco returned to Victoria College, but taught only half-time to keep himself available for directing opportunities. He was invited by two community theatre groups to direct for them that winter, commuting to Cobourg to stage *The Odd Couple* and to Kingston to stage John Herbert's *Fortune and Men's Eyes*. Herbert's protégé at the Garret Theatre, Ken Gass, came to Kingston to see this production, and that meeting eventually led to Glassco's quick acceptance at the Factory Theatre Lab later that year.

Throughout this period, Bill Glassco's wife, Jane, had become increasingly involved in his theatrical interests. Jane Glassco, like her husband, had grown up among Toronto's business elite. Her father, Walter Gordon, was a partner in one of Canada's leading financial consulting firms, and had been a controversial federal finance minister in the 1960s. (Indeed, some wags referred to the Glasscos' marriage in 1961 as a 'merger.') While absorbing some characteristics of their upper-crust upbringing, however, both Glasscos were more free-spirited than the average member of Toronto's Establishment. By 1970 Bill was looking for work in professional theatre, and Jane was interested in finding a job in which she could share some time with her busy husband and their two small children. With her excellent administrative and interpersonal skills, Jane Glassco was well suited to managing a theatre, and took the opportunity to do so – for the fun of it, as she recalls. In the spring of 1970, the Glasscos decided to rent the Red Barn

Theatre in Ontario's 'cottage country' to produce a season of summer stock.

The Red Barn Theatre was a summer theatre located near the resort town of Jackson's Point, Ontario. It was first converted from a barn to a 300-seat summer theatre by Alfred Mulock in 1949, and operated most summers in the 1950s under a variety of producers (including Shaw Festival founder Brian Doherty and long-time Stratford actress Amelia Hall). In its second decade, under the determinedly stable management of Marigold Charlesworth and Jean Roberts (1959–62), the Red Barn attracted some of Canada's leading actors, expanded into winter operations in Toronto, and became the best known of Ontario's 'straw hat' companies.[8] This stability deteriorated toward the end of the decade, however: when Bill Glassco announced his 1970 season, Herbert Whittaker described the Red Barn as 'Ontario's most-managed summer theatre.'[9] For his summer company, Glassco recruited several experienced professionals such as Betty Leighton and James B. Douglas, along with some younger actors he had worked with in university and community theatre such as David Hemblen and Steve Whistance-Smith. A new play opened each week for eight weeks, with five of them directed by Glassco.[10] The discipline of directing weekly stock and the challenge of managing a marginal theatre company, as he recalls, were important learning experiences for both Glasscos:

We didn't lose money, we delighted the community, we did a good season of plays ... we had reasonably good houses, good enough to break even. Most importantly, Jane and I discovered we could run a theatre, we were quite good at that. We could handle our apprentices quite well, we kept everybody happy, we got on with it.

In the 1970–71 season Glassco took his final preliminary steps toward founding Tarragon Theatre. Having finally quit his teaching position at the University of Toronto, he became involved with the fledgling Factory Theatre Lab on his return from Jackson's Point. There, in Ken Gass's single-minded determination to produce new Canadian drama, Glassco found a vision and a dream which his own work had been lacking. Although he had no experience with plays-in-progress, Glassco plunged himself into the tasks of reading new manuscripts, improving them through workshops with actors and playwrights, and staging them for the public. He also solicited a script from David Freeman, a writer with cerebral palsy whom Jane Glassco had met in her teens while working at a summer camp for the handicapped. Encouraged by such friends as the Glasscos and actor Don Cullen (best known at the time as the founder of the Bohemian Embassy coffee-house), Freeman had overcome his handicap to graduate from McMaster University and to publish some of his writing. Now Glassco wanted another look at a play Freeman had once shown him about cerebral palsy victims in a sheltered workshop. Glassco's production of this play, *Creeps*, became the greatest sensation of a sensational year for new Canadian drama, the first of an unprecedented number of popular indigenous plays which dominated Toronto theatre in the early 1970s. While *Creeps* has since received more polished productions, including the one which opened Tarragon Theatre later in 1971, the impact of its first performance was unique. 'Nothing was more exciting than the first week of playing *Creeps*,' recalls Glassco. 'Nothing was more meaningful, nothing was more amazing, nothing was more dangerous.'

Working with Gass at the Factory Lab, Bill Glassco acquired a passion for presenting a Canadian audience with new Canadian plays. However, he was unhappy with what he considered slapdash production habits there. He felt that good new plays such as *Creeps* would not find a wider audience unless they were presented in the best possible light. While Gass was devoted to the Canadian playwright, he seemed less concerned with the Canadian theatre-goer. Productions at the Factory were regularly under-financed, under-produced, and under-rehearsed, with attention to detail often sacrificed to the sheer volume of activity. Moreover, while audience inconvenience had become something of a design style at Theatre Passe Muraille, the offhand squalor of the Factory bespoke nothing but indifference, as Nathan Cohen indicated in his review of the Factory's very first production:

The theatre is the second floor of a garage. One of the actors' entrances is the heaviest, noisiest roll-on door this side of the Casa Loma. The decor for the in-the-round staging includes barbed wire that reaches from the ceiling to the floor. To drink the coffee sold in the lobby is to risk your life.[11]

In Jane Glassco's view, alternative theatres in 1970 seemed indifferent, even antagonistic, to their audience. Certainly personable house management and colourful surroundings were not part of the alternative theatre aesthetic at that time. The importance the Glasscos placed on their audience as collaborator remained a major distinction between their work and that of more avant-garde Toronto theatres. At Tarragon, Jane Glassco's personal contact with her audience, in the lobby and through her newsletter, was to contribute greatly to the way her theatre was perceived.

After *Creeps* opened in February 1971, Glassco left for Fredericton to direct *The Playboy of the Western World* at Theatre New Brunswick, his first fully paid directing job. While returning to Toronto, where he was to direct *Branch Plant* at the Factory, he learned that Nathan Cohen had died suddenly. As a former board member of the Crest Theatre, which had suffered some of Cohen's most vitriolic criticism, Glassco saw him as a negative influence on theatrical enterprise in Toronto because of the fear which he inspired. On hearing the news of Cohen's death, recalls Glassco, 'I remember thinking very strongly, "My life is going to change."'

Back at the Factory, the success of *Creeps*, and its implications regarding production standards and audience development, further widened the rift between Glassco and Gass. Glassco wanted to remount the play, making improvements in both script and production, and to run it for as long as the Toronto audience would support it. This was antithetical to Gass's goals for the Factory: new scripts and more productions, a theatre to develop playwrights rather than audience. Glassco's position was that a playwright cannot develop without the opportunity to rewrite, to see the play produced under the best conditions possible, and to reap the rewards of popular success if the play deserved it. (As the report of the Niagara conference put it a few months later, the playwrights wanted 'to be exploited as imaginatively and widely as possible, even to the point of becoming rich, or famous, or both.') This conflict with Gass provided the final stimulus for Glassco to start his own company. As he later said, 'A lot of Tarragon came out of what I thought Ken Gass had been doing the wrong way.'[12]

At first the Glasscos wished to rent a theatre in which to remount *Creeps*. However, they found that available rental spaces were expensive and poorly suited to the play, and so they decided instead to look for a permanent space of their own. Although they considered several sites, Bill Glassco kept returning to a vacant warehouse at 30 Bridgman Avenue because 'it felt the most like a theatre.' The warehouse was located near the crosstown railway tracks, just north of Toronto's Annex neighbourhood, less than two blocks from the Factory Lab. Built as a casting factory shortly after World War II, it was currently for sale or lease, but at a monthly rate which the Glasscos felt their company could not afford. However, some dashing salesmanship by a friend of theirs, a young lawyer named Barry Stuart, brought the rent down to a manageable level. As Glassco later described it,

Without his charm and chutzpah Tarragon might never have opened at all. When I despaired that we would never be able to afford the rent on this magical space, it was Barry who propelled me into one of the boldest acts of my life. We telephoned the owner of the building, who told us his wife was responsible for all decisions concerning rent and tenants. Barry asked to speak to her, asked her what she liked to drink, and two hours later we were on her doorstep with chilled glasses and bottles of gin and vermouth. I was convinced they'd throw us out, but no, the lady was intrigued (bless her), and awfully impressed that we wanted the place so badly we'd brought our own martinis. The rent came down, and the rest is history.[13]

Tarragon Theatre began as a family operation under Bill and Jane Glassco. Indeed, the third director of the company (legally required for incorporation) was a Rosedale neighbour who merely provided her signature whenever it was needed. Although Jane Glassco was listed as the publicity director, her influence in shaping Tarragon's policies could be better described as managing partner with responsibility for staff and public relations. Soon the company acquired a theatre manager (Ann Kewley) and a technical director (Mark Freeborn), whose duties were also far more eclectic than their titles indicated. Glassco recruited three associate directors with whom he had worked closely: Brian Meeson, James B. Douglas, and Steve Whistance-Smith, who was also listed as dramaturge that first season. Finally, the new theatre's business manager was Bernie Bomers, formerly the business manager of Rochdale College. Born in Holland in 1942, Bomers came to Canada in his teens and later studied commerce at the University of Toronto. As an executive member of the Campus Co-op, he was heavily involved in the planning for Rochdale College. In 1968 Bomers resigned his executive-trainee position with the Toronto-Dominion Bank to work for Rochdale, later serving as finance minister in Jim Garrard's monarchy. After leaving Rochdale the next year, Bomers began making and selling bean-bag furniture, at which time he met the Glasscos. 'Bernie the Beanbagger,' as he was known, also played a walk-on role in *Creeps* at the Factory. He was the perfect choice as manager for the Glasscos' new theatre. He brought to Tarragon his business training and experience, along with a perverse affection for improbable projects. As Bomers puts it, 'There is a whole world beyond rational maximizing-profit-making behaviours.'[14]

The name of the company was actually coined (rather whimsically) a year before it was founded, when Glassco needed to invent a legal title for his Red Barn venture. Now he felt it sounded right for his new theatre on Bridgman Avenue. As he told the press, 'The only thing I can make is salad and, as tarragon is my favourite herb, I use it a lot. We did think of Parsley Productions, but decided against it. What we mostly wanted to avoid was anything with "workshop," "studio" or '"lab" in it.'[15] The name 'Tarragon,' then, was a reaction against the kind of alternative theatre which promised half-realized artistic experiments. Instead, it offered the imagery of the kitchen: a bright comfortable workplace where carefully chosen ingredients are skilfully combined to bring pleasure to one's guests. It also suggested the well-bred courtesy of the Glasscos' upbringing, of a style not to be found at Passe Muraille or the Factory. Nonetheless, the alternative impulse to change the audience's conception of theatre was also a part of Tarragon, albeit in a more understated way. At Tarragon, change was to be effected in the manner of Rosedale, not Rochdale, through persuasion rather than confrontation.

One cannot review Glassco's career from 1966, when he directed his first play, to 1971, when he founded Tarragon Theatre, without being struck by the very numerous but very small steps he took toward his goal of becoming a professional director. The direction of his ambitions was unwavering, and the progress toward them was constant; but Glassco's self-confidence was never so strong as his self-awareness, so that each small step demanded a renewed effort. Finally, however, by the summer of 1971, he had collected the experience and the resources he needed. He had found a theatre space that could balance his conservative aesthetics and the experimental quality of the venture. He had gathered a staff which suited the collaborative managerial style which he and his wife favoured. Most importantly, he had found a mandate, which he clearly elucidated a few weeks before his theatre opened:

WHY TARRAGON?

I decided to start a theatre last February as a result of working on new Canadian scripts at the Factory Theatre Lab. While there I learned several things; namely, a) there are many exciting playwrights in Canada, and particularly in Toronto, who are as yet unproduced. b) Many of them could benefit from working with actors and a director on their scripts. They need to learn more about shaping a play, or how to write for actors. c) A new play should be produced modestly because of the financial risk involved. It is essential, however, if a playwright is to learn from the experience, and if his play is to have a chance of further life, that the play also be produced with as much care and expertise as is possible. This is not easy to do, but if it is not done, the end result can be more harmful than beneficial to the writer.

By far the most important discovery for me was simply finding both a meaningful context to work in and a meaningful *way* to work. To produce plays of one's own culture, and to be a part of their inception through the act of collaboration with a playwright is for me, in 1971, preferable to any other way of working in the theatre. It is the means I have of creating a distinctive kind of theatre, one which, hopefully, can make a contribution to this country's culture. Tarragon's success will be measured not only by box office returns but by the number of good plays it is able to produce. To nurture Canadian playwriting talent is Tarragon's primary aim. Canada and its theatres *need* their *own* plays. If the regional theatres in this country do not have Canadian plays to do, they must fall back on the classics or recent West End or Broadway successes. They cannot be expected to do Canadian plays out of a sense of duty (theirs or the public's) or to please the grant-giving bodies. Nor can they be expected to choose them over commercially successful plays of another culture unless they have available Canadian plays that have already proved their intrinsic excellence and/or box office potential elsewhere. Part of Tarragon's function will be to act as a testing ground for new plays, to provide a source from which other Canadian theatres can draw.

It is impossible to know how inclined the Toronto public is to take a genuine interest in new Canadian plays. From my experience, the public attends not because the play is Canadian but because it is entertaining. Tarragon will not expect to survive on the strength of its Canadian policy, but on the excellence of its productions. Quality will create the need.[16]

From its inception, then, the goal of Tarragon Theatre was production excellence for contemporary Canadian plays, in order to build an appreciative audience for such plays first locally and then nationally. The most remarkable aspect of Tarragon's first four seasons was the extent to which it achieved its stated goals.

Production at Tarragon, 1971–75

As Jane Glassco recalls, it cost only $9000 to renovate the warehouse on Bridgman Avenue and to open *Creeps* in it. Bernie Bomers scavenged lumber from a wrecking company to build risers for audience seating, and plywood chairs were purchased at a school auction. The new version of *Creeps* opened in October 1971, with the same principal actors as in the earlier production at the Factory. In Bill Glassco's view, the second production was much improved, particularly in the script, set, and lighting. To those for whom the excitement of alternative theatre was its most important quality, however, the improvements were counter-productive. As Tom Hendry wrote,

Sadly, something had gone wrong in the move from one production to another. The caustic edge had been taken off; the obvious jokes at the expense of Shriners and other do-gooders had embarrassingly multiplied and were now too-heavily underlined; the cast which previously *experienced* the play as a scaldingly focussed look at what it is like to be alive, were now '*acting*' and acting for all they were worth.[17]

However, the critical response to this production was even more enthusiastic than for the play's Factory debut, led by Urjo Kareda's assertion that 'the performance itself is quite beyond praise.'[18] The first night of *Creeps* was one of Kareda's first assignments as lead critic for the *Star* (following the death of Nathan Cohen), and he was understandably nervous about it. This nervousness was exacerbated when, in the lobby before the performance began, a man with cerebral palsy spilled coffee all over Kareda's jacket, then apologized in loud halting tones which could not be understood. It was playwright David Freeman.

The long popular run of *Creeps* was followed by four productions which did not attract sizeable audiences. Reviews were seldom discouraging, but the plays' word-of-mouth reputations were poor and ticket sales were slow. The first of these was *Cabbagetown Plays* by David Tipe. It comprised three one-acts, each with two characters, linked by themes of loneliness and fantasy. While Whittaker found the writing commanded respect, Kareda saw these playlets as only a necessary kind of exercise for a beginning playwright.[19] As with *Creeps*, Kareda praised Glassco's direction, commending 'his customary attention to detail and atmosphere ... and his usual skill with handling actors.' The only oddity of this comment is how few of Glassco's productions Kareda had ever seen. Tarragon's next play was *See No Evil, Hear ...* by Jack Cunningham, a psychological thriller with brooding Pinteresque dialogue. This time Kareda criticized the script as wilfully obscure, and the direction (by Brian Meeson) as tending toward pretentiousness. 'The mystery of the situation, and the hypnotic effect of that mystery,' he wrote, 'would emerge more shrewdly if the cast didn't appear to know that it was performing a spiritually profound mystery.'[20]

From this point the season went from bad to worse. *Surd Sandwich* by James Blumer, directed by Steve Whistance-Smith, was not long enough for a full evening's entertainment, so Glassco suggested presenting a curtain-raiser of Blumer performing his own songs. Critics found both the concert and the play interminable. As Kareda put it, 'The blurred sense of language, the vague ideas, the awkward poetry all drag the evening to a standstill.'[21] *Surd Sandwich* was followed by Sheldon Rosen's *The Wonderful World of William Bends Who Is Not Quite Himself Today*, directed by James B. Douglas, critically appraised as a very bad play by a very good playwright. Box-office returns were bad for all four plays following *Creeps*, with that for *Surd Sandwich* the worst of all.

Glassco had not directed these last three productions, nor had he put much energy into the development of the scripts, as his attention was monopolized by a new project. The struggling writer/actor David French had written a long one-act play based on his own Newfoundland family transplanted to Toronto. After seeing a pay-what-you-can matinee of *Creeps*, French decided that Tarragon Theatre would be the best place to submit his play. Glassco read the script and liked it immediately, but he also felt that it needed a lot of reworking before it would be ready for production. He arranged to meet French in the theatre's green room to discuss the play. When Glassco offered some admittedly nebulous criticisms and suggestions, the insecure playwright flew into a rage. As French later recalled, 'We had a fierce fight. Bill told me that he liked the play but that it hadn't realized its full potential. I grabbed the script. I called him names and left the theatre. Bill came after me saying, "I'm your friend." I went back in and we talked. That was the only fight we ever had.'[22]

The revised play, *Leaving Home*, opened at Tarragon Theatre in May 1972. It focused on the generational conflict between French's alter ego, a sensitive young man, and his blustery argumentative father, brilliantly played by the veteran actor Sean Sullivan. The Glasscos, worn down by the lack of public response since *Creeps*, had decided that if *Leaving Home* did not succeed they would close their theatre. French alluded to this situation in his later hit play *Jitters*, a backstage comedy containing many allusions to the early years of Tarragon: 'This theatre's done four turkeys in a row. We need a hit or else.' *Leaving Home* received a standing ovation on opening night, newspaper reviews were excellent, and word spread rapidly. This was the success that enabled Tarragon Theatre to endure.

Before the 1972–73 season opened, Mallory Gilbert joined the staff of

Tarragon, the last of what might be called Tarragon's founding family. An American by birth, Gilbert trained at Dennison College in Ohio, and came to Canada in 1967 when her husband accepted a teaching position at the University of Toronto. She began working on productions at the University Alumnae Dramatic Society's Coach House Theatre, a converted synagogue at Huron and Cecil streets not far from the university. This amateur group was a significant local antecedent for alternative theatre in Toronto. Founded in 1918 by female graduates of University College, the club initially allowed only its members to take part in productions, but soon invited males as guests to play male roles or to direct. In 1957 it rented its first permanent theatre (a converted coach house seating thirty-five) with prize money won at the DDF final competition, and in 1962 it purchased the Huron Street building. In the period spanning the decline of the Crest Theatre in the early 1960s and the rise of the alternative theatres at the beginning of the next decade, Toronto's 'Aluminum Ladies' produced the plays that theatre people wanted to see. The Alumnae's repertory featured distinguished playwrights of earlier Art theatre movements (Chekhov, O'Neill, and Somerset Maugham), new writers of post-war Europe (Sartre, Pinter, and Ugo Betti), and a continuing interest in new Canadian plays. In 1968, before Theatre Passe Muraille had yet performed in public, the Alumnae introduced both American and British radical theatre to Toronto with productions of Megan Terry's *Viet Rock* and David Halliwell's *Little Malcolm and His Struggle against the Eunuchs*. With its interest in literate contemporary plays from Canada and abroad, with its continuing informal connections with the University of Toronto, with tough-minded women in its management, with its mixture of aspiring professionals and middle-class middle-aged theatre hobbyists in all areas of production, the Alumnae was an especially important antecedent to Tarragon. Bill Glassco and Dennis Lee co-produced a summer season there in 1964; Brian Meeson directed several plays there before joining Tarragon; and Mallory Gilbert worked there as a producer and a lighting technician when she first came to Canada, alongside such directors as Meeson, Herbert Whittaker, and Urjo Kareda. Gilbert was also producer of Meeson and Glassco's summer season at Trinity Square in 1968; and when her marriage disintegrated a few years later, she embarked on a career as a professional stage manager. In the fall of 1972 she joined Tarragon as theatre manager, where she quickly became Bernie Bomers' protégé in the office. Gilbert succeeded Bomers as general manager in 1975, and remained in that position when Kareda became artistic director in 1982.

Tarragon's 1972–73 season saw the company take its first steps toward infiltrating Canada's regional theatres with its homegrown repertory. The season opened with a three-week reprise of *Leaving Home*, after which the production was filmed by CBC and transferred to Centaur Theatre in Montreal. New productions of *Leaving Home* were given by Theatre Calgary, Neptune Theatre, and Theatre New Brunswick within a year, and many other productions followed. Tarragon's next play that season, *The Last of the Order* by Richard Benner, attracted no such interest. Set in a seedy mission in Mexico, *The Last of the Order* was the story of a broken-down priest, his ex-showgirl companion, and a wandering matador. Kareda wrote the most damning criticism of Brian Meeson's production, calling the script 'unrelieved drudgery' with its ending 'compounded of equal parts of sanctimoniousness and sentimentality.'[23] The next play, however, was another of Tarragon's landmark successes, and introduced another writer who was to become strongly identified with Glassco and the Tarragon. The play was *Forever Yours, Marie-Lou* by Michel Tremblay, a much-produced new playwright, but heretofore only in Quebec and only in French.

Like many of Glassco's major projects, this one started in a casual way. With his difficulty in finding quality scripts during that first season, Glassco had been wondering what potential there might be in new Quebec drama. He met John Van Burek, the director of a fledgling francophone group in Toronto called Le Théâtre du P'tit Bonheur, when Van Burek was helping to put up horror film posters in the Tarragon lobby for the opening of *See No Evil, Hear* .... Glassco asked him if he knew of any Quebec plays that might be appropriate for Tarragon. In response, Van Burek prepared a list of such plays, none of which Glassco had heard of, with accompanying scenarios. When they met to discuss the list, Van Burek described Tremblay's *A toi, pour toujours, ta Marie-Lou* as 'a string quartet,' which greatly appealed to Glassco's musical instincts. As soon as *Leaving Home* opened in May 1972, Glassco and Van Burek began working on a translation of *Forever Yours, Marie-Lou*, and later (with some difficulty) persuaded Tremblay to allow Tarragon to produce it. It opened at Tarragon in November 1972, the first of six Tremblay plays they translated together, and the first of nine Tremblay plays produced at Tarragon by 1988. The following spring, Toronto Arts Productions' version of Tremblay's *Les Belles Soeurs*, again translated by Glassco and Van Burek, brought still more attention to new Quebec drama in English-Canadian theatre.

Glassco's production of *Forever Yours, Marie-Lou* was the third major new Canadian play produced at Tarragon in little over a year, following *Creeps* and *Leaving Home*. It was also a groundbreaking triumph of another sort. To English-speaking Canadians the culture of Quebec had always seemed somehow more exotic and self-sufficient than their own. This impression grew stronger with the greater traffic between the cultures in the late 1960s, under the influence of Expo in 1967, 'Trudeaumania' in 1968, and the Official Languages Act of 1969. The English-language première of Quebec's favourite new playwright was a cultural event in Toronto even before it opened. 'The acclaim given Tremblay's play sharpened our interest, and our expectations,' wrote Herbert Whittaker, himself from Montreal. Still, he found Tremblay's dramatic technique surprisingly familiar: 'We were watching hard to see what makes Tremblay tick, of course, but also to see what makes the Montrealers tingle, theatrically. Our response, we recognized, was hedged by an element of curiosity and envy. As we appreciated the skill with which Tremblay led us over old, rocky ground, we had to suppress an urge to pop up and say "I knew that! Teacher, I knew that. Everybody knows that!"'[24]

For Glassco and Tarragon Theatre, the success of Tremblay in Toronto was significant in another way as well. While not a playwright himself, Glassco was broadening Toronto's understanding of what a Canadian playwright was. While the Factory Lab and the recently opened Toronto Free Theatre were producing plays by and about each other, exploring the human condition of young urban Torontonians, Tarragon and Theatre Passe Muraille were bringing their audiences portrayals of Canadians *other* than themselves: Newfoundlanders or Québécois, farmers or the handicapped. Tarragon and Passe Muraille were the theatres that reached *out* for their material, not just inward. The introduction of Quebec playwrights to anglophone audiences became one of Tarragon Theatre's signal, and continuing, achievements.

The fourth play of Tarragon's 1972–73 season was *The Stag King*, Sheldon Rosen's adaptation of an eighteenth-century Italian comedy. After the sombre tone of the preceding plays, Jane Glassco's handwritten press release promised some levity for Christmas. 'No social issues, no heavy drama, no realism,' she proclaimed; instead 'a vision of oriental splendor filled with satire, suspense and enchantment ... a fairy tale for children of all ages.' Gift certificates and colouring books were marketed for the holiday season, and reviewers were encouraged to bring a child or an elderly aunt on their second ticket. However, the production's creators (Rosen, designer Mary Kerr, and director Stephen

Katz) wished to avoid the label of children's theatre: 'It is being staged for adults,' wrote Jane Glassco, 'but we think children will enjoy it too.'[25] While Kareda found the production 'handsome and often amusing' and praised in particular 'Mary Kerr's dazzlingly coloured and layered costumes and John Mills-Cockell's enchanted score,' he felt the boisterous good humour of the production failed to exploit the imaginative potential of a fairy tale. 'It may seem wretchedly unfestive to carp at a production which has opted for fun,' wrote Kareda, 'but it simply doesn't seem enough to settle for a campy, self-deprecatory approach, when the material – and the exceptional resources of talent you have on hand – are open to so much more.'[26]

An anecdote about *The Stag King* illustrates the distinction between the literate high-toned experimentation at Tarragon and the more risqué experimentation which the public had come to expect of the other alternative theatres. As Jane Glassco later reported,

THE STAG KING was beautiful, but some people were confused by the title. We had calls asking about the cover charge, and was the show running continuously from 2:30 p.m. Finally we were visited by the Morality Squad. They asked if THE STAG KING was a dirty movie or a strip. We asked would they like to see for themselves. They had every intention of doing so. They left after fifteen minutes rather embarrassed, having discovered that 'stag' at Tarragon meant male deer. We blame whoever coined the phrase 'off-Yonge St' theatres for the small theatres, for this delightful confusion.[27]

There is perhaps more significance to this story than just another joke at the expense of the philistines of the morality squad. The phrase 'off-Yonge-Street,' taken from 'off-Broadway,' described not only the location of the small Toronto theatres between 1968 and 1970, but also the radical American origins of their most noteworthy productions, such as Passe Muraille's *Futz* and the Studio Lab's *Dionysus in 69*. But with the emergence of the Factory Theatre Lab in the 1970–71 season, followed by Tarragon Theatre the next year, the geographic focus shifted from off-Yonge-Street northwest to Dupont Street, and the dramaturgical focus from American alternative theatre to new Canadian plays. The garish Yonge Street strip flaunted the hedonism and permissiveness which accompanied the pursuit of 1960s ideals. By 1972, however, these dreams were perceived as false idols, and Yonge Street as just a dismal row of sex shows, hawkers, and prematurely haggard prostitutes. At

Tarragon, on the fringe of the Annex neighbourhood, rooted in values of the family, with long intricate connections with established Toronto culture, 'stag' had always meant male deer; and as Toronto reverted to its native conservatism in the early 1970s, Tarragon's values became, if not quite voguish, at least more artistically acceptable. Tarragon presented plays that were risky but not reckless, arresting but not offensive, a theatre with good manners, good sense, and good taste. 'Apple juice and cookies,' sneered one veteran of the early years at Passe Muraille, alluding to the polite gentility of even the intermission refreshments at Tarragon. But Tarragon's aesthetics reflected that which endured from the turbulent 1960s into the 1970s; and the company's success is partly attributable to its good fortune in having the right aesthetic at the right time.

Bill Glassco returned to Tarragon's customary seriousness with his next production, *Battering Ram* by David Freeman, which opened in February 1973. Another realistic piece, this play was about a wheelchair-bound man who uses his handicap as emotional blackmail when he moves in with a social worker and her teenage daughter. Freeman felt the pressure of high expectations after the success of his first play. 'In fact,' he said, 'working on *Battering Ram* I sometimes felt that the failure of *Creeps* would have been easier to handle.'[28] Pay-what-you-can previews did an overflow business, opening night reviews were full of praise, and *Battering Ram* set new records at Tarragon's box-office as almost all the performances sold out. After its successful run in Toronto, *Battering Ram* was transferred to the Studio Theatre at the National Arts Centre in Ottawa, and new productions followed in Lennoxville, Vancouver, Edmonton, and London (Ontario) in the ensuing two years.

Amid all this euphoria, however, theatre people who disliked naturalism felt that Tarragon's success was undermining the artistic potential of Toronto's alternative theatres. The most articulate of Tarragon's detractors was Brian Boru in *That's Showbusiness*, who took the occasion of the opening of *Battering Ram* to pour scorn on the conservative aesthetics of the Tarragon Theatre:

Its presence on the stage of Tarragon Theatre marks an appallingly low point in the already undistinguished history of Canadian drama. As an indicator of Battering Ram's poverty of thought and expression (not to mention its utter disregard for theatrical achievements of the past seventy years), the play is both set and staged in a most uncompromisingly naturalistic way, certainly the most retrograde and limiting of the theatre's molds.[29]

By 'theatrical achievements' Boru evidently meant the anti-realistic experiments of the avant-garde, which he felt were essential to any theatrical development in Canada:

I find it nearly impossible to believe that the artistic management of Tarragon Theatre could be so blind to the nature of the theatrical event, so crashingly *derrière garde* and so impervious to experimentation. This play and its production would make David Belasco do flip-flops in his clerical collar. Yet Tarragon blithely offers it up as a 'new' work. There may be a theatrical dish stewing in this country, but Tarragon is clearly not part of the recipe.

Kareda, with his love of Chekhov, took an opposite critical stance. He may have been prepared to accept quality in whatever style he found it, but he found it mainly in naturalism. As he wrote in his introduction to the published version of *Leaving Home*,

The strength of that revolutionary 1971–72 season lay with old-fashioned, naturalistic drama, unaccountably considered archaic and unworkable. In new drama, it is the most difficult form to master because it requires reserves of self-discipline. It is heartening that some of the best young writers are willing to commit themselves to a style which must, to many, seem virtually primitive. Perhaps the reward lies in the intensity of public response.

While realism may lack theoretical respectability, as Tom Wolfe has pointed out, it will outsell the avant-garde in an open market. The Glasscos knew on which side of the fence their audience could be found. Indeed, Jane Glassco (apparently with tongue in cheek) used the phrase 'The Latest in Tarragon Realism!' in her pre-show publicity for Freeman's next play the following season.

Tarragon's conservative aesthetics also fed its early rivalry with the Factory Lab. In fact, as Glassco recalls, the competition was healthy for both companies. Since both were dedicated to developing Canadian plays, they were in effect competing for scripts. While Tarragon's comparatively high production standards made it more attractive to some writers, the sheer volume of opportunities available at the Factory fostered a group spirit among others who held naturalism in contempt, notably George Walker and Ken Gass himself. The active development of promising playwrights was the one area in which Tarragon was falling behind. Accordingly, Tarragon's next project was, as Jane Glassco wrote, 'an attempt to extend our range.'[30] Sponsored by the du Maurier

Foundation and evidently inspired by the Factory's *Works* festival, this project involved the staging of six new one-act plays. The plays, with whimsical omnibus titles created by Bill Glassco, ran on alternate evenings for four weeks. *Gifts* was made up of Ken Mitchell's 'This Train' and David Tipe's 'Street Light,' while *Turtle Songs* comprised 'Fish' by David Tipe, 'Electric Gunfighters' by Bryan Wade, 'By the Sea' by James Osborne, and 'Lying under My Tombstone Watching the Subway Go By' by Lance Weisser and Glen Sharp. Directors included filmmaker Allan King, Creation 2's director Louis Capson, and John Plank, later head of the Arbor Theatre in Peterborough. Without the Factory's cavalier attitude toward production exigencies, however, Tarragon's version of *Works* became an organizational nightmare. Reviews were mediocre, and houses poor. The next year, Tarragon turned to public readings instead of performances to develop new scripts.

Tarragon's second season closed with a play that was, in retrospect, a disappointment, *A Quiet Day in Belfast* by Andrew Angus Dalrymple. Dalrymple's experience as a television journalist in Belfast led him to write this play 'to satirize the part played by TV newsmen in the continuing drama of catholics vs protestants in the Northern Ireland feuding.'[31] The script apparently had mainstream potential: Broadway producer Jed Harris had seriously considered purchasing it, and Toronto Arts Productions took out an option to remount it at the St Lawrence Centre. Finally, however, Harris decided it was too controversial for New York (although reviews indicate it was perhaps too glib for Toronto),[32] and TAP's option was not exercised. The most important fringe benefit of this production was that it introduced director Keith Turnbull into the Tarragon family. Over the ensuing two years Turnbull would stage the first productions of James Reaney's celebrated Donnelly trilogy, which was to become one of Tarragon's most enduring accomplishments.

The second season had built on the success of the first. While the first season had been experimental simply in terms of starting a professional theatre dedicated to new Canadian scripts, the second had featured new explorations in terms of repertory, script development, and corporate expansion. The successes were seized and exploited in the following seasons – more plays from Quebec, more co-productions with regional theatres – while the less successful experiments were dropped or changed (such as *The Stag King* and the hectic du Maurier Festival). At this time Bernie Bomers created a second legal company to serve as

Tarragon's publishing arm. This company was named Sage Productions to continue the herb motif at Tarragon (where even the washroom doors were labelled 'Rosemary' and 'Basil'). Sage served not only as agent for *Leaving Home* and some other Tarragon plays (similarly to Great North at the Factory Lab), but also as producer for Tarragon's studio performance series at the Poor Alex Theatre in the 1973–74 season.

In the summer of 1973, Jane and Bill Glassco travelled to Halifax where the Donnelly workshops were under way. Keith Turnbull and James Reaney had assembled a dynamic and talented group of actors, most of whom were also working for Neptune Theatre at the time. There they were conducting daily workshops to develop Reaney's extraordinary research and sense of language into a play – which finally turned into three plays. The Donnelly project had already been discussed with the Glasscos, who at this point committed Tarragon to producing the whole trilogy. That summer, the Glasscos also visited David French in Prince Edward Island, where he was writing a sequel to *Leaving Home* entitled *Of the Fields, Lately.* Jane Glassco's September newsletter promised her audience the Reaney and French plays, a third by David Freeman, and another by Michel Tremblay, plus some scripts which were not finally produced. In her breezy personal style, Glassco aired a few of her pet peeves as publicity director: customers not phoning to cancel their reservations, advertising rates going up, students seeking easy information for assignments on Canadian theatre. Although Tarragon needed donations and volunteers to survive, she wrote, 'most of all, we need you and your friends and families as audiences again. You are the final ingredient to any successful production.' She also reported that the company's fiscal position was excellent: 'We ended the season $600.00 in debt. But that's good in the theatre. It's some kind of miracle in theatre just to meet the payroll week after week for two years.' Glassco was too polite to add that this financial picture was aided by the very small salaries which she and her husband drew.

Tarragon's 1973–74 season, its third, started with three of its strongest productions ever. In September came *Of the Fields, Lately,* which was reviewed in even more glowing terms than *Leaving Home* had been.[33] After six weeks at Tarragon, averaging 95 per cent attendance, *Of the Fields, Lately* was transferred to the Centaur Theatre in Montreal and then to the Neptune Theatre in Halifax, with inquiries also received from the Vancouver Playhouse, Theatre New Brunswick, and the Manitoba Theatre Centre. In November came *Sticks and Stones,* the first of the Donnelly trilogy, performed by the sparkling company which was later established as NDWT. For Tarragon audiences accustomed to realism either stolid (*Leaving Home*) or offbeat (*Creeps*), the verbal and visual poetry of Reaney's play and Turnbull's production was, as Kareda said, 'just plain overwhelming.' Critics were sent scrambling for superlatives, even comparing the play to Greek tragedy and Elizabethan popular drama. The effusive praise was crowned by a letter to the *Globe and Mail* from a teaching colleague of Reaney: 'It is not only the best Canadian play yet written, it is among the best poetic dramas ever written, better, for example, than any of the plays of Yeats, Eliot and Fry to which they might be usefully compared.'[34] *Sticks and Stones* was followed by David Freeman's third play, *You're Gonna Be Alright, Jamie Boy*, in January 1974. Dealing with emotional rather than physical handicaps, this was a bitter comedy about a troubled teenage boy and his bickering insensitive family, all trapped together at home on their 'family night' in front of the TV set. While it received more mixed reviews than Tarragon's two preceding plays, *Jamie Boy* was successfully transferred to the MTC Warehouse and the Centaur Theatre, and has been remounted elsewhere many times.

While 'Tarragon' playwrights French, Reaney, and Freeman held the stage at Bridgman Avenue to begin the 1973–74 season, Sage Productions presented some unusual departures (for Tarragon) at the Poor Alex, a long-established studio theatre off Bloor Street. Sage's first production there, in October 1973, was *The Group of Seven and the Case of the Glowing Pine*. It was a comedy revue written and directed by four former students of Yale's School of Drama, Canadians Bill Peters and John McAndrew and Americans Joe Grifasi and Jim Burt. *The Group of Seven* received excellent reviews, and brought the first Toronto fame to guest performer Fiona Reid. The Poor Alex was also used for Tarragon's production of *Blitzkrieg*, Bryan Wade's offbeat play about the domestic life of Adolf Hitler, featuring a stellar performance by Brenda Donohue as Eva Braun. *Blitzkrieg* was, as Whittaker noted, 'a curious excursion for Tarragon, but one which must be forgiven them for their more significant work elsewhere. But I hope they don't make a habit of this Factory Theatre Lab whimsy.'[35] As the play's director, Eric Steiner, recalls, Jane Glassco also thought it was the wrong kind of show for Tarragon, and nearly closed it prematurely on a couple of occasions. That spring, the Poor Alex was also used to present two touring productions, 'monodramatist' David Watmough's *Pictures from a Landscape* (reminiscences from Cornwall and British Columbia) and Centaur Theatre's *Mr. Joyce Is Leaving Paris*. Operating two theatres at the same time overextended Tarragon's energy if not its finances; indeed, it was the strain of the 1973–74 season which Glassco cited when he announced his sabbatical a year later.

That spring at Bridgman Avenue, Keith Turnbull staged a double-bill of Canadian poetic drama, *Four to Four* by Michel Garneau and *One Man Masque* by James Reaney. Both plays depicted condensed life-cycles, the first through four Quebec women representing four successive genera-tions, the second through a soliloquy performed by Jerry Franken, one of the featured actors of the Donnelly plays. The season there concluded with yet another tumultuous success, Michel Tremblay's *Hosanna*, one of the most celebrated Canadian productions of its decade, featuring the Canadian classical actor Richard Monette in the title role. *Hosanna* is the story of a Montreal transvestite who, dressed as Elizabeth Taylor was in the film *Cleopatra*, re-examines 'her' relationships and self-image after being humiliated at a gay Hallowe'en party. Of all critics, Kareda was least distracted by the play's implicit homosexuality ('Hosanna is about homosexuality only in the way that Othello is about miscegenation'), and his review concluded with awestruck praise: 'The play, the production, these actors make playgoing a privilege.'[36] *Hosanna* played to large houses for seven weeks at Tarragon, was remounted at the Global Village Theatre in the fall, and then was transferred to Broadway for a further three weeks. While the short New York run could not be considered an unqualified success, it seems that American producers as well as Canadian regional theatres were beginning to take notice of Tarragon's record for discovering marketable plays. In an article in the *New York Times*, Kareda noted that *Hosanna* was one of three Tarragon plays to be produced in New York within a year.[37]

Offstage, Tarragon Theatre continued to consolidate its gains and expand its sphere of influence, in a season in which it had also mounted a total of nine productions. The Bridgman Avenue building had been for sale since Tarragon first rented it in 1971, and as Jane Glassco wrote in her newsletter, 'The For Sale signs were so big and prominent people kept asking us why we didn't call Tarragon the *For Sale Theatre*.' During the 1973–74 season the building finally changed hands, and Tarragon was in danger of joining Passe Muraille and the Factory Lab among the homeless. This threat was averted when a five-year lease was successfully negotiated with the new owners. After *You're Gonna Be Alright, Jamie Boy* opened, Glassco travelled west to direct *A Doll's House* at the Vancouver Playhouse, his first external directing assignment since founding Tarragon, and the first non-Canadian script as well. Reviewing the production's subsequent run at the National Arts Centre, Kareda applauded Glassco's excursion into modern classics, and accorded perhaps the greatest compliment a Chekhov scholar could give a director:

But his [Glassco's] strength is emotional complexity (what a Chekhov director he will make some day!) and it is pleasing to report that Glassco's production is as rich an emotional experience as Glassco's David French productions. May he have time, and opportunity, and energy for many more of both.[38]

Indeed, modern classics became a significant part of Tarragon's repertory after Glassco's sabbatical during 1975–76.

In the fall of 1974, a season-long writers-in-residence program was initiated to improve Tarragon's script development process. As the *Toronto Star* reported,

It will give as many as 10 writers a chance to learn all aspects of the production process by attending rehearsals and production meetings, discussing works in progress with dramaturge Bena Shuster, and ultimately mounting some modest professional productions of their own works.

Participants will be selected in September on the basis of work submitted – prose, poetry or whatever – and will include relative beginners and writers with experience in other media.[39]

Shuster chose nine writers with varied backgrounds, assigned them readings on theatre, and brought in established playwrights to discuss specialized genres such as documentary, translation, and adaptation. She also arranged for the writers to attend rehearsals at Tarragon and productions all around Toronto. 'Eventually,' Kareda reported, 'when mutual trust and confidence were built up and deadlines confronted, the writers began to bring their own work into the group, subjecting it to their peers' evaluation.'[40] The group's work culminated in May and June of 1975 with public workshops of their plays, each performed only twice. Although the actors were of high calibre, admission was free and publicity was minimal to try to avoid any counter-productive pressure to succeed. The dynamic and admittedly arrogant Shuster remained dramaturge for two more seasons. A similar play-development program was instituted under Kareda in 1982.

The writers could not have asked for a more intriguing season to observe than the Tarragon's 1974–75 season, its fourth, the last before

Glassco's sabbatical. It opened with *The Night No One Yelled*, a prison drama by ex-convict Peter Madden, produced by the Beggars' Workshop company from Montreal. Madden's first play, *Criminal Record*, had created a stir at a regional Theatre Ontario festival in 1971 because all its cast members (including Madden) were prison inmates. A film documentary about this theatre behind bars led to a job offer from the National Film Board in Montreal and a parole for Madden. Peter Duffy, a physician and founding director of the Beggars' Workshop, staged *The Night No One Yelled* in Montreal. Glassco heard about it, travelled to Montreal so that the company could read it for him, and invited the production to open Tarragon's season while *Hosanna* was tuning up for New York.

The second play of the 1974–75 season was *The St. Nicholas Hotel*, also the second play of the Donnelly trilogy, developed in another summer of workshops in Halifax. As anticipated, audiences were enthusiastic, and the production ran for over two months. At the same time, however, this production set off a public furore over adequate funding for Tarragon. Even before *The St. Nicholas Hotel* opened, Tarragon was using the critical success of the Reaney plays to battle a financial squeeze of which they were partly the cause. Actors Equity had recently upgraded Tarragon's classification, which nearly doubled the minimum wage required for its actors.[41] For its part, the Theatre Office of the Canada Council was unable or unwilling to help make up the difference, even though Tarragon felt it had been underfunded by the Council already. *The St. Nicholas Hotel*, like *Sticks and Stones*, received ecstatic reviews, but only 70 per cent houses – due in part to the longer scheduled run. And the economic realities of producing such a large-cast show in such a small theatre were painfully obvious. As one critic put it, responding to the Glasscos' warnings, 'The Donnellys' trilogy may mean the beginning of the end for the Tarragon Theatre, birthplace of so many native successes. The theatre cannot produce many successes of this magnitude and with this large a cast – 15 players – without digging its own financial grave.'[42] The Donnelly plays were expensive to develop, to mount, and to run, and Bill Glassco made it known that the theatre might have to curtail its current season, or even close permanently, if more generous operating grants were not received. 'I'm not trying to blackmail anyone in public,' he said, 'but it doesn't make sense to go on, considering the money problems we have.'[43]

Critics and the theatre-going public were aghast that funding difficulties might prevent the Donnelly trilogy from being completed. A feature article by critic David Billington, syndicated in the Southam newspaper chain, was the strongest statement of this feeling, and was used extensively by Tarragon as it continued to battle for better funding. 'The treatment of the Tarragon theatre is a national disgrace,' wrote Billington, 'and there is not one member of the Canada Council who should not hang his or her head in shame over their narrow, bureaucratic obscurantism.'[44] Tarragon's management apparently recognized that the completion of the Donnelly trilogy was their strongest weapon in this dispute. As Jane Glassco said, 'To put off the production would risk the break-up of the cast and it's a risk we don't want to run.' Added Billington, 'Nor should they be asked to.' With a guaranteed masterpiece as incentive, funding was finally obtained from two private foundations and a major brewery.[45] The trilogy was completed that season, but not before Glassco's announcement of a sabbatical prompted further rumours of financial trouble at Tarragon. The public debate surrounding the Donnelly plays was very important for the small theatres in Toronto. Besides emphasizing the great impact these companies had had on Canadian dramatic literature in only half a decade, it served to illustrate that they absolutely required public subsidy due to their small size. A success could be just as financially debilitating as a failure in a small house, and much more difficult to close. The high price of success has remained a persistent paradox in Toronto's alternative theatres to the present day.

Tarragon's fourth season concluded in a most appropriate fashion, with three new plays by three 'Tarragon' playwrights. In February 1975 came *Bonjour, Là, Bonjour*, Tremblay's dreamlike allegory of the incestuous love of two young Québécois alienated from their stifling matriarchal family. Uncharacteristically, Whittaker and Kareda disagreed completely about the quality of this play: for Whittaker it was 'the most fascinating of the Montreal playwright's work,' while for Kareda it was 'the most deeply flawed of his plays that we've seen in Toronto.'[46] In March *Handcuffs* brought the Donnelly trilogy to a triumphant close, amid misleading rumours of financial trouble at Tarragon and of friction with the NDWT company. The 1974–75 season ended with *One Crack Out*, David French's pool-hall drama, which received excellent reviews despite a script which both French and Glassco felt was flawed.[47] Perhaps the reviews were coloured by the critics' admiration for the accomplishments of French, Glassco, and Tarragon Theatre in the three years since *Leaving Home*.

Tarragon's sabbatical was announced in March 1975, near the end of the run of *Bonjour, Là, Bonjour*. The press release began:

After four seasons and 24 productions of original Canadian plays, Tarragon Theatre will not be producing next season. Bill Glassco, founder and artistic director of Tarragon, will take a year off to rethink and plan a future direction for the theatre. Our original intention was 'to produce new plays of our own culture as well as possible, to nurture Canadian playwriting talent, to act as a testing ground and as a source of new plays from which other Canadian theatres could draw.' We believe we have come very close to reaching these goals, but at this stage we feel it is impossible to go further without taking time to assess what we have done and to think about where we want to and should be going. We need to find a new direction as meaningful as the first.

The theatre itself would be heavily utilized for the 1975–76 season, however:

Since we want to continue serving our audience, we are in the process of inviting other companies from across Canada, who have been developing new plays to use our theatre space. We have asked the Canada Council and the Ontario Arts Council staffs for assistance with this proposal and their response has been positive and enthusiastic.

In addition, said the release, the playwrights-in-residence program would continue under the direction of Bena Shuster. 'Since the focus of Tarragon will continue to be the nurturing of new writing,' it read, 'this programme provides an important continuity from our present work to future seasons.'[48]

The first response to this announcement was the suspicion that it was euphemistic, that Tarragon was near bankruptcy, a rumour no doubt based on the company's threats not to complete the Donnelly trilogy. However, Glassco quickly assured the press that the reasons given were genuine. 'We need a year off to assimilate all that we've accomplished to date in four seasons, and to re-think our direction for the future,' he said. 'The main factor in the decision is that we're really not excited right now about running a theatre. We've done what we set out to do.'[49] As usual, Kareda delivered the most thoughtful analysis of Glassco's decision. He pointed out that creative artists need time away from their work, although few are able to take it. There is added pressure in a small theatre, he said, because the very existence of the company often depends on the energy of one man. In Tarragon's case, moreover, the company was like a family with Glassco assuming the added burden of father-figure. And, as everyone had noted, it was Tarragon's very success which brought about its current weariness. 'It's much more mental than physical exhaustion,' Glassco told Kareda, 'and I think it was last year, when we took plays to so many places, rather than this one that's done us in.'[50] As he did with most of Glassco's artistic judgments, Kareda agreed wholeheartedly with the idea of a sabbatical:

It seems to me that Glassco's decision is excellently timed. He is stopping at the end of one of Tarragon's most splendid seasons; he is stopping not because he is disillusioned with the small theatre or the new play scenes, but because he wants to consider how they can develop; he is stopping, knowing that the theatre will not be empty next season, but rented to other companies; and, best of all, he is stopping because he knows he must stop. Like most fine artists, Bill Glassco is the first to know what is best for him.

Once again, Tarragon's sabbatical achieved what it set out to. With its funding still in place, the theatre performed (in Mallory Gilbert's words) a 'National Arts Centre function' for the 1975–76 season. Theatre Calgary brought W.O. Mitchell's *Back to Beulah*, the first professional show in Canada for director Guy Sprung, an opportunity which Bill Glassco was instrumental in arranging for him. The Mummers Troupe of Newfoundland brought a collective entitled *What's That Got to Do with the Price of Fish?* Tarragon's theatre was also used by some Toronto companies which did not have their own home, including Black Theatre Canada, Young People's Theatre, and Open Circle. With the sabbatical came changes to Tarragon's founding family. Bernie Bomers left for Vancouver, succeeded by Mallory Gilbert. Jane Glassco left to return to school, later embarking on a career in journalism and television production. Through Kareda's new influence at Stratford, Bill Glassco was engaged to direct Robert Patrick's *Kennedy's Children* at the Stratford Festival in 1975, and *The Merchant of Venice* the year after. *Merchant* was Glassco's first attempt at Shakespeare since *The Winter's Tale* in 1968, and the results were equally disheartening. In addition, the Glasscos' marriage dissolved in separation and then divorce, so that it was a greatly altered Tarragon Theatre which resumed production in 1976.

Tarragon after 1975

After the sabbatical, although the majority of its plays were still Canadian, the most obvious difference at Tarragon Theatre was the inclusion of European and American plays in its repertory. In the

1976–77 season, for instance, Bill Peters directed his own adaptation of Wedekind's 'Lulu' plays, and Glassco directed Chekhov's *The Seagull* in a new translation by David French. Except for this expanded repertory, however, Tarragon continued in the pattern it had established in its first five years. Following the sabbatical, guest productions were a regular occurrence: Vancouver's Tamahnous Theatre in 1976, the Mummers Troupe in 1978, and co-productions with Theatre Passe Muraille, the National Arts Centre, and other Canadian companies. Tarragon also continued to produce Quebec playwrights in English, primarily Michel Tremblay, but also Roland Lepage (*Le Temps d'une vie*, 1978) and Jovette Marchessault (*The Saga of Wet Hens*, 1982). The company's stylistic horizons were greatly expanded by two productions co-directed by master puppeteer Felix Mirbt, Strindberg's *The Dream Play* (1977) and the Brecht/Weill musical *Happy End* (1981). In addition, Glassco continued to bring in younger directors to help share the load, giving needed opportunities to newcomers such as Guy Sprung, Bill Peters, Jack Blum, and Cecil O'Neal, as well as to alternative theatre veterans such as Eric Steiner, Timothy Bond, and William Lane. Finally, Glassco's interest in script development and professional training led to Tarragon's expansion in 1980 with the opening of the Maggie Bassett Studio, named after a long-time Tarragon and community theatre volunteer.

After the sabbatical, too, Tarragon's role as an 'alternate' theatre grew more paradoxical. Tarragon generally produced either established Canadian playwrights (French and Tremblay in particular) or new writers' second or third plays rather than their initial ones. During Bill Glassco's tenure, for example, only one script (Basya Hunter's *Johannes and the Talmud* in 1976) ever progressed from Tarragon's playwrights-in-residence program to its mainstage season. Through its careful methods and conservative aesthetics, however, Tarragon became, in the eyes of the regional theatres, the chief source of readily transplantable new Canadian drama. As Kareda wrote in the *New York Times*, 'A hit at Tarragon can significantly influence repertory in theaters all across Canada in a season or two.'[51] On the management side, in 1976 Tarragon offered (effectively) the first subscriber series in Toronto's alternative theatre, the 'Week One Club,' a reduced-price package for the first week of each production. Most importantly, Tarragon had given its mainstream audience an alternative theatre with which it could cope. This achievement is well summarized in the comments of a Torontonian who was asked to arrange an evening of theatre for out-of-town guests:

Nothing grand, they said. Not the Royal Alex, or the O'Keefe. And nothing smooth, foreign or overpowering either. They wanted to be stimulated by a local entertainment, preferably one that was well reviewed.

As they fidgeted through a vigorous improvisation in a loft that smelled of old tires and the straw mats from which we watched, I realized something: alternate theatre can wear many faces, some of them quite unlovely to all but hard core urbanites. What my friends wanted was the kind of local theatre where the seats are comfortable, the coffee good, the audience eclectic, the artistry soundly organized, and the intelligence ample. I should have taken them to Tarragon.[52]

Before the sabbatical, Glassco's choice of directing assignments was very narrow: nine of the first ten plays he directed at Tarragon were written by Freeman, French, or Tremblay. After the sabbatical, he expanded his directorial range both in Tarragon productions and beyond, with Mirbt's unusual techniques or with outside assignments in opera. Finally, however, after a decade of running Tarragon Theatre, Glassco wished to move on to a larger company. 'I've got to work on large stages to grow as a director,' he said, 'and I've got to run a theatre because there's no way to affect theatre in this country if you don't.'[53] Glassco stepped aside in 1982, appointing Urjo Kareda as his successor.

In 1985 Bill Glassco was named artistic director of CentreStage (the renamed Toronto Arts Productions), completing his rise to command the flagship of mainstream theatre in Toronto. The appointment had the aura of a homecoming. Glassco still worked within sight and sound of the railway tracks, the main line now, in the handsomely redesigned proscenium house of the St Lawrence Centre. His priorities had not changed since Kareda's observation, in 1974, that 'Glassco knows – and this, I think, is the strength of his perspective – that what really matters is the Canadian audience.'[54] At CentreStage, too, Glassco provided challenging (though hardly offensive) plays for the audience he knew so well. Meanwhile Tarragon, after a mediocre first season under Kareda, regained the position of leadership it held between *Leaving Home* and *Handcuffs*.[55] A new Tarragon family became established, producing high quality (though hardly surprising) plays in its same location. The company's stability was underscored in 1987 with the purchase of the Bridgman Avenue building for $1.3 million, making Tarragon only the third theatre company in Toronto (after Theatre Passe Muraille and TWP) to own the space in which it performed. Bill Glassco still directed new Tremblay plays there. Mallory Gilbert was still general manager. And at intermission, you could still buy apple juice and cookies.

6

Toronto Free Theatre

I have a personal belief, which mainly stems from looking at a lot of old photographs, that during its early period Free Theatre had a visual and a production sense which nobody has matched in this country.[1]

Martin Kinch, 1982

The survival of any new theatre company depends on leadership, environment, and chance. In the rise of Toronto's alternative theatres, it appears that survival also depended on each company's ability to find and proclaim (in an appropriate manifesto) a mandate which had so far gone unfulfilled. The Factory Lab, for example, proclaimed itself the home of the Canadian playwright at a time when no other companies were filling that need – or even knew that such a need existed. Tarragon Theatre created a similar role for itself, but with an entirely different style. The alternative theatres which followed Theatre Passe Muraille each developed as alternatives not only to the mainstream, but also to each other. Thus, the beginnings of Toronto Free Theatre, the last of the four major alternative companies, were profoundly influenced by the stature and style of the companies which preceded it. From its initial planning stages, 'the Free' set forth organizational and artistic aims which would differentiate it from its rivals.

Toronto Free Theatre's first distinguishing feature was its group leadership. It was founded with Tom Hendry as managing director, Martin Kinch as artistic director, and John Palmer as literary director. The collective experience of this triumvirate greatly exceeded that of any other alternative theatre in Canada, and of most regional theatres as well. In particular, Tom Hendry had been a co-founder of the Manitoba Theatre Centre, the prototype Canadian regional theatre, and had also served as executive secretary of the Canadian Theatre Centre and as literary manager of the Stratford Festival. The second distinguishing feature of Toronto Free Theatre was that it was established on public funds. Indeed, unlike the other alternative theatres, the stimulus which created the Free was administrative rather than artistic. A trained accountant, Hendry seized upon the sudden availability of LIP grants to provide seed money for a new theatre. From its inception, the Free was able to hire a salaried staff, including what was intended to be a permanent acting company. The idea of a permanent company, made possible because of the LIP money, was the crux of the new theatre's new mandate, as Martin Kinch explained:

The original idea for Toronto Free Theatre was a response to what had been lacking. We wanted to approach a new work with a fairly permanent company to bring more to bear on any given script than we've done in the past.

These days, almost any given Canadian play can get a production. But there is no process of development. The Factory Theatre Lab develops playwrights, the Theatre Passe Muraille develops directors, and we wanted to develop a relationship between actor, director and playwright in a resident sense.[2]

Like its artistic mandate, the Free's most celebrated distinguishing feature was made possible by its instant financial stability: the novelty of free admission. This was no piece of profligate whimsy, explained the founders' proclamations, but was deeply rooted in a philosophy of cultural accessibility. As Tom Hendry later said,

In those days the fact that we were free meant more than that you didn't have to pay. It was a gesture against the notion of theatre as commodity. We were saying, no, it's a service; it's something that a civilised community should have complete access to, like a church, public library or museum. It should be doing the work of its own citizens and should be criticizing and celebrating the life around it.[3]

The name 'Toronto Free Theatre' had a double meaning. It signified not only admission without charge, but also liberty for the theatre artist. As Martin Kinch pointed out, amid the flurry of articles which accompanied the theatre's founding, 'when you're free at the box office, you're free in a lot of ways. You don't go around trying to pick hits and all that nonsense, you're free to find things that will be good things for your people as artists. You're free.'⁴ As at Rochdale College, the joy of freedom at the Free was soon overtaken by the banality of day-to-day business, especially after the job-creation grants began to disappear and fundraising sapped so much of the company's collective energy.

These distinguishing features did not last long. They turned out to be more useful for creating the company than for sustaining it. Within a year, the group leadership had been eroded by jurisdictional disagreements, particularly between Kinch and Palmer. After 1973 Palmer spent much of his time in New York, although he came back to work on specific shows, and Hendry too had other projects which often kept him away from the Free. The permanent company also dissipated within TFT's first year of operation. Casting from a fixed group of actors proved inefficient, as soon as the company began taking on scripts which were not written with their specific actors in mind. Free admission too was soon eroded by new fiscal realities. The glory days of LIP and OFY lasted only about two years before a tourniquet was applied to federal job-creation funds. (Ironically, a factor in stemming this flow of public money into the arts was the Canada Council, which objected to the erosion of its authority in determining relative amounts of government funding for arts organizations.) In theory, free theatre was supposed to appeal to a new audience, a more working-class audience, but in practice the Free's early plays were full of moody intellectuals and unhappy dilettantes. Kinch had envisioned the Free as a kind of theatrical art gallery, where the public would come to view the creations of a certain group of artists. In this analogy, the opening of each new production would correspond to a gallery's change in display. It was an idea that never caught on.

Unlike the Glasscos' Tarragon, then, the theatre which the Free's founders created was not the one they intended to create. What remained after its proclaimed mandates all lay broken, and what gave the Free Theatre a unique place in Toronto's cultural community, was the stylish urban tone of its productions. This tone was mainly due to the productions of Martin Kinch. The gory decadence of many of his shows earned Kinch the nickname 'Mr Sex-and-Violence' and prompted the comment (sometimes attributed to Paul Thompson) that the sum of the Free's artistic intent was to gross out their parents. While this dismissal is not entirely fair, it is true that the Free's productions tended to be more visceral, both in tone and in content, than those of the other alternative companies. While Hendry's skilled grantsmanship had literally made the company possible, it was Kinch's sensibility that was seen on stage. At the same time, a distinctive Free Theatre 'look' was developed largely by Miro Kinch, who was in effect the company's resident designer. While the founders of TFT originally set out to create a laboratory and a forum for showcasing their own talents, the company they created accomplished much more than that. However, the lesson they had learned from Toronto's earlier alternative theatres was that, for directors as well as playwrights, new plays were the most effective way of gaining recognition in their chosen field.

Background to 1972

Tom Hendry was responsible for the founding of Toronto Free Theatre, and in a proprietary sense it remained his company well into the 1980s. Hendry's career in Canadian theatre is perhaps unmatched in its breadth. Born in Winnipeg in 1929, Hendry trained as a chartered accountant, but his passion was always theatre. He began by acting in many amateur theatre productions locally, and also acted professionally on CBC radio. In 1957, dissatisfied with the scarcity of opportunities available in theatre in Winnipeg, Hendry founded a semi-professional company with another young Winnipegger, John Hirsch. They called their venture Theatre 77, because it was located seventy-seven paces from the famous intersection of Portage and Main. At the same time, the board of the Winnipeg Little Theatre realized that the establishment of the Canada Council would create unprecedented opportunities to fund new professional arts organizations. In the summer of 1958, the board invited Hirsch and Hendry to lead a new professional theatre company, initially formed by a merger of Theatre 77 and the Winnipeg Little Theatre, to be called the Manitoba Theatre Centre. Under the tireless leadership of Hirsch and Hendry, and with the financial support of the new Canada Council, the Manitoba Theatre Centre became the model for the network of Canadian regional theatres which spread in the 1960s from sea to sea.

Hendry left the MTC in 1963 to accept a Canada Council Senior Arts Grant, the first to be given for administrative study, to evaluate information systems in theatre management. He recalls that the Council's intention was to standardize business practices and to establish a consulting service in what was becoming a growth industry in the Canadian professional arts. Hendry's report, based on observations of arts management systems in Europe and the United States, became a blueprint for a revamped Canadian Theatre Centre, which had operated as a volunteer agency since 1956. After the expiry of his grant, and after a short stint as administrator for the Canadian Players, Hendry was appointed the first full-time executive secretary of the Canadian Theatre Centre. Funding from the Canada Council and the federal Centennial Commission enabled the CTC to greatly expand its operations along the lines Hendry had recommended. With the CTC, as in other positions before and since, Hendry concentrated on organization and communications. Under his direction, the CTC inaugurated a magazine entitled *The Stage in Canada*, a precursor to *Canadian Theatre Review*; a *Theatre Yearbook*, precursor to *Canada on Stage*; and a directory of theatre artists, precursor to ACTRA's professional directory *Face to Face*. He also advised new professional groups on how to structure their administrative organizations, and brought arts administrator Danny Newman from the United States to help existing professional groups to establish subscription series.

Hendry left the CTC in the spring of 1969 to join the Stratford Festival as its first literary manager, which combined the previous functions of dramaturge and public relations director. A Festival press release described Hendry's new position in this way:

As Literary Manager, Mr. Hendry will work in an area concerned with the relations between writers and the theatre. He will read original scripts and seek out new playwrights, and his own writing will involve commissioned works and play adaptations. Mr. Hendry will also assist the artistic and administrative staffs with ideas on repertory, workshops and project developments, and will act as a spokesman for the Stratford National Theatre of Canada.[5]

But his immediate duties in Stratford were less high-flown than these. Stratford's two directors, Jean Gascon and John Hirsch, did not get along very well, and it was felt that Hendry could help make their working relationship less abrasive. In addition to generally greasing the wheels, Hendry would write the book and lyrics for Hirsch's pet project for the coming season, *The Satyricon*, a new musical with the potential (they hoped) for a transfer to Broadway.

The Satyricon, loosely drawn from several Roman comedies, was mounted with the combined sensibilities of 1960s permissiveness and old-time vaudeville, resembling in places both *Hair* and *A Funny Thing Happened on the Way to the Forum*. Like *Futz* at the Central Library and Palmer's production of *Tango* at the DDF finals, both that same year, *The Satyricon* became something of a *succès de scandale* due to the choice of venue as much as the choice of material. Hendry recalls that students and taxi drivers adored the production, and that the gay community of southwestern Ontario turned out *en masse* to its opening. On the other hand Dora Mavor Moore, the godmother of theatre in Ontario, sternly upbraided Hendry on opening night at the Avon Theatre: 'This is not Stratford,' she said, 'it is nothing but entertainment!'[6] The highly publicized arrests and convictions in the *Futz* affair had taken place while *The Satyricon* was in preparation and in rehearsal. As a result, the issue of nudity on stage was prominent in the minds of Ontario's theatrical community, and presumably of Ontario's police as well. Rumours were abroad that *The Satyricon* would exhibit the Festival's first onstage nudity, and the Stratford police had threatened to press charges against any such display. While in the end *The Satyricon* used G-strings and pasties beneath sheer fabrics, there was another show in Stratford in which the nudity was less demure. This was John Palmer's new play *Anthem*, across the street at the Canadian Place Theatre. Palmer too was threatened with possible police action, and he called the Festival's literary office to solicit Hendry's support. Hendry, of course, was aware of the *Futz* conviction and of the possible implications for Canadian theatre in general and for *The Satyricon* in particular. He quickly agreed to attend Palmer's opening night. There he told some police officers in attendance that he would serve as a defence witness if the play were charged. The police were not heard from again, and Kinch and Palmer's company continued to play to minuscule audiences for the rest of the summer. Hendry, already discouraged by the Festival's slowness to respond to his ideas, became the only Stratford manager to take an interest in their operation (although some younger Festival employees such as Paul Thompson and Anne Anglin also supported it). During this difficult time for Hendry – his wife, Judith, was away in Niagara-on-the-Lake working for the Shaw Festival – he found this exuberant young company especially appealing, and became a regular at their parties and late-night discussions. Playwrights Hendry and Palmer also found that, besides their iconoclastic attitudes toward the Festival, they shared an evangelical fervour for getting Canadian plays produced, especially their own.

Tom Hendry survived the mixed reception of *The Satyricon*, although both director Hirsch and composer Stanley Silverman left Stratford in its aftermath.[7] As Hendry's hostility toward the Festival's management continued to grow, so did his inclinations toward the new Canadian theatre being created by Toronto's underground companies. 'At that

time,' he recalls, 'things were happening in Toronto. Passe Muraille had
started, and gotten into trouble, and that defined a constituency. Either
you were in favour of *Futz*, or you weren't.'[8] For the 1970 Festival season,
Hendry lobbied vigorously for an adventurous series of modern
European plays to occupy the Avon Theatre, a venue which the Festival
had used primarily for opera and for modern classics in previous years.
The obscure plays which he championed – Wesker's *The Friends*,
Mrozek's *Vatzlav*, and Arrabal's *The Architect and the Emperor of Assyria* –
had very weak advance sales, and Hendry's poor commercial/literary
judgment led to his being released at the end of the 1970 season.[9]
Hendry remained resident in Stratford until the summer of 1971, when
he moved to Niagara-on-the-Lake to join Judith.

In the two years following *Futz* and *The Satyricon*, Toronto's alternative
theatres had taken a decidedly nationalistic turn. This new nationalism
was spurred on by playwrights such as Palmer who demanded a place in
Canadian theatre, and by new companies such as the Factory and
Tarragon which were committed to producing only indigenous scripts.
Hendry, himself a widely produced Canadian playwright, took part in
some of the Factory's early playwriting workshops, and was one of only
four delegates to attend both 1971 conferences on Canadian playwriting.[10] Having been involved in producing new Canadian plays in
alternative theatres, in regional theatres, and even at the Stratford
Festival, Hendry adopted the cause of the Canadian playwright. He
helped form a professional association called the Playwrights Circle
(which spawned the Playwrights Co-op as a publishing service), and
wrote passionately on the need to implement the recommendations of
the two playwriting conferences.[11] This issue spread beyond a special-
interest lobby when Hendry's subsequent brief to the Canada Council,
co-sponsored by the Playwrights Circle and the Association of Canadian
Radio and Television Artists, was the subject of a featured interview on
CBC radio.

At the conference in Niagara-on-the-Lake, Hendry heard of a new
federal government program designed to create publicly funded jobs
based on locally identified priorities. This Local Initiatives Program, as it
was called, was based on political exigencies as much as economic ones:
the Liberals' anti-inflation measures had driven unemployment figures
to new post-war heights, and the October Crisis of 1970 had shaken the
public's faith in Prime Minister Trudeau's vision of participatory
democracy and a 'Just Society.' During his tenure at Stratford, Hendry
had drawn up a plan for a theatre company dedicated to nurturing new

plays. In the fall of 1971 he applied to LIP for funds to put his plan into practice. He wished to create a company which would make theatrical use of non-theatrical spaces, concentrating on good lighting, acting, direction, and of course script development. Because marketing unknown plays had proven to be such a headache, at Stratford and elsewhere, and because salaries would be paid by LIP funds regardless of the attendance, Hendry also proposed that admission should be free. At first LIP officials balked at the concept of free theatre, but finally Hendry persuaded them of its value. LIP in turn, having no particular expertise in theatre, sought the opinion of the Ontario Arts Council on Hendry's proposal. Charlotte Holmes of the OAC, the same administrator who had steered Garrard toward Rochdale College in 1968, now advised that Hendry must enlist some co-directors in the project before she could recommend its approval. Hendry asked Kinch and Palmer to come in on the project, and they readily agreed.

Since coming to Toronto after the Canadian Place season in 1969, Kinch and Palmer had become the most prominent directors in an extremely fluid alternative theatre scene. The progress of Kinch's career showed a steady climb toward mainstream credibility through these alternative structures. For Passe Muraille he had directed *Tom Paine*, *Sweet Eros*, *In His Own Write*, *Separate Cell* (for the FUT festival), and *Spring's Awakening*. He had also scored a huge critical and popular success at Passe Muraille with *Vampyr*. For a time, even while artistic director there, Kinch also retained his position as consultant with the Central Ontario Drama League, for which he set up a new training centre in Toronto. He also directed Tom Hendry's *Fifteen Miles of Broken Glass* for a CODL regional festival, where it was judged the best production of a Canadian play. In 1971 Kinch was hired by the mainstream Toronto Arts Productions to direct workshops of two new Canadian plays, Brock Shoveller's *Westbound 12:01* and Michael Ondaatje's *The Collected Works of Billy the Kid*, in the Town Hall of the St Lawrence Centre. He was an assistant director with the Stratford Festival in both 1970 and 1971, and then directed *Tango* at the National Theatre School and *A Touch of God in the Golden Age* at the Factory Lab. Early in 1972, with Toronto Free Theatre just starting up, Kinch staged the Toronto première of George Ryga's controversial *Captives of the Faceless Drummer*, again presented by TAP at the Town Hall. In this production he used several performers making the transition with him from Passe Muraille to Toronto Free Theatre, including Clare Coulter, Brenda Donohue, Peter Jobin, Booth Savage, and Phil Schreibman.

In this period, John Palmer's star was rising even faster than Kinch's. After directing *Memories for My Brother, Part I* at Passe Muraille in 1969, Palmer retreated to Ottawa before returning with his quirky production of *A Doll's House* for the FUT festival. In the 1970–71 season he created *Out to Breakfast* at Passe Muraille and directed a workshop production of his own play *Bland Hysteria* for TAP at the Town Hall. He also took part in playwriting workshops at the Factory Lab, where he soon became dramaturge. In the fall of 1971, with Canadian playwriting a highly publicized issue, three different companies proudly announced projects centred on Palmer. He would direct *Charles Manson a.k.a. Jesus Christ* for Passe Muraille, his play *A Touch of God in the Golden Age* would be presented at the Factory Lab, and, finally bridging the gap to the mainstream, his play *Memories for My Brother, Part II* would open New Year's Eve on the main stage of the St Lawrence Centre. *Memories, Part II* was a disaster, as it turned out, but up to its opening Palmer was the hottest property in Toronto theatre. It was no wonder that Herbert Whittaker dubbed him 'man of the year' in Toronto theatre for 1971.[12] Clearly, Tom Hendry was out to recruit the best young talent in town.

At Kinch's suggestion, Hendry made the fortunate choice of Shain Jaffe as general manager of his new company. Raised in Ohio, Jaffe had studied creative writing and business administration in college, and had run his own small business after graduation. But in 1969 Jaffe's life was thrown into disarray when his marriage dissolved, he was summoned for military service, and he fled to Canada. After settling in Toronto in August 1969, although he had never been involved in theatre before, Jaffe spent some weeks in his room writing a play. He then called several theatres listed in the telephone directory to see if they would produce it. When only the Garret Theatre showed any interest, he rushed over to meet the Garret's director, John Herbert. Herbert, perhaps soliciting for more students, advised Jaffe to take some acting workshops in order to gain some familiarity with theatre, which he did. Jaffe's business background immediately became a valuable asset to Toronto's alternative theatre scene. He helped straighten out Passe Muraille's books when Kinch took over as artistic director in 1969, and later showed Paul Thompson how to maintain them. The next year he gave similar assistance to Ken Gass's Factory Lab. Jaffe was one of the first of a new generation of theatre administrators who, no less than the new generation of directors, made these theatres possible. Along with other unique personalities such as Bernie Bomers and Ralph Zimmerman, Jaffe was a dedicated and creative problem-solver working in a management field which had no established precedents to follow. For such managers, a group which also included June Faulkner at TWP and later Dian English at Passe Muraille, this period became a golden era in all ways except financial. Jaffe's eclectic background was typical of Toronto's alternative arts scene of the time; he was also just one of many Americans who came to Toronto in the waning years of the Vietnam War.

Having recruited some of the best talent available in Toronto's alternative theatre, Hendry again turned his attention to organizational matters. At first he wanted to call his company 'Toronto New Theatre'; but when he learned that there was already a group called New Theatre, he settled on 'Toronto Free Theatre' as being equally descriptive. The name 'Free Theatre' also had fine historical precedents in the celebrated experiments of André Antoine's Théâtre Libre and Otto Brahm's Freie Bühne in the 1880s. At this time Hendry also created a community-based board of directors such as the regional theatres had, the first board of its kind among Toronto's alternative theatres. Hendry's board included influential friends such as television personality Adrienne Clarkson, publisher Richard Schouten, and advertising executive K. Gray Perkins. However, the Free's board differed from regional theatre boards in its strong representation from the artistic side, including its three founding directors. Later, regular actors such as Peter Jobin and Bill Webster also served on the board of Toronto Free Theatre.

The first press release of this new company, issued in January 1972, announced plans to mount a season of new Canadian plays at Hart House Theatre in June, following a month of work-in-progress previews at a location to be announced. While the plays were not yet chosen, the philosophy of the company was clearly spelled out:

TFT aims to develop a repertoire of Canadian material; membership in the company is planned to be entirely Canadian; strenuous efforts will be made in the area of audience development to encourage attendance by persons who, for one reason or another, do not attend the legitimate theatre at present. TFT plans to work in co-operation with theatres having aims similar to its own, to collaborate particularly closely with Factory Theatre Lab [where Palmer was dramaturge] and to maintain close liaison with the newly-founded Playwrights Co-op [of which Hendry was co-founder]; TFT supports completely the recommendations of the Gaspe and Niagara-on-the-Lake playwrights' conferences, and the position of the Playwrights Circle as set out in its recent brief to the Canada Council.[13]

This press release added that, as a matter of company philosophy, admission to TFT's productions would be free of charge.

Hendry chose Hart House Theatre partly because he had managed to persuade the University of Toronto to let him use it rent-free. However, this plain 450-seat proscenium theatre was obviously a poor venue for new experimental plays. When Hendry learned that his new company would be responsible for paying the house stagehands their union wages, an estimated $3000 for the month, the hunt began for a 'found' theatre space. Shain Jaffe led his three directors to a derelict brick gas works on Berkeley Street, a run-down industrial area of the city just a few blocks east of the St Lawrence Centre and the O'Keefe Centre. 'The place was in a hell of a mess,' Kinch later recalled, 'but after we climbed over a wall, waded through broken glass up to our ankles and took a look at the inside we figured it would be ideal.'[4] What they had found was a large interior space, fifty-five feet square by forty-five feet high, in effect their own version of 11 Trinity Square although lacking its fine acoustic properties.

The eventual home of Toronto Free Theatre was constructed in the late 1880s as part of the Consumers Gas Company, which manufactured coal gas for city-wide distribution. After the gas company moved in 1955, its ramshackle buildings lay derelict until 1971, when the Greenspoon Brothers demolition firm was offered a contract to tear them down. The Greenspoons were so impressed with the beauty of their Victorian brick facades and with their potential for redevelopment, that they offered to buy the buildings instead. They hoped to turn the site into a cultural and commercial centre modelled on San Francisco's Ghirardelli Square, a chic waterfront shopping complex reclaimed from an old chocolate factory. Toronto Free Theatre was exactly the kind of first tenant the Greenspoons wanted, one dedicated to bringing Berkeley Street back to life by making it part of Toronto's expanding cultural community. In May 1972, after some sand-blasting and general clean-up, the company moved into the handsome central structure of the complex, sometimes called the Old Opera House because the Canadian Opera Company had once used it as a scene shop. As Bill Greenspoon later admitted, 'When the theatre company came in to rent the place, I took one look at them and gave them three months, maybe six months at best. We were all very gratified when they proved me wrong.'[5]

The acting company was chosen by February 1972, and rehearsals began in temporary premises on Queen Street West. Toronto Free

Theatre had assembled an impressive corps of actors, some of whom were becoming stars in their own right in Toronto's alternative theatres. Besides Coulter, Donohue, Jobin, and Savage, the original resident acting company comprised George Dawson, Carole Galloway, Don MacQuarrie, and Marrie Mumford, some of whom were working under their first Equity contracts. While their salary of one hundred dollars per week does not seem sumptuous, then or now, it was nonetheless a considerable luxury for these actors to obtain continuing paid employment in the theatre. Coulter and Savage recall earning five dollars per week at Trinity Square only two years earlier, and being happy to have the work. The founding of Toronto Free Theatre, on a fully paid and professional basis, operating within the guidelines of Actors Equity, was a triumph of Hendry the mainstream administrator (as opposed to Hendry the alternative playwright). This accomplishment, in the watershed year of 1972, fundamentally altered the nature of alternative theatre in Toronto. It drove the other alternative companies, reluctantly in most cases, toward providing similar pay scales, and heralded a new concern for adequate compensation among young theatre professionals in Toronto. If the gloss came off this 'Golden Age' shortly thereafter, perhaps the reliable paycheque was as important a factor as the simple passage of time.

Since the advent of the Canada Council in the 1950s, public subsidy had been an essential factor in the creation of a professional arts community in Canada where none had existed previously. In advocating free theatre, Hendry pointed out that the difference between paying eight dollars per seat at the ballet, and paying nothing at all at Toronto Free, was merely a matter of degree. Ironically, because of his company's relatively low fixed costs, the free performance actually cost the taxpayer less than the paid one. As Martin Kinch explained early in 1972, 'We'll need a per-seat-occupied subsidy of about $1.75. Stratford needs more than $2.00 in subsidy for every ticket they sell, the National Ballet needs probably $6.00 or $7.00, St. Lawrence Centre at least three dollars, probably more, Manitoba Theatre Centre about four dollars. In terms of ultimate cost to society – it's cheaper to be free.'[16]

TFT was not the first Toronto company to offer free performances, but it was the first to do so as a matter of policy and ideology. As the company presented it, free admission was not just a gimmick, nor just a way of attracting large audiences to a potentially inferior product. Rather, it was a fundamental philosophical statement about the nature of public accessibility to works of art. Herbert Whittaker's review of the company's first production began by treating the concept flippantly: 'So what's for free? Well, not much these days, as you may have noticed.' But Whittaker knew the experiment was a serious one, led by such a high-profile team, and he had followed Canadian theatre for long enough to see their experiment in historical perspective. As he wrote,

The whole enterprise is one that bears watching. Torontonians have always taken it for granted that theatre must pay for itself, largely because of the continuing presence here of touring houses bringing in imported entertainment for short periods, at little or no financial risk to the city.

But with the development of locally created theatre, and the recognition that such contributions must be paid for by subsidy, the concept of a theatre entirely subsidized has not been slow to come. Now we shall see whether our audiences will accept drama when no direct payment is involved. If they do in numbers, further subsidy will likely be forthcoming.[17]

Production at the Free, 1972–75

Toronto Free Theatre was the first of the alternative theatres to be born fully grown. It had a paid staff, paid actors, and its own theatre space. Its directors were not neophytes struggling for first recognition, but were highly experienced professionals. For these reasons, as well as for the noteworthy innovations of free admission and a resident acting company, the critics treated TFT's first productions as events of some significance. However, the very stability of the new enterprise undermined one of Hendry's goals, that of establishing a working theatre in a minimalist style which would emphasize the script development process. Kinch and Palmer, it must be remembered, had been working under hand-to-mouth conditions for years, and not by choice. The opportunity to command resources which would better satisfy their artistic needs was a major factor in their decision to leave Theatre Passe Muraille. Months of rehearsal and weeks of preview performances were the rule for the Free's opening summer season at Berkeley Street. These luxuries of time would have been unthinkable in a theatre dependent upon ticket revenue for its survival, but were perfectly appropriate for the kind of art theatre its founders envisioned. Yet in another way, Hendry felt that his eager young partners had missed the point of the experiment:

What they wanted was a traditional theatre. I was frankly shocked, when we did our first season, to discover how much set and everything we had ...

See, I'd been *through* running a theatre – I'd run Rainbow Stage, I'd run Manitoba Theatre Centre, I'd helped run Stratford – and to me there was no great thrill ... What I wanted to do was to find out how much communication could be established on a minimalist basis ... That did not appeal to them. They were like the third world, they wanted pollution.[18]

Ironically, Hendry's own play which inaugurated the new theatre demanded as much set as any of the others, and even opened with a maid dusting a very bourgeois grand piano.

As at the Canadian Place Theatre, it seems that the critics wanted to like these first productions, but could not bring themselves to do so. The actors, they said, were talented and attractive, but the scripts were disappointing. The first show, Hendry's *How Are Things with the Walking Wounded?*, directed by Kinch, was set at a cocktail party in Montreal during Expo 67, where a homosexual couple was celebrating their first anniversary with some decadent friends. Kareda expressed surprise, considering the gusto of TFT's 'pioneering spirit,' that the play contained so many theatrical commonplaces, notably that of a party which degenerates into 'bitchery, confessions and bleary-eyed early morning truths.'[19] A week later *Walking Wounded* was joined in repertory by Larry Fineberg's *Hope*, which Whittaker found 'an amiable but aimless Gothic comedy ... touched up here and there by John Palmer's chic direction.'[20] Kareda also found much to admire in Palmer's direction, and a few redeeming qualities in the script, but summarily dismissed the characters as comic-book stereotypes ('Little Orphan Annie meets the Munsters').[21] The third play of the summer, Kinch's production of *The End* by John Palmer, certainly brought the best critical response. While praising both the staging and the performances, however, Whittaker worried that the playwright 'has yet to learn to quit when he's ahead. He is a Calvinist after all and the price he pays for using all those naughty words is that he can't stop talking.' Whittaker also noted the potential for narcissism built into this company, established essentially by playwrights to produce their own works. 'When a playwright gets his own theatre,' he wrote, 'nobody's going to stop him when he boils over.'[22]

By the fall of 1972, all of Toronto's alternative companies had achieved some critical success, public credibility, and a fairly dependable constituency. At this time, Urjo Kareda sounded the most thrilling call to arms that the alternative theatres ever inspired. In an article in the *Toronto Star*, Kareda articulated for these theatres a context, a cause, and a public image:

The alternative theatre rushes in where the commercial theatre fears to tread. The alternative theatre continues a ceaseless flirtation with chaos and ruin. The alternative theatre carries hope for the future.

The pattern for these alternative theatres is almost ritualistic. They are born out of a dissatisfaction with existing forms, a frustration and bewilderment in the face of commercial pressures, and a desire to explore new works, new techniques. Catching a foothold is the greatest hurdle; survival is a matter of tenacity.[23]

Kareda's article focused on Kinch, 'nervous, chain-smoking, hortatory,' and his artistic goals with the company. Apparently the idea of giving free performances was perceived as unfair competition by some other small theatres, and Kinch was hurt by their criticism. 'I just think we're building a larger audience for theatre in Toronto,' he said. 'I don't understand the defensive attitude. The theatre in this country is a kind of moribund private club, trying to keep alive a tradition that has no meaning.'

Kareda's enthusiasm for the alternative theatres, which helped promote them as a cultural asset both locally and nationally, was fully vindicated by their many successes over the next few seasons. However, these successes would be of a palpably different nature after 1972, successes of conventional theatre art rather than of alternative modes of expression and communication. Inexorably, the Toronto public began to perceive theatre as an activity which took place in converted warehouses; otherwise, the new mainstream theatre functioned much the same as the old one had.

Kinch admitted in this article that Toronto Free Theatre 'had begun without adequate thoughtful preparation.' That fall, the cracks began to show. *The End* was rewritten and remounted in September, with disastrous results barely averted when the set collapsed the day before the show opened. Palmer as director met this crisis with his customary aplomb, and actually garnered critical praise for his more stripped-down production. The theatre was not so lucky with its next production, however, Kinch's modern-dress version of *Hedda Gabler*, stylistically reminiscent of *Vampyr*, featuring Chapelle Jaffe (Shain's wife) as a demonic Hedda. Performances were suspended when (with the theatre empty, fortunately) a beam fell from the rafters onto the stage some thirty feet below. For the safety of the company and the audience, the theatre was closed while the rafters area was made secure. Office space, dressing rooms, and makeshift heating were also installed that fall, all of which added to financial pressure on the company.

The Free's first season concluded with two highly successful productions in the new year. The first was *Gabe* by Carol Bolt, directed by newcomer Robert Handforth from Ottawa, which opened in February 1973. Although no sets or beams fell down, *Gabe* was a near-disaster of another kind. In rehearsal, huge puppets were used to draw pointed parallels between the contemporary Métis characters (Louis and Gabe) and their historical referents, Louis Riel and Gabriel Dumont. As opening night approached, the play remained long, ponderous, and baffling, but it was rescued with the help of John Palmer. Palmer was usually at his best in a crisis (the production of *Memories, Part II* at the St Lawrence Centre was a notable exception), and he suggested cutting these allegorical elements. *Gabe* finally opened as a spare story of modern drifters, with muted allusions to their ancestors adding to the poetic realism. The play retained these changes when it was published. *Gabe* was followed in April by *Me?*, a fine first play by Martin Kinch, directed by John Palmer. *Me?* was a realistic drawing-room tirade, a bit like a 1970s version of *Look Back in Anger*, about an egotistical but talented young writer besieged by his estranged wife, his current mistress, and his homosexual best friend. Critics were intrigued that Kinch served as playwright and Palmer as director, a reversal of their usual working roles; oddly, Palmer's extensive directing experience was largely ignored, or perhaps not well known. *Me?* caused quite a stir in Toronto's theatre community, in no small measure due to its recognizably autobiographical content. As William Lane put it, in his introduction to the published play, 'every one of the four major characters of the play were in the audience that [opening] night.'[24] Critics applauded Kinch's 'well-written and perceptive script' and Palmer's 'strong and subtle direction.' Miro Kinch's set was unforgettable, an apartment interior dominated by 'a rusty, dented, topless, golden four-door sedan as part of the sitting room's furniture.'[25]

Toronto Free Theatre had, in retrospect, a highly successful first season. Although the opening plays by Hendry and Fineberg did not appeal to the critics, the four subsequent productions were very well received. Moreover, two of these plays (*Gabe* and *Me?*) were soon remounted elsewhere and published, to become part of the growing repertory of stageworthy new Canadian drama. In a newsletter sent to its supporters in June 1973, TFT summarized the year's activities. Its six productions had played to more than 17,000 people, averaging 98.5 per cent of capacity in their 99-seat house. Its Monday night series entitled 'Poetry and People,' featuring such readers as bp Nichol and Dennis Lee, attracted 685 people to ten performances. Special events had included experimental music, community workshops, midnight performances by outside groups, and two evenings of poetry and electronic music given by Fabian Jennings and Allan Rae, the team which had created *Charles Manson a.k.a. Jesus Christ*. In this newsletter, a new manifesto trumpeted the company's accomplishments in its first year, not just in surviving, but also in affecting the nature of alternative theatre in Toronto, and therefore the nature of theatre in Canada:

WHY FREE?

The TORONTO FREE THEATRE, through its policy of free admission, has created a large and diverse audience. We have found that our audience responds enthusiastically and with discrimination when presented with something of quality and relevance, refuting those who implied lack of general public interest in the performing arts. This audience makes highly creative demands on the theatre's ability to communicate and on the nature and contents of that communication. Unencumbered by the necessity to produce 'commercially acceptable' work which tends toward the slick or competent applications of formula technique, free theatre has allowed the freedom conducive to the highest degree of exploration, experimentation and the resultant rise in quality.

We are pioneering a dimension in cultural accessibility comparable to the first experiments in free public education during the nineteenth century. It is interesting to note that many of the individuals involved in the creation and development of the TORONTO FREE THEATRE are among those who pioneered the concept of alternative theatre in Canada and have established it as the most exciting theatrical force in this country today.

Until the emergence of these small theatres, economics, programming and availability precluded attendance by the vast majority of the community. Now, through more relevant programming, reduced admission prices, and the concurrent development of a truly Canadian style, the market potential and the scope of the theatre has substantially increased. With the birth of TORONTO FREE THEATRE the first truly accessible theatre now exists.[26]

For the next season, this newsletter promised seven productions, an expanded program of playwriting and directing workshops (under the title 'Open Space'), and an expanded series of music and poetry readings as well. In addition, it said, the policy of a fixed company of artists was changed to one of 'associate artists,' to allow for a broader creative input and a greater diversity in play selection.

The first season's successes had been largely those of Kinch and Palmer: Hendry had not been involved in a specific production since

Walking Wounded had opened the theatre. In the summer of 1973, both Kinch and Palmer were away. (Indeed, Palmer was to return infrequently, arriving at points of crisis from New York or Ottawa like an absentee governor.) Hendry had written a play he wanted produced, although it was little more than a scenario when rehearsals began, and persuaded Eric Steiner to come over from the Factory Lab to direct it. The play was *Gravediggers of 1942*, a bitter musical revue about the Dieppe fiasco suffered by Canadian troops in World War II. As with *Maybe We Could Get Some Bach* the previous year, Steiner managed to find an ironic edge to the production which reflected the subject matter, while he and the cast improvised wildly and Hendry scrambled to provide new rewrites. Brenda Donohue's performance in *Gravediggers* was widely praised, but a throat ailment forced her to leave the show a few days after it opened. This was the first of a series of illnesses afflicting this brilliant young performer, ending with her death of cancer in 1979 at the age of twenty-nine.

The Free Theatre's ensuing production, *Clear Light* by Michael Hollingsworth, is the one for which its early years are most vividly remembered. As with *Futz* in 1969, the pre-show publicity for *Clear Light* focused on the sensational elements of the play – although in this case the sensational elements *were* the play to a great extent. It begins quietly enough, with two couples playing cards in a squalid apartment while a saxophone plays offstage; but soon it degenerates into an orgy of hallucinogenic drugs, mix-and-match sexual coupling, and offhanded violence. As Kareda described it,

The play's incidents are a dark nauseating reflection of the characters' moral, physical, psychological emptiness. There is a very great deal of sex – heterosexual, homosexual, lesbian – almost always connected with humiliation, violence, rape fantasy. Excrement, semen, vomit, all in their midst, are accepted casually. Brutality is squalid and inevitable. In the play's most stomach-turning moment, we discover (but do not see) that an infant is found in an oven. Parts of him are subsequently devoured.[27]

Hollingsworth claimed that the title *Clear Light* was taken from the Tibetan Book of the Dead, although it was common knowledge at the theatre that this was also a nickname for a certain strain of LSD. It was reported that a number of actors had refused to appear in the production; indeed, the cast list includes none of the Free's original acting company nor any of its 'associate artists' of the time. Even the director's feelings toward the play were ambivalent, if not perverse. Said Kinch: 'The play revolts me. The people in it revolt me. I hope that disgust is creative. The play should be done.'[28]

While the Free Theatre rejected the domestic realism that had brought success to Tarragon Theatre, it explored a different kind of realism, one that became popular a decade later in gory films aimed at adolescent audiences. It was the very effectiveness of this realism which Kareda found was the only distracting element of the production: 'How do you convincingly show an iron pipe striking a bald head so that blood spurts in the air? How do you simulate a razor slashing a naked chest? What do you use to represent cooked human flesh?' For Kinch, the play was worth doing because of its social message, which at bottom was very puritanical. For Hendry, it was worth doing because of the unique voice of a new playwright. And for the 23-year-old Hollingsworth, a former rock musician, it was a way of making a name for himself in Toronto theatre. 'When I wrote *Strawberry Fields* and *Clear Light* I wanted to be notorious,' he said. 'I was the beast walking Toronto and I was happy with that role. Of course I missed the implications of what that meant. I got them later when I didn't work for three years.'[29]

While Kareda and other reviewers put forth metaphorical explanations for the play's degradation and depravity, the older Whittaker seemed to feel angry, even betrayed, that the support he had given these young artists should have led to such gratuitous shock tactics:

I get the impression from time to time that the Toronto Free Theatre is desperately trying to attract attention ... even from the morality squad.

Tom Hendry's all-out venture may well get that this time, for any one of the people who walked out on the opening night looked as if he might stop by at the police station. People don't want pornography even when it's for free, I guess.[30]

From a critic of Whittaker's stature, this invitation to the police is indeed shocking, especially considering his tongue-in-cheek toleration of nudity and sexuality in alternative theatre productions in preceding years. It is safe to say that Whittaker himself was deeply offended. His original interest in the Free Theatre's experiments with existing subsidy and repertory practices went completely sour in the next year. He was, one must remember, one of John Palmer's most important boosters, and certainly respected Tom Hendry's formidable theatre experience. But in the end, Martin Kinch's fascination with and facility for staging explicit sex and violence exhausted even Whittaker's seemingly endless supply of good will.

Police action on *Clear Light* was neither swift nor harsh. Morality squad officers watched the play on Friday October 26, almost a week after its official opening. After the show they advised the cast and theatre staff that they would recommend that obscenity charges be laid. The following Monday, TFT's lawyer Patrick Sheppard requested a meeting between representatives of the police and of the theatre (himself, Jaffe, and Kinch). Also invited were representatives of Actors Equity. That evening, when the whole company met to discuss the events of the day and to vote on possible courses of action, Equity representatives arrived too. But their only interest, the company soon realized, was in protecting their members; they had no interest whatsoever in opposing police censorship. As Sheppard later complained to Equity's counsel,

> They refused to permit the general meeting of the Theatre to go ahead; they insisted on meeting with their members prior to the general meeting of the [company's] membership; they took a separate vote in the matter; they not only successfully drove a wedge between the Equity members and the rest of the company, but they heavy-handedly dealt a destructive blow to the whole process of Free Theatre ... the results of the vote were almost unanimous for the curtailing of *Clear Light*, which was then done and the police were advised, thus avoiding any Criminal charges being laid. [31]

In Equity's view, evidently, the theatre was simply an employer whose actions had placed their members at risk.

Censorship was an issue once again. Kareda, who like much of the theatrical community was revolted by *Clear Light* but admired it nonetheless, reported that the morality squad's 'relative lack of success' in recent years (especially in the final outcome of the *Futz* case) had 'led us to a false sense of security.'[32] At a public meeting on the issue two months later, police inspector John Wilson pointed out that the Free Theatre had been given a number of options which might have kept the play open; indeed Wilson, probably unaware of Equity's role in the matter, seemed surprised that the theatre had not exercised any of these options.[33] There were a number of reasons why the producers of *Clear Light* capitulated more easily than those of *Futz*. The producers of *Futz* had been forced to defend themselves at any cost because of the possibility of disbarment, and because charges had already been laid. In the case of *Clear Light*, however, the charges were merely threatened, and could be (and were) averted completely. Closing *Clear Light* also represented little financial loss to the company, since box-office revenues were not a major consideration.[34] On the other hand, a lengthy court case could easily exhaust the company's resources, and any lingering emphasis on pornography could greatly damage its ability to secure public and private funding. The Free also wished to continue operating as an Equity company, an issue which had not affected either Jim Garrard or Trio Productions. In all these arguments, the Free Theatre had nothing to gain by keeping the show running, but plenty to lose. Kinch and Hendry discussed keeping the show open on principle, with a staged reading by the theatre's permanent staff. Only then, says Hendry, did they discover that this staff included some American draft dodgers and deserters who would face lengthy prison terms if repatriated. As Hendry put it, 'I couldn't afford to be a hero at the expense of these people.'[35] So *Clear Light* was extinguished, although its brief sensational run remains something of a legend of its time. Among some critics, however, there lingered a sense of betrayal at the way in which the Free buckled under official pressure.[36]

The Free's 1973–74 season resumed in November in less spectacular fashion with Marc Gélinas' production of *Vallières!*, by Paul Thompson and Penny Williams, a documentary drama about the Quebec revolutionary Pierre Vallières. Originally a radio play, *Vallières!* was performed with only a single actor, several tape-recorded voices, and a *son et lumière* show which seemed improvised and haphazard. By all accounts *Vallières!* was an excruciating bore. Shain Jaffe, house manager as well as general manager, recalls the tenacious actor Chris Kelk giving a spirited performance to an audience of one, a man who had evidently dozed off during the first act. The tiny houses it drew, however, vindicated Tom Hendry on one point: that audiences would not come to see free theatre if it was of poor quality. This show was followed, in February 1974, with *Red Emma* by Carol Bolt, a musical biography of Russian-American anarchist Emma Goldman. Kinch's production of *Red Emma* drew generally glowing reviews, although the Free's nagging health problems recurred when laryngitis struck lead actress Chapelle Jaffe and the show's opening date had to be postponed.[37] The Free's second season ended in May with *Troll* by Des McAnuff, yet another new script directed by Kinch. *Troll* was a gothic science-fiction story about two women imprisoned in a modern research laboratory so that their disfiguring skin disease could be observed by malevolent male scientists. McAnuff, a theatrical prodigy from Toronto and later an award-winning stage director in the United States, spent the following season as assistant to Kinch at Toronto Free.

In January 1974 the Free announced that cutbacks in LIP funding made it necessary to start charging admission for some performances; and by the end of the season it was obvious that job-creation grants would not support the theatre much longer. Despite the erosion of free performances, the philosophy of cultural accessibility was still considered fundamental to the Free. Therefore, the company embarked on a fundraising campaign to gain more support from non-public sources in order to expand its seating capacity. A handsome brochure was printed for this campaign, outlining TFT's formidable accomplishments in its first two years of operation. In appealing for a share of business' promotional and charitable budgets, the brochure stressed the Free's mainstream organization and stability:

A down to earth, widely representative Board of Directors works together with a management that is the most dynamic and flexible in the country. Their combined efforts have made TFT a model of union-management relations, of debt-free orderly growth and of imaginative, practical aspiration. Stable but never static, TFT finds that experience and excitement make a winning combination.[38]

This brochure also described the company as leaving its Inception Period (1972–74) to move into a Development Period (1974–76) which was to feature 'carefully controlled expansion.' At the same time, TFT printed a coil-bound booklet entitled *Toronto Free Theatre: Corporate Fundraisers Guide* as information for volunteer fundraisers helping in this campaign. Because of its purpose, this document is a remarkably thorough summary of the company's origins, personnel, ideals, and plans for the near future. It even includes box-office percentages for all TFT productions to date, from *How Are Things with the Walking Wounded?* through *Troll*, and the result of a survey of TFT's audience composition which had been commissioned by the Arts and Cultural Branch of the Secretary of State. In this kind of grantsmanship, the influence of Tom Hendry's mainstream experience is unmistakable. The alternative theatre may still have required guerrilla administration in its day-to-day work, with the problem-solving skills of general managers like Jaffe tested to their limits. However, through Glassco's familiarity with the Toronto business elite, and through Hendry's experience in navigating proper channels, Toronto's alternative theatres acquired a mainstream methodology and vocabulary for administrative process.

Despite continued financial pressure, the Free Theatre recaptured some of its excitement in 1974–75. The season opened in October with Michael Ondaatje's *The Collected Works of Billy the Kid*, one of Kinch's finest productions in Toronto. Earlier versions had been presented in 1971 in a workshop production at the St Lawrence Centre (also directed by Kinch) and in 1973 at Stratford's Third Stage. In his review of *Billy the Kid*, Kareda compared Ondaatje's poetry to Reaney's in the Donnelly trilogy ('words that dare to be extraordinary') and praised the humour and eroticism evident in Kinch's direction.[39] Whittaker, however, showed no inclination to forgive the company that had given him *Clear Light*. 'Kinch is less concerned with the poetic and mythological aspects of Ondaatje's view of the American folk figure than he is with exploring its basis in violence.' As a result, he wrote, Ondaatje's images seemed to have been 'ripped untimely from his deep-rooted vision [and] held up, still bleeding.' Whittaker also added, cryptically, that 'you'd probably get the most out of him [Nick Mancuso's Billy] if you got stoned first.'[40]

The production to follow *The Collected Works of Billy the Kid* was planned to be a musical by George F. Walker and Steven Jack (who had written and performed the music for *Gravediggers of 1942*). Less than three weeks before the announced opening, however, the director, John Palmer, realized there was a crisis brewing, and he rose to meet it. Palmer informed Jaffe and Kinch that the planned production could not be completed in the time remaining and, with their assent, cancelled work on the production. Overnight, Palmer devised a new scenario for a non-musical play to be called *The Pits*, which would be collectively created by the cast. The physical design was an important part of the premise, Palmer explained to his actors. They were to portray the daily activities in a seedy Toronto rooming-house. The skeleton of the house itself would occupy the middle portion of the theatre, entirely surrounded by eight-foot-tall platforms from which the audience would view the action. The audience would also be free to move about to follow certain characters more closely (anticipating the later 'environmental' hit *Tamara*), or even to descend stairs to the floor level if they wished. *The Pits* was very well received, and a thrill for its creators. Produced under great duress, *The Pits* called upon the ensemble spirit which had permeated the earliest successes of Toronto's alternative theatres, and brought out some of the best improvisational qualities of those times. The success of both *Billy the Kid* and *The Pits* represented a last tip-of-the-hat to the glory days of Kinch and Palmer at Trinity Square.

Kinch remembers his final production of the 1974–75 season, *Heat* by American playwright William Hauptmann, as one of his best. Based on a series of real-life murders in Texas in the 1960s, the play was dismissed by Kareda, however, as an 'academic piece of playwriting' heavily influenced by Büchner's *Woyzeck*.[41] Whittaker on the other hand praised the design, directing, and acting in *Heat*, but still felt compelled to express his distaste for the Free Theatre's preoccupation with sex and violence. 'Heat is a tawdry horror story,' he wrote, 'with which Kinch's vigorous directorial instincts invest the fascination the subject has for him.' And, noting that the real-life model for the play had recently been stabbed to death in an Arizona prison, he added, 'That vote of confidence out in Arizona should attract the right kind of audience to the Free Theatre.'[42] It was Whittaker's last slap at Kinch and the Free, as he retired from the *Globe and Mail* a few months later.

Toronto Free Theatre had produced only three plays in 1974–75 – *Billy the Kid, The Pits,* and *Heat*. The company was obviously suffering from the creative exhaustion that afflicted all the major alternative theatres at mid-decade. These companies had been so successful in reforming the sensibilities of Toronto theatre that, in only a few years, they were perceived as stable institutions, even as an inbred establishment, by new young artists who continued to gravitate to Toronto. At this time Martin Kinch, through a series of interviews and articles, became something of a spokesman for creative exhaustion in Toronto. In one such interview, just before the opening of *Heat,* Kinch pondered the absurdity of finding himself in a position of leadership so early in his career, with so few role models for himself in the larger theatres. At the same time, he felt he was no closer to his goal of taking over, or at least affecting, the larger regional theatres. With Tarragon's Glassco ceasing production for the 1975–76 season, Kinch reflected on the malaise which had overtaken the initial successes of these companies: 'It's damn hard to keep up the excitement,' he said. 'I got very depressed about the situation last year. There seemed to be creative exhaustion everywhere. We had fulfilled the first promise and many of us simply didn't know where to go from there.'[43]

Ironically, part of this malaise was due to the more widespread financial rewards which these companies fought so hard to achieve for their writers and actors, particularly at Toronto Free Theatre. CBC drama, for example, was becoming increasingly active, revitalized to some extent by writers groomed in the alternative theatres, and provided better pay and more recognition for writers and actors than the small theatres could. (Kinch himself left theatre for the CBC a few years later.) But Kinch also recognized that the problem went deeper, that the aggressive idealism of the 1960s which once fuelled their projects had subsided, grown old perhaps; and despite their years of toil, there still seemed to be no opportunity for growing into larger theatre experiences within the Canadian context. A career in Canadian theatre, he felt, was still a dead end:

> What should be happening now, and is to a small extent, is that the people – the writers and actors and directors – who have worked their way up in the Toronto theatres, be allowed into the major theatrical institutions of the country. That will make room for the new ideas coming up here, which is what will keep our particular perspective alive and help renew the larger institutions. If this process doesn't happen, I don't really like to think of what will become of places like the Free Theatre – or the big theatres for that matter. Everything will stagnate.[44]

The Free after 1975

The Free's 1975–76 season consisted entirely of new Canadian plays. These included Kinch's *April 29, 1975*, Alianak's *Passion and Sin* (each directed by the author), and Lawrence Russell's *The Mystery of the Pig Killer's Daughter* directed by William Lane. Each play had a violent foreboding tone and was experimental in some respect. Nonetheless, it was apparent that the creative exhaustion of which Kinch had spoken was debilitating Toronto Free Theatre. Already disappointing, the season came to a dreadful close with Tom Hendry's *Byron*, directed by Kinch. In this play, set on the eve of Lord Byron's fatal decision to go to Greece to fight for freedom, Hendry was striving for a baroque richness of language in an anti-realistic style. The criticism it provoked was brutal. 'Byron an egotistical drama of stupendous tedium,' pronounced the *Globe and Mail*, whose new critic, John Fraser, in a lengthy vivisection of its failures, offered this insight into the symptoms of creative exhaustion: 'The production has a weird feeling of everyone – director, actors, designer, composer – trying to pretend their hearts are all there, indeed going overboard to prove the point, when in reality they have been left three miles back, mired in common sense.'[45] Equally damning was the production's curt dismissal by the *Star*'s new critic, Gina Mallet ('flop is too kind a word ... Catastrophe is more apt'),[46] whose acid commentaries and anglophile reputation so infuriated the smaller theatres over the ensuing years. It must have been with some sense of relief that Toronto Free Theatre shut up shop in May 1976, exactly four years after moving into 24 Berkeley Street, to undertake major renovations and expansion.

Judith Hendry, who replaced Shain Jaffe as general manager that year, shepherded the company through the difficult renovation period. In January 1977, after expenditures of a half million dollars, the renovated theatre reopened with its original capacity increased from 99 to 175. A second theatre ('Theatre Upstairs') was created in another brick building in the old gas works, and a handsome glass-and-steel lobby was built between the two. The renovations reflected the Free's continuing ambitions toward mainstream status. As the *Star* put it, 'With its new complex and an operating budget of $300,000, Toronto Free Theatre is stepping from the ranks of experimental theatre into shouting distance of such institutions as the St. Lawrence Centre.'[47] One problem with the renovations, however, was that they did not create a theatre large enough for the Free to take this step effectively. Indeed, the Free's revenue-producing capability, box-office and otherwise, has never kept pace with its mainstream ambitions.

Although revitalized by the new plant for a short time, the Free was considered moribund by the end of the decade. This was partly the result of the company's slowness to rejuvenate its leadership despite an obvious need to do so. Since 1975 Kinch had clearly been grooming William Lane as his successor. Lane, a director from Ottawa, joined the company as dramaturge in 1975, became associate artistic director in 1977, and stepped up to acting artistic director in 1979 when Kinch left for a year's sabbatical. However, when Kinch chose not to return to the Free, accepting a position with CBC television instead, Hendry decided that Lane was not the artistic director he wanted. Accordingly, Hendry appointed himself resident producer of the Free, and named a nebulous artistic advisory board composed of eight directors, including Lane, Kinch, Steiner, and John Hirsch. Another member of this advisory board was Guy Sprung, a young director from Montreal, whose touring production of *Paper Wheat* had been the biggest draw of TFT's 1979–80 season. Sprung was named consulting director in 1981, and artistic director in 1982. At that time, Hendry also gave up his position as president of Toronto Free Theatre.

Sprung's tenure at the Free was characterized by mainstream ambitions even more obvious than Kinch's and Hendry's had been. He arrived with an outstanding record for staging new Canadian plays, a record he enhanced with his first production at the Free, Anne Chislett's *Quiet in the Land*. Thereafter, however, few of Sprung's best-known productions were new plays, and most were classics, including *The Changeling, Hamlet,* and *A Midsummer Night's Dream*. The *Dream*, given for free in 1983 and 1984 in a beautiful hillside setting in Toronto's High

Park, re-established the company's tradition of offering free theatre, and greatly raised its profile and popularity locally. As in its early days, Sprung's TFT barely survived cash-flow crises on several occasions; but in April 1986, its mainstream ambitions made headlines once again when Sprung and Bill Glassco announced a planned merger between Toronto Free Theatre and CentreStage (the renamed Toronto Arts Productions). The merger was consummated over the ensuing two years, the new supercompany finally adopting a new name, the Canadian Stage Company, in 1988. Sprung and Glassco's ambition in this was to create a company of 'national importance and scope,' an eerie echo of Kinch's hope (expressed a decade earlier) that Toronto Free Theatre would become 'the true national theatre of Canada.'[48] The merger also represented a perfect amalgam of the original nationalist and mainstream ambitions of the St Lawrence Centre, Tarragon Theatre, and the Free.

7
The Off-Yonge-Street Theatres

The major influence on current Canadian theatre is neither classical nor Canadian ... Rather it is Off-Broadway.[1]

Herbert Whittaker, November 1969

While Jim Garrard's Theatre Passe Muraille was the most prominent of the alternative theatres founded in the late 1960s, it was by no means the only one. Because these companies all displayed influences of off-off-Broadway theatre, and because they were all located off Yonge Street, the press sometimes referred to them as the 'off-Yonge-Street' theatres. The influence of American alternative theatre in Toronto reached its peak in the 1969–70 season, the year of *Sweet Eros* at Passe Muraille, *Dionysus in 69* at the Studio Lab, and *Hair* at the Royal Alex. When Toronto's interest in American alternative theatre declined after 1970 (again, the FUT festival is a useful landmark), the term 'off-Yonge-Street' disappeared. In 1971 and 1972, audience interest shifted away from American models and toward new Canadian drama. At the same time, the centre of Toronto's alternative theatre shifted from Yonge Street northwest to Dupont Street, where both the Factory Lab and Tarragon Theatre were located.

After Theatre Passe Muraille, the three most important of these off-Yonge-Street theatres were Ernie Schwarz's Studio Lab Theatre, Robert and Elizabeth Swerdlow's Global Village Theatre, and Louis Capson's Creation 2. In retrospect, the rise and fall of these theatres also shed some light on the remarkable perseverance of Theatre Passe Muraille. What separates Passe Muraille from the others is that it successfully left its radical origins behind, first to flourish as a nationalist theatre, then to find a mainstream audience. The ways in which the other off-Yonge-Street theatres failed to join this new mainstream are as numerous as the companies themselves. Like Passe Muraille, each of them moved away from their American influences and toward Canadian content, yet they somehow failed to become as important a part of the nationalist 'Toronto movement.' While these companies were part of the greater theatre community of Toronto, they were not acknowledged to be as important to its artistic leadership. It is significant, for instance, that the New Directors Group chose not to include Schwarz, Swerdlow, or Capson (or even George Luscombe) among its members, even though Creation 2 and the Global Village played important roles in the FUT festival.

As critical and popular acclaim began to accrue to Toronto's four major alternative theatres during their nationalist stage, these other companies produced fewer successes and attracted less critical attention. Perhaps this, like the sudden popularity of Canadian scripts, was also due to that most elusive of theatrical qualities, fashion. What is certain is that the eventual demise of these companies was mourned only perfunctorily by Toronto's theatre community, and that their contribution to the alternative theatre scene is largely forgotten nowadays. Like their more durable contemporaries, these off-Yonge theatres helped to revitalize Toronto's theatrical self-image, and thus helped to establish a receptive environment for the city's subsequent triumphs in producing new Canadian drama.

Studio Lab Theatre

The Studio Lab Theatre was well known as a children's theatre company before it began presenting experimental plays for adults. It was founded as the Studio Theatre in 1965 by Ernest J. Schwarz, who taught acting classes and produced children's theatre to support his company. In 1968 the acting workshops he had been leading began to present public performances, essentially bringing audience participation techniques of children's theatre to off-off-Broadway experimental plays. Between *Futz* in 1969 and *Creeps* in 1971, alternative theatre became an established force in Toronto but had not yet found its nationalist voice. In this period, the Studio Lab was the leading rival of Theatre Passe Muraille because of the popular success of a single production, *Dionysus in 69* (later *Dionysus in 70*). Despite this success, however, the Studio

Lab was an accepted member of neither the mainstream theatre nor the underground. After *Dionysus in 70* finally closed, the Studio Lab produced two successive failures, lost its home theatre to urban development, abandoned its Toronto base, and ceased to have any influence in Toronto theatre.

Ernest J. Schwarz was born in 1934 in Cleveland, Ohio, and was educated at Allegheny College (in Pennsylvania) and at the Yale School of Drama. Between terms at Yale, where he received an MFA in 1959, Schwarz worked in summer stock in Ohio and Michigan. He started his professional career as a set painter, but quickly rose to become designer, technical director, and stage director in summer stock. After graduation, Schwarz directed several amateur productions in Detroit, and this led to a position with the Sun Parlour summer theatre in Leamington, Ontario, thirty miles southeast of Windsor. There he directed at least eleven plays in 1960 and 1961. Between summers in Leamington he settled in Toronto, studying acting and dance with Basya Hunter and Bianca Rogge respectively, and supporting himself by teaching English at the Ryerson Institute of Technology. He also produced and directed several plays under various auspices in the early 1960s: Ionesco's *Jack, or the Submission* at the Bohemian Embassy, Pirandello's *Six Characters in Search of an Author* at an after-hours jazz club, and Giraudoux's *Ondine* at Ryerson, among others. In those days, the CBC had attracted a lot of talented performers to Toronto, but there were not many stage companies to employ them. As Schwarz recalls, 'If you had the gumption, it was easy to get a show on.'[2]

In 1965 Schwarz founded his 'Studio Theatre' in a ground-floor studio on Front Street, in a building later demolished to make way for the St Lawrence Centre. His intention was to create a permanent company by uniting one group of actors which had been studying with him and another which had been working with George Luscombe at TWP. Schwarz began to produce children's plays almost by accident, beginning with touring productions of *Pinocchio* and *Jack and the Beanstalk*. He quickly discovered, however, that there was an unfulfilled demand for such programming. A pattern developed in which Schwarz would devise a children's script in workshops, design and direct the play himself, and present it at the Don Mills Library on Saturdays and the Colonnade Theatre on Sundays. By giving four such performances each weekend, he was finally able to form a full-time company, although salaries were small. The next year, with his Front Street studio scheduled for demolition, Schwarz moved his company to a new location on Collier

Street (off Yonge north of Bloor). By 1968 Schwarz had also produced *Cinderella*, *The Lion and the Lollipop*, *Hansel and Gretel*, and a rock-music version of *Aladdin* for young audiences. His company would travel throughout metropolitan Toronto and beyond, performing on weekends and school holidays in neighbourhood libraries and available theatre spaces. Other professional children's theatres were being developed at the same time in Toronto, most notably Susan Rubes' Toronto Museum Children's Theatre (later established as Young People's Theatre). The outstanding feature of the Studio Theatre, however, was its extensive use of audience participation, which required the kind of improvisational skills which Schwarz taught in his classes and workshops.[3] At this time, the Studio Lab was recognized as 'the best children's theatre in operation here,' and Schwarz himself as 'the golden boy of Toronto children's theatre.'[4]

In September 1968 Schwarz rented the dilapidated Orange Hall at 53 Queen Street East (off Yonge) for his own performing space. (As with both his Front and Collier studios, the fact that the Orange Hall was slated for demolition helped keep the rent low.) At this point his Studio Theatre was renamed the Studio Lab Theatre to avoid confusion with a local cinema. At the same time, on weekend evenings, Schwarz began producing experimental theatre in the small Collier Street studio. In both his productions there, Schwarz attempted to introduce elements of audience participation into experimental plays from New York and London. The first one was Megan Terry's *Comings and Goings*, an off-off-Broadway collection of blackout scenes on themes of courtship, sex, and love. The novelty in this show was that Schwarz would sit on a high stool, blow a whistle to interrupt the play, and choose a numbered card at random. The audience member whose seat corresponded to the numbered card would then be allowed to replace any performer currently onstage with another member of the company. The other production at Collier Street was Paul Ableman's *Tests*, a similarly loose collection of short playlets with surreal dialogue. After a set first act, the actors solicited snippets of dialogue from the audience to create their own short surreal improvised pieces for the second act. Meanwhile, the Studio Children's Theatre program continued in an expanded format at the Orange Hall, with after-school performances three times daily during the busy Christmas shopping period. Late that autumn, again just one step ahead of the wrecker's ball, Schwarz abandoned his Collier studio and moved his entire operation to Queen Street. There he opened his next adult production in February 1969, the controversial American play *The Beard* by Michael McClure.

Critics in Toronto, as elsewhere, commented on the profusion of obscene language in *The Beard*, but generally liked Schwarz's production nonetheless. The comedy inherent in the play was well realized, and one critic actually preferred the Studio Lab version to the 'ponderous and juvenile' production of the original San Francisco company.[5] Less than two weeks after *The Beard* opened on Queen Street, however, the opening of Passe Muraille's *Futz* at the Central Library Theatre raised the dual spectres of obscenity and censorship in Toronto theatre. A few days later, amid the sensational publicity generated by *Futz*, the morality squad visited Schwarz to suggest that *The Beard* too might be legally obscene. Although he was fond of his production, Schwarz felt that his highly regarded children's theatre company could not afford to be associated with an obscenity controversy. He therefore closed his production immediately and issued a public disclaimer. Nathan Cohen, although he had reviewed neither *Futz* nor *The Beard*, was one of the most vocal opponents of the police action regarding *Futz*. In response to Schwarz's disclaimer, Cohen vigorously defended Passe Muraille on the grounds of artistic freedom, and attacked Schwarz's position in withering terms:

For the perfect combination of sanctimoniousness and pusillanimity, consider the following announcement by Ernest Schwarz's Studio Lab Theatre:

'In light of the recent sensational publicity (with which we do not wish to be associated) on modern experimental drama, The Beard has been withdrawn.'

The 'sensational publicity' refers to the trouble that Theatre Passe-Muraille [*sic*] has been having with the morality squad for its production of Futz at the Central Library Theatre.

First Studio Lab imputes [*sic*] the integrity of that company, suggesting it deliberately courted police attendance and summons. Then, priggishly and cautiously, it jumps back to a safe position for fear that it too might suffer some harassment by the law. How's that for cant?[6]

Schwarz's refusal to support this *cause célèbre* of Toronto's underground theatres meant his permanent exclusion from what was (in effect) a club of like-minded young directors. He was not invited to join the New Directors Group or to enter a play in the FUT festival; and for his own part Schwarz felt he had little in common with these younger directors.

After *The Beard* closed, Schwarz quickly mounted another experimental production, Arrabal's allegorical *Automobile Graveyard* in March 1969, after which he resumed his concentration on youth projects. That summer, the company operated a leadership training program in the arts, called 'Sagitta-II,' out of the Orange Hall. That fall, the Studio Lab made its first children's theatre tour of northern Ontario, which it was to reprise for many years thereafter. At the end of November 1969, the Studio Lab resumed its adult performances with previews of another American experimental play, *Dionysus in 69*.

Richard Schechner's original production of *Dionysus in 69* had opened in New York in June 1968, and quickly became an international sensation. The play was a contemporary recasting of Euripides' *The Bacchae*, created with Schechner's acting students at New York University and performed in a warehouse in Greenwich Village. Schechner's Performance Group, in the new tradition of New York's Living Theatre and Open Theatre, helped to popularize a style of 'poor theatre' in North America, typically with actors dressed in jeans and leotards attempting to break down traditional boundaries between actors and audience. In Schechner's case, the power of the printed word was also a factor: he was editor of *The Drama Review* at that time, America's leading journal for experimental theatre, and his published pictorial record of *Dionysus in 69* did much to disseminate the production's influence. Incidentally, Schechner's production also contained two celebrated nude scenes which sometimes spilled over into the audience, and which helped earn the epithet 'group grope' for this style of theatre. With *Viet Rock* and *Futz* recently performed in Toronto, with *Tom Paine* running at Theatre Passe Muraille, and with *Hair* scheduled to open the new decade at the Royal Alex, the Studio Lab's *Dionysus in 69* was certainly in the mainstream of theatrical fashion in Toronto.

Dionysus in 69 soon became as singular a phenomenon in Toronto as it had been in New York. Cohen praised Schwarz's production for containing not only less sensationalism than Schechner's in its use of nudity and political rhetoric, but also 'more integrity and a more genuine quality of audience involvement.'[7] In Schwarz's hands, in fact, *Dionysus in 69* became less a contemporary exploration of ritual than an audience participation play for adults. As the actors grew more comfortable with the improvised participation, audiences (especially of university students) warmed to the opportunities to join in. Capacity houses became the rule for weekend performances, and some audience members returned again and again. The production ran for six months, finally closing in May 1970 only because Schwarz was committed to another children's theatre tour of northern Ontario. *Dionysus in 69* reopened in June for two months, then was remounted in October as

Dionysus in 70, with several cast changes. This was a more confident and accomplished version, according to the reviews, and ran for another three months, finally closing for good in January 1971. Its 165 performances, to audiences totalling more than 44,000, made it the longest-running non-musical play ever produced in Toronto to that time. To the veteran critic Herbert Whittaker, a long-time booster of homegrown professional theatre, lengthy runs of locally produced plays (such as *Dionysus in 69/70*, *Chicago 70* at TWP, and *Hair* at the Royal Alex) represented a great step forward. 'Toronto has entered into a period in which only imported shows will have short runs,' he predicted, 'a complete reversal of the original condition of the town's theatre.'[8] Schechner, who visited Toronto at Schwarz's invitation, also commented on the city's new cultural climate. 'Toronto has changed enormously since I was here before,' he said. 'Then it was as if it were in a corset laced three holes too tight. Now it doesn't even seem to be wearing a bra.'[9]

With this production, the Studio Lab had become the first of Toronto's alternative theatres to score a long-running popular success. (Remember that *Futz*, for all its notoriety, ran for only three weeks.) This success enabled Schwarz to create two separate companies, one for adults and one for children. Indeed, by late 1970 the Studio Lab was Toronto's second-largest employer of theatre talent, after only the St Lawrence Centre.[10] Schwarz even allowed himself some condescending comments on the FUT festival, from which his underground hit had been excluded. 'I think that what we're doing is more experimental than a lot of what went on during the theatre festival,' he said. 'Maybe they're not basing the definition of underground on the degree of experimentation, but on the degree of success – if you're not a failure you're not underground.' He discovered, however, that his company's extraordinary recent success did not mean its financial position was any more stable: 'with our income, our seating capacity, and our expenses – remember we do all our children's theatre work here – any real profit is out of the question.'[11] To make matters worse, the Canada Council refused to give the company operating grants because of its semi-professional status and its emphasis on theatre for young audiences, both areas which the Council classified as outside its mandate. The Studio Lab's administrative director, Bill Reid, added that a single box-office failure could imperil the whole organization. Reid was proven correct when, still unable to gain Canada Council support, the Studio Lab produced two consecutive failures after closing *Dionysus in 70*.

The first of these was *The Brothers*, an adaptation of the Roman comedy by Terence, which opened in January 1971. The new script was by Rex Deverell, a former Baptist minister who was later to gain fame as resident playwright for Regina's Globe Theatre. (Deverell's wife, Rita, was an actress who had appeared in *Dionysus in 70*.) In *The Brothers*, Schwarz tried to do for Roman comedy what Schechner had done for Greek tragedy: to re-express its themes in a contemporary idiom. In effect, he tried to appeal to the audience's taste for sexy comedy as Schechner had done to its taste for sexy ritual. As always, audience participation was central to Schwarz's production concept. But *The Brothers* failed to find the magic which had animated *Dionysus in 69/70*, and the production seemed energetic but pointless. As Herbert Whittaker put it,

At the moment The Brothers seems to have more cute ideas than genuine directorial inspiration. The audience participation is high, as before. This time you can go up on stage, appear in living tableaux and illustrate the rather wobbly reformer's lecture; read dirty words from the Lab's early show, The Beard, or announce publicly how you first had sex. No wonder True Davidson left at half-time.[12]

The play's weak structure, the cast's clumsy handling of verbal obscenity, and the forced charm of the program notes suggested an uncomfortable mixture of summer stock and off-off-Broadway, which was perhaps the central contradiction of the Studio Lab. The second failure was *Where Do We Go from Here?*, a farewell revue hastily mounted when the Orange Hall was finally scheduled for demolition and the company's monthly tenancy was terminated. This revue featured songs by Obie-award-winner Tom Sankey, recently arrived from New York, and improvised skits which allowed for audience participation in the Studio Lab style. The show received very poor reviews, and was poorly attended.

After these two failures, the Studio Lab's work in adult theatre was greatly curtailed, and the company was again reorganized as primarily a children's theatre. It also continued to offer a wide range of theatre classes in successive interim homes on Lombard Street and Adelaide Street. Widespread construction had made inexpensive downtown studio spaces harder and harder to find. Without its own performing space, the Studio Lab concentrated on touring productions, and its presence in Toronto diminished. In the fall of 1971, the company took its *Aladdin* to an international festival of children's theatre in Venice, after which it toured Italy with financing from Canada's Department of

External Affairs. Later that fall, the Studio Lab received a LIP grant of more than $200,000 to become the resident company in a new arts centre in Sudbury, Ontario. When it did perform again in Toronto, almost two years after the loss of the Orange Hall, Whittaker reviewed the production as a piece of nostalgia. He appreciated, he said, this memento of 'the Schwarz method of improvised and freewheeling audience communication,' but gently pointed out that 'Toronto has moved on a little past the Studio Lab Theatre style.'[13]

Federal job-creation grants turned out to be a mixed blessing for theatre in Toronto. Part of the company's reason for relocating to Sudbury was that it could no longer support itself in Toronto by producing children's theatre, because new groups funded by LIP or OFY had sprung up which would perform for free. In 1974 Schwarz returned to Toronto and leased the Bathurst Street Theatre as a 'permanent' home; however, he found its auditorium poorly suited to children's theatre, and used it mainly as a rental house. Even his touring activity declined: as expenses of touring increased, Schwarz was discouraged by trying to mount downscaled versions of his earlier children's productions. The Studio Lab was finally closed in 1976, and Schwarz himself abandoned the theatre business for several years. However, he returned in the 1980s to become one of Toronto's most important independent producers of commercial theatre.

The Studio Lab had the misfortune to lose its Orange Hall at precisely the time when it most needed to capitalize on the success of *Dionysus in 69/70*. Then it left town at precisely the time when new companies, new playwrights, and a massive injection of LIP and OFY money created unprecedented theatrical opportunities in Toronto. When the Studio Lab returned, forced back onto the resources of a single overworked person and into its previous role as a touring children's theatre, its style seemed old hat, and Schwarz seemed unable or unwilling to start all over again. 'In theatre, fashion is everything,' said Tom Hendry. In retrospect, it appears that the Studio Lab flourished when its style was blessed by fashion, and floundered when fashions changed. It also suffered for lack of a support network, of the kind that carried Passe Muraille and the Factory Lab through some tough times. Because it was not an accepted member of Toronto's alternative theatre community, the Studio Lab's contributions to the Toronto theatre scene are seldom acknowledged nowadays. It should be remembered, however, that the Studio Lab was for a time the most successful of Toronto's alternative theatres, and the first to gain a broad audience.

Global Village Theatre

From its inception, the Global Village Theatre had a greater affinity with
the artistic community of New York than with the theatrical community
of Toronto. It was founded by advertising writer Robert Swerdlow and
choreographer Elizabeth Swerdlow as a venue for a dance-drama which
she had created. Because of Robert's commercial instincts and because
of the connections both Swerdlows had with other Toronto artists, the
Global Village quickly became a meeting place for a variety of Toronto
subcultures. Their warehouse theatre on St Nicholas Street (off Yonge)
became the most eclectic after-hours club the city had ever seen, and the
focus of an artists' colony in the style of New York's Greenwich Village.
While this activity raged at the Global Village, the Swerdlows collaborat-
ed on a series of original musicals, the first of which (*Justine*) ran for
several months both off-Yonge-Street and off-Broadway. Despite scor-
ing the first international success of Toronto's alternative theatre,
however, the Global Village (like the Studio Lab) was not an accepted
member of that community. The Swerdlows felt that Toronto critics
were unappreciative, and spent much of their time in New York, where
their work attracted more commercial interest. By the time the
Swerdlows gave up their New York ambitions and again turned their
attention to Toronto, the decline of the teeming street activity of the late
1960s, of which their theatre had been the crossroads, had undermined
its position. Toronto's major alternative theatres had become part of
the city's mainstream culture by then, but the Global Village was not
included in it. In addition, poor fiscal management drove the company's
deficit up to $80,000 by 1975.[14] In that year the Swerdlows separated,
the company folded, and a fire later destroyed their theatre.

Robert Swerdlow was born in Montreal in 1938, the son of a diplomat
and grandson of an actor. A musical prodigy, he was trained as a classical
pianist, but abruptly changed direction in his late teens. 'To be
facetious,' he said, 'I guess I discovered girls, love, sex, I discovered
another form of expression. I began to improvise, and I found magically
that I could sit down at the piano and play, just play.'[15] He stopped taking
piano lessons, started haunting jazz clubs, and studied composition at
McGill University before leaving for advanced study at the Vienna State
Conservatory of Music. There, in 1960, the Austrian government gave
him the signal honour of commissioning an original score for a Young
People's Concert.

After returning to North America, Swerdlow became very popular as a ballet-class pianist because of his uncanny ability to improvise in the style of various classical composers. While accompanying classes at New York's American Ballet Theatre in 1964, he met dancer Elizabeth Szathmary, a native of New York City and the daughter of a respected American composer-arranger. Robert and Elizabeth went to Europe together and worked in ballet in Paris and Monte Carlo, before Robert took a job in Montreal in 1966 as a writer-director with the National Film Board. They moved to Toronto in 1967, Robert giving up music and film for the advertising business and Elizabeth continuing her dance career with Toronto's first modern dance company, the newly formed New Dance Group of Canada. She performed in this group's first concert in December 1967, and in the first concert of its successor, Toronto Dance Theatre, the following year.

In the summer of 1968, just before Toronto Dance Theatre was formed, Elizabeth Swerdlow established her own company called Modern Dance Theatre of Canada. Its performers were drawn from the modern dance class of the National Ballet of Canada, some of whom had also performed with the New Dance Group. The impetus for this company seems to have been a rejection of the Martha Graham model on which TDT was explicitly based, seeking instead an original style. Its first production would be a full-length ballet entitled *Blue S.A.*, which Elizabeth Swerdlow spent nine months in creating. The glossy program, which Robert had had designed and produced through his many contacts in the advertising business, described the work as 'a lucid dance rhetoric on the spiritual and moral decline of America today.' When it was time to go into production, however, the Swerdlows could not find a rental house in Toronto which they felt was an appropriate performing space for such revolutionary material. As Elizabeth Swerdlow put it, 'We went to all the theatres, and they weren't right. You can't do a ballet like Blue S.A. with its social comment in a theatre in which the audience is so far removed from the performers.'[16]

At about this time, the Swerdlows saw *Dionysus in 69* at Schechner's Performance Garage in Greenwich Village, which inspired them to build their own theatre in Toronto instead of renting one. With money from options sold on Robert's new invention, a four-track magnetic audio technique for 16 mm film, the Swerdlows leased what was once an RCMP stables on St Nicholas Street. Appropriately, it was just a few doors from the site of the Bohemian Embassy, Toronto's leading coffee-house of the early 1960s. In its large high warehouse, reminiscent of Schechner's austere Performance Garage, the Swerdlows and their friends built their own theatre in less than three weeks. Indeed, Robert Swerdlow found that his friends in advertising were eager to help with this exciting new venture, just for the fun of it. He also found that businesses could be persuaded to donate building materials and other supplies, as if to align themselves with the liberal conscience of the 1960s. He recalls obtaining five thousand square feet of plywood and thousands of sheets of styrofoam in this way, and hiring transient hippies off Yonge Street for day-labour. ('The biggest expense,' he recalls, 'was the hammers.') The theatre's name, 'the Global Village,' taken from Toronto's popular communications theorist Marshall McLuhan, reflected its energetic beginnings and the busy Toronto street scene of 1969.

Critical rejection, later an infuriating theme for the Swerdlows, began with the opening of *Blue S.A.* in June 1969. One reviewer found it 'simple-minded and pretentious at the same time,' while another described the evening as 'a choreographed mess, an incoherent hodgepodge of nonsense and naivete.'[17] But there were two episodes in the ballet, neither of them involving dance, which captivated critics and audiences and led to later successes for the Global Village. One was the appearance of the then-unknown Salome Bey, recruited by the Swerdlows in a typically unorthodox fashion. When Elizabeth decided she needed a black blues singer for her *Blue S.A.*, the Swerdlows went to dinner at a local soul-food restaurant and asked the manager if he knew of any talent of that kind. The manager recommended his wife, Salome Bey, who earned great acclaim in that show and in many since. Another audience favourite in *Blue S.A.* was a female impersonator named 'Sacha,' whose popularity led to a new show the next month. This show, entitled *Facad,* was an original revue of female impersonators, consisting mainly of songs mimed to recorded music. The androgynous performers in their flamboyant costumes, wrote one reviewer, yielded 'a strange blend of Kurt Weill sadness, Mae West humor and Follies Bergere sensuality.'[18] *Facad* not only attracted excellent houses, it also initiated a vogue for 'drag' shows in Toronto. Toronto impresario Ed Mirvish paid $10,000 for the right to remount *Facad* at the Royal Alex, where it also proved very popular.

Despite this infusion of money from Mirvish, the Global Village was on the brink of collapse by October 1969, unable to pay its rent or install heating. 'I've put $60,000 into it, and I've got no money left,' said Robert Swerdlow, '[but] I'll go and hawk my shoes before I'll let the theatre fold.'[19] He started a coffee-house in the Global Village with the ironic name 'Waiting for Teperman,' an allusion to a well-known Toronto demolition firm. The coffee-house soon turned into an after-hours club which featured an enormous range of entertainment – experimental plays, kabuki theatre, jazz, blues, folk, rock, even improvised Dixieland jazz with Robert Swerdlow at the piano. By February, up to five hundred customers could be expected on a Saturday night, 'mostly young, fringed, beaded, and long-haired,' according to the press, with the Global Village assuming (in Nathan Cohen's words) 'the same role on the Toronto scene that the Bohemian Embassy used to have, though of course for a different, younger generation.'[20] The weekend concert stage, called 'Platform,' hosted some of the country's most prominent entertainers: recording groups Crowbar and Lighthouse, *Hair* authors James Rado and Gerome Ragni, poet Irving Layton, comedians John Candy and Gilda Radner before they became television stars. While some of Passe Muraille's gloomier offerings were playing to a handful of patrons at Trinity Square, the Global Village was full of noise, colour, and people. Visiting celebrities would rub elbows with advertising executives, gaudy homosexuals, black musicians, graphic artists, photographers, filmmakers, actors, and hippies. It was the closing party of the Age of Aquarius, and everyone came as they were.

This eclectic activity spilled over into theatre productions at the Global Village. Robert Swerdlow distrusted theatre designers because he felt their finished work always looked too conventional. (He preferred casting untrained actors for the same reason.) Instead, he recruited designers from among talented young artists of other media, sculptors for sets, painters and figure-skaters for costumes. In turn, the design opportunities afforded these artists added to the upbeat activity surrounding the Global Village, and increased its stature in the broader artistic community as well. Such designers could make wonderfully creative use of 'found' materials. In Swerdlow's *Copper Mountain*, for example, a children's musical first produced in December 1969, scavenged set and costume materials were used to create a magical visual style. Initially offered free of charge to underprivileged city children, *Copper Mountain* proved so popular that it was remounted every Christmas for five years.

Evening theatre performances resumed in the new year, with audiences for the late-night 'Platform' often lining up outside while the evening's play was still performing. In January 1970, Ionesco's *Exit the King* (with music by Robert Swerdlow) was staged by David Martin, a young filmmaker. In March came *Transmission,* a new episodic dance-drama created by Elizabeth Swerdlow. This production, which she concluded with her own nude solo dance, was described by Nathan

Cohen as 'a 65-minute denunciation by Elizabeth Swerdlow of the state of the world, and particularly such institutions as marriage, organized religion, and political parties in the west.'[21] Cohen was offended not by the nudity, it seems, but by the dancers' dirty feet. He also criticized the company's professed dedication to Grotowski, of whom he felt their efforts were entirely unworthy. Like *Blue S.A.*, *Transmission* generally provoked anger and confusion among the critics. Already the Swerdlows felt that lack of critical favour was damaging their theatre. This theme became crucial to their next production, the musical *Justine*, which opened in May 1970. For *Justine*, critics were partly responsible for both its international success and its near-collapse in New York.

Justine was the story of a small-town girl seeking adventure in the big city, who is discouraged by the evil she finds but is finally redeemed through love. It was written and directed by Robert Swerdlow, who had never before directed a stage play. Nonetheless, *Justine* received an unmitigated rave from Nathan Cohen, who suggested it ought to be remounted at Stratford or the St Lawrence Centre.[22] Cohen's extravagant praise quickly attracted the notice of some American producers looking for a hit in the manner of *Hair*. The Swerdlows were soon swept up in script revisions for a New York opening, and in the backstage infighting for which Broadway's commercial theatre is famous. Although the Swerdlows disagreed with many of the changes made, *Justine* (retitled *Love Me, Love My Children*) finally opened off-Broadway in November 1971. Perhaps the long delay prevented the show from fully capitalizing on the brief vogue for hippie rock musicals – certainly Robert Swerdlow thinks so. When it received a dreadful review from the influential Clive Barnes of the *New York Times*, the producers wanted to close the show immediately. Virtually overnight, however, Swerdlow and his director, Paul Aaron, found enough capital to keep the show running. Their faith was rewarded: subsequent reviews were very positive, and the show developed a knot of dedicated admirers. *Love Me, Love My Children* finally ran for an impressive 187 performances, the first successful transfer from Toronto to New York, with Salome Bey winning an Obie award in the process.

While rewrites were underway in New York for *Justine*, the Swerdlows also embarked on the Global Village's most famous production in Toronto, *Spring Thaw '71*. This annual revue, created by Dora Mavor Moore's New Play Society in 1948, began as a lark for that fledgling company, and turned into a national tradition. Some of Canada's favourite performers were among its regulars, including Don Harron,

Jane Mallet, and Mavor Moore. *Spring Thaw* had had a topical new script each year, usually written by a committee. After purchasing the production rights from Mavor Moore, however, Swerdlow decided to discard the revue format. Instead, he wrote the entire show himself, a 'book' musical about sexual concerns among contemporary urban couples. A film director, Dennis Miller, was hired to stage it, but he was replaced by Elizabeth Swerdlow after a week of rehearsals. Written with one eye on Broadway, *Spring Thaw '71* never got off St Nicholas Street. Despite genial reviews, ticket sales were slow, the run was cut short, and a planned provincial tour was cancelled. Producer Andrew Alexander blamed the poor box-office on 'a negative backlash' to the show's reputation as old-fashioned entertainment. 'We paid nearly $1000 for the rights to call our show Spring Thaw because we felt it had a built-in audience,' he said. 'Of course, once that was so. But no more.' However, another producer asserted (in the picturesque language of show business) that 'it was the show, not the title, that people were not coming to see.'[23] He suggested that Alexander's argument might be tested by reopening *Spring Thaw '71* under a different title.

While the Swerdlows seemed unable to please Toronto critics, their success with *Love Me, Love My Children* attracted the interest of commercial producers in New York. Robert Swerdlow was given a retainer of $20,000 for two consecutive years to write for United Artists. He also recalls an Americah music publisher advancing $15,000 for the publishing rights to *Spring Thaw '71*, although the show did not finally go anywhere. Despite their acceptance by and fascination with the world of commercial theatre, the Swerdlows were horrified, even humiliated, by the experience of producing *Love Me, Love My Children* in New York. As Robert Swerdlow put it, 'There's this particular brand of New York producers and directors; egomaniacal, avaricious, the knife-in-the-back smilers who feed on naive playwrights. My wife, Elizabeth, warned me. She was born and bred in New York, but I didn't believe her.'[24] As they did with other aspects of their personal lives, the Swerdlows put their New York experience on stage. The result was *Rats*, which opened at the Global Village Theatre in November 1972. This was a musical satire about the problems of taking a musical to New York, inspired by an incident in which *Justine*'s American producers insisted on cutting some coarse language. *Rats*, observed Herbert Whittaker, was 'the cry of a deeply wounded ego.'[25] As with *Spring Thaw '71*, *Rats* was written with hopes of attracting some commercial interest, but it did not do so.

From the time when *Justine* diverted their attentions toward New

York, the Swerdlows had little to do with the day-to-day management of their theatre. During this period, from 1971 to 1974, the Global Village became an important rental and transfer house for small companies other than the major alternative theatres, as well as the Swerdlows' base for their own new shows. With its role as a theatrical crossroads revived, the accessibility of the Global Village served many theatre artists on their way to greater glory. For example, Ray Whelan (who later founded Open Circle Theatre) directed Janet Amos in one production, while John Gray (of *Billy Bishop* fame) made his Toronto debut in another. Perhaps the most significant rental of this period was for Camus's *Les Justes* in September 1972. It was presented by W.W. Productions and directed by Paul Bettis, a partnership which later emerged as Theatre Second Floor in the late 1970s. The stage manager of *Les Justes* was Mallory Gilbert, later to become Tarragon Theatre's long-time general manager. Her assistant stage manager was Paul Reynolds, later producer of the Shaw Festival.

By 1974 the Global Village was still recognized locally for producing excellent children's theatre and unusual original musicals, but it had not received the acclaim that Toronto's four major alternative companies had. The Swerdlows felt that their theatre's poor public profile was due to a 'weak chain of command' in the preceding years. Accordingly, for the 1974–75 season they 'reassumed total control of their enterprise and reassessed the philosophy behind the theatre.'[26] Their goals were stated more explicitly than before, and were brought in line with those of other alternative theatres: developing new Canadian talent, producing new musicals, and emphasizing the Global Village as a theatrical development centre. As part of this program the Swerdlows converted their studio living space adjacent to the theatre into a rehearsal and instructional area which they called 'The Inner Stage.' Here they developed *Cosmic Jack*, a contemporary reconsideration of 'Jack and the Beanstalk,' presented as a 'work-in-progress' in February 1975. While Kareda dismissed it as 'another of Robert Swerdlow's ponderous allegorical musicals,'[27] Swerdlow himself remembers it as his best show ever. At about the same time, Elizabeth Swerdlow discovered a new personal commitment to children's theatre through another workshop production, *Peter and the Wolf*. At what appeared to be the threshold of a new direction, personal problems destroyed the Global Village in the space of a few months in 1975. The Swerdlows' personal relationship deteriorated, and Robert Swerdlow abruptly left for San Francisco, where he resumed his career of playing piano for dance classes.

Elizabeth Swerdlow formed a company called the New Global Village with two partners, a director and a management consultant, but the partnership survived only one production. As 'The St Nicholas Street Theatre,' the Global Village was the venue for a few unremarkable commercial productions before being gutted by fire the next year.

The heyday of the Global Village is still fondly remembered by theatre veterans of that time. Besides its role as the night-club of Toronto's counter-culture and as the social centre of the FUT festival, it was the place where a tremendous number of theatre professionals, alternative and mainstream, got their start. When the Swerdlows returned from New York, however, the 1960s ethos was over, the street activity which was the life-blood of the Global Village had subsided, and Toronto theatre was firmly in the hands of theatre people once again. Moreover, despite the Swerdlows' deeply ambivalent feelings about American culture, New York remained the dominant artistic referent of the Global Village while new Canadian drama flourished all around it. As a business, the management of the Global Village was always a mess. As an artistic laboratory, it was so personal that it hovered between self-indulgence and self-destruction. As Robert Swerdlow put it,

We broke too many traditions at the same time. We were trying to stop a war in Viet Nam, we were trying to get together with our parents, we were trying to make the world a better place to live, we were trying to make a living, and we were also trying to put on a show, and all of the above was in the show.[28]

It is a tribute to the optimism of the age and the resilience of these people that the experience did not leave them embittered. Said Elizabeth, still producing children's theatre on St Nicholas Street, those were 'wonderful, growing years.' Said Robert, still writing musicals, 'I've stayed young and I'm not afraid to start again.'

Creation 2

The beginnings of Creation 2 are strikingly similar to those of Theatre Passe Muraille. Creation 2 was led by a single charismatic director, Louis Capson, a Canadian who (like Garrard) had gone outside Canada for his advanced training. Inspired by techniques of American radical theatre, Capson (like Garrard) formed a company centred in a communal residential experiment in Toronto, with developmental workshops forming the basis for rehearsals and performances. But there were two major differences between Creation 2 and the more durable Passe Muraille. First, Creation 2 was rooted in a Christian brotherhood, so that its artistic goals were often indistinguishable from its religious ones. Second, and more critically, as the group attained some stature in Toronto theatre, its development turned inward rather than outward. Whereas Garrard expanded the membership of Theatre Passe Muraille to include the best talent he could recruit, in order to enhance its artistic potential, Capson cultivated the fixed population of his small company, in order to preserve its spiritual foundation. As Creation 2 moved from its street-theatre beginnings to more conventional theatre spaces, its audiences of curious onlookers dwindled. Critics too grew impatient with the wilful obscurity and shallow political allegories of Capson's plays. By the mid-1970s, a reduced tolerance for formal experiment and artist-centred expression greatly damaged the credibility of Creation 2. It gradually became isolated from other alternative theatres, received some extremely negative reviews, and responded with self-righteous anger. There is no record of Creation 2 performing in Toronto after 1977.

Born in Fredericton, New Brunswick, in 1944, Louis Capson completed his BA in English and theatre at the University of Victoria (BC) in 1966. There his play *The Potter's Field* received a mainstage production directed by the theatre department's founder, Carl Hare. Capson then took an MFA at the Yale School of Drama, where his anti-bureaucratic iconoclasm nearly resulted in his expulsion.[29] At Yale he came into contact with several leaders of American radical theatre, including Julian Beck, Judith Malina, and Joseph Chaikin, and their hortatory and highly physical performance styles were later reflected in Capson's own work. In May 1969 Capson formed his Creation 2 company in a large communal house in Toronto's Annex neighbourhood. Initially it operated under the umbrella of the Religion and Theatre Council at 11 Trinity Square, in the same summer that Garrard ran his theatre drop-in centre there. Creation 2's first performances were parable-plays in a guerrilla theatre style, written by Capson or created collectively by the company, presented without advance notice in public plazas, parks, and shopping centres. 'Our purpose in doing this is to get people to respond to us by creating a spontaneous experience,' explained one young performer. 'And it's to present what we believe is God's gift of love and our personal relationship with Jesus Christ.'[30] Although little evidence survives of its street-theatre phase, Creation 2 is known to have performed at 11 Trinity Square in 1969, at the Festival of Underground

Theatre in 1970, and at Peterborough's Trent University in January 1971. This was followed by a two-month tour of British Columbia, sponsored by that province's Centennial Commission.

By 1971 the explosion of alternative theatre in Toronto had acquired a nationalistic tone, particularly with the availability of OFY/LIP grants for artistic projects. From this time, Capson's plays began to mingle Canadian political themes with those of anti-establishment spiritual quests. The Christian foundation of the company was seldom mentioned in press releases and programs thereafter. Instead, the company stressed its all-Canadian membership, its performances for the BC government and several universities, and what it called its increasing responsibility as a 'resource bank for the development of a new theatre in Canada.'[31] By this time Creation 2 had also abandoned guerrilla theatre for more conventional theatre spaces. It received excellent reviews for Capson's *I Love You Billy Striker* at the Factory Lab in August 1971, the story of an Orwellian future in a Canada controlled by a Big Brother from Saskatoon. In this play, Capson freely mingled images of Canadian, American, and Nazi nationalism – the maple leaf, the stars and stripes, and the swastika. By the end of the year, Capson had written two additional 'Billy Striker' plays to complete a trilogy entitled *The True North Blueprint*, which was performed in repertory at the University College Playhouse at the University of Toronto. The generally positive critical reaction was led by Urjo Kareda, who praised the group's 'dazzling' performance technique which overcame a script 'often maddeningly vague and obscure.'[32] A LIP grant allowed the company to continue its explorations in form, culminating in a production entitled *Prosix 16*, again at the University College Playhouse, in May 1972.

Next came Creation 2's greatest debacle, Capson's *Midway Priest*, which opened in August 1972 at the National Arts Centre Theatre. Like *The True North Blueprint*, *Midway Priest* presented a futuristic retrospective of contemporary Canadian society, this time set in a Quebec which had already separated from Canada. As with most Capson plays, *Midway Priest* depicted the personal and spiritual struggles of a central martyr figure, this time a socially concerned priest, in a repressive, polarized society. Quebec critics were deeply offended by the implication that separation would necessarily lead to a totalitarian state. Capson's shallow knowledge of this volatile issue was widely criticized, particularly the fact that he had never lived in Quebec. When the play's director, Gary Reeves, tried to defend Capson by saying the playwright had read about Quebec and talked to Quebeckers, his condescending tone infuriated their critics all the more. Reeves pointed out what was surely obvious to the Creation 2 company, that the play had a religious rather than a political aim. However, his explanations were overwhelmed by the angry responses of a region still deeply troubled by the October Crisis of 1970. Perhaps it was Creation 2's blithe insensitivity that was most galling: fumed one Quebec commentator, 'Is the question of Quebec's separation any more to English Canadians than subject matter for plays?'[33]

With this production at the National Arts Centre, and another the following month at the St Lawrence Centre, Creation 2 was clearly attempting to gain the ear of a mainstream audience. The problem was that Capson and his company had no feeling for what a mainstream audience wanted to hear. Creation 2 continued to mount new productions over the next few seasons in various locations, with very little popular or critical encouragement. In reviewing one of Capson's new plays in 1973, Whittaker noted that there were more people on stage than there were in the audience. From this time on, most of the company's new work was done outside Toronto, where it was felt the audience would be more receptive.

During this period, the company's relations with the rest of Toronto's theatre community also declined. A planned collaboration with Bill Glassco was not carried through because, as Capson put it, 'he didn't want to fight with me.'[34] At the Stratford Festival in 1976, Reeves was ejected from a performance of *Hamlet* when he began to heckle Richard Monette in the title role. The following summer, Creation 2 chose to open its version of *Richard III* in Toronto the same night that Robin Phillips' celebrated production of *Richard III* opened in Stratford. Creation 2's production drew such a vitriolic review from the *Globe and Mail* that it elicited an angry protest from the managing editor of the *Canadian Theatre Review*.[35] This was apparently Creation 2's last production.

Although it is forgotten now, Creation 2 was an important company in its time. Kareda praised its stylistic accomplishments in *The True North Blueprint* in the same way that he praised such later landmark productions as *The Farm Show* and *Sticks and Stones*. 'For once,' he wrote, 'a company of actors has developed an original idiosyncratic style and has worked intelligently to relate that to a serious consideration of our national experience.'[36] When these qualities were not nurtured and built upon, Kareda responded first with anguish and later with contempt: 'Where and when did Creation Two go astray? How could their earlier gifts have been submerged so completely? Do they really see the work they're doing now as an advance?'[37] Both in his praise of its early work and in his later censure, Kareda was mistaken in equating the goals of Creation 2 with those of other alternative theatres. Whittaker was more perceptive when he noted that 'this is theatre for the individual making it, [not for] the outsider, the public.'[38] While some of Creation 2's work was reminiscent of the formal concerns of Garrard's Passe Muraille or the nationalist ambitions of Gass's Factory Lab, it is clear now that the company began as, and remained, a theatrical pulpit for a young man whose messianic tendencies eventually overcame his considerable talent. The themes of Capson's plays, as well as the self-martyring pattern of his leadership, strongly suggest he identified himself and his company with Christ and his Church. Jim Garrard, we remember, had a messianic style as well; but he discarded it as easily as an actor discards his role when it no longer served his artistic needs.

8

The Second Wave

Like the so-called underground theatres before them, the second wave small theatres were founded with a certain sense of mission. But the second wave theatres have had a slightly different focus to their aims. Benefiting from the experience, and often the mistakes of some of the older small theatres, the second wave theatres have been more selective in their aims, more knowledgeable about their audiences, and more concerned about developing their basic theatrical capabilities.[1]

Greg Leach, April 1976

This quotation is given for its ironic value. It is taken from an excellent series of articles on Toronto's alternative theatres published in *That's Showbusiness* during the 1975–76 season. Leach's misfortune in this case was to mistake current events for long-term trends. Several times during the 1970s, especially around mid-decade when the energy of the four major alternative theatres was noticeably flagging, other small companies would elbow their way to the front rank of theatre in Toronto. But the new pattern for Toronto theatre was already set by 1972, and ultimately the later companies were not able to change it.

The second-wave companies discussed in this chapter – New Theatre, Open Circle, and Phoenix Theatre – were all founded in the early 1970s. (Another second-wave company, NDWT, is discussed next in its own chapter because it cannot be grouped comfortably with these.) They all flourished at or after mid-decade, and all expired in the early 1980s. Why these companies failed is a slippery question; it is more surprising, more strange, that the earlier ones should have survived. The Second Wave may have produced some bad shows, but surely no worse than *A*

Bond Honoured or *Vallières!* The Second Wave also mounted some excellent productions, such as *The Relapse* and *Automatic Pilot*, and some controversial ones such as *Chinchilla*. The real problem for the Second Wave was that it arrived too late to have an impact comparable to the first. The four major alternative theatres had gobbled up all the broad-based mandates, leaving little room in which the second-wave companies could manoeuvre. Whether a genuine need existed for the earlier alternative theatres is a moot point, but they were able to create an *impression* of need which (real or not) lent their very survival a sense of urgency. They set a new pattern for theatre in Toronto, a pattern to which the later companies were marginal. The element of timing is crucial in theatrical success – a third wave of small theatres in Toronto, founded during the late 1970s and early 1980s, has proven more durable than the second.

The fashion for warehouse theatres, particularly earnest nationalistic ones, subsided after mid-decade. Those first-wave theatres which had established a stable audience, particularly the Tarragon, continued to enjoy good health. Those which had not, most notably the Factory Lab, barely survived. The new fashion which supplanted it was commercial theatre. Whereas critics and granting agencies once lavished their attention on new theatres which could demonstrate their good intentions and their value to the community, more attention was now paid to theatres which could demonstrate popular appeal. With the nationalist critics Cohen, Whittaker, and Kareda all gone from the Toronto scene by mid-1975, the new fashion was presided over by Gina Mallet, the most prominent (and quotable) of their heirs. In this climate, the second-wave theatres were caught without a *raison d'être*. They had no established audience. They had no clear mandate. While they instinctively responded to the public's need for commercial theatre, they did not occupy commercial playhouses, nor did they have enough money to break out of warehouse production styles. In fact, the most noteworthy shows of the Second Wave – successes and failures – were those in which the contrast was most obvious between the companies' counter-culture antecedents and their new commercial leanings.

A final oddity of the three companies discussed here is that they all expired soon after moving into the comfortable renovated theatre complex called Adelaide Court, which opened in 1978. The building which housed Adelaide Court was an old courthouse on Adelaide Street, dating from 1852. It had also housed the city council chambers in the nineteenth century, and was home to Toronto's Arts and Letters Club for a few years after 1910. Derelict for many years, the old courthouse was brought back to life by a $2.3 million renovation program spearheaded by Open Circle's general manager, John Fisher. The renovated building was to house not only two theatres (seating about 130 and 270 respectively) but also restaurants and bars which would help sustain the operation. What happened instead was that the move to Adelaide Court, a shared space, damaged whatever unique identity each of its tenant companies had developed. (A notable exception here was Le Théâtre du P'tit Bonheur, a francophone company whose identity and whose audience were more clearly defined than the others at Adelaide Court.) The companies' operating costs skyrocketed, and those which had left other spaces (New Theatre and the Phoenix) could no longer weather financial storms. Adelaide Court itself went into receivership less than a decade after it opened. It represented an attempt by the second-wave theatres to establish a mainstream presence in downtown Toronto. If successful, it would have shot them past the first-wave companies, which were all struggling to hold on to their modest warehouse theatres. But the theatre spaces at Adelaide Court were too small to support the building's mainstream expenses, and the public was indifferent to the whole development.

It is tempting to call these second-wave companies 'The Adelaide Court Theatres' because of their common tenancy, but this would be misleading. They were not created for Adelaide Court, or even at Adelaide Court. Their origins and emphases were very different from the building in which they all expired, and from one another. What they shared was the frustration of being in the Second Wave, and they all ended up at Adelaide Court for the same reason – desperation. They were trying to find an acceptable commercial identity without giving up their small-theatre ambience, trying to find a comfortable house in an uncomfortable climate. For each of these companies, struggling to make ends meet, the chance to move to Adelaide Court was like an anchor thrown to a drowning man. Only the Bathurst Street Theatre rivalled Adelaide Court as a graveyard of small theatre companies, albeit for entirely different reasons.

New Theatre

Although the first productions under the name 'New Theatre' appeared in 1971, the company was not firmly established until 1973. At that time, New Theatre's co-founder Jonathan Stanley leased a meeting hall in the

Bathurst Street United Church complex, a large downtown church with a dwindling population which rented office and performing space to many arts groups during the 1970s. Within the theatre community, New Theatre became known for its adventurous repertory of unusual new European and North American plays. During its early years, the critical reputation of New Theatre varied greatly from one show to the next. At mid-decade, however, it mounted a series of highly respected productions, including Picasso's *Four Little Girls* (in 1975), Peter Handke's *The Ride across Lake Constance* (1975), and Robert Patrick's *Kennedy's Children* (1976). But in 1977 New Theatre embarked on two widely promoted projects that proved financially disappointing. One was renting the St Lawrence Centre for a star-studded production of Tom Stoppard's *Travesties*, and the other was moving its operations to Adelaide Court. After two years there, ending with the popular success of Erika Ritter's *Automatic Pilot* in 1980, New Theatre abruptly closed as Stanley moved on to other projects.

Jonathan Stanley was born in 1946, grew up in Wales, and came to Canada in the late 1950s. In the mid-1960s, while studying English literature at the University of Toronto, he was enthusiastically involved with the Trinity College Dramatic Society and Hart House Theatre. After graduating in 1968, he spent a year as an assistant director at the Manitoba Theatre Centre under such directors as Keith Turnbull, John Hirsch, and Edward Gilbert. In 1970 Stanley and fellow Trinity College graduate Andrew Bethell rented Passe Muraille's hall at 11 Trinity Square for a summer theatrical activity centre for teenagers, called 'Toronto Theatre-Go-Round.' One of their resource staff there was a Czech mime teacher named Adolf Toman. Born in 1942, Toman had trained at Prague's Academy of Theatre Arts and performed with the Czech national theatre company, until the Soviet occupation of 1968 left him stranded abroad in France. He immigrated to Canada in 1969, and worked at odd jobs for two years while trying to gain employment in theatre. Toman teamed up with Stanley again in 1971, at a time when Theatre-Go-Round had the use of a rehersal hall in the St Lawrence Centre.

In the fall of 1971, Stanley and Toman launched New Theatre, its name taken from a well-known company in Cardiff, Wales. (Later that fall, the existence of their company caused Tom Hendry to name his company 'Toronto Free Theatre,' instead of 'Toronto New Theatre' as he had planned.) It opened with a production of *The Importance of Being Earnest* at the Colonnade Theatre. The Colonnade was an urban architectural experiment, opened in 1963, which combined residential and commercial premises on Bloor Street near Avenue Road. Developer Irwin Burns and architect Gerald Robinson, prime movers of the project, had included a 190-seat thrust theatre on the Colonnade's second floor as a multi-purpose display and performance space. Burns and Robinson were both friends of George Luscombe, who along with playwright Jack Winter had offered informal advice on the theatre's design. The Colonnade Theatre opened in April 1964 with the Winter/Luscombe collaboration *Before Compiegne*. Their plan was for the Colonnade to serve as a downtown showcase for Luscombe's more marketable shows, with Toronto Workshop Productions having veto power on the theatre's programming. Instead, the Colonnade soon functioned as a rental space for college, community, and semi-professional groups in the same way as the Central Library Theatre did, although the Colonnade was never as popular a venue.

Stanley scheduled a number of matinees for *The Importance of Being Earnest* in hopes of attracting school audiences. Indeed, as Herbert Whittaker reported, this inaugural production 'drew some of the Colonnade's best houses in recent years.'[2] Stanley and Toman did not collaborate on any further productions. Stanley independently went on to direct Tennessee Williams' *Garden District* (a double bill of *Something Unspoken* and *Suddenly Last Summer*) at the Colonnade. The following season, Toman leased the Colonnade Theatre for a new company of his own, named Classical Stage Productions, which presented some familiar classics by Molière, Ibsen, and Strindberg, and an acclaimed version of Dostoevski's *White Nights*. However, a mounting deficit forced this operation to close after only one season. Toman later reappeared as a commercial producer in Toronto, as founder and director of Aladdin Theatre for children (1975–) and of Limelight Dinner Theatre (1977–).

Stanley, meanwhile, spent time in broadcasting, working for CBC radio and CITY-TV. On his return to the theatre early in 1973, he re-established New Theatre in the Bathurst Street United Church complex. With the help of Community Producers, a LIP project which he started at about the same time, Stanley refurbished a meeting room in the church to provide flexible seating for up to 220. New Theatre's first production there, in April 1973, was Oscar Wilde's *Salomé*, directed by Jiri Schubert. This was followed in May with Sam Shepard's *The Tooth of Crime,* directed by Clarke Rogers, later the artistic director of Theatre Passe Muraille. The 1973–74 season saw only two productions, Heathcote Williams' *AC/DC*, directed by Tim Leary, and Michel Tremblay's *Montreal Smoked Meat* (a translation of *En Pièces Détachées*), directed by Stanley. New Theatre survived that winter on personal loans from Stanley and his wife.[3]

Although the 1974–75 season started in controversy, it marked the beginning of two years of critical success for New Theatre. During rehearsals for David Storey's *Home*, persistent conflicts between director Stanley and actor Patrick Boxill led to the entire cast resigning. But when *Home* finally opened two weeks behind schedule, with a new cast and a new director, it received an excellent review from Herbert Whittaker.[4] The company's next production, Pablo Picasso's *Four Little Girls*, directed by Hrant Alianak, was praised by Urjo Kareda as 'ravishing ... the most successful and original work that New Theatre has yet given us.' Another highly experimental work, Peter Handke's *The Ride across Lake Constance*, directed by Robert Handforth, prompted Kareda to comment that New Theatre's 'quality of production is beginning to approach the adventurousness of the plays chosen.'[5] This critical success continued through the 1975–76 season with Larry Fineberg's *Human Remains*, Robert Patrick's *Kennedy's Children* (directed by Stanley), and *Miss Margarida*, a one-woman show written and directed by Brazilian playwright Roberto Athayde. *Kennedy's Children* was New Theatre's most popular production to date, playing for six weeks to excellent houses. It appears that New Theatre was trying to invite comparisons with Tarragon Theatre and Bill Glassco during Tarragon's sabbatical year: *Human Remains* had originally been scheduled for Tarragon, and *Kennedy's Children* had been staged by Glassco the previous year at Stratford.

Coping with this kind of success became an acid test for Toronto's small theatres. As Tarragon had proven with the Donnelly trilogy, a popular show in a small house could bring as many problems as an unpopular one. Because of the limited number of seats available, holdovers (even sold-out ones) were slow to recoup production expenses. Moreover, since actors' salaries are smaller in smaller houses, busy actors making low salaries would want to move on to other work rather than to continue a long run in an alternative theatre. In addition, Equity had shown that it would interpret full houses as a sign that actors' salaries and working conditions needed upgrading, even when the producing company subsisted on marginal funding. But marginal companies really had no choice but to pursue growth, if only to raise their standard of cultural living with adequate equipment and more support staff. They aspired to the same stability and public recognition as had accrued to such companies as Passe Muraille and Tarragon.

Following its successful 1975–76 season, New Theatre prepared a brief to persuade arts councils that the company's accomplishments demonstrated that it deserved far greater financial support.[6] The dominant theme in the brief, aside from the boosterism typical of such documents, is the incongruity between New Theatre's financial situation and its ambitions. Offstage, it appealed to the arts councils for increased operating funds to support its work in renovated quarters at the old Adelaide Street courthouse. Onstage meanwhile, New Theatre would present a new rock musical by Michael Hollingsworth, *White Noise*, at its Bathurst Street location. And finally, in something of a coup, Stanley had obtained the performance rights to Tom Stoppard's West End and Broadway hit *Travesties*. To help finance a large production needed to pay the high royalties, he enlisted the aid of two co-producers, then rising stars in Toronto's entertainment business, Garth Drabinsky and Moses Znaimer. (Stanley had already co-produced *Miss Margarida* with Znaimer.) Arnold Edinborough, in the *Financial Post*, hailed the innovative marriage of public and private funding to produce *Travesties*, a practice which was to become more common in the 1980s. 'New Theatre,' he wrote, 'has not only put new life consistently into the Toronto theatrical scene, it has also been given a new method of financing which may begin a move in theatre away from high seriousness to solid entertainment – with beneficial effects for authors, writers, producers, and audiences.'[7]

All three projects proved disastrous. *White Noise*, based loosely on the Electra myth and directed by Clarke Rogers, opened in February 1977 to unanimously terrible reviews. In April came *Travesties*, co-produced by Znaimer and Drabinsky and directed by Stanley. The producers rented the St Lawrence Centre and reportedly paid Barry Morse $2000 per week to star in it. Reviews were mixed, and attendance far from capacity – not all that surprising for a small theatre presenting a single production without the benefit of subscriptions. In some quarters, the results were perceived as a just come-uppance for a young director (as Gina Mallet put it) 'displaying an imagination rather bigger than his current abilities.'[8] Finally, the move to Adelaide Court proved a debilitating expense to New Theatre. During two years there (1978–80), the company produced Sam Shepard's *The Curse of the Starving Class*, a new version of John Palmer's *The Pits*, Erika Ritter's *Automatic Pilot*, and Barry Collins' *Judgement*, a one-man show featuring R.H. Thomson. Of these, only *Automatic Pilot* attracted sizeable audiences, while confirming Ritter and actress Fiona Reid as two of the brightest talents in Canadian theatre. Ironically, because of the tight scheduling necessary at Adelaide Court, New Theatre was unable to extend the run of *Automatic Pilot* in what was supposed to be its own building. Originally produced in January 1980, *Automatic Pilot* was remounted at Toronto Free Theatre in February and again at the Bayview Playhouse in June. The program for the Bayview run reported that Stanley was 'in the process of relinquishing his position with New Theatre and concentrating his energies on ARTSTRUST, a production and investment partnership.' It was New Theatre's last production.

Open Circle Theatre

Open Circle Theatre began as a melding of George Luscombe's social consciousness and Peter Cheeseman's documentary methods. It sought to redefine the term 'community theatre' within a professional context, as the program notes from its first production proclaimed: 'It is the aim of this company to unite the professional artist with the community. We are interested in articulating the needs of the community by establishing a cycle of research and contact within it.' In practical terms, Open Circle created its early productions by identifying an issue of local interest, creating a text from interviews with people affected by the issue, and making the resulting show accessible to them. Since most people in this target audience were not habitual theatre-goers, Open Circle also tried to present its shows with a popular performance style, for a low admission price, and in a convenient location. The company defined this policy very clearly at its inception, and adhered to it closely for two seasons. While it found a mandate, however, it did not find an audience. (Perhaps it is a romantic delusion to believe one can convert non-theatre-goers to the theatre.) After enduring poor attendance for most of its productions, Open Circle drifted away from its documentation of specific local problems toward producing scripts of more general social concern. In this broadening process, it lit upon a wildly successful commercial production, Israel Horovitz's *The Primary English Class*, the skilful marketing of which extended the life of the company by several years. Even this unexpected hit, however, could not sustain the company through its move to Adelaide Court, which greatly increased Open Circle's operating expenses while further dissipating its artistic identity. After a brief return to overtly political comedies, the company suffered a fatal financial collapse, unfortunately on the eve of opening another show.

Open Circle Theatre was founded in 1973 by the husband-and-wife team of Ray Whelan and Sylvia Tucker. Whelan had been a child performer in his native Dublin, a singer-impersonator at age ten and an actor at fourteen. He came to Canada in 1960 and, as he said, 'spent years trying to scrounge acting work in the barely-existent Toronto theatre scene.'9 Whelan worked with George Luscombe at Toronto Workshop Productions from 1967 to 1972, appearing in many productions (including title roles in *The Good Soldier Schweik* and *The Resistible Rise of Arturo Ui*) and conducting workshops in documentary theatre on Luscombe's behalf. There he also met Sylvia Tucker, born and educated in the United States, who had come to Toronto in the mid-1960s to help U.S. draft resisters. In Toronto, Tucker acted at the Colonnade Theatre, at TWP, and at the Central Library in Jim Garrard's notorious production of *Futz*. While seeking to combine their social concerns with their desire to make a living in professional theatre, Whelan and Tucker met Peter Cheeseman, the celebrated British director from Stoke-on-Trent who visited Theatre Passe Muraille in 1972. As Herbert Whittaker reported, 'Whelan took the British director around the province to give workshops on the Cheeseman school of documentary theatre. Hooked, Whelan won support from the Canadian Directors in Britain scheme, and went to England to work under Cheeseman.'10 Apparently the experience with Cheeseman was not what Whelan and Tucker expected, for they returned to Canada after only three months instead of the allotted six. On their return, they founded Open Circle Theatre with goals and methods similar to Cheeseman's. Their company's founding members, drawn mainly from their former colleagues at Toronto Workshop Productions, included Diane Grant, Marcella Lustig, and Michael Marshall.

Open Circle's first production was *No Way, José*, a 'documentary revue' about welfare and unemployment in Toronto, which opened in April 1973 at St Paul's Church, Avenue Road. The dialogue was created by editing interviews conducted by the company as part of their research process, with songs written by Tucker, musical director Pierre Gallant, and actor Michael Kirby. Kareda felt the company had a promising idea in this format, something which had yet to be supplied by the growing number of small theatre companies in the city. It had found, in other words, an unfulfilled mandate. 'Toronto's theatre has needed a company which could provide the dramatic equivalent of a monthly news magazine,' wrote Kareda, 'who could absorb the events of a given period of time and, while they were still fairly fresh in our memory, re-produce them in a satirical way.'[11] However, despite its deliberately populist material and popular style, despite generally favourable reviews, and despite 'pay-what-you-can' admission for all performances, only nine hundred people attended the twenty performances of *No Way, José*, and only $950 was collected. Financing of the show had been marginal from the outset: besides a $600 grant from Theatre Ontario, production expenses were met by donations from company members, whose salaries were only ten dollars per week.[12]

The success of *The Farm Show* a few months earlier showed that documentary theatre could be successful with both critics and audiences. In fact, emulating the success of *The Farm Show* became a goal for Open Circle, in order, as Whelan said, 'to do the same kind of thing for people in Toronto.'[13] (This goal eluded even Paul Thompson for several years, as we have seen.) For Open Circle's second production, the model of *The Farm Show* was closely followed. This was a musical revue about the community of the Toronto Islands, entitled *I'm Hanlan, He's Durnan, He's Ward*. Financed by an OFY grant, the company researched the history and current attitudes of people on the Toronto Islands by interviewing island residents. They then edited the material into a revue format, and performed it in the Ward's Island Association Club House in July 1973. The production not only received positive reviews, but also delighted the local residents who, it was reported, 'came out in full force, even providing a nightly feast of cakes and pies.'[14] This documentary pattern was also followed in Open Circle's next show, *COP*, a collective creation about the relationship between Toronto's police force and its citizenry, which opened in November in a rented hall off College Street.

The following summer, in 1974, an invitation from the Island community and another OFY grant enabled Open Circle to return to Ward's Island to create a new show. This time it was *Business As Usual*, an acerbic satire on lead pollution in Toronto. Lead poisoning was an issue which deeply affected a western portion of the city, but not the Toronto Islands; and, to the disappointment of the Open Circle company, the Island audience which they had cultivated so carefully in the previous summer stayed away from *Business As Usual*. Perhaps the show was too serious or too remote for the Islanders, who had so enjoyed Open Circle's light-hearted flattery the previous year.

Business As Usual was remounted at St Paul's Church, Avenue Road, in the fall of 1974, but public response remained very slight. Two performances were even cancelled in its first week due to lack of audience. Faced with such public indifference, Open Circle abandoned its documentary revue format. Ultimately this left the company with no distinctive style to distinguish its work from the collectives of Passe Muraille, the new modern repertory of New Theatre, or the socialist commitment of Toronto Workshop Productions. Open Circle was also weakened by the splintering of new groups which followed the initial success of the first wave: as Open Circle had (in effect) split off from TWP and Theatre Passe Muraille, so two actresses from Open Circle (Diane Grant and Marcella Lustig) left to found their own company, Redlight Theatre. Only a couple of years earlier there had been strength in this kind of diversity, but now it seemed that the splintering process was accelerating and that the alternative theatres were suffering by it. As Kareda wrote,

Are there simply too many small theatres? Too much unnecessary competition? Does the proliferation of small groups thin out the community of creative artists, thin out potential audiences, and most frighteningly, thin out the money available from granting agencies? ...

Thus, the multiplication of small groups is in some ways self-defeating. The other side of the dilemma, however, is that it is necessary. That independence of ambition might yet produce something unusual and original. If Bill Glassco hadn't set out from the Factory Lab, we wouldn't have Tarragon. If Martin Kinch and John Palmer had not moved away from Theatre Passe Muraille, we wouldn't have Toronto Free Theatre. Setting out on one's own may be the catalyst for creative growth, but it takes time to discover whether it has happened.[15]

In the case of Open Circle, this creative growth had taken place, but the community did not support it.

As the company drifted away from its original mandate, it moved toward greener but overcrowded pastures. Like many other alternative theatres, it began to trade in scripted drama rather than collectives, conventional presentation rather than satiric song-and-dance, general social issues rather than specifically local ones. In 1975 Open Circle produced three scripted plays in various locations. *A Soupsong* by Ralph Brockhouse retold Gay's *The Beggar's Opera* as a story about world food shortages in the near future. (Brockhouse earlier had served as dramaturge for *Business As Usual*.) *The Life and Times of Grey Owl* by Martin Lavut and Arnie Gelbart was a stage biography of the famous English-born Canadian impostor and conservationist. *The Blood Knot* by Athol Fugard, the company's first play without music, explored issues of interpersonal and interracial relations against the background of South African apartheid.

In its last play of the 1975–76 season, Open Circle returned to specifically local issues with David Lewis Stein's *The Hearing,* a play about the process of adjudicating real estate development proposals in Toronto. This play flew in the face of both the ideology and the aesthetics on which Open Circle had been founded. Because the play presented an unsympathetic view of left-wing anti-development forces, reported the *Globe and Mail,* 'the company nearly stopped the production for fear of alienating its core audience and furthering an outlook it had no sympathy for at all.'[16] In addition, neither the author, Stein, nor the director, Jeremy Gibson, wanted anything to do with Open Circle's customary workshop methods or multiple roles. While *The Hearing* received good reviews, these internal conflicts further undermined the company's original artistic methods and ideology. Growing problems of identity were compounded by the company's lack of a permanent performing space: since leaving Ward's Island, every Open Circle production had been presented in a different rented location.

Open Circle Theatre would have probably succumbed quietly at this time were it not for its production of Israel Horovitz's *The Primary English Class,* a comedy about racial stereotypes set in a language school for immigrants. *The Primary English Class* opened to glowing reviews in February 1977 at New Theatre on Bathurst Street. It was remounted at Tarragon Theatre that summer and again at the Bayview Playhouse that fall, and spawned two touring versions. There was some social commentary implicit in the play, but it was incidental to a lot of low comedy. In fact, there were persistent criticisms that *The Primary English Class* was not so much a lampoon of ethnic intolerance as an exploitation of it. As cast member Michael Macina wrote, in reporting on Horovitz's visit to Toronto,

There is throughout Horovitz' work to date an unwillingness to meet issues head on in a way which is both theatrically effective and honest. Audience members present at the first discussion struck out straightaway at Horovitz' betrayal of ethnics in *The Primary English Class,* in an emotionally honest response to the play; the theatre community likewise based a hovering mistrust on a gut-level desire for honesty, issues and methods.[17]

In a companion article, another commentator agreed that, racist or not, the play was so insubstantial as to be irrelevant to the genuine social problems of immigrants in the community.

Sylvia Tucker later admitted that she was not particularly fond of the play. Nevertheless, she threw herself into marketing it, with considerable success.[18] With the profits from this production, Open Circle was able to complete its plans to move into the Adelaide Court Theatre complex along with New Theatre and Le Théâtre du P'tit Bonheur, which further diluted Open Circle's already weak identity.

As far as an artistic mandate was concerned, Open Circle found itself hemmed into a smaller and smaller area of middle ground, as this program note from *The Primary English Class* suggests:

We define ourselves as an alternative theatre. The work offered is not only an alternative to the obviously 'commercial' form, it is also alternative to the more esoteric experimentation one can encounter in other small theatres.

Our subject matter reflects a strong social consciousness, never forgetting however that the major aim is to ENTERTAIN.

As Tucker herself later commented, 'The combination of Primary English Class and the move to Adelaide Court brought in new people and new emphases, and we were trying to please too many masters. The company basically fell apart. We didn't have our own audience any more. And I couldn't distinguish us from the Free Theatre or the Tarragon.'[19]

Open Circle's first production at Adelaide Court was another Horovitz play, *Mackerel*, which opened in October 1978. *Mackerel* was a play about a giant fish which was itself a huge flop. Its permanent staff reduced to two (Whelan had left by then), the company produced very few shows thereafter. In March 1982, the day before previews were to begin for its third Dario Fo play in three years, Open Circle was unable to renew its two-week salary bond with Actors Equity. An expected Canada Council grant was delayed due to late paperwork, the board of directors declined to personally guarantee a line of credit, and the company suspended operations indefinitely.[20] The theatre community was evidently saddened by the demise of Open Circle, but its sense of loss was tempered with a sense of release, as if a terminally ill friend had died and his suffering finally over. As Gina Mallet observed, Open Circle 'never seemed quite at home trying to make a buck with quasi-commercial productions.'[21] It was the second Adelaide Court tenant to shut up shop, and was followed the next year by Phoenix Theatre.

Phoenix Theatre

Strictly speaking, the Phoenix Theatre arose too late to be part of this study. However, it has several characteristics which argue for its inclusion. First, it was the most critically successful of the later alternative theatres, through a series of productions in the late 1970s. Second, it was built on a foundation of local amateur theatre which is largely missing in other Toronto companies. Finally, it completes the trio of second-wave theatres which expired at Adelaide Court. The paradoxes of an alternative theatre courting success in a commercial age were never illustrated so clearly as in the Phoenix Theatre.

With so many other companies promoting new Canadian work in the mid-1970s, Phoenix initially sought a mandate by staging modern international drama (mainly British) which was not commercial enough to fill the St Lawrence Centre or the larger touring houses. Its two founders, Graham Harley and Bryan Foster, had worked extensively in amateur theatre in Toronto, and wished to turn their avocation into a career. Because both Harley and Foster were unknown in the established professional theatres, alternative or mainstream, and because they did not profess any dedication to new Canadian drama, the Phoenix was at first dismissed as an amateur group aspiring only to 'the status of a provincial English repertory company.'[22] This image was reinforced by the company's financial reliance, in its early unsubsidized years, on productions of that solid gold chestnut *The Mousetrap*. Eventually, however, the Phoenix under Harley won the admiration of the theatre community with its tenacity, its adventurous programming, and some excellent productions. In 1980, when other alternative companies were producing fewer original works, the Phoenix Theatre abruptly reversed its field. It began to present new Canadian plays for the same reason it had once shown modern British drama or Restoration comedy: because these were good plays which might otherwise not be seen. In the ensuing years, however, the Phoenix fell prey to the public demand for more comfortable surroundings, to the rising cost of rented theatre space, to a loss of public identity due to the loss of its own theatre, and to administrative exhaustion due to chronic underfunding and resulting lack of support staff. It closed permanently in 1983.

Phoenix Theatre is rightly identified with Graham Harley (b. 1942), artistic director throughout the company's existence. Born in England's industrial Midlands, Harley studied literature at Oxford, taught in universities in Scotland and the United States, and in 1972 came to Canada to teach at the University of Toronto. Harley had done quite a bit of acting as an undergraduate at Oxford, and some directing as well, but the constraints of trying to complete his doctorate while teaching full-time had kept him away from the stage until he reached Toronto.

'Once I'd finished the PHD in the early '70s,' he recalls, 'I found psychologically that was what really had kept me in the university.'[23] Like Bill Glassco, Harley found himself disenchanted with the prospect of a career in university teaching. His new ambition was to run his own theatre company. He resumed his acting with a number of amateur companies in Toronto, mostly at the Central Library Theatre. One of these groups, called Menagerie Players, was run by Australian Bryan Foster, who (like Harley) wished to move into professional theatre. With Menagerie Players, Harley acted in Pinter's *The Birthday Party* in November 1973, and directed Albee's *All Over* in September 1974.

The opportunity to form a new company arose when a studio space on Dupont Street became available early in 1975. It was then occupied by the Toronto Centre for the Arts, an organization formed in January 1974 by the union of a private theatre training centre (Toronto Actors' Studio, founded 1963) and an affiliated performance group (Actors' Theatre, founded 1971). The studio theatre itself was a former woodworking shop upstairs at 390 Dupont Street, just two doors from the original Factory Theatre Lab, an intimate performing space seating about 120. Neither the Actors' Theatre nor the short-lived Toronto Centre for the Arts had much critical success with their productions, and suffered by comparison with the major alternative theatres in the early 1970s. By the end of 1974 the Toronto Centre for the Arts was about to close, and needed to unload its lease obligations. Harley and Foster found two other partners, pooled $6500 to buy the former company's equipment, and arranged to assume the lease. The name 'Phoenix Theatre' was an apt one, since the new company was rising from the ashes of the earlier ones.[24]

The Phoenix's first production, in April 1975, was *Butley* by Simon Gray, with Harley playing the title role of an embittered English professor. By that time the initial euphoria of discovering new Canadian drama had subsided, and there was a growing concern that Toronto's approach to repertory had become too parochial. To produce a healthy cultural climate in Toronto, went this reasoning, the new Canadian drama and its accompanying emphasis on collective creation needed to be balanced with exposure to good international playwrights. As one commentator put it, in praise of *Butley*, 'We are fortunate that people like Graham Harley sense the need for "checks and balances" in theatre, and can give us first-rate productions of plays we might otherwise not see in Toronto.'[25] While *Butley* was well received critically, audiences were unfamiliar with it and box-office was poor. This immediate financial setback prevented the Phoenix from hiring Equity actors for the next two years. During this period, with no significant subsidy for their theatre, Harley and Foster drew no salary from the Phoenix. They lived by part-time employment, mainly teaching, and kept (for their trouble) the proceeds from selling intermission refreshments at their theatre. Nonetheless they persisted, following *Butley* with productions of a Pinter double-bill, *The Lover* and *The Collection*, and Ann Jellicoe's *The Knack*. These plays helped to define the Phoenix Theatre's repertory: good modern plays which were not Canadian enough for the established alternative theatres, but not commercial enough for the regionals.

Phoenix Theatre opened its 1975–76 season with *The Mousetrap*, Agatha Christie's popular mystery, which saved the company from early financial collapse. The profits from this production enabled Harley and Foster to mount *Fortune and Men's Eyes* in November 1975, which won a belated Chalmers Award for John Herbert and brought Phoenix Theatre its first recognition in the theatre community. 'It put us on the map,' recalled Harley, 'people took notice of us.'[26] A second run of *The Mousetrap* enabled them to mount Stoppard's *Rosencrantz and Guildenstern Are Dead* the following spring, as well as an eccentric double-bill directed by John Herbert, his own *Close Friends* (earlier staged in 1970 at the FUT festival) and Tennessee Williams' *The Gracious Lady*. Profits from *The Mousetrap* also enabled Harley and Foster to buy out their original partners at this time. *The Mousetrap* also introduced Ann Antkiw to the Phoenix, a veteran of community theatre who became general manager when Foster left the next year.

In the summer of 1976, the Phoenix produced two profitable English farces, *No Sex Please, We're British* and *What the Butler Saw*. Once again, these commercial successes allowed the company to produce some unusual international plays for its third season, Ferenc Molnár's *The Play's the Thing* and John Hopkins' homosexual drama *Find Your Way Home*. Another farce, *Pajama Tops*, financed the Toronto première of Joanna Glass's *Canadian Gothic and American Modern*, for which the Phoenix was able to hire two Equity actors and an outside director. Two Equity actors were also hired for the Phoenix's next offering, Harley's production of Edward Bond's *The Sea*. If *Fortune and Men's Eyes* put Phoenix Theatre on the map, *The Sea* put it in the vanguard of Toronto theatre. Ecstatic reviews quickly spread the word that this was the best production in town. As the *Globe and Mail* reported, 'The first night audience was papered, the next night only 40 people turned up and then Saturday, when the first of the rave notices came in, it sold out. Since then, according to artistic director Graham Harley, the theatre has been sold out every night.'[27]

Having established itself in Toronto's cultural community, Phoenix Theatre acquired Equity status for its next project, a production of Alan Ayckbourn's comic trilogy *The Norman Conquests,* presented in repertory from July through October 1977. Harley has often said he tried to take on a new challenge each year at the Phoenix, and his choice of plays now as sole artistic leader of the company was certainly adventurous. Following *The Norman Conquests,* Harley produced Pinter's *Old Times,* Orton's *Loot,* and David Rudkin's *Ashes. Ashes,* in particular, is a difficult and challenging play which sets the story of a young couple trying to conceive a baby in counterpoint to the modern sectarian violence in Northern Ireland. It was directed by Pam Brighton (who had also directed its original production in England), featured two young stars of the Canadian theatre in R.H. Thomson and Fiona Reid, and received outstanding critical acclaim.

The following season saw the Phoenix's most conspicuous triumph, the Restoration comedy *The Relapse* by Sir John Vanbrugh, a play on which Harley had written his doctoral thesis. The audacity of a small theatre with limited resources staging such a sprawling period piece delighted the audience as much as the splendid performances did. As Mallet put it, 'This tiny theatre with perhaps the worst space in Toronto has once again pushed itself out in front of every other theatre in town.'[28] *The Relapse* ran for thirteen weeks on Dupont Street, and was revived the following season for a co-production with Theatre London.

After all these successes, the 1979–80 season was a somewhat bitter one. It opened with Harley's most controversial production, *Chinchilla* by Robert David MacDonald, originally produced at the Citizens' Theatre in Glasgow. *Chinchilla* was an impressionistic play about the flamboyant Russian choreographer Diaghilev and his hedonistic homosexual lifestyle. A controversy over Ray Conlogue's scathing review in the *Globe and Mail* soon overshadowed the production itself, and audience opinion remained divided as to the play's merits.[29] Lead actor Robert Benson appealed for word-of-mouth support from the audience following the second night's curtain call, and Harley placed a paid advertisement in the *Globe and Mail* protesting Conlogue's review and quoting extensively from another critic's enthusiastic praise in the *Toronto Sun.*[30] *Chinchilla* was followed by O'Neill's *Long Day's Journey into Night,* which received poor notices despite the presence of Donald Davis and Doris Petrie in the cast. The season closed with the remounted co-production of *The Relapse*. The high cost of success was already evident at the Phoenix: despite capacity houses, *The Relapse* was allowed to run only two weeks in Toronto, or else it would have started to lose money.

After his successes with British plays, Harley startled Toronto's theatre community in the 1980–81 season by suddenly producing a succession of original Canadian comedies. These included Allan Stratton's *Nurse Jane Goes to Hawaii*, one of Canada's most-produced plays; John Ibbitson's *Mayonnaise*; and Stratton's *Rexy!* about eccentric Canadian prime minister Mackenzie King. The season ended with *Hamlet*, presented for the Toronto Theatre Festival in May 1981. This was the Phoenix's last production on Dupont Street. The lease was about to run out, and there was to be a substantial increase in rent. Moreover, as Harley later recalled, 'There was pressure from both Actors Equity and the city to make improvements. We would have had to spend $250,000 to $500,000 to renovate, and we still would have ended up with a 166-seat theatre and a 16-foot ceiling.'[31]

Harley decided to join Open Circle and Le Théâtre du P'tit Bonheur as tenants at Adelaide Court, taking the place of the recently folded New Theatre. Typically, Harley first revived a commercial success, *Nurse Jane*, in January 1982, then embarked on a daring summer season of international plays. These plays were *President Wilson in Paris* by Australian Ron Blair, *True West* by Sam Shepard, and *The Kite* by W.O. Mitchell. Despite an outstanding acting company, reviews were mixed for these productions and box-office receipts were disappointing. In preceding years Harley would have suspended production and rented out his theatre, but this was not possible at Adelaide Court. By November 1982, with the Phoenix Theatre on the brink of collapse, the theatre community rallied to Harley's support. As he gratefully recalled, 'I was knocked for a loop. In three days, we raised $40,000 ... from people who are not by tradition very well paid. It was really quite humbling. Suddenly, I felt we had a whole new responsibility, not just to theatre, but to a whole community of people out there.'[32] From his beginnings as an interloper, then, Harley's dogged hard work, adventurous artistic sense, and signal accomplishments had made him a respected figure in Toronto theatre. Still this was not enough to save the Phoenix. After three more productions of Canadian plays (the final one with the prophetic title *Last Call!*), the Phoenix Theatre gave up trying to pay its rent with good reviews. In July 1983 its board of directors voted to dissolve the company.

The Phoenix's move to Adelaide Court had reduced its public profile, its personal contact with its supporters, and its revenue-producing capabilities, while greatly increasing its operating expenses. Perhaps if the Phoenix had not lost its home on Dupont Street, as Harley believes, the company would still be operating. But the space was lost, not due to carelessness or cupidity, but due to its insuperable architectural inadequacies. It was a good enough theatre for an experimental company, but not for an established one. Moreover, the psychological exhaustion afflicting the Phoenix's only two permanent employees, Harley and Antkiw, left them unable to persist through new fiscal emergencies as they had in the company's earlier years. As Harley joked a few months before his theatre was finally closed, 'I've never regretted it for a minute. I don't know, however, if I could do it now. As Nicky Pennell would say, 'I'm too old, too tired, and too talented.'[33] The passing of the Phoenix was mourned by the theatre community as if it were the death of a respected colleague. 'The Phoenix was scrappy, irritating and irresistible all at once,' wrote Ray Conlogue, the object of Harley's wrath over *Chinchilla*. 'It will be missed.'[34]

9

NDWT

The major preliminary work [for the Donnelly tour] has been done, and that was the creation of an innovative performing style. No arts council or impresario can touch that; it is NDWT's special glory.[1]

Urjo Kareda, April 1975

It is appropriate that this study should end with the NDWT company, because the company's gestation period spans the whole of the period under scrutiny. NDWT is usually considered a second-wave company because it was not founded officially until 1975. However, the seeds of NDWT were sown in 1966 at the University of Western Ontario, when student Keith Turnbull and English professor James Reaney produced Reaney's play *Listen to the Wind*. That year Turnbull was the first of the new generation of Canadian directors to present a season of exclusively Canadian plays; Reaney, in turn, was one of the few Canadian writers already established as a playwright when the alternative theatres turned toward Canadian drama in the early 1970s. The founding members of NDWT were assembled seven years later, in 1973, when Reaney's and Turnbull's paths crossed again with another production of *Listen to the Wind*, this time at the Neptune Theatre in Halifax. In the interim, Turnbull had completed an astonishingly quick rise and fall through the ranks of established Canadian theatre, while Reaney had been busy researching a play about the Donnelly massacre, a celebrated piece of local history in southwestern Ontario. Reaney and Turnbull agreed to collaborate on the Donnelly project, which became a landmark in the history of Canadian drama and theatre. Although the Donnelly plays

were first produced by Tarragon Theatre, it was always understood that
the company which created them, under the direction of Reaney and
Turnbull, was a separate entity. By the time the last of the trilogy
reached the stage in 1975, this distinction was made official with the
founding of a new company, named (mysteriously) NDWT.

Keith Turnbull (b. 1944) was born in Lindsay, Ontario, and raised in
London. Although he studied political science at university, Turnbull's
main interest was always theatre. As a teenager he directed plays at high
school and worked in production at the London Little Theatre. In 1964
he became involved in a summer theatre project sponsored by the
University of Western Ontario's Summer School and Extension Department. The repertory of this company was far more challenging than was
usual for summer stock, including such modern classics as *Look Back in
Anger*, *The Caucasian Chalk Circle*, and *Antigone*. The following summer,
Turnbull became the group's producer. Frustrated by what he perceived as unnecessary red tape at the university, Turnbull moved
Summer Theatre 65 to downtown London. He rented a second-storey
strip club, the Oasis Restaurant Theatre, where he presented another
challenging season of plays, including *Summer and Smoke*, *A Taste of
Honey*, and *The Balcony*.

For Summer Theatre 65, Turnbull also decided that one of his
productions ought to be a Canadian play. While trying to choose such a
play, Turnbull discovered (as Ken Gass did a few years later) that there
were very few Canadian plays in print. However, someone mentioned to
him that there was a Canadian playwright living in London and teaching
at Western. This, of course, was James Reaney, then forty years old;
Turnbull had never heard of him. Reaney had completed a PHD under
Northrop Frye at the University of Toronto, and gone on to teach at the
University of Manitoba and at Western. He had already won three
Governor-General's awards, the first two for volumes of poetry, and the
third for a collection of poetic drama published in 1962 entitled *The
Killdeer and Other Plays*. In the 1960s, Reaney's emphasis as a writer
shifted from poetry to a growing personal involvement in producing
original drama. He also developed strong connections with the best
Canadian theatres of the time. Reaney's own early plays had been
produced at the Alumnae Theatre and Hart House in Toronto; and his
ideas on drama had been deeply affected by seeing two important
experiments in arena staging, the first plays at the Stratford Festival and
George Luscombe's *Hey Rube!* in the park at Stratford. (Is it a
coincidence that both of these took place in a tent?) While Reaney was

living in Winnipeg, the Manitoba Theatre Centre was founded by one of his former students, John Hirsch. Hirsch later directed the first productions of some of Reaney's plays, including *Names and Nicknames* at the MTC (1963) and *Colours in the Dark* at the Stratford Festival (1967).

As a result of meeting Reaney, Turnbull presented a double-bill of Canadian plays in Summer Theatre 65. It consisted of two previously unproduced plays, Rae Davis' *Transistor* (directed by the author) and Reaney's *The Sun and the Moon* (co-directed by Reaney and Turnbull). The program for this production contains a number of familiar names.[2] Artist Jack Chambers painted the landscape panels, while another artist, John Boyle, appeared in the cast. Martin Kinch, who directed *The Balcony*, acted in both *Transistor* and *The Sun and the Moon*. The production's stage manager was Paul Thompson, who left that fall for his first season in Lyons with Roger Planchon. In some ways, the University of Western Ontario's summer theatre was the cradle of later alternative theatre in Toronto.

At the end of the summer, at John Hirsch's suggestion, Turnbull left to travel in Europe and see theatre there. His first stop was the Citizens' Theatre in Glasgow, where Reaney's *The Killdeer* was being produced in a festival of Commonwealth theatre. (Canadian commentators at this festival included John Hirsch, Michael Langham, and Herbert Whittaker.) Turnbull then went to London, England, where he was able to work in a television studio through some Canadian connections. He also travelled to Lyons and stayed with Paul Thompson for several weeks. In Europe, Turnbull found an institutional commitment to the training of young talent which he had not seen in Canada. Despite having laid little groundwork for his trip, he was allowed to observe rehearsals in Lyons, in Milan, in Munich (where the resident playwrights were Dürrenmatt and Anouilh), and at London's Old Vic. Wherever he went, he saw new work being produced and heard experts tell him that Canada would never have a mature theatre until new work was part of its life.

When Turnbull returned home to Ontario to produce another summer season, he arranged for seminars to be given to his company by Hirsch and David William (who staged Glasgow's production of *The Killdeer*), both of whom were directing that summer at Stratford. Hirsch argued that a company needed to define its function, and suggested that Summer Theatre 66 ought to produce an all-Canadian bill.[3] Over the objections of many of the project's previous supporters, Turnbull discarded the international plays which had already been selected, and chose Canadian plays to take their place. Each play was given five performances, in an auditorium on campus, with a new play opening each week. Turnbull himself directed *Down Wellington*, a revue written by the company, and *The Audition* by Dan Daniels. Other productions were *Listen to the Wind*, written and directed by James Reaney; *Marise* by Jack Cunningham, co-directed by Kinch and Thompson; and *Riel* by John Coulter, directed by Stratford assistant director Tim Bond. (*Riel* was the only production which was not a première, and the only one for which the director received a fee.) Besides the innovation of Canadian content, the audience was encouraged to remain after each performance to discuss the play with its author. Fringe activities added to the festive atmosphere of the summer season, with a play for children (Reaney's *Names and Nicknames*) and with two medieval plays performed outdoors. Some high-profile actors and directors came down from Stratford to see this experiment, as did Nathan Cohen from Toronto. While not enthralled with the production he saw, Cohen was full of praise for the principles behind Turnbull's all-Canadian season. 'Whatever the dangers, artistic and at the box-office,' he wrote, 'Mr. Turnbull has right on his side. He knows that a dynamic theatre cannot exist on the borrowings from the past and present of other peoples. The reason the Canadian theatre, for all the interest in it, has not taken hold at home, or made any impression abroad, is that it does not have its own sources of nourishment.'[4]

The following winter, Turnbull served as Reaney's assistant at a community centre for artistic projects, 'Alphacentre,' which Reaney established in London. (Reaney's own literary journal and print shop, *Alphabet* and the Alphabet Press, were already fixtures in London's artistic community.) One of their activities there was a series of Saturday morning 'Listeners Workshops' initiated in response to the summer's production of *Listen to the Wind*. In these, Reaney used techniques of creative drama with a mixed group of adults and children, to develop the interpersonal and theatrical sensitivity required for the kind of theatre he wished to pursue. In these Listeners Workshops, Reaney himself developed the methods which he was to use to create the Donnelly trilogy with NDWT.

The next summer, after working at Expo 67, Turnbull began his five-year association with the Manitoba Theatre Centre. To Turnbull (and to many others), the MTC represented the aspiration of the Canadian theatre artist to work as a professional in his own country. First Turnbull drove to Winnipeg just to *see* this shrine; then he drove east to the Shaw Festival to offer himself to Edward Gilbert, Hirsch's successor at the MTC, as an unpaid assistant, in effect a 'stagiaire' in Winnipeg. At the MTC that fall, Turnbull just sat and watched rehearsals for two shows, before graduating to assistant director on Gilbert's acclaimed production of *The Three Sisters*. At the same time, Turnbull began directing studio projects in the Theatre Across-the-Street, a small open space which had been used mainly for the MTC's educational programs. Turnbull's productions there during 1967–68 included *Endgame, La Voix Humaine*, and a one-hour version of *Hamlet*. In Winnipeg as in Stratford, company members who wanted to explore their craft beyond their current mainstage duties would work on these studio productions, unpaid, whenever their schedules permitted. For young directors such as Turnbull, this was their first opportunity to work with experienced professional actors.

In the spring of 1968, Turnbull joined the Stratford Festival company as an assistant director. In his first season there he assisted Douglas Campbell on *Romeo and Juliet*, Jean Gascon on *The Seagull*, and Hirsch on *A Midsummer Night's Dream* and *The Three Musketeers*. At the end of the summer, he returned to Winnipeg with a new mandate for Theatre Across-the-Street. In other regional centres as well as in Toronto, new artists and ideas were inundating the mainstream theatres. As a result, between 1968 and 1972 several regional theatres established their own alternative stages to try to accommodate this new activity and the smaller audience to which it would appeal. One of the first of these regional second stages was the MTC's Theatre Across-the-Street (precursor to its more famous Warehouse), which Gilbert wanted Turnbull to make a centre for new experimental drama. In his 1968–69 season there, Turnbull directed Beckett's *Happy Days*, Ionesco's *Exit the King*, de Ghelderode's *Red Magic,* and an improvised play about Che Guevara entitled *How the Puppets Formed a Government*. Adding to his directorial range, Turnbull also staged a classic there, *School for Wives*, and a Canadian play, *Fortune and Men's Eyes*. Theatre Across-the-Street's experimental tone and daring repertory were a breath of fresh air in a bad time for the MTC. That season, its original Dominion Theatre home was being demolished, and its mainstage productions were being presented in the cavernous Centennial Concert Hall while the new MTC building was under construction. During this transitional period, Gilbert's attempts to program for this difficult space proved disastrous: for instance, a Broadway touring production of *Funny Girl* was cancelled at the last minute, resulting in some bad press and in lawsuits threatened by both the MTC and the show's New York producer. Meanwhile, Theatre Across-the-Street flourished. Nathan Cohen (again) travelled to Winnipeg to see Turnbull's experiment, and found it the only encouraging aspect of the MTC's dismal 1968–69 season.[5]

Turnbull's star continued to rise the following year as he commuted between Winnipeg, Halifax, Stratford, and wherever the Stratford company was touring. He assisted on three more Stratford productions, including Hirsch's production of *The Satyricon* which proved to be such a crossroads for Tom Hendry and the future Toronto Free Theatre. Turnbull also travelled to Ottawa with the Stratford company, where he restaged Hirsch's *Hamlet* for the NAC Theatre, and staged his own production of the off-off-Broadway play *America Hurrah* in the NAC Studio. In the 1969–70 season, Turnbull also directed two more plays for MTC's Theatre Across-the-Street and three for the Neptune Theatre in Halifax, where the MTC's former educational director, Robert Sherrin, was artistic director. Meanwhile, back in Winnipeg, the MTC's new artistic director, Kurt Reis, was having a difficult time with his board of directors, and finally resigned after a series of disputes. Surprisingly Keith Turnbull, only twenty-six years old, was appointed his successor.

Turnbull's two seasons at the MTC began in confusion, and ended in bitterness. He arrived to find the MTC's staff decimated after Reis's departure, and no season in place with which to open the new MTC building. Turnbull was deeply committed to the community-theatre ideals of the MTC and to broadening its audience base. He wished to produce a truly balanced season for his audience, including some very challenging plays (such as Hirsch's production of *A Man's a Man* which opened the new theatre) and some new Canadian work as well. However, Turnbull was never comfortable with the social niceties of his position, particularly with the society-page puffery surrounding the opening of the new theatre. It also appears that the MTC board was never comfortable with its choice of this Canadian *wunderkind*: in that first season Turnbull was listed as 'Resident Director,' not artistic director, while Hirsch was listed as 'Consultant Artistic Director.' Turnbull believes that his insistence on programming some new Canadian drama, in the wake of the 'Gaspé Manifesto' with which he agreed so thoroughly, finally led to his abrupt dismissal. In April 1972, while rehearsing the last play of his second season, Turnbull was informed that his contract would not be renewed. In its press releases the MTC's board tried to give the impression that he had resigned, but Turnbull quickly set the record straight. He also left no doubts as to what he thought of the MTC's board. 'Although I regret having to leave Manitoba and having to sever my full-time relationship with this fine theatre,' he said, 'I am happy to be relieved of the creativity-stifling pressures of the theatre's archaic and ill-managed board structure.'[6]

Leaving Winnipeg, Turnbull was quickly hired as director of Neptune Theatre's Second Stage, another regional theatre response to experimental theatre and new Canadian drama. Turnbull remained director of this LIP-financed project for only a few months, then moved to England determined to make his theatrical career in an environment which he felt would be more receptive. But a prior commitment to Neptune brought him back to Canada to direct a new production of Reaney's *Listen to the Wind* in January 1973. For Turnbull, having endured so much at the MTC, directing *Listen to the Wind* represented a reaffirmation of his roots in southwestern Ontario, and of his beginnings as a director. As Turnbull wrote, while in rehearsal for this show, 'Producing "Listen to the Wind" with James Reaney [in 1966] was one of the most exciting experiences in theatre I've ever had. It gave me a deep understanding of the basic thing in producing theatre, which I discovered then was much more than just writing off for the script to New York or London. Reaney taught me "the making of theatre." With his plays, I can create something which is related to how I see things around me. I can draw on my own experiences of growing up in Canada.'[7]

While in Halifax, Turnbull talked with Reaney about the Donnelly project, which Turnbull had wanted to produce at the MTC. Still in Halifax, he received his first professional offer to direct a new Canadian play when Bill Glassco telephoned from Tarragon Theatre about *A Quiet Day in Belfast*. These new opportunities reawakened Turnbull's ambitions to make his career in Canada. His English agent, a veteran of the Guthrie years at Stratford, warned him against returning to a situation which had devoured so many youthful ideals. 'I was there with Bill Needles and Bill Hutt,' she said, 'and don't you think they didn't have just as much get-up-and-go as you have.'[8] But the opportunity to work with Reaney on his Donnelly project was too great a temptation. By the time developmental workshops began in Halifax that summer, the actors, the director, the playwright, and Tarragon Theatre were all committed to producing what became the Donnelly trilogy.

The NDWT company coalesced around these workshops conducted by Reaney and Turnbull in the summer of 1973. These were similar to the Listeners Workshops of 1966–67, but with two significant differences:

they were conducted daily instead of weekly, and they were conducted with professional actors alongside amateurs, students, and children. One of these professionals was Patricia Ludwick, who was to play Mrs Donnelly, born in British Columbia but trained at the London Academy of Music and Dramatic Art (LAMDA), a youthful veteran of Stratford tours and several regional theatres. Another was Jerry Franken, born in Edmonton but raised and trained in California, who was to make James Donnelly, Sr, his most famous role. Other key members were David Ferry, a native of Newfoundland who trained at Canada's National Theatre School, and Tom Carew from England. Some other actors who took part in the workshops did not finally appear in the trilogy: Richard Donat, who never seemed comfortable with the material; Blair Brown, who eventually became a movie star instead; and Michael and Susan Hogan, who rejoined NDWT a few years later. The company lived on Neptune work when they could get it, and slept on Turnbull's floor when they had nowhere to stay. To these intelligent and talented actors, Reaney's material represented an opportunity to stretch the limits of their craft, an opportunity not normally available to them in regional theatres. It also represented (for them as well as for Turnbull) a return to the idealism which they had brought into the theatre business, but which they had felt slipping away. Many personal and professional sacrifices were made for the sake of work they could believe in, sacrifices which became a common bond within the company. What began as a summer of workshops turned into a commitment of up to three years.

The first play of the trilogy, *Sticks and Stones*, opened at Tarragon Theatre in November 1973, and played for a month to overflow houses. Critical reaction, as we have seen, was ecstatic. The next summer, another series of Donnelly workshops was held in Halifax, where Turnbull was again directing for Neptune Theatre. The second Donnelly play, *The St. Nicholas Hotel*, opened at Tarragon in November 1974. As anticipated, audience response was again enthusiastic, and performances continued for nine weeks. Credit for the development of the company's unique presentational style, dubbed by Whittaker 'The Reaney-Turnbull Method,'9 was given equally to the playwright, director, and actors. When Tarragon was able to secure corporate funding to complete the trilogy, workshops for the third play were held in Toronto, and *Handcuffs* opened in triumph in March 1975. In his review of this last production, Kareda noted that the 'controversial originality and demanding complexity' of the trilogy had created a kind of cult following, so that fragments repeated from the preceding plays would 'send a ripple of recall through the audience.' Part of this fascination, he noted, was the palpable sense of commitment which the cast had brought to these plays. It was an experience, he said, that would 'leave its mark forever on the people who helped create it.'[10]

Having won the admiration of their Toronto audiences, Turnbull and his devoted company of Reaney-philes now wished to bring these remarkable productions to a Canadian audience beyond the small house at Tarragon. The NDWT company was formed in April 1975 specifically to accomplish this. The name of the company, long kept a tantalizing secret, came from an ironic self-description from the Halifax workshops, 'Ne'er-Do-Well Thespians.' Making up new slogans for the initials NDWT became a persistent whimsical pastime within the company: 'Not Done With Tarragon' celebrated NDWT's newly declared independence, and 'No Dough With Turnbull' described NDWT's salaries. The split with Tarragon sparked some false rumours of friction between the two companies, but in fact the Glasscos and Mallory Gilbert were of immense help in organizing the tour and in obtaining corporate and governmental support. Shortly after *Handcuffs* closed at Tarragon Theatre, Turnbull and company manager Richard Carson, along with company member Keith McNair and his dog, piled into a third-hand Datsun and drove across the country to Vancouver, booking as they went. Rehearsals began in mid-August, in space obtained by Reaney at the University of Western Ontario. Reaney himself, on sabbatical that year, travelled with NDWT on the tour.

NDWT's repertory for the tour included the three Donnelly plays plus *Hamlet*. Given the limited resources and rehearsal time for a company already overloaded with poetic drama, *Hamlet* was not a successful production artistically. It was a good choice financially, however, as school matinees became the bread-and-butter of the tour, often booked by principals who had never *heard* of Canadian drama. Public performances began in London in late September, followed by shows in Winnipeg, Vancouver, Edmonton, Calgary, Medicine Hat, Ottawa, Hamilton, and several cities and towns in New Brunswick and Nova Scotia. The final performances of the tour were originally scheduled to open a community theatre in Port Perry, Ontario; but when the company found that the renovations would not be finished in time, Toronto's Bathurst Street Theatre was booked for a one-week run. That run ended on Sunday, 14 December 1975, when for the first and only time the entire trilogy was performed in a single day. It was the culmination of years of work for the company, and a celebration for their many admirers. (Mallory Gilbert organized a huge gourmet lunch.) Hearing the echoes between the trilogy's opening speech that morning and the closing speech that night, Reaney himself felt as much a celebrant as the audience was. 'Unless I had had the devoted, skillful, and energetic help of maybe fifty people all told, not counting audience,' he wrote, 'I couldn't have shown just how that first unguarded speech on Mrs Donnelly's part results, with terrible logic, through a series of complex events lasting years and years, in the second speech and its fiery setting. That's worth being born and worth being a writer for.'[11]

Despite the triumphant tone of its finale, the tour had been a difficult one. Generally speaking, while the trilogy received critical praise, the *Hamlet* was poor, and was often performed under poor conditions. There was also some resistance in British Columbia and Alberta, in this time of Western separatism, to the 'national' pretensions of the trilogy in light of its clearly regional content. The company also found frustrating the indifference of Canada's regional theatres to this widely hailed masterpiece. Except for the four performances at Neptune, where NDWT's adventure had started three years earlier, no regional theatre would help the company with its bookings. Even the MTC, where Turnbull had been artistic director, refused to let NDWT have its Warehouse space. And even at Neptune, artistic director John Wood did not come to see any of NDWT's performances, which resulted in his being punched in the face by a furious NDWT actor. In the absence of mainstream support, the company tended to be booked into university and high-school theatres, often with inadequate promotion by non-professional local sponsors. At Simon Fraser University, for instance, no posters had been put up, and Turnbull had to telephone newspaper critics at their homes to invite them to the show. Similar surprises awaited them in New Brunswick, where, Turnbull recalls, the tour would have collapsed without on-the-spot school bookings of *Hamlet*. Living in each other's pockets for so long also put a strain on NDWT's interpersonal relations: at one matinee, a school audience was treated to a very loud (and very obscene) backstage argument between Lord Hamlet and the Player King. The final discouraging word was that, when the results were tallied, the tour lost $13,000.

Not surprisingly, the company returned home totally drained both artistically and personally. Turnbull seemed both proud and bitter about the whole experience: 'Why should the mounting of a Canadian work which is hailed as a masterpiece,' he asked, 'have been such a difficult, energy consuming, totally exhausting experience?'[12] By the time NDWT returned to Toronto, all the existing alternative companies were suffering from similar exhaustion. As they grew into their thirties, these artists found it more and more difficult to meet the high personal cost of artistic idealism. In this vein, an odd note appeared on a publicity handout for the Donnellys' last stand in Toronto: 'and to end it all ... 3 in one day – Bear the Agony of Nine Hours of Theatre.'[13]

NDWT after 1975

Despite this exhaustion, Turnbull and NDWT were determined to continue their operations beyond the Donnelly tour. For a permanent home they leased the Bathurst Street Theatre, the large sanctuary of the Bathurst Street United Church. In the 1960s the congregation of this church had become too small to support the rambling old stone building, which then found a new role for itself as a centre for social services and cultural groups. In the 1970s it was used a great deal as an inexpensive medium-sized transfer house seating between four and five hundred, which Toronto's alternative theatres otherwise lacked. Its most celebrated rental at this time was for the notoriously successful run of *I Love You, Baby Blue* in 1975. The Bathurst Street Theatre was intended to serve NDWT as a home base for what was essentially a touring company, as its production and administrative centre, as its own performing space, as a revenue-producing rental hall, and (as NDWT reported) 'as a road house for Canadian productions from across the country, thus stimulating national Canadian theatre by providing for it access to the large Toronto marketplace.'[14] On balance, the building did accomplish these goals, but it was also a source of many problems. Much of the company's initial energy went into preparing and maintaining the theatre; and, as the years went by, the well-intentioned blundering of the church's pastor drove NDWT and several other tenants to distraction. NDWT's first productions there, in the fall of 1976, were *I Wanna Die in Ruby Red Tap Shoes*, a musical satire on the Toronto theatre scene, and *Baldoon* by James Reaney and Marty Gervais, based on true incidents of an Ontario pioneer family beset by poltergeists. In its *Annual Report* for 1976–77, the company admitted that both productions suffered from lack of sufficient preparation.

Like Theatre Passe Muraille, NDWT's greatest achievements in the ensuing years occurred far from its Toronto base. Reaney's new play *Wacousta!*, workshops for which had been the centrepiece (in 1977) of the first of three annual street festivals at the Bathurst Street Theatre, was toured through northern Ontario early in 1978 before being brought to Toronto. In a poetic journal of this tour, actress Patsy Ludwick described how poorly the play was received by 'urbanites who refuse to be carried away into romance,' but how receptive audiences were in more remote areas.[15] The company's initials, they joked, now stood for 'No Drama Without Travel,' or 'Northward Driver, We're Touring.' A revue entitled *Northern Delights* was created for an even more far-flung northern tour the next season. Like *Wacousta!*, this production was greeted with great enthusiasm by communities which seldom saw any theatre, but was savaged by the Toronto press on its return. NDWT's northern connections were strengthened by the tour of *Radio Free Cree* (1979), a comedy by broadcaster Paulette Jiles about a community radio station in a remote Indian settlement, and by the establishment in 1980 of a new community theatre in Sioux Lookout, Ontario, called the Northern Delights Theatre Company. Its first production was another comedy by Paulette Jiles, *Northshore Run*, directed by Jerry Franken. Significantly, neither *Northshore Run* nor *Radio Free Cree* was brought to Toronto to face what the company considered the false sophistication of urban audiences and critics.

Financial instability was a problem which the company grappled with but could not solve. One cause of this instability was the very style which had brought NDWT its fame. Large casts and lengthy periods for script development made its productions much more expensive than, say, Passe Muraille's small-cast multi-role collectives. Another cause was the Bathurst Street Theatre itself: while it enabled the company to survive by giving it a home and a source of rental income, the building was also the greatest weight in a crushing administrative and artistic burden on a company which, because of chronic underfunding, did not have enough staff to handle the load. The major complication, and a difficult one to analyse, was timing. Both government subsidy and corporate support were harder to obtain in the mid- to late-1970s than had been the case when the major alternative theatres had become established. Artistic matters were affected by timing as well: in this regard, it is instructive to compare the careers of Keith Turnbull and Martin Kinch, two directors of the same age, from the same city, with similar training. It appears that Turnbull's quick ascension to regional theatre success by 1970, while Kinch continued to struggle toward a stable career in Toronto's 'underground' theatre, kept him out of Toronto until the public enthusiasm for homegrown drama had largely subsided. In any event, lack of funds (along with frustration at the church's ineffectual management) forced NDWT to give up its Bathurst Street home in 1980. It moved to Adelaide Court for a short time, then mounted productions at both Tarragon and Toronto Free Theatre in 1981. In February 1982, the company announced that it would suspend operations for a year. The chairman of NDWT's board of directors assured the public that this fallow period would be used 'to pay off the deficit and re-establish the company on a sound financial basis.'[16] However, operations were never resumed.

NDWT was the most important alternative company to expire before 1982, the year that Passe Muraille, Tarragon, and Toronto Free all appointed new artistic directors. It is important mainly because of the rehearsal techniques, script development methods, and performance style which were developed to give definitive first productions to the new works of a major Canadian playwright. Keith Turnbull and his loyal corps of actors are not always given the credit they deserve for their contribution to Reaney's drama. This collaboration between playwright and director, now such an accepted part of the development of new Canadian plays, had its most spectacular success with NDWT. As Urjo Kareda put it, 'Keith Turnbull's contribution as Reaney's collaborator and director is surely revolutionary, creating a performing style as extraordinary and original as the text to be performed. His most stunning skill is in assembling textures, linking words and objects ... sounds and silences, the keen professionalism of some of his actors with the eloquent, untrained simplicity of others.'[17] But Reaney's later scripts seldom attained the quality of his Donnelly plays, and no other playwright emerged to fill the needs of the company. Its dependence on one playwright for material, and on one director for an increasingly broad range of leadership tasks, finally bankrupted the company, first artistically then financially.

NDWT is still remembered for its energy, integrity, and commitment to new work, which endured in spite of declining idealism in Toronto theatre. While other alternative theatres aspired to mainstream success, Turnbull and NDWT started with that success, and gave it up to pursue their vision of a better Canadian theatre. NDWT is also remembered for its innovative performing style, an extraordinarily successful melding of text and performance. Indeed, the most striking of the many anomalies surrounding NDWT is that, in a company with such a highly physical style, the text should have held such primacy. Finally, NDWT is remembered for its all-day Donnelly performance on 14 December 1975, which remains a significant event in the history of Canadian drama and theatre.

10

Making Myths

There was a 'Judy's father has a barn period' which lasted for about four years – the
FUT festival of 1970 and very early Passe Muraille, the Canadian Place Theatre.
Probably only two years was truly extraordinary, a period when one actually believed
that one could do anything, and sometimes did.[1]

Martin Kinch, 1982

Toronto's alternative theatres captured the imagination of the critics
and the theatre-going public during a period of great social upheaval
and then retrenchment, and contributed immeasurably to the explosion
of new Canadian drama in the early 1970s. The four major companies
also had wide-ranging effects on theatre in other cities across Canada:
Theatre Passe Muraille, initially for its counter-culture flamboyance,
then for its play-creation methods; the Factory Theatre Lab, for
insisting there were Canadian plays begging to be produced, then
finding them and producing them; Tarragon Theatre, for creating
conditions under which new Canadian drama could infiltrate the
repertory of the regional theatres; and finally Toronto Free Theatre,
for bringing mainstream subsidy and promotion to the smaller theatres.

Ironically, the nationalistic accomplishments of these theatres owe a
great deal to the influence of American values in Canada during the
1960s. Canadians were very attuned to the crescendo of protest voiced
by America's youth. Whatever the cause, the message conveyed was one
of confidence and freedom. In their world, it seemed, individuals had
the right to pursue their own concepts of morality, and society had no
right to impose a consensual one. To Canadians, for whom liberty and

pursuit of happiness have traditionally been overshadowed by order and good government, the voice of young America was a siren song. We felt the brotherhood and heard the music of the Woodstock generation; we didn't see the garbage and the bad trips until much later. In the afterglow of our own Expo 67, we embraced their nationalism and their confidence as qualities to emulate. Our love of the American way of disputation, even when it was channelled into anti-American protests, was strengthened by the dominance of American television, and by the influx of articulate Americans to our rapidly expanding academic and cultural scenes. While only a few of these Americans were draft-dodgers, they all came to Canada for similar reasons. They sought a more nurturing environment than the highly competitive and violent society which they found in contemporary America. Canada in the late 1960s met American emigrants half-way. Canada had a benign social environment which valued the Americans' outspokenness and initiative. In the arts, Canada also provided many more opportunities for individual achievement through its tradition of government patronage. While we often hear of Canadians who crossed the border to find their stardom, we seldom hear of the many Americans who crossed the border to find steady work – and work which they could believe in. The American influence in Toronto's alternative theatres had less to do with a few individuals in key positions than it had to do with the spirit of the time.

The early days of the alternative theatres are surrounded by a great deal of myth. Partly this is due to the deliberate myth-making activities of their leaders, who realized that creating a mythology was essential to creating a new kind of theatre. These leaders, in general, were fully conscious of their mythologizing. As Paul Thompson said in 1974, 'Garrard was the original myth-maker. He created the myth of Theatre Passe Muraille and it was the myth that allowed it to survive. Not the reality of it ... I think I'm creating a new mythology.'[2] The first myth of Toronto's alternative theatre was that of a radical theatre. Initiated in 1968 with the opening of Rochdale College, it invoked imagery of the American protest movement and the 'hippie' subculture. This myth declined rapidly after the Festival of Underground Theatre in 1970; perhaps it had just run its course, or perhaps it could not survive its own commercialization in vehicles such as *Hair*. The second myth was that of a nationalist theatre. It invoked imagery of a popular uprising in which, as one critic put it, 'small theatres with meagre budgets and minimal physical resources developed to challenge the cultural imperialism of the more solvent Regional theatres.'[3] This myth was fuelled by revolutionary rhetoric, much of it written by Ken Gass and Tom Hendry, and gained momentum with the inauguration of the LIP/OFY programs in 1971. As in the radical stage, the nationalist leaders were very conscious of their goals, and making myths to support these goals.

On the last day of 1971, the revolutionary goals of this nationalist theatre were dealt a crippling blow by the failure of John Palmer's *Memories for My Brother, Part II* at the St Lawrence Centre. Here was the opportunity for which the nationalists had been lobbying so stridently, and had achieved so quickly: a production of its best playwright, under one of its best directors (Henry Tarvainen), with a large professional cast and the support of the city's finest mainstream staff and facility. *Memories, Part II* put mainstream resources at the service of the new nationalist theatre. The results, everyone agreed, were disastrous, although there was no such agreement as to where the blame lay.

If *Memories, Part II* proved anything, it was that the methods developed in the nationalist stage were not equal to the task of producing mainstream theatre in Toronto. It was a lesson thoroughly absorbed by the men whose theatres were the dominant ones in Toronto in the ensuing three years: Paul Thompson, Bill Glassco, and Tom Hendry. While retaining some of the vocabulary of the radical and nationalist stages, these leaders helped create a new mainstream theatre in their converted warehouses and church halls. The myth of the new mainstream relegated Toronto's civic professional theatre, the St Lawrence Centre, to the same category as the Royal Alex and the O'Keefe: a significant building, to be sure, but somewhat beside the point in Toronto theatre. Thompson pursued new audiences, Glassco wooed existing ones, and all of them contributed to a new myth, an institutional one, the myth of stability and permanence in an ongoing alternative. At this time, 'Alternative to what?' became the question that had no answer.

In creating their myths, the alternative theatres had ready-made allies in Toronto's theatre critics. As Ken Gass wrote in 1979,

It would be nice to think that we serious-minded artists were above that sort of concern, but the reality is that we live in a media-oriented society where the press is our most vital link to an audience. In fact, it was the excitement echoed in the papers in the early 1970s that helped launch the Alternate Theatre movement by creating a myth around several isolated endeavours. It wasn't that the ratio of bad versus good reviews was any different ... It was that somehow the press exuded a passion and a contagious excitement that made the work seem important. It mattered.[4]

Nathan Cohen and Herbert Whittaker had been dedicated cultural nationalists for at least two decades before these young upstarts appeared. Cohen's sympathy for the underdog and Whittaker's generosity toward any indigenous theatre brought the alternative companies, in their embryonic stages, a disproportionate amount of press coverage. In addition, other critics such as Don Rubin, David McCaughna, and Brian Boru believed these companies to be the first worthwhile theatre to ever happen in Toronto – probably because they were new to Toronto themselves. Finally, Cohen's successor, Urjo Kareda, in his four years as lead critic of the *Toronto Star,* became the most important promoter of these small theatres and their new drama. Indeed, Kareda's enthusiasm and influence had a great deal to do with bestowing mainstream status on these theatres.

In 1975 Whittaker retired and Kareda left the *Star* for Stratford. Their departure greatly sapped the sense of vitality surrounding the alternative theatres, whose energy was flagging anyway. The critics which followed them never gained the same kind of respect in the theatre community, nor did they give the community the same kind of support. At the *Globe and Mail,* several lead critics followed Whittaker in quick succesion. The first (in 1975) was John Fraser, the *Globe's* award-winning dance critic, who wrote about the theatre scene with intelligence and wit. However, Fraser left his theatre beat less than two years later, succeeded in turn by Bryan Johnson (in 1977) and Ray Conlogue (in 1979). At the *Star,* meanwhile, Kareda's position went unfilled for almost a year. Both newspapers, it seems, considered the power and influence which had accrued to Cohen, Whittaker, and Kareda as somehow unhealthy, as were their intimate connections with theatrical enterprise in Toronto. Before 1975, Toronto's leading critics saw themselves as an integral part of the theatre community. After 1975, they more often saw themselves as journalists reporting entertainment news or providing a consumers' guide to local theatre. As one of them said, in 1980, 'I am commenting on art and culture. I'm not here to pull the boulder up the hill.'[5]

In June 1976 the *Star* finally appointed Gina Mallet to succeed Kareda. Mallet was born in Britain, but came to Canada from the United States, where she wrote on entertainment for *Time* magazine. On her arrival in Toronto, Mallet quickly incurred the wrath of the theatre community with her curt dismissal of Hendry's *Byron* and with a nasty preview article on the Shaw Festival. It was a hard time for cultural nationalists – within a year, the Stratford Festival, the Canadian Opera Company, and the National Ballet had all appointed new artistic directors from abroad. When the *Star* followed suit by appointing Mallet lead critic, a number of individuals and organizations (including Actors Equity) called a press conference to protest. There, a statement read by Ken Gass complained of Mallet's 'total disregard for the history, traditions and development of Canadian theatre': 'Why hire someone completely unfamiliar with and inexperienced in the wide range of theatre in Canada? And where is The Star's commitment to the development of our own critics, who are essential to the future of Canadian theatre and Canadian journalism?'[6]

These were sensible questions to ask, but they sounded like self-serving jingoism to those unfamiliar with Toronto's critical traditions. Mallet soon became the most influential critic in Toronto, building her reputation on her capacity for vitriol. She relished her role as the nationalists' villain, and delighted in criticizing, as she put it, the 'blinkered and parochial vision of directors and playwrights and bureaucrats' in Canadian theatre.[7] Her own background as an internationalist, and her own reverence for commercial success, crystallized the mood of Toronto theatre in the second half of the decade just as Kareda's attitudes had in the first half. With Mallet, companies such as Tarragon or the Factory could expect no critical leniency out of respect for their past contributions. In addition, it seems that Mallet wanted to 'discover' her own small theatres, as if to dispel the lingering influence of Kareda. The Phoenix Theatre, for instance, greatly benefited from Mallet's praise, and marginal companies striving for mainstream success (such as New Theatre with *Travesties*) were given excellent pre-opening coverage. But over the long haul, Mallet's emphasis on large-scale commercial success was an unattainable goal for the alternative theatres.

At the same time, in the second half of the 1970s, the alternative theatres entered a period of introspection in which the myths of success and of stability were superseded by one of stagnation. In a pivotal article in September 1975, John Fraser summarized the accepted myths of Toronto's alternative theatres at the time, and articulated the emerging one:

All the innovative or underground theatres ... are at a crossroads today. The past five or six years have been dazzling, probably revolutionary, for theatre in this country. We have moved from a century of mostly derivative drivel to a half decade of indigenous creativity and excitement and leading us all was the new and cocky Toronto theatre movement.[8]

Tarragon's sabbatical and Passe Muraille's dependence on familiar playmaking conventions, said Fraser, indicated different kinds of problems ahead:

These are not yet symptoms of a disease, but they *are* hints of a worrying malaise. The initial burst of energetic creativity has been spent and the less glamorous, but more demanding, task of building on all those foundations is what faces the small theatres today. It won't surprise me if some of them never make it; those that do will have proved the worth of the early efforts.

Although Fraser was new to this community, he astutely identified the element which had disappeared from the alternative theatre – a sense of excitement – and the place where it had gone – Stratford:

The major commodity that is in danger of leaving Toronto is the atmosphere of innovation which has infused so many of the hallmarks of the new theatre here and allowed it to transcend the rigid structures of value judgments over what was a good or bad production. Almost imperceptibly during the summer, this atmosphere was drifting towards Stratford where Robin Phillips' pyrotechnics won so much attention, and where the superficial glibness of three productions ... was largely forgotten in the euphoria over a great theatre renewing itself.

In fact, Phillips' reign at Stratford (1975–80) dominated theatre in Ontario for that period.

Fraser was surely correct in discerning the mood of the theatre community. Indeed, alternative theatre leaders were less concerned with refuting this opinion than with apportioning blame for it. Ken Gass blamed the 'thoroughly conservative' nature of Toronto. Tom Hendry blamed the loss of LIP/OFY funds, allegedly through the malevolence of the Canada Council.[9] As in the mid-1960s, the self-image of Toronto theatre in the late 1970s was unjustifiably low. To outside observers of this very busy theatre scene, even the self-examination seemed absurd. Critic Ronald Bryden, a recent arrival from England, pointed this out in 1978:

Theatre in Toronto is a puzzle; not only to foreigners, apparently, but also to itself. Its bustle and air of prosperity are dumbfounding. Its confidence seems close to nil. Every season seems to bring the opening of some handsome, lavishly found new theatre premise. Every season, at least two or three artistic directors step down or threaten to, agonizing publicly about the crossroads their theatres and Canada's stand at; their need to find some new policy, impetus, or audience. Usually, they will throw in at least two references to 'colonialism.'[10]

The most perceptive of these self-examinations came from Martin Kinch. While he objected to Fraser's 'prophecies of gloom and doom,' he seems to have accepted that malaise as a starting point. Kinch chose to blame both the alternative theatre's success and its inability to capitalize on that success:

The major alternative theatres were rapidly turning themselves into producing institutions. Subsidy was growing and the theatres were becoming dependent ...

New works had to be found; but the theatres, having more money to spend, were already becoming conservative. Young playwrights began to find their way into workshop programs instead of onto the stage. Often these programs acted as a sop for withholding large production resources. The theatres, spending more and more on individual works, relied on a small and shrinking group of writers.[11]

The victory of the alternative theatre, argued Kinch, was built on twin illusions: that the change in audience tastes was permanent, and that this change would be supported by regional theatres which had seen the error of their colonial ways. In fact, Kinch wrote,

Very few realized how uncommitted the regional theatres really were. Certainly they needed and welcomed actors and directors from the Toronto Scene – but their response to the playwright was largely dictated by fashion, and federal promptings ...

In Toronto, neither the money nor the expertise existed for the transfer of productions into larger houses for indefinite runs. This failure to create a system for the exploitation of success not only created unnecessary financial problems for the theatres, but also motivational problems for writers looking for a reasonable return on their work. Without the glamour of the long run, the Canadian playwrights were absurdly regarded by the regional theatres as experimental ... The playwrights cut off from further theatrical advancement moved partially or completely into television and film. The fashion began to fade as quickly as it had grown.

It seems that the malaise in this new mainstream ought to have created opportunities for the Second Wave, but it did not. The new pattern was established, and it proved impossible to break into it. The real failure of the Second Wave of Toronto's alternative theatres was that they were unable to create a myth which would help them survive. The public considered them desirable, but not essential in the way that Passe Muraille or Tarragon had become. One reason was that they were not blessed with the same consistent encouragement from the press. Another was that, by the mid-1970s, there were many more theatres competing for survival. But most critically, the second-wave theatres had great difficulty articulating a permanent mandate. It seemed a more difficult task, and probably was, to find a source of public interest that had not been tapped out. The second-wave companies had all folded, or were about to, by the time of a thorough changeover in the established alternative theatres which took place in 1982. At that time Thompson, Glassco, and Hendry all stepped down, and were replaced (respectively) by Clarke Rogers, Urjo Kareda, and Guy Sprung. The mainstream inclinations of the retiring leaders, if further demonstration were needed, may be seen in their subsequent activities. Hendry wrote policy studies for the City of Toronto and for the National Arts Centre. Glassco became artistic director of CentreStage, the renamed Toronto Arts Productions, and effected its merger with Toronto Free Theatre in 1986. Thompson was named head of the National Theatre School in 1987. Meanwhile, those alternative leaders who had been most vehement in rejecting the old mainstream, like Gass and Palmer, were themselves ignored by the new one.

The broad outline of these myths are still common currency in Toronto's theatre community, but the details surrounding them have dissipated very quickly. While those people who created the alternative theatres wish to have their stories told, the people who now run them generally do not. It is not in their interest. Their job is to sell each season as something new and exciting – and the need to market a 'new and improved' version, as with toothpaste, gives them no vested interest in the old one. Budding theatre historians should be warned that theatre people keep records to promote their own activities, not to help explain those of their predecessors. I have encountered some exceptions to this rule, but the tendency is beyond question. Those now in charge have no wish to remember, and those who wish to remember are scattered farther and farther afield. Files are thrown out, memories fade, and nostalgia fogs the rear-view mirror.

The word 'myth,' unfortunately, has come to mean something false. Instead, I use it to mean a story which contains a valuable truth. The myths of the alternative theatre are mainly true for the same reason that any myth is mainly true. Inevitably, however, the story of Toronto's alternative theatre has been retooled to serve the needs of today's publicists, or heightened by sentimentality as the myth-makers have grown older. And there was a lot to be sentimental about. Even nostalgia can contain some important truths, as illustrated in this story which Martin Kinch tells about that first summer season at Toronto Free Theatre:

I remember, for example, for Larry Fineberg's *Hope* this extraordinary setting was designed that was well beyond the abilities of anybody in our circle. The day before the show opened the entire thing fell down. John Palmer 'improvised' and mounted his 'brilliant minimalist production' of the play in one day. That kind of story always tends toward sentimentalization. The truth of the matter is that we were tearing our hair out.

But, in another way, the truth is that immense amounts of theatre were being created, some of it good, some of it terrible. I think the thing that we lose track of is that we made contact with an audience that for various reasons had no means of cultural expression ... And there was a very close bond between the audience and that theatre. Why that has disappeared is a very difficult question. But I don't think there is any question that it has.

... You know, it is really quite fashionable to laugh at the Sixties and the early Seventies but there was an extraordinary idealism then, a belief amongst actors, directors and writers that we were breaking through to a new balance between performers and audience. Along with everything else that relates to the late-Sixties idealism, it has now dissipated. Theatres have become more concerned with desperate attempts to keep their heads above water, the desire to make commercial choices, the careerist aspirations of the people involved.[12]

The alternative theatres may have been awash in the rhetoric of their time, but at least they lived up to it, or tried to. They changed the face of Canadian theatre, and how that happened is worth remembering.

Chronology

1951 The report of the Massey Commission is published

1953 The Stratford Festival opens with *Richard III*

1954 The Crest Theatre opens with *Richard of Bordeaux*

1957 The Canada Council is established

1958 The Manitoba Theatre Centre opens in Winnipeg

1959 Workshop Productions opens on Fraser Avenue in Toronto

1960 The O'Keefe Centre opens with the pre-Broadway tryout of *Camelot*

1961 Workshop Productions presents *Hey, Rube!*

1962 The St Lawrence Centre is proposed by Toronto city planners

1963 President Kennedy is shot

1964 The Beatles arrive in North America
–   Canada's Parliament debates the national flag
–   Tom Hendry joins the Canadian Theatre Centre

1965 Paul Thompson goes to Lyons, France, to apprentice under Roger Planchon

1966 The Crest Theatre and the Canadian Players cease operation
Aug. James Reaney and Keith Turnbull stage *Listen to the Wind* in London, Ontario
Sept. Jim Garrard goes to London, England, to study theatre

1967
Jan. *Spring Thaw* embarks on its Centennnial tour
Feb. *Fortune and Men's Eyes* opens off-Broadway
Apr. Expo 67 opens in Montreal
July John Palmer's 'New Vic Players' perform in a coffee-house in Stratford
Sept. Bill Glassco goes to New York to study theatre
– Martin Kinch and John Palmer go to Britain as apprentice directors
Dec. TWP moves to its new location on Alexander Street

1968
Jan. Theatre Toronto opens its first of two winter seasons at the Royal Alexandra Theatre
Apr. Martin Luther King is shot
– Pierre Trudeau becomes prime minister
– Jim Garrard begins conducting workshops under the banner of Rochdale College
June Robert Kennedy is shot
July Bill Glassco produces *The Winter's Tale* at Trinity Square, later the home of Theatre Passe Muraille
– Richard Schechner produces *Dionysus in 69* in Greenwich Village in New York
Aug. Police and anti-war protesters riot outside the Democratic National Convention in Chicago
Sept. Rochdale College opens
– Trio Productions opens three shows in a week
– The Studio Lab begins experimental theatre performances
Nov. Richard Nixon is elected president of the United States
Dec. Theatre Passe Muraille opens with a single performance of *Tom Paine* at Rochdale College

1969
Jan. Theatre Toronto's production of *Edward II* triggers Clifford Williams' resignation

Mar.   Trio Productions and Theatre Passe Muraille present *Futz* at
        the Central Library Theatre
Apr.   Tom Hendry becomes literary manager of the Stratford Festival
 –   John Palmer's production of *Tango* scandalizes the DDF final
        competition in Kelowna, BC
May   John Lennon and Yoko Ono begin their 'bed-in' for peace
        in Montreal
 –   Theatre Passe Muraille takes up residence at Trinity Square
June   Jim Garrard and the *Futz* producers are tried for obscenity
 –   The Global Village opens with *Blue S.A.*
July   The Canadian Place Theatre opens in Stratford
 –   *The Satyricon* opens at the Stratford Festival's Avon Theatre
 –   Jim Garrard directs *Home Free*, his first production at Trinity
        Square
 –   Neil Armstrong walks on the moon
Aug.   The Woodstock Festival draws a half million people to a farm
        in upstate New York
Dec.   *Dionysus in 69* opens at the Studio Lab
 –   *Hair* previews at the Royal Alex, and runs there for over a year

1970
Jan.   The double-bill of *Sweet Eros* and *In His Own Write* opens
        at Theatre Passe Muraille
Feb.   The St Lawrence Centre finally opens
May   Four student protesters are shot to death at Kent State
        University
June   Bill and Jane Glassco open their summer theatre at the Red
        Barn in Jackson's Point, Ontario
July   The Factory Theatre Lab opens on Dupont Street with *We
        Three, You and I*
Aug.   The Festival of Underground Theatre opens at the St Lawrence
        Centre and the Global Village
Oct.   'The October Crisis': Prime Minister Trudeau invokes the War
        Measures Act

1971
Feb.   *Creeps* opens at the Factory Theatre Lab
Mar.   Nathan Cohen dies at the age of forty-seven
July   The Canada Council sponsors the Gaspé conference on
        Canadian playwriting

Aug.   The Shaw Festival sponsors the Niagara-on-the-Lake conference on Canadian playwriting

Oct.   Tarragon Theatre opens with a remount of *Creeps*

Dec.   *Memories for My Brother, Part II* opens New Year's Eve at the St Lawrence Centre

1972

Jan.   *The Black Queen Is Going to Eat You All Up* marks the end of the Garrard era at Theatre Passe Muraille

Feb.   *Wedding in White* opens at the Poor Alex, the first Toronto show financed by LIP or OFY grants

Apr.   Keith Turnbull is fired as artistic director of the Manitoba Theatre Centre

–   Peter Cheeseman, director from Stoke-on-Trent, conducts workshops as a guest of Theatre Ontario

May   *Leaving Home* opens at Tarragon Theatre

June   Toronto Free Theatre opens with *How Are Things with the Walking Wounded?*

Aug.   *The Farm Show* opens in a barn in Clinton, Ontario

Sept.   Paul Henderson scores the winning goal in the first Canada-Russia hockey series

Nov.   *Forever Yours, Marie-Lou* opens at Tarragon, the first production in English of a Michel Tremblay play

Dec.   The Factory's *Works* festival is shut down by Actors Equity

1973

Jan.   Theatre Passe Muraille presents *1837*

Mar.   The Factory Lab presents *Bagdad Saloon*, its last show on Dupont Street

Apr.   Open Circle Theatre opens with *No Way, José*

–   New Theatre opens on Bathurst Street with *Salomé*

May   The U.S. Senate Watergate hearings begin on television

Sept.   The Factory Lab opens a festival of Canadian plays in London, England

Oct.   Toronto Free Theatre closes *Clear Light* under threat of prosecution

Nov.   *Sticks and Stones* opens at Tarragon

–   Robin Phillips is appointed artistic director of the Stratford Festival, provoking a nationalist protest from Toronto's theatre community

1974
Jan.   Theatre Passe Muraille is finally evicted from Trinity Square
–   The first issue of *Canadian Theatre Review* is published
Feb.   TWP presents *Ten Lost Years*
Aug.   President Nixon resigns

1975
Mar.   Bill Glassco announces his sabbatical
Apr.   Phoenix Theatre opens with *Butley*
–   Theatre Passe Muraille closes *I Love You, Baby Blue* after
         a four-month run
Aug.   Herbert Whittaker retires from the *Globe and Mail* and Urjo
         Kareda leaves the *Toronto Star*
Oct.   NDWT embarks on its national tour of the Donnelly trilogy

1976   Theatre Passe Muraille moves into its new home on Ryerson
         Street

1978   Ken Gass resigns as head of the Factory Theatre Lab

1982   Paul Thompson, Bill Glassco, and Tom Hendry step aside as
         heads of Theatre Passe Muraille, Tarragon, and Toronto Free

1986   George Luscombe steps aside as head of Toronto Workshop
         Productions

Toronto Playlist, 1968–1975

What follows is a list of selected plays produced in Toronto from 1968 through 1975. It is appended here to balance the company-by-company structure of this study and to give some sense of the nature of Toronto theatre in a given cross-section of time. The list may also be useful in helping other researchers to find reviews of specific productions.

The list includes all productions by local mainstream companies (Theatre Toronto, Toronto Arts Productions, and Theatre Plus), all productions by the four major alternative companies, and all significant productions by other alternative theatres in Toronto. It also includes a few productions by other companies (such as *Viet Rock* and *Hair*) which had some impact on locally produced professional theatre. The playlist does not generally include dance, mime, opera, revues, children's theatre, university theatre, amateur theatre, foreign touring shows, or productions in French or in foreign languages. Neither does it include any production which ran for less than a week, unless (as with the Rochdale *Tom Paine*) it has some special historical significance. 'Number of weeks' is calculated as number of weekends, excluding previews, for which performances were announced in the daily newspapers. Abbreviations used in the table are as follows:

ad.	adapted from
Alum	University Alumnae Dramatic Society
Bath	Bathurst Street Theatre

Bayv	Bayview Playhouse
Cent	Centaur Theatre (Montreal)
CLT	Central Library Theatre
Cr2	Creation 2
CSP	Classical Stage Productions
Fire	Firehall Theatre
FTL	Factory Theatre Lab
Garr	Garret Theatre
GV	Global Village
Home	Homemade Theatre
n/a	not available
New	New Theatre
OC	Open Circle Theatre
O'K	O'Keefe Centre
PA	Poor Alex Theatre
Pho	Phoenix Theatre
(r)	(in repertory)
RA	Royal Alexandra Theatre
Red	Redlight Theatre
seed	Theatre Passe Muraille 'seed show'
SLC	St Lawrence Centre
Stu	Studio Lab Theatre
T+	Theatre Plus
TAP	Toronto Arts Productions
Tarr	Tarragon Theatre
TCA	Toronto Centre for the Arts
TF	Theatre Fountainhead
TFT	Toronto Free Theatre
TID	Theatre in the Dell
TPM	Theatre Passe Muraille
Trio	Trio Productions
TSF	Theatre Second Floor
TT	Theatre Toronto
TWP	Toronto Workshop Productions
WW	WW Productions

An asterisk denotes the first production of a continuing company.

Year	Date of Opening	No. of Wks	Company or Venue	Author	Title
1968	(Dec./'67)	7	CLT	J. Herbert	Fortune and Men's Eyes
	Jan. 10	5	TWP	J. Carew	Gentlemen Be Seated
	*Jan. 17	3	TT	J. Basile	The Drummer Boy
	Feb. 7	3	TT	J. Feiffer	Little Murders
	Feb. 16	3	TWP	B. Jonson	The Alchemist
	Feb. 27	8	CLT	D. Harron	Here Lies Sarah Binks
	Feb. 28	3	TT	R. Hochhuth	Soldiers
	Mar. 20	3	TT	J. Hearn	Festival of Carol's
	Apr. 4	2	TWP	A. Miller	A View from the Bridge
	Apr. 15	8	RA	various	Spring Thaw '68
	Apr. 18	4	Alum	D. Halliwell	Little Malcolm and His Struggle against the Eunuchs
	May 1	2	TWP	E. McColl	The Travellers
	May 28	10	TWP	N. Kline	Faces
	June 20	12	Garr	A. Keogh	Incident at Rosedale
	*Sept. 24	5	Trio	P. Shaffer	White Lies Black Comedy
	Sept. 26	6	Trio	C. Dyer	Staircase
	*Sept. 26	6	Stu	M. Terry	Comings and Goings
	Oct. 2	4	Trio	P. Weiss	Marat/Sade
	Oct. 7	5	RA	D. Harron	Anne of Green Gables
	Oct. 8	4	CLT	H. Livings	Eh?
	Oct. 17	3	Alum	M. Terry	Viet Rock

Year	Date of Opening	No. of Wks	Company or Venue	Author	Title
1968	Nov. 5	5	TWP	G. Grass	Flood
	Nov. 11	2	RA	M. Moore	Sunshine Town
	Nov. 14	4	Stu	P. Ableman	Tests
	Nov. 26	4	CLT	M. Fratti	The Victim
	Dec. 10?	0	TPM	P. Foster	Tom Paine
	Dec. 17	5	TWP	M. Fratti	Che Guevara
1969	Jan. 9	3	TT	C. Marlowe	Edward II
	Jan. 30	3	TT	G.B. Shaw	In Good King Charles's Golden Days
	Feb. 20	3	TT	C. Goldoni	The Servant of Two Masters
	Feb. 21	2	Stu	M. McClure	The Beard
	Feb. 25	7	TWP	ad. Hasek	The Good Soldier Schweik
	*Mar. 5	3	TPM/Trio	R. Owens	Futz
	Mar. 13	3	TT	F. Marcus	The Killing of Sister George
	Mar. 27	3	CLT	G. Divers	Take a Litter
	Mar. 27	3	Stu	F. Arrabal	The Automobile Grave-yard
	Apr. 21	5	RA	various	Spring Thaw '69
	Apr. 22	7	TWP	collective	Mr Bones
	May 30	12	Garr	J. Herbert	The World of Woyzeck
	June 18	2	YMCA	collective	Plague ... So Far
	*June 18	3	GV	E. Swerdlow	Blue S.A.
	June 26	4	Stu	collective	Sagitta II

Year	Date of Opening	No. of Wks	Company or Venue	Author	Title
1969	June 27	1	TPM	J. Levy	Portrait Itch
	July 3	2	TPM	M. de Ghelderode	Escurial
	July 17	2	TPM	L. Wilson	Home Free
	July 31	2	TPM	J. Genet	The Maids
	Aug. 22	2	RA	various	Facad
	Aug. 26	4	GV	ad. Ibsen	Peer Gynt
	Nov. 4	2	TPM	J. Palmer	Memories for My Brother, Part I
	Nov. 20	5	TPM	P. Foster	Tom Paine
	Nov. 25	3	TWP	Shakespeare	The Tempest
	Dec. 11	32	Stu	ad. Euripides	Dionysus in 69
	Dec. 11	4	GV	R. Swerdlow	Copper Mountain
1970	Jan. 6	5	GV	E. Ionesco	Exit the King
	Jan. 11	52	RA	Rado/Ragni	Hair
	Jan. 13	2	TWP	C. Bolt	Daganawida
	Jan. 29	8	TPM	T. McNally Lennon et al.	Sweet Eros In His Own Write
	Feb. 16	10	Bayv	various	Spring Thaw '70 Is a New Bag
	Feb. 26	8	Garr	I. Burgess	Horseshoe House
	*Feb. 26	7 (r)	TAP	J. Languirand	Man, Inc.
	Feb. 27	9 (r)	TAP	J. Gray	Striker Schneiderman
	Mar. 1	9 (r)	TAP	B. Vian	The Knacker's ABC

Year	Date of Opening	No. of Wks	Company or Venue	Author	Title
1970	Mar. 5	5	GV	E. Swerdlow	Transmission
	Mar. 10	11	TWP	Luscombe et al.	Chicago 70
	Mar. 26	3	TPM	J. Osborne	A Bond Honoured
	Apr. 21	5 (r)	TAP	Goethe	Faust
	May 7	2	TPM	ad. Germain	Notes from Quebec
	May 11	2	o'κ	D. Harron	Anne of Green Gables
	May 19	60	TID	R. Cook	Oh! Coward
	May 27	3	TPM	D. Helwig	The Hanging of William O'Donnell
	June 4	24	GV	R. Swerdlow	Justine
	*July 30	2	FTL	S. Ross W. Greenland	An Act of Violence We Three, You and I
	Aug. 19	3	SLC		Festival of Underground Theatre
	Oct. 5	2	SLC	various	Love and Maple Syrup
	Oct. 8	3	TPM	F. Wedekind	Spring's Awakening
	Oct. 9	2	TPM	L. Del Grande	Six of a Kind
	Oct. 26	2	Cr2	L. Capson	Dead Sun Rise
	Oct. 31	10	Stu	ad. Euripides	Dionysus in 70
	Nov. 10	10 (r)	TAP	C. Fry	A Yard of Sun
	Nov. 13	14 (r)	TAP	P. Zindel	The Effect of Gamma Rays on Man-in-the-Moon Marigolds
	Nov. 18	3	FTL	F. McEnaney	A Bedtime Story

Year	Date of Opening	No. of Wks	Company or Venue	Author	Title
1970	Nov. 19	3	TPM	R. DeCanio	I Had It but It's All Gone Now
	Nov. 20	9 (r)	TAP	ad. Ibsen	An Enemy of the People
	Nov. 24	3	TWP	N. Jowsey	The Piper
	Nov. 27	2	TPM	P. Hopcraft	Niobe
1971	Jan. 7	4	TPM	collective	Out to Breakfast
	Jan. 19	3	TWP	B. Behan	The Hostage
	Jan. 22	9 (r)	TAP	J. Kerr	Mary, Mary
	Jan. 28	5	Stu	ad. Terence	The Brothers
	Feb. 3	5	FTL	M. Mirolla	Snails
				D. Freeman	Creeps
	Feb. 5	2		'Renaissance 71' festival	
	Feb. 11	6	TPM	Jaffe et al.	Vampyr
	Feb. 12	7	Bayv	ad. Synge	The Heart's a Wonder
	Mar. 5	5 (r)	TAP	B. Brecht	Puntilla and Matti, His Hired Hand
	Mar. 9	4	TWP	A. Jellicoe	Shelley, the Idealist
	Mar. 11	4	Stu	Sankey et al.	Where Do We Go from Here?
	Mar. 17	5	GV	R. Swerdlow	Spring Thaw '71
	Mar. 17	5	FTL	J. Addison	Two Countries
	Apr. 1	1	TAP	J. Palmer	Bland Hysteria
	Apr. 2	5	TPM	collective	Doukhobors
	Apr. 15	1	TAP	B. Shoveller	Westbound 12:01

Year	Date of Opening	No. of Wks	Company or Venue	Author	Title
1971	Apr. 20	4	TWP	F. Dürrenmatt	The Visit of an Old Lady
	May 1	4	FTL	H. Markowitz	Branch Plant
	May 6	8	GV	Collins et al.	The Late Late Crisis Show
	May 13	3	TPM	L. Del Grande	Wrestler's Son
	May 20	3	Bath	ad. Shakespeare	The THOG Hamlet
	June 2	4	FTL	H. Hardin	Esker Mike and His Wife, Agiluk
	June 20	2	FTL	S. Bordeniuk G. Walker	Gin Rummy The Prince of Naples
	July 2	2	FTL	S. Rosen G. Walker	The Love Mouse The Prince of Naples
	July 14	4	FTL	ad. Mair	The Red Revolutionary
	July 22	13	GV	T. Sankey	The Golden Screw
	Aug. 29	2	FTL	D. Hayes	The Death of Artaud
	Sept. 10	10	PA	D. McAnuff	Urbania
	Sept. 29	6	GV	R. Tavel	The Life of Lady Godiva
	Sept. 30	3	TPM	collective	Free Ride
	*Oct. 5	11	Tarr	D. Freeman	Creeps
	*Oct. 19	4	New	O. Wilde	The Importance of Being Earnest
	Oct. 21	3	TPM	L. Del Grande F. Parman	Me, You, Us and the Raincoat Renegade in Retrospect
	Oct. 25	6 (r)	TAP	B. Brecht	Galileo
	Oct. 27	3	FTL	R. Canale	The Jingo Ring

Year	Date of Opening	No. of Wks	Company or Venue	Author	Title
1971	Oct. 29	6 (r)	TAP	J. Orton	What the Butler Saw
	Nov. 5	3	Cr2	L. Capson	The True North Blueprint
	Nov. 11	4	TWP	B. Brecht	The Resistible Rise of Arturo Ui
	Nov. 19	7	TPM	Jennings/Rae	Charles Manson a.k.a. Jesus Christ
	Dec. 2	2	GV	T. Sankey	Phuque
	Dec. 7	2	FTL	G. Walker	Ambush at Tether's End
	Dec. 22	4	FTL	J. Palmer	A Touch of God in the Golden Age
	Dec. 23	5	TWP	J. Winter	Pickwick
	Dec. 28	6 (r)	TAP	E. Bond	Narrow Road to the Deep North
	Dec. 29	4	Tarr	D. Tipe	Cabbagetown Plays
	Dec. 31	5 (r)	TAP	J. Palmer	Memories for My Brother, Part II
1972	Jan. 13	4	TPM	Powley et al.	The Black Queen Is Going to Eat You All Up
	Jan. 26	2	FTL	L. Fineberg	Stonehenge Trilogy
	*Feb. 2	9	WW/PA	W. Fruet	Wedding in White
	Feb. 9	4	Tarr	J. Cunningham	See No Evil, Hear ...
	Feb. 14	2	TAP	G. Ryga	Captives of the Faceless Drummer
	Feb. 17	3	TWP	collective	Fanshen
	Feb. 17	3	TPM	collective	Bethune!

Year	Date of Opening	No. of Wks	Company or Venue	Author	Title
1972	Feb. 22	3	TAP	A. Chekhov	The Three Sisters
	Feb. 23	5	FTL	L. Kardish	Brussels Sprouts
	Mar. 15	3	Tarr	J. Blumer	Surd Sandwich
	Mar. 24	4	TPM	H. Alianak	Tantrums
	Mar. 29	3	New	T. Willams	Garden District Suddenly Last Summer
	Mar. 30	4	TWP	Carew et al.	Mr Bones
	Apr. 5	4	FTL	G. Walker	Sacktown Rag
	Apr. 13	3	Tarr	S. Rosen	The Wonderful World of William Bends Who Is Not Quite Himself Today
	Apr. 24	6	TPM	G. Hamel	Deadline FLQ
	May 1	2	Cr2	collective	Prosix 16
	May 10	4	FTL	L. Del Grande	Maybe We Could Get Some Bach
	May 11	3	WW	J. Barbeau	The Way of Lacrosse Manon Lastcall
	May 16	6	Tarr	D. French	Leaving Home
	May 19	3	TPM	Bolt et al.	Buffalo Jump
	May 25	9	TWP	L. Peterson	The Workingman
	June 1	63	RA/Bayv	J. Tebelak	Godspell
	June 9	3	FTL	J. Nichol	The Book of Solomon Spring
	*June 19	5 (r)	TFT	T. Hendry	How Are Things with the Walking Wounded?

Year	Date of Opening	No. of Wks	Company or Venue	Author	Title
1972	June 27	3 (r)	TFT	L. Fineberg	Hope
	Aug. 13	5	TFT	J. Palmer	The End
	*Sept. 5	4	CSP	Molière	The Hypochondriac
	Sept. 6	2	Cr2/SLC	L. Capson	The Everlasting Salvation Machine
	Sept. 7	4	WW/GV	A. Camus	Les Justes
	Sept. 11	3	Tarr	remount	Leaving Home
	Sept. 20	4	FTL	L. Russell	Foul Play
	Sept. 21	4	TPM	collective	The Farm Show
	Oct. 2	10	TID	T. Hendry	Seance You Smell Good to Me
	Oct. 4	4	CSP	C. Goldoni	Mirandolina
	Oct. 10	4	Tarr	R. Benner	The Last of the Order
	Oct. 25	5	TPM	ad. de Vega	Dog in the Manger
	Oct. 26	4	FTL	remount	Esker Mike and His Wife, Agiluk
	Oct. 31	5	CSP	H. Ibsen	Hedda Gabler
	Nov. 3	2	TPM	H. Alianak	The Violinist and the Flower Girl
	Nov. 7	4	TAP	ad. Kafka	The Trial
	Nov. 9	4	WW	U. Betti	Goat Island
	Nov. 14	4	Tarr	M. Tremblay	Forever Yours, Marie-Lou
	Nov. 23	7	GV	R. Swerdlow	Rats
	Nov. 29	3	TPM	K. Campbell	Pilk's Madhouse

Year	Date of Opening	No. of Wks	Company or Venue	Author	Title
1972	Dec. 5	2	FTL	various	'Works' festival
	Dec. 5	5	TFT	ad. Ibsen	Hedda Gabler
	Dec. 5	4	CSP	F. Dostoevski	White Nights
	Dec. 7	6	TWP	remount	Hey, Rube!
	Dec. 12	5	TAP	Shakespeare	Twelfth Night
	Dec. 20	5	Tarr	ad. Gozzi	The Stag King
	Dec. 27	3	Cr2	L. Capson	Four Plays
	Dec. 27	3	TPM	B. Nye	The Separate Condition
1973	Jan. 2	4	CSP	N. Machiavelli	The Mandrake
	Jan. 12	4	FTL	M. Hollingsworth	Strawberry Fields
	Jan. 13	6	TAP	E. O'Neill	A Touch of the Poet
	Jan. 18	5	TPM	Salutin et al.	1837
	Jan. 25	4	TWP	N. Gogol	The Inspector General
	Jan. 30	4	CSP	A. Strindberg	Miss Julie
	Feb. 6	6	Tarr	D. Freeman	Battering Ram
	Feb. 8	4	GV	L. Fineberg	Eyes
	Feb. 14	5	TFT	C. Bolt	Gabe
	Feb. 26	5	FTL/CLT	remount	Brussels Sprouts
	Feb. 27	4	CSP	A. Chekhov	The Bear A Jubilee
	Feb. 27	4	TAP	Euripides	Electra
	Mar. 2	3	TPM	W. Seymour (= P. Hopcraft)	The Master

Year	Date of Opening	No. of Wks	Company or Venue	Author	Title
1973	Mar. 15	3	TWP	A. Kopit	Indians
	Mar. 15	5	GV	R. Swerdlow	The Big Apple
	Mar. 22	3	TPM	Bolt et al.	Pauline
	Mar. 26	4	Tarr	various	Gifts Turtle Songs
	Mar. 28	4	FTL	G. Walker	Bagdad Saloon
	Apr. 3	4	TAP	M. Tremblay	Les Belles Soeurs
	*Apr. 5	4	New	O. Wilde	Salomé
	*Apr. 5	5	OC	collective	No Way, José
	Apr. 11	2	TPM	remount	The Farm Show
	Apr. 29	5	TFT	M. Kinch	Me?
	May 3	4	TWP	ad. Twain	Letters from the Earth
	May 8	3	Cr2	L. Capson	Psychocrockery E.S.M. Edict
	May 9	3	Home	collective	The Show of Shows
	May 9	7	Tarr	A. Dalrymple	A Quiet Day in Belfast
	May 11	4	TPM	H. Alianak	Brandy
	May 11	2	New	S. Shepard	The Tooth of Crime
	May 15	5	GV	P. Schaus	Glorification
	June 12	3	TWP	remount	The Good Soldier Schweik
	*July 5	3	T+	J. Orton	Loot
	July 7	8	TFT	T. Hendry	Gravediggers of 1942

Year	Date of Opening	No. of Wks	Company or Venue	Author	Title
1973	July 12	3	OC	collective	I'm Hanlan, He's Durnan, He's Ward
	July 31	4	T+	Waterhouse/Hall	Say Who You Are
	Sept. 4	4	T+	J. Guare	The House of Blue Leaves
	Sept. 19	4	TPM	collective	Under the Greywacke
	Sept. 27	4	New	H. Williams	AC/DC
	Sept. 29	7	Tarr	D. French	Of the Fields, Lately
	Oct. 2	1	Cr2	L. Capson	The Lonely Ventriloquist
	Oct. 6	7	Tarr	Peters et al.	The Group of Seven and the Case of the Glowing Pine
	Oct. 10	3	TPM	H. Alianak	Noah's Kiosk
	Oct. 16	4	TAP	Molière	The Misanthrope
	Oct. 17	2	TPM	collective	Crime and Punishment Cod on a Stick
	Oct. 20	2	TFT	M. Hollingsworth	Clear Light
	Oct. 23	3	TWP	McKenna/Bush	Richard Thirdtime
	Oct. 25	3	TPM	L. Del Grande	So Who's Goldberg?
	Nov. 14	3	GV	J. Crossland	Bigger than Both of Us
	Nov. 20	4	TAP	A. Strindberg	The Dance of Death
	Nov. 21	5	OC	collective	COP
	Nov. 22	2	TWP	J. Anouilh	Thieves Carnival
	Nov. 22	5	TFT	Thompson/ Williams	Vallières!
	Nov. 24	5	Tarr	J. Reaney	Sticks and Stones

Year	Date of Opening	No. of Wks	Company or Venue	Author	Title
1973	Nov. 26	3	TPM	L. Fineberg	All the Ghosts
	Nov. 28	3	TPM	remount	Cod on a Stick
	Dec. 12	2	TPM	H. Alianak	Christmas
	Dec. 18	4	TWP	remount	Richard Thirdtime
1974	Jan. 5	5	FTL	L. Rooke	Ms America
	Jan. 8	4	TAP	A. Pinero	Trelawney of the Wells
	Jan. 9	2	TPM	collective	Toronto Pixie Caper
	Jan. 9	3	TPM	remount	Cod on a Stick
	Jan. 12	4	Tarr	D. Freeman	You're Gonna Be Alright, Jamie Boy
	Feb. 7	15	TWP	Winter/Smith	Ten Lost Years
	Feb. 12	4	TAP	M. Cook	Colour the Flesh the Colour of Dust
	Feb. 14	3	TPM	Salutin et al.	Adventures of an Immigrant
	Feb. 16	6	Tarr	B. Wade	Blitzkrieg
	Feb. 20	5	TFT	C. Bolt	Red Emma
	Mar. 7	5	New	M. Tremblay	Montreal Smoked Meat
	Mar. 7	4	OC	collective	Nuts and Bolts The Storm of Blackdeath Prison
	Mar. 12	2	FTL	D. Hayes	Spaces
	Mar. 19	4	TAP	B. Brecht	The Good Woman of Setzuan
	Mar. 27	5	TCA	E. Whitehead	The Foursome

Year	Date of Opening	No. of Wks	Company or Venue	Author	Title
1974	Mar. 30	5	Tarr	M. Garneau J. Reaney	Four to Four One Man Masque
	*Apr. 4	3	Red	collective	Entrances
	Apr. 9	4	FTL	G. Walker	The Prince of Naples Demerit
	Apr. 10	3	TPM	T. Johns	Naked on the North Shore
	Apr. 11	5	GV	R. Swerdlow	Hey, Justine!
	Apr. 17	3	Tarr	T. Gallacher	Mr Joyce Is Leaving Paris
	Apr. 24	2	TPM	ad. Shakepeare	The Tempest
	May 8	3	Red	D. Grant	What Glorious Times They Had
	May 10	3	TPM	various	Rail Tales
	May 11	4	FTL	G. Walker	Beyond Mozambique
	May 14	7	Tarr	M. Tremblay	Hosanna
	May 14	3	TFT	D. McAnuff	Troll
	May 22	3	GV	R. Swerdlow	Beethoven's 5th
	June 4	4	T+	C. Hampton	The Philanthropist
	June 7	3	Red	M. Terry	Ex-Miss Copper Queen on a Set of Pills The Gloaming Oh My Darling
	June 27	4	GV	collective	Bull Durham
	July 9	4	T+	L. Hellman	The Little Foxes
	July 10	7	OC	collective	Business as Usual
	Aug. 2	3	Cr2/TFT	ad. Dostoevski	Crime and Punishment

Year	Date of Opening	No. of Wks	Company or Venue	Author	Title
1974	Aug. 13	3	T+	H. Leonard	The Au Pair Man
	Sept. 10	4	T+	J. Anouilh	The Rehearsal
	Sept. 10	5	TAP/MTC	J. Hirsch	The Dybbuk
	Sept. 11	3	Tarr	remount	Hosanna
	Sept. 11	6	TPM/PA	ad. Service	The Spell of the Yukon
	Sept. 12	4	TPM	Salutin et al.	1837: The Farmers' Revolt
	Sept. 19	3	TWP	McKenna/Bush	From the Boyne to Batoche
	Sept. 24	5	OC	remount	Business as Usual
	Oct. 2	4	Tarr	P. Madden	The Night No One Yelled
	Oct. 15	3	FTL	G. Engler	Sudden Death Overtime
	Oct. 16	3	TPM	remount	Them Donnellys
	Oct. 16	3	Red	remount	What Glorious Times They Had
	Oct. 17	5	GV	Rose/Campone	Jubalay
	Oct. 22	4	TAP	M. Scott	Wu-Feng
	Oct. 23	2	Cr2	T. Hendry	Aces Wild
	Oct. 24	6	Codco	collective	Sickness, Death and Beyond the Grave
	Oct. 26	3	CLT	A. Fugard	Hello and Goodbye
	Oct. 31	5	TFT	M. Ondaatje	The Collected Works of Billy the Kid
	Nov. 5	5	New	D. Storey	Home
	Nov. 16	9	Tarr	J. Reaney	The St Nicholas Hotel

Year	Date of Opening	No. of Wks	Company or Venue	Author	Title
1974	Nov. 20	2	TPM	Schreibman et al.	The Joke Show
	Nov. 26	4	TAP	R. Sheridan	The Rivals
	Nov. 30	6	FTL	K. Gass	Hurray for Johnny Canuck
	Dec. 4	2	seed	P. Melnick	Brutal Paradise
	Dec. 10	4	GV	R. Swerdlow	Peter and the Wolf
	Dec. 12	4	TWP/Bayv	remount	Ten Lost Years
	Dec. 17	2	TWP/SLC	remount	Mr Pickwick
	Dec. 21	4	seed	ad. Lee	Alligator Pie
	Dec. 22	3	FTL	H. Alianak	Christmas Mousetown
	Dec. 31	4	TWP	J. Winter	You Can't Get There from Here
1975	Jan. 18	15	TPM	collective	I Love You, Baby Blue
	Jan. 21	4	TAP	A. Solzhenitsyn	Article 58
	Jan. 22	4	TFT	collective	The Pits
	Jan. 23	7	OC	collective	A Soupsong
	Feb. 1	7	Tarr	M. Tremblay	Bonjour, Là, Bonjour
	Feb. 5	3	seed	M. Sestito	Tony's Woman
	*Feb. 12	5	TSF	D. McAnuff	Leave It to Beaver Is Dead
	Feb. 19	3	Home	collective	The Show of Shows
	Feb. 25	5	TAP	R. Davies	Question Time
	Feb. 26	3	seed	J. Roy	Follies of Conviction

Year	Date of Opening	No. of Wks	Company or Venue	Author	Title
1975	Feb. 27	4	TWP	C. Zuckmayer	The Captain of Kopenick
	*Mar. 8	3	TF	W. Soyinka	The Swamp Dwellers
	Mar. 12	3	seed	collective	Family Entertainment
	Mar. 12	2	New	P. Picasso	Four Little Girls
	Mar. 13	3	TPM	R. Salutin	The False Messiah
	Mar. 15	3	Red	E. Siminovitch	Strange Games
	Mar. 29	6	Tarr	J. Reaney	Handcuffs
	Mar. 29	3	TAP	remount	Trelawney of the Wells
	Apr. 2	4	TFT	W. Hauptmann	Heat
	Apr. 2	3	New	P. Handke	The Ride across Lake Constance
	Apr. 8	3	FTL	various	'Works II' festival
	*Apr. 19	4	Pho	S. Gray	Butley
	Apr. 23	4	TPM	collective	Alive
	Apr. 24	4	TWP	J. Winter	Summer '76
	May 5	2	O'K	C. Jones	Kronborg: 1582
	May 7	3	Red	Grant et al.	The Most Beautiful Girl in the World
	May 7	3	TPM	H. Alianak	Night
	May 14	2	seed	P. Melnick	Monomania
	May 20	4	FTL	B. Wade	Underground
	May 24	6	Tarr	D. French	One Crack Out
	May 30	4	Fire	E. Moore	The Sea Horse

Year	Date of Opening	No. of Wks	Company or Venue	Author	Title
1975	June 4	3	T+	M. Tremblay	Forever Yours, Marie-Lou
	July 2	4	T+	T. Williams	A Streetcar Named Desire
	July 3	3	Pho	H. Pinter	The Collection The Lover
	Aug. 6	4	T+	A. Gurney	Children
	Aug. 21	3	Pho	A. Jellicoe	The Knack
	Aug. 25	2	TWP/SLC	remount	Ten Lost Years
	Sept. 9	4	GV	E. Swerdlow	High Lights
	Sept. 10	3	T+	F. Dürrenmatt	The Physicists
	Sept. 18	4	TPM	collective	City: The Toronto Show
	Sept. 30	6	Pho	A. Christie	The Mousetrap
	Oct. 10	4	Cr2	L. Capson	Face Crime
	Oct. 14	5	New	L. Fineberg	Human Remains
	Oct. 15	4	TFT	M. Kinch	April 29, 1975
	Oct. 22	3	TAP	M. Tremblay C. Bolt	Surprise! Surprise! Shelter
	Oct. 28	3	FTL	J. Crossland	Peaches and Poisonned [sic] Cream
	Oct. 29	3	TPM	ad. Shakespeare	Titus Andronicus
	Oct. 30	3	OC/TWP	Lavut/Gelbart	The Life and Times of Grey Owl
	Nov. 12	6	TSF	S. Beckett	Waiting for Godot
	Nov. 20	5	Pho	J. Herbert	Fortune and Men's Eyes
	Nov. 22	3	TWP	L. Peterson	Women in the Attic

Year	Date of Opening	No. of Wks	Company or Venue	Author	Title
1975	Nov. 26	3	TAP	S. O'Casey	The Plough and the Stars
	Dec. 3	3	TFT	L. Russell	The Mystery of the Pig Killer's Daughter
	Dec. 6	5	OC	A. Fugard	The Blood Knot
	Dec. 10	1	Bath	J. Reaney	The Donnelly trilogy

Notes

Throughout these notes, the abbreviation MTL signifies the Performing Arts Files of the Arts Department, Metropolitan Toronto Library. Other abbreviations used are CTR (*Canadian Theatre Review*), GM (the Toronto *Globe and Mail*), *Tele* (the Toronto *Telegram*), and *TStar* (the *Toronto Star*).

CHAPTER 1 Before the Flood

1 Respectively, Whittaker, 'The Alternate Theatre in Toronto,' *The Stage in Canada* 7, no. 1 (Sept. 1972), 6; and Kareda, 'Alternative theatre offers hope for the future,' *TStar*, 16 Sept. 1972
2 Quoted by Gina Mallet and David McCaughna, in 'Free Theatre leaps into the bigtime,' *TStar*, 30 Dec. 1976
3 Peter Hay, 'Cultural Politics,' CTR 2 (Spring 1974), 10
4 Kareda, 'Canada's new playwrights have found a home at home,' *New York Times*, 24 Nov. 1974
5 Respectively, John Palmer, 'Canadian Playwright Crisis: The Twelfth Hour,' *Performing Arts in Canada* 8, no. 3 (Fall 1971), 7; and Martin Kinch, 'Canadian Theatre: In for the Long Haul,' *This Magazine* 10, nos. 5–6 (Nov.–Dec. 1976), 4
6 Whittaker, 'The Theatre,' in *Culture of Contemporary Canada*, ed. Julian Park (Ithaca: Cornell University Press 1957), 165. This summary of Canadian theatre is especially intriguing because it was written just before the Canada Council was established and the regional theatre network began.
7 Murray Edwards, *A Stage in Our Past* (Toronto: University of Toronto Press 1968), 36
8 *The Awkward Stage: The Ontario Theatre Study Report* (Toronto 1969), 181

9 Ken Gass, 'Toronto's Alternates: Changing Realities,' *CTR* 21 (Winter 1979), 127

10 The Crest's productions are listed in *CTR* 7 (Summer 1975), 45–51.

11 Donald Davis, 'Interview,' *CTR* 7 (Summer 1975), 43. This issue contains several articles on the Crest controversy.

12 Whittaker, 'Canada's roving players come to rest,' *GM*, 9 Apr. 1965

13 Quoted by Blaik Kirby, in 'Theatre Toronto is dead! Long live Theatre Toronto!,' *GM*, 12 Apr. 1969

14 Quoted by Vincent Guy, in 'Clifford Williams in Interview,' *Plays and Players* 16, no. 11 (Aug. 1969), 57

15 Cohen, 'The new theatre season,' *TStar*, 22 Aug. 1964

16 Davis, 'Interview,' 44

17 More detailed discussions of Canadian workers' theatre may be found in Robin Endres' introduction to *Eight Men Speak and Other Plays from the Canadian Workers' Theatre* (Toronto: New Hogtown Press 1976), and in Toby Gordon Ryan's memoir *Stage Left: Canadian Theatre in the Thirties* (Toronto: *CTR* Publications 1981).

18 Adjudicator Harley Granville-Barker commented on the irony of the audience response: see the Ottawa daily newspapers, 23 Apr. 1936.

19 Biographical details are taken from Alan Filewod's *Collective Encounters: Documentary Theatre in English Canada* (Toronto: University of Toronto Press 1987); from an interview with Dr Neil Carson, who is currently working on a book on Luscombe and *TWP*; and *MTL*.

20 The Theatre Workshop is the subject of a fine history and memoir by company member Howard Goorney, in *The Theatre Workshop Story* (London: Eyre Methuen 1981).

21 Antony Ferry, 'Ten good people and an idea,' *TStar*, 5 Dec. 1959

22 See Dennis Braithwaite, 'New theatre group,' *TStar*, 21 Mar. 1959; and Joan Ferry, 'Experiences of a Pioneer in Canadian Experimental Theatre,' *Theatre History in Canada* 8, no. 1 (Spring 1987).

23 Mavor Moore, 'A protest against conformity,' *Tele*, 9 May 1960

24 Cohen, *TStar*, 11 Feb. 1961

25 See Antony Ferry, '"Hey, Rube!" paid peanuts, but created big impact,' *TStar*, 13 Mar. 1961.

26 Whittaker, 'Luscombe's merit shines in play,' *GM*, 29 Dec. 1961

27 Cohen, 'A remarkable achievement,' *TStar*, 17 Apr. 1963

28 Quoted by Michael Enright, in 'Luscombe, Mysterious Keeper of the Flame,' *Globe Magazine* [in *GM*], 14 Jan. 1971, p. 9

29 Filewod, *Collective Encounters*, 51

30 Biographical details are taken from Ronald Bryden's preface to *Whittaker's Theatre* (Greenbank, Ont., 1985).

31 Quoted by John Fraser, in 'Kareda: the critic who jumped the fence and joined Stratford,' GM, 26 Mar. 1977
32 Quoted by Ray Conlogue, in 'Kareda and Tarragon: each the tonic the other needs,' GM, 26 Sept. 1981
33 Kareda, 'An almost forgotten dramatic style,' TStar, 14 Feb. 1972
34 Kinch, 'Long Haul,' 7
35 Kareda, Introd., Leaving Home (Toronto: New Press 1972), ix

CHAPTER 2 Theatre Passe Muraille to 1970

1 Cohen, 'Passe Muraille is Toronto's "other" theatre,' TStar, 9 Jan. 1971
2 Interview with Jim Garrard, 12 June 1985. Unattributed quotations from Garrard which follow are taken from the same source.
3 Quoted by Don Rubin, in 'The Insurgent Theatre,' Egg 2 [Oct.? 1969], 18. Egg, a local radical newsmagazine, seems to have survived only two issues. These may be found in the special collections of the John P. Robarts Library, University of Toronto.
4 Quoted by Lynda Hurst, in 'Old folks take over hippie palace,' TStar, 1 Mar. 1980, p. B6
5 This brief overview of Rochdale College is summarized from the clippings files in the University of Toronto archives, and from the appendices to Adelman's The Beds of Academe (Toronto: James Lewis and Samuel 1969), which promulgates his theories on student housing.
6 The complex financial dealings surrounding Rochdale, such as the inclusion in these formulas of the value of land which the Co-op already owned, would require a forensic auditor to untangle. While my research was in progress, two new books appeared on the topic of Rochdale: Rochdale: The Runaway College, by David Sharp (Toronto: Anansi 1987); and Dream Tower: The Life and Legacy of Rochdale College, by Henry Mietkiewicz and Bob Mackowycz (Toronto: McGraw-Hill Ryerson 1988).
7 'Rochdale Drama Project,' a typescript, on the microfiche 'Theatre Passe Muraille – History,' MTL. Ensuing quotations in this and the next paragraph are from the same document.
8 Don Rubin, 'Sleepy Tunes in Toronto,' CTR 20 (Fall 1978), 93
9 Reviewed by Whittaker, 'It's a busy week for the Unitarians,' GM, 19 Mar. 1968. The origins of the Colonnade, a modern arena theatre seating two hundred, are described briefly in chapter 8.
10 Quoted by Marci McDonald, in 'Futz brings nudity, bestiality to Toronto stage,' TStar, 5 Mar. 1969. Unattributed quotations in the next two paragraphs are from the same article.

11 Quoted in 'Appeal court frees Futz producers of indecency charge,' *TStar*, 3 Apr. 1970

12 Respectively, Jack Jones, 'The Futz Hassle,' on the microfiche 'Central Library Theatre – Reviews,' MTL; and an unidentified cast member quoted in 'Futz troupe summoned, goes on,' *GM*, 8 Mar. 1969. Jones was a prominent member of Rochdale's governing council.

13 Quoted by Whittaker, in 'Playwright bewildered over police crackdown on Futz,' *GM*, 19 Mar. 1969

14 Stan Fefferman, 'The Rape of Futz,' *Tele*, 8 Mar. 1969

15 Don Rubin, 'Futz is essentially a fatuous play,' *TStar*, 6 Mar. 1969. This is the most detailed description of the first act, and the most careful analysis of the cast's difficulties with it.

16 Quoted in 'Detective and theatre critics disagree on obscenity in Futz,' *GM*, 26 June 1969

17 For instance, Bolsby was involved in another controversy the following month when he had a Legal Aid counsel ejected from his courtroom. See 'Judge Bolsby's tough on lawyers but they respect him all the same,' *TStar*, 18 July 1969, p. 2.

18 Quoted in 'Futz trial airs *the* 4-letter word,' *TStar*, 26 June 1969

19 Quoted in 'Does freedom of expression mean barnyard talk? Futz Judge asks,' *GM*, 27 June 1969

20 Quoted in 'Futz hit with $1300 fines,' *Tele*, 30 June 1969, p. 2

21 This quotation is a compromise between the *Star* and the *Telegram* reports of the verdict, both dated 30 June 1969. In both papers, the story was on the front page.

22 *TStar*, 3 July 1969, p. 6

23 Quoted in 'Judge questions authors' right to use language of "barnyard,"' *TStar*, 27 June 1969

24 Quoted in '4 letter word not obscene: Cleric,' *Tele*, 27 June 1969

25 Cohen, 'The strange silence in the Futz case,' *TStar*, 14 May 1969. See also Marci McDonald, 'A huge free-form happening,' *TStar*, 24 June 1969.

26 Cohen, 'Hair's endurable but terribly insufficient,' *TStar*, 12 Jan. 1970

27 Cohen, 'Morality squad specialists next?' *TStar*, 7 Apr. 1970

28 Wayne Grady, 'A Man's Garden of Verse,' *Saturday Night* 98, no. 11 (Nov. 1983), 74

29 Undated report, on the microfiche 'Theatre Passe Muraille – History,' MTL. Unattributed quotations in the next two paragraphs are from the same source.

30 Interview, 22 May 1985

31 See Whittaker, 'Two Canadian plays accepted for festival,' *GM*, 14 Feb. 1966

32 Interview with John Palmer, 14 July 1985. Unattributed quotations from Palmer which follow are taken from the same source.

33 Gale Garnett, 'The Triple-headed Monster-genius of Toronto Free Theatre,' *Performing Arts in Canada* 9, no. 2 (Summer 1972), 50

34 Quoted by Tom Hendry, in 'The Canadian Theatre's Sudden Explosion,' *Saturday Night* 87, no. 1 (Jan. 1972), 24–5

35 Whittaker, '1971 saw Canadian theatre's greatest leap forward,' GM, 1 Jan. 1972

36 *Visions of an Unseemly Youth* was produced at Le Hibou the year before by Gilles Provost, a francophone director whom Palmer credits for giving him early encouragement.

37 Cohen, 'CBC upset at games' cost rise,' *TStar*, 17 July 1967

38 'Contemporary play didn't please adjudicator,' *Tele* [CP], 23 May 1969. Elaine Reed later became a theatre administrator, and (as Elaine Calder) served as general manager of Toronto Free Theatre from 1982 to 1984.

39 Everyone seems to have forgotten this American source for the CPT's name, but it was reported by Herbert Whittaker in 'Stratford may not want Canadian plays,' GM, 5 Aug. 1969.

40 Palmer directed *Occasional Seasoning* and *Anthem*, while Kinch directed the other two.

41 Don Rubin, 'Stratford offspring needs more than encouragement,' *TStar*, 9 July 1969

42 According to Kinch, interview, 13 May 1986

43 Respectively, Whittaker, 'Nude Memories swing about jungle gym,' GM, 6 Nov. 1969; and Cohen, 'Muraille chooses badly for opener,' *TStar*, 6 Nov. 1969

44 Cohen, 'A story that needed to be plainly told,' *TStar*, 22 Nov. 1969

45 Respectively, Whittaker, 'Creative forces at work on World Theatre Day – and a welter of sadism, incest, blood and laughs,' GM, 27 Mar. 1970; and Cohen, 'Osborne all wrong at Trinity Square,' *TStar*, 31 Mar. 1970

46 Quoted in 'Collective Conversation: The Space Show,' CTR 6 (Spring 1975), 27

47 Cohen, 'Director and cast failed customers,' *TStar*, 4 June 1970. See also Whittaker, 'Muddled treatment of a massacre,' GM, 28 May 1970.

48 Quoted by Betty Lee, in 'Can these directors come up with an answer?' *Globe Magazine* [in GM], 21 Feb. 1970, p. 14

49 See Daniel Stoffman, 'Panic Theatre's play a Tarzan take-off,' *TStar*, 4 Sept. 1970.

50 Cohen, 'Splendid news: The Balanchine ballet returns,' *TStar*, 5 Sept. 1970

CHAPTER 3 The Factory Theatre Lab

1 Hendry, 'Sudden Explosion,' 28
2 See, for instance, Whittaker, 'What chance now for Canadian playwrights?'
   GM, 24 Oct. 1970.
3 Gina Mallet, '"Navel-gazing days" are over for theatre,' TStar, 21 Nov. 1981
4 Gass's articles also included a feature on Theatre Passe Muraille and an
   attack on the university's summer teacher-training program, in which he
   had been enrolled the preceding year. This latter article provoked a lively
   debate in the pages of the 1969 Summer Varsity.
5 Don Rubin, 'The Trials of John Herbert,' Egg 1 [Oct.? 1969], 10 [Special
   Collections, John P. Robarts Library, University of Toronto]
6 Herbert's story of his early theatrical influences, brushes with the police,
   and his subsequent arrest and imprisonment is most fully told in his
   contribution to Stage Voices, ed. Geraldine Anthony (Toronto: Doubleday
   1978), 170–92.
7 Cohen, 'Brundage shuns play offers,' TStar, 15 May 1967
8 This play had originally been intended for George Luscombe at Toronto
   Workshop Productions in 1964; but when he and Herbert had a falling-
   out, Luscombe instead produced a version adapted by his resident playwright, Jack Winter.
9 Audiotapes made by Ken Gass, 1978, and deposited in the National Film,
   Television and Sound Archives, National Archives of Canada. Unattributed quotations from Gass which follow are taken from this source. Gass's
   review of The World of Woyzeck, along with a profile of Herbert, appeared
   in the Summer Varsity, 1 Aug. 1969.
10 Ken Gass, Introd., The Factory Lab Anthology (Vancouver: Talonbooks 1974),
   7–8
11 Cohen, 'Act of Violence quite lamentable,' TStar, 6 Aug. 1970. See also
   Susan Perly, 'Factory Theatre Lab presents experiments in racism,' Summer Varsity, 7 Aug. 1970.
12 Although The Factory Lab Anthology cites the Factory's 1970 production as
   the first performance of We Three, You and I, prior performances are
   recorded at the University of British Columbia and at Theatre Passe
   Muraille. Gass did not direct its première at UBC.
13 Quoted by Betty Lee, in 'It's still a bumpy road for Canadian plays, playwrights,' GM, 10 Oct. 1970
14 Snails was partly sponsored by Renaissance '71, a Canada-wide universities
   arts festival centred at the University of Toronto, in which Gass, Shain
   Jaffe, and Jane Glassco were all involved as organizers. A summary of this

festival is given in *Performing Arts in Canada* 8, no. 2 (Summer 1971), 18. Gass's audiotaped memoirs suggest that Renaissance '71 was an excellent concept destroyed by sloppy administration.

15 DuBarry Campau, 'Play little more stimulating than reading annual report,' *Tele*, 3 May 1971. The Dunlop plant controversy is summarized in Alexander Ross, 'Tale of a plant closure: no pat answers for 597,' *Financial Post*, 28 Mar. 1970, p. 7.

16 Whittaker, 'Tale of Eskimo life stark and engrossing,' *GM*, 11 June 1971

17 Walker had had some earlier plays workshopped, but *The Prince of Naples* was his first play to be produced.

18 Kareda, 'Theatre Lab's rehearsal was an involving experience,' *TStar*, 21 June 1971

19 Don Rubin, 'Theatre draws its sabre on Americans,' *TStar*, 5 Aug. 1971

20 While this project was accepted, Gass never submitted the paperwork required to complete his MA.

21 See Don Rubin, 'I Love You Billy Striker a fascinating and disturbing drama,' *TStar*, 12 Aug. 1971; and Don Rubin, 'Two intelligent productions worth seeing,' *TStar*, 1 Sept. 1971.

22 'A Strange Enterprise: The Dilemma of the Playwright in Canada' (n.p., 1971), p. 1. Copies of the reports of both conferences, originally distributed by the Canadian Theatre Centre, may be found in the Tarragon Theatre Archives, University of Guelph, and in the papers of the Canadian Theatre Centre, National Archives of Canada. In addition, summaries of the recommendations of the 'Gaspé manifesto' are given in *The Stage in Canada* 6, no. 9 (Jan. 1972), 12–14, and by Tom Hendry in 'The Natives Are Restless,' *Performing Arts in Canada* 8, no. 4 (Winter 1971), 30–1.

23 For samples of such commentary, see 'Canadian quotas and subsidized theatres,' *That's Showbusiness*, 6 Jan. 1972, pp. 1–2; and the issue of *The Stage in Canada* cited above.

24 From Doherty's letter of invitation, quoted in 'Report on a Playwrights Conference, Niagara-on-the-Lake' (n.p., 1971), p. 1

25 The last non-Canadian play produced by Passe Muraille had been Kinch's production of *Spring's Awakening* almost a year earlier.

26 Palmer, 'Canadian Playwright Crisis,' 6

27 Typescript, datestamped Oct. 1971, on the microfiche 'Factory Theatre Lab – History,' MTL

28 Interview, 30 Apr. 1986

29 Respectively, Whittaker, 'Jingo Ring unoriginal but full of flair,' *GM*, 28 Oct. 1971; and Kareda, 'This poor writer is at the mercy of his director,' *TStar*, 28 Oct. 1971

30 Whittaker, 'One-liners play's main ploy,' GM, 9 Dec. 1971
31 Respectively, Whittaker, 'Touch of God: talent as well as gab,' GM, 23 Dec.
    1971; and Kareda, 'A Touch of God in the Golden Age a curious work,'
    TStar, 23 Dec. 1971
32 Tom Hendry, letter to the editor, TStar, 10 Jan. 1972, p. 7
33 Kareda, 'Brussels Sprouts remarkable play,' TStar, 24 Feb. 1972
34 Kareda, 'Sacktown Rag a new play with creaky past,' TStar, 6 Apr. 1972
35 Retitled Forty-Two Seconds from Broadway, Bach was produced on Broadway
    in March 1973, but closed after a single performance.
36 At the Factory, Del Grande had also acted in A Touch of God in the Golden
    Age. His productions at Theatre Passe Muraille included Six of a Kind,
    Wrestler's Son, Tantrums, and Dog in the Manger, all mentioned in chapter 4.
37 Whittaker, 'Unsentimental look at the Grand Tour,' GM, 24 Feb. 1972
38 The Brock Bibliography indicates it was published by the Canadian Theatre
    Centre in 1966, but apparently it was not widely circulated.
39 Respectively, Kareda, 'Solomon Spring is a crudely crayoned TV-like melo-
    drama,' TStar, 12 June 1972; and Whittaker, 'Acting too light in The
    Book of Solomon Spring,' GM, 12 June 1972
40 Kareda, 'Foul Play decked in enough trappings to hold attention,' TStar, 21
    Sept. 1972
41 Respectively, Kareda, 'Factory Lab's Esker Mike a monumental achieve-
    ment,' TStar, 27 Oct. 1972; and Whittaker, 'New Esker Mike version
    lacks its original drive,' GM, 27 Oct. 1972
42 Kareda, '"Short" play festival a killing marathon,' TStar, 7 Dec. 1972
43 From Gass's press release and his letter to Equity discussed immediately
    below, in the file 'Factory Theatre Lab – Publicity,' MTL
44 It should be pointed out that the Factory honoured its verbal agreement
    with the actors, and that the complaint did not originate with any of the
    Works participants. Gass recalled it came from Canadian international star
    Barry Morse, whose daughter Melanie Morse had been offered a role
    and the fifty-dollar fee.
45 Respectively, Kareda's preview article 'A horrifying vision worth a second
    look,' TStar, 8 Jan. 1973; and Whittaker, 'No merit in Factory's latest,'
    GM, 12 Jan. 1973
46 Ken Gass, Introd., Three Plays, by George F. Walker (Toronto: Coach House
    1978), 10
47 Kareda, 'Bagdad Saloon: Young playwright leaps forward,' TStar, 29 Mar.
    1973
48 Quoted in 'Theatres support Factory Lab,' TStar, 6 Apr. 1973

49 Brian Boru, 'Factory Theatre Lab: out of Gass,' *That's Showbusiness*, 22 May 1974
50 Kareda, 'Theatre Lab's comic book romp is for kiddies,' *TStar*, 4 Dec. 1974
51 Respectively, Sheldon Rosen's *The Box* and Thomas Cone's *Cubistique*; James de Felice's *The Jumper* and Elizabeth Boyle's *Unliberated Lady*; *Aliens*, an earlier play by Bryan Wade; and Henry Beissel's *The Curve*, an adaptation of a 1960 play by Germany's Tankred Dorst.
52 Both in Kareda, 'Factory Theatre shows its old pep,' *TStar*, 4 Apr. 1975
53 Ken Gass, 'Perspective,' *Theatre Notebook* 1, no. 1 (Oct. 1975), 1. This theatre newspaper, published by the Factory Theatre Lab, seems to have survived only one issue. Copies may be found in file 'Factory Theatre Lab – Publicity,' MTL, and in the University of Guelph Theatre Archives.
54 In 'Postscript: Interview with Ken Gass,' CTR 12 (Fall 1976)
55 Ken Gass, 'The Boy Bishop,' CTR 12 (Fall 1976), 91
56 Gass, 'Perspective'

CHAPTER 4 Theatre Passe Muraille after 1970

1 Kareda, 'Craziness on Trinity Sq.,' *TStar*, 14 Jan. 1974
2 Quoted by Merle Shain, in 'Pursuing the need for guerilla theatre,' *Tele*, 1 Mar. 1969
3 Bob Bainborough, 'Recollections of the Making of Paper Wheat,' in *Paper Wheat: The Book* (Saskatoon: Western Producer Prairie Books 1982), 34. The historical and stylistic connections between Thompson's collectives and *Paper Wheat* are well documented elsewhere. See, for instance, Don Kerr's introduction to *Paper Wheat: The Book*, and Alan Filewod's chapter on *Paper Wheat* in *Collective Encounters*.
4 John Gray, Preface to '18 Wheels,' in *Local Boy Makes Good: Three Musicals by John Gray* (Vancouver: Talonbooks 1987), 20
5 Paul Thompson, Introd., *The Farm Show* (Toronto: Coach House 1976), 7
6 John Gray, Introd., *Billy Bishop Goes to War* (Vancouver: Talonbooks 1981), 6
7 Quoted by Robert Wallace, in 'Out of Place: Western Adventures of Two Theatrical Dudes,' CTR 42 (Spring 1985), 36
8 Interview with Paul Thompson, 31 Mar. 1986. Unattributed quotations from Thompson which follow are taken from the same source. The most thorough description of Thompson's work in France, and the effect it had on his work in Canada, is given by Paul Wilson, 'Blyth Spirit,' *Books in Canada* 12, no. 4 (Apr. 1983).

9 Quoted by Whittaker, in 'Come wrecker's ball or poverty, Passe Muraille means to survive,' *GM*, 28 Oct. 1972

10 Maruska Stankova's *I Am Coming from Czechoslovakia*. The play is described in stories in the *Montreal Star*, 28 Nov. 1968 and 3 Dec. 1968.

11 Quoted by Wilson, in 'Blyth Spirit,' 11

12 Cohen, 'Some good things have happened on theatre scene,' *TStar*, 26 Oct. 1970

13 Quoted by Whittaker, in 'Sexless stripping useful artifice in Doukhobors,' *GM*, 3 Apr. 1971

14 Paul Thompson, Introd., *Doukhobors* (Toronto: Playwrights Co-op 1973), 2

15 Quoted by Wilson, in 'Blyth Spirit,' 11

16 Interview, 17 June 1985. Quotations from Garrard which follow are taken from the same source.

17 Respectively, Whittaker, 'Play a well-disorganized happening,' *GM*, 14 Jan. 1972; and Kareda, 'Only performers are delighted with inane play,' *TStar*, 14 Jan. 1972

18 Kareda, 'Theatre manages to make Dr. Norman Bethune a bore,' *TStar*, 17 Feb. 1972

19 Kareda, 'Exciting new show at Passe Muraille almost too good,' *TStar*, 24 Mar. 1972

20 Whittaker, 'An ingenious Buffalo Jump,' *GM*, 22 May 1972

21 Kareda, 'Buffalo Jump: A play on Depression misery,' *TStar*, 19 May 1972

22 Quoted by Robert Wallace, in 'Paul Thompson at Theatre Passe-Muraille: Bits and Pieces,' *Open Letter* 2nd ser., no. 7 (Winter 1974), 59

23 Quoted by Wilson, in 'Blyth Spirit,' 11

24 Interview, 14 July 1985

25 In the film *The Clinton Special*, dir. Michael Ondaatje, Mongrel Films, 1974

26 Quoted by Linda West, in 'Passing comment on Passe Muraille,' *That's Showbusiness*, 25 Sept. 1974, p. 5

27 In *The Clinton Special*

28 Liza Williams, 'Clinton area theatre opening left audience agog, talking,' *Goderich Signal-Star*, 17 Aug. 1972

29 Kareda, 'The Farm Show: A rich theatrical experience,' *TStar*, 22 Sept. 1972

30 Quoted by David Fox, interview, 1 Dec. 1986

31 Interview, 25 Nov. 1986

32 Rick Salutin, Preface to '1837: The Farmers' Revolt,' in *1837: William Lyon Mackenzie and the Canadian Revolution* (Toronto: James Lorimer 1976), 195–6. The glimpse here of the cast's reactions to the dispute between Equity and the Factory Lab (p. 191) is also a revealing one.

33 In Kareda, 'Passe Muraille's biographical play remains oblique,' *TStar*, 23 Mar. 1973

34 Quoted by Whittaker, in 'Passe Muraille is back on the Farm,' *GM*, 23 Apr. 1973

35 Ibid. A tour of New England towns was also planned, but not carried through.

36 Quoted by Whittaker, in 'Passe Muraille booming in Cobalt,' *GM*, 9 Aug. 1973

37 See the introduction to Alianak's collection *Return of the Big Five* (Toronto: Fineglow 1975).

38 See Kareda, 'It's non-stop comedy with Cod on a Stick,' *TStar*, 10 Dec. 1973; Kareda, 'It's them Donnellys, and how!' *TStar*, 17 Nov. 1974; and Brian Boru, 'History, Mystery, and Myth: The Donnellys,' *That's Showbusiness*, 12 Dec. 1973.

39 Interview, 25 Nov. 1986

40 Kareda, 'Good idea tossed away,' *TStar*, 5 Nov. 1973

41 Kareda, 'Craziness on Trinity Sq.,' *TStar*, 14 Jan. 1974

42 Quoted by Frank Rasky, in 'Director takes theatre to immigrant audiences,' *TStar*, 14 Feb. 1974

43 Kareda, 'Adventures of an Immigrant has its moments,' *TStar*, 15 Feb. 1974

44 Quoted by Debra Sharp, in 'It's Newfound*land*[.] Under*stand?*' *GM*, 13 Oct. 1979, *Fanfare* supplement, p. 10. The following quotation is from the same source.

45 Thompson, quoted by Frank Rasky, in 'The Newfie joke is on us, folks!' *TStar*, 5 Nov. 1974

46 Whittaker, 'Passe Muraille's Oil tribute to Petrolia,' *GM*, 26 June 1974

47 Quoted by West, in 'Passing comment'

48 A scripted treatment of the same story, by Leonard Peterson, was first produced by Toronto's Young People's Theatre in 1970.

49 Quoted in an interview by Ted Johns, 'The Trial of Baby Blue,' *CTR* 13 (Winter 1977), 7. Unattributed quotations from Thompson which follow are taken from the same source.

50 Kareda, 'Negative show of nudity ignores the joy of sex,' *TStar*, 20 Jan. 1975

51 Quoted by Candace Bullard et al., 'I Love You, Baby Blue: Two Inside Views,' *York Theatre Journal* 5, no. 2 (Winter 1976), 29. Actor Howard Cooper added sourly that the show 'met with an appropriate end' (p. 34) when it was closed by police.

52 Linda Griffiths, Introd., *Maggie and Pierre* (Vancouver: Talonbooks 1980), 7

53 Wilson, 'Blyth Spirit,' 13

CHAPTER 5 Tarragon Theatre

1 Kareda, 'One Crack Out a daring play,' *TStar*, 26 May 1975
2 Respectively, John Fraser, 'Tarragon, Glassco back in business,' *GM*, 6 Mar. 1976; and Renate Usmiani, *Second Stage: The Alternative Theatre Movement in Canada* (Vancouver: University of British Columbia Press 1983), 28
3 Robert Wallace, 'Growing Pains: Toronto Theatre in the 1970's,' *Canadian Literature* 85 (Summer 1980), 74
4 Interview with Bill Glassco, 29 Nov. 1985. Unattributed quotations from Glassco which follow are taken from the same source.
5 Quoted by Kareda, in 'Academic drop-out puts his all into theatre by the railroad tracks,' *TStar*, 4 Oct. 1971
6 Lee, who later became a celebrated poet, editor, and prime mover of the Rochdale College experiment, was a teaching colleague of Glassco at Victoria College. Hamlin, later a professional director in England, was a Victoria College alumnus and had been resident stage manager at the Crest for its 1963–64 season.
7 Kareda, 'Winter's Tale is midsummer madness,' *TStar*, 19 July 1968
8 This stability continued under Patricia Carroll Brown, who was artistic director of the Harlequin Players at the Red Barn, 1963–66.
9 Whittaker, O'Keefe adopts airline standby system,' *GM*, 6 Apr. 1970
10 Glassco directed *The Hypochondriac*, *Lovers*, *The Late Christopher Bean*, *Rope*, and *The Owl and the Pussycat*. Other productions were *Barefoot in the Park* and *Fallen Angels* directed by Lawrence Ewashen, and a double-bill, *The Private Ear* and *Black Comedy* directed by Brian Meeson.
11 Cohen, 'Act of Violence quite lamentable,' *TStar*, 6 Aug. 1970
12 Quoted by Joseph Erdelyi, in 'Theatrical miracle worker believes in Canadian drama,' *Citizen* [Ottawa], 6 Apr. 1974
13 Bill Glassco, Introd., *The Tarragon Theatre Cookbook* (Toronto: Tarragon Theatre 1982), 7. Stuart left Toronto shortly afterwards and later became chief justice of the Yukon.
14 Interview, 6 Jan. 1986
15 DuBarry Campau, 'Home for Irish, Canadian drama,' *Tele*, 17 Sept. 1971
16 Undated press release, datestamped 27 Sept. 1971, on the microfiche 'Tarragon Theatre – History,' MTL
17 Hendry, 'Sudden Explosion,' 25
18 Kareda, 'New theatre's first production beyond praise,' *TStar*, 6 Oct. 1971. See also Whittaker, 'Creeps excellent starter for Tarragon Theatre,' *GM*, 6 Oct. 1971
19 Respectively, Whittaker, 'Cabbage town [*sic*] Plays: low-key Tipes,' *GM*, 30

Dec. 1971; and Kareda, 'Tarragon Theatre gives playwright first-rate assist,' *TStar*, 30 Dec. 1971

20 Kareda, 'See No Evil, Hear keeps shifting but finally stuns,' *TStar*, 10 Feb. 1972

21 Kareda, 'Play's sharp jokes contrast with foggy language,' *TStar*, 16 Mar. 1972

22 Quoted by C. Eileen Thalenberg and David McCaughna, in 'Shaping the Word: Guy Sprung and Bill Glassco,' CTR 26 (Spring 1980), 37. This article contains a useful review of the collaboration between Glassco and French. French describes how he came to write *Leaving Home* in Anthony, ed., *Stage Voices*, 233–50.

23 Kareda, 'Characters imprisoned in new Tarragon play,' *TStar*, 11 Oct. 1972. More charitable reviews appeared in the other two Toronto dailies. Incidentally, Benner later wrote and directed one of Canada's most acclaimed feature films, *Outrageous* (1977).

24 Whittaker, 'Forever Yours offers some familiar novelty,' GM, 15 Nov. 1972

25 Undated press release and handout, in the file 'Tarragon Theatre – Publicity,' MTL

26 Kareda, 'The Stag King: A handsome fantasy-farce-fairy tale,' *TStar*, 22 Dec. 1972

27 Tarragon newsletter, dated March 1973, in the file 'Tarragon Theatre – Publicity,' MTL

28 Freeman, quoted in Anthony, ed., *Stage Voices*, 265. The inception and development of each of Freeman's plays is described here, pp. 251–74.

29 Brian Boru, 'Onstage: Voyeurism of spiritual nakedness,' *That's Showbusiness*, 7 Mar. 1973

30 Tarragon newsletter, March 1973

31 Undated press release, in the file 'Tarragon Theatre – Publicity,' MTL

32 See Whittaker, 'Quiet Day in Belfast travels a worn path,' GM, 10 May 1973; and Kareda, 'Quiet Day in Belfast: Well-organized success,' *TStar*, 10 May 1973. Glassco himself later recalled the play as too commercial for Tarragon (in Ray Conlogue, 'The Glassco era,' GM, 3 Oct. 1981).

33 Not surprisingly, Brian Boru was a notable exception: see 'A blight in Strawberry Fields,' *That's Showbusiness*, 31 Oct. 1973.

34 Letter from Ross Woodman, GM, 5 Dec. 1973, p. 7. See also Kareda, 'It's just plain overwhelming,' *TStar*, 26 Nov. 1973; Whittaker, 'Donnellys: legend celebrated,' GM, 26 Nov. 1973; and Whittaker, 'Canada's own Greek tragedy,' GM, 27 Nov. 1973.

35 Whittaker, 'Blitzkrieg elusive bit of whimsy,' GM, 21 Feb. 1974. See also Kareda, 'A star shines in witty play,' *TStar*, 18 Feb. 1974.

36 Kareda, 'Shimmering production at Tarragon Theatre,' *TStar*, 16 May 1974
37 Kareda, 'Canada's new playwrights.' The others were *Creeps* and *Leaving Home*.
38 Kareda, 'Director Bill Glassco seeks new challenges,' *TStar*, 26 Apr. 1974
39 'Writers given chance at Tarragon Theatre,' *TStar*, 14 Aug. 1974
40 Kareda, 'Tarragon program helps playwrights to develop,' *TStar*, 21 June 1975
41 The minimum salary was still very low, $125 per week rather than $65.
42 Joseph Erdelyi, 'The Donnellys triumph again,' *Citizen* [Ottawa], 23 Nov. 1974
43 Quoted by Sid Adilman, in 'Tarragon Theatre's budget can't keep up with success,' *TStar*, 6 Dec. 1974
44 David Billington, 'Canada Council ignores our best stage,' *Gazette* [Montreal], 17 Dec. 1974
45 They were the Richard Ivey Foundation of London, the Laidlaw Foundation of Toronto, and John Labatt Limited. The Ivey grant was specifically to finance the workshops required for *Handcuffs*.
46 Respectively, Whittaker, 'Bonjour La, Bonjour a fascinating creation,' GM, 3 Feb. 1975; and Kareda, 'Cast stranded in new play lacking reality,' *TStar*, 3 Feb. 1975
47 See Thalenberg and McCaughna, 'Shaping the Word,' 43
48 Press release, on the microfiche 'Tarragon Theatre – History,' MTL
49 Quoted, respectively, by David Billington, in 'Tarragon's not quitting just taking a year's rest,' *Spectator* [Hamilton, Ont.], 11 Mar. 1975; and by Sid Adilman, in 'Local theatre won't produce next season,' *TStar*, 12 Mar. 1975
50 Quoted by Kareda, in 'Director needs time to restore his creative energy,' *TStar*, 15 Mar. 1975
51 Kareda, 'Canada's new playwrights.' Tarragon also figured prominently in a subsequent *New York Times* article on new Canadian drama, Henry Popkin's 'Canadian theater is enjoying a "naissance",' 15 Jan. 1978.
52 Anne Montagnes, 'The passionate alternate: Bill Glassco's Tarragon,' *Performing Arts in Canada* 14, no. 3 (Fall 1977), 36
53 Quoted by Conlogue, in 'The Glassco era'
54 Kareda, 'Canada's new playwrights'
55 One indication of this is the annual Dora Mavor Moore awards for theatre in Toronto, for which Tarragon received more nominations than any other company in both 1985 and 1986.

CHAPTER 6 Toronto Free Theatre

1 Quoted in Robert Wallace and Cynthia Zimmerman, eds., *The Work:*

Conversations with English-Canadian Playwrights (Toronto: Coach House 1982), 344

2 Quoted by Kareda, in 'Alternative theatre offers hope for the future,' *TStar*, 16 Sept. 1972

3 Quoted in Wallace and Zimmerman, eds., *The Work*, 175–6

4 Quoted by Tom Hendry, in 'Toronto Free Theatre,' *Toronto Citizen*, 27 Jan. 1972, p. 13. The *Citizen* was a community newspaper of downtown Toronto, particularly of the Annex neighbourhood, published biweekly from 1970 to 1974.

5 Press release of the Stratford Festival, 14 Apr. 1969 on the microfiche file 'Tom Hendry', MTL

6 Quoted by Tom Hendry, interview, 8 Aug. 1985

7 The team of Silverman and Hendry later appeared as composer and lyricist of the musical *Dr. Selavy's Magic Theater*, which ran off-Broadway for four months during 1972–73.

8 Interview, 8 Aug. 1985

9 The Festival press release for this occasion, dated 31 Aug. 1970, contained its president's comment that 'Mr. Hendry brought a fresh viewpoint which we have appreciated greatly.' Press releases on such occasions can be admired for their dry ambiguity.

10 The other three were Carol Bolt, David Gardner, and Jack Gray.

11 See, for instance, his article 'The Natives Are Restless,' *Performing Arts in Canada* 8, no. 4 (Winter 1971), 30–1.

12 Whittaker, '1971 saw Canadian theatre's greatest leap forward,' *GM*, 1 Jan. 1972

13 Press release, dated 18 Jan. 1972, to be found in the archives of the Canadian Stage Company

14 Quoted by Myron Galloway, in 'The work paid off,' *Montreal Star*, 22 Jan. 1977

15 Quoted by Tom Hendry, in 'Toronto Free Theatre Is Off and Running,' *Centre Stage Magazine* 2, no. 5 (Jan./Feb. 1977), 24. During the 1976–77 season, this house magazine of the Royal Alexandra Theatre carried a series on Toronto's small theatres.

16 Quoted by Hendry, in 'Toronto Free Theatre'

17 Whittaker, 'Inaugural play shows few worthwhile flashes,' *GM*, 21 June 1972

18 Interview, 8 Aug. 1985

19 Kareda, 'Walking Wounded works in a way despite trashiness,' *TStar*, 21 June 1972

20 Whittaker, 'Hope: an amiable but aimless comedy,' *GM*, 30 June 1972

21 Kareda, 'Orphan Annie meets the Munsters,' *TStar*, 4 July 1972

22 Whittaker, 'Palmer almost fulfills promise with off-beat sex farce, The End,' *GM*, 14 Aug. 1972

23 Kareda, 'Alternative theatre offers hope'
24 William Lane, Introd., *Me?* (Toronto: Coach House [1975], 7
25 Respectively, David McCaughna, 'Me?' *Toronto Citizen*, 18 May 1973, p. 12; Kareda, 'Play explores versatility of theatre,' *TStar*, 30 Apr. 1973; and DuBarry Campau, 'Nary a dropped stitch in Tarragon play,' *Toronto Sun*, 15 May 1973
26 TFT 1, no. 2 (n.d. [June 1973]), to be found in the archives of the Canadian Stage Company
27 Kareda, 'Clear Light revolts, horrifies, succeeds,' *TStar*, 22 Oct. 1973
28 Quoted by Kareda, in 'Horrific play must be done director says,' *TStar*, 9 Oct. 1973
29 Quoted in Wallace and Zimmerman, eds., *The Work*, 189
30 Whittaker, 'Clear Light morality squad's meat?' *GM*, 22 Oct. 1973
31 Patrick Sheppard, letter to Laura Legge, Q.C., 12 Nov. 1973: I am indebted to Martin Kinch for providing me with a copy of this letter, which clearly explains the sequence of meetings which led to the closing of the play.
32 Kareda, 'Traditions fail in gloomy week for theatre,' *TStar*, 3 Nov. 1973. Kareda's use of the first person is indicative of his own strong identification with Toronto's alternative theatres.
33 See Tom Slater, 'Censorship versus the theatre,' *TStar*, 11 Jan. 1974.
34 Hendry later claimed that the closing damaged the financial backing of the company. However, it seems more likely that the scandal, rather than the closing, would have been responsible for a decline in private donations.
35 Interview, 8 Aug. 1985. He used the same phrase in an interview with Ray Conlogue, *GM*, 20 Mar. 1982. While Hendry's explanation became the theatre's 'official' position, it seems unlikely that he would not have known that Jaffe (for instance) was an American deserter. Another position sometimes reported, but not true, is that Kinch decided to close the show rather than make cuts demanded by the morality squad.
36 It is curious, for instance, that CTR's special issue on 'Obscenity and the Theatre' (*CTR* 13, Winter 1977) analyses official suppression of modern drama in America and in Canada, both in general and in reference to particular productions, yet makes no mention of *Clear Light*.
37 Reviewed, for instance, by Kareda, 'Free Theatre's Red Emma a wonderful, disciplined play,' *TStar*, 21 Feb. 1974; and Whittaker, 'Red Emma a bouncy little musical,' *GM*, 25 Feb. 1974. The health problems which plagued the Free are described by Kareda, 'Laryngitis hits star[;] opening postponed,' *TStar*, 8 Feb. 1974. Before the incident with Chapelle Jaffe, there had been two such incidents involving Brenda Donohue and one with William Webster.

38 Untitled promotional brochure, n.d. [1974], in the file 'Toronto Free Theatre – Publicity,' MTL

39 Kareda, 'This is where Billy really belongs,' *TStar*, 31 Oct. 1974

40 Whittaker, 'Billy the Kid: a legend skinned alive,' *GM*, 31 Oct. 1974

41 Kareda, 'Playwright's talent gets overheated,' *TStar*, 3 Apr. 1975

42 Whittaker, 'Heat tawdry but fascinating chiller,' *GM*, 3 Apr. 1975

43 Quoted by Kareda, in 'Young director sees his position as slightly absurd,' *TStar*, 29 Mar. 1975

44 Quoted by John Fraser, in 'The revolution's over in underground theatre,' *GM*, 27 Sept. 1975

45 John Fraser, 'Byron an egotistical drama of stupendous tedium,' *GM*, 22 Apr. 1976

46 Gina Mallet, 'One-liner is a three-act flop,' *TStar*, 22 Apr. 1976

47 Gina Mallet and David McCaughna, 'Free Theatre leaps into the bigtime,' *TStar*, 30 Dec. 1976. Several other small theatres were also trying to provide larger, more comfortable places for their audiences: see Sandra Souchotte, 'Toronto's Baby Building Boom,' *CTR* 21 (Winter 1979), 35–46.

48 Quoted, respectively, by Salem Alaton and Ray Conlogue, in 'TFT, CentreStage merger is announced,' *GM*, 16 Apr. 1986; and Mallet and McCaughna, in 'Free Theatre leaps'

CHAPTER 7 The Off-Yonge-Street Theatres

1 Whittaker, 'The current influence is Off-Broadway,' *GM*, 20 Nov. 1969. Whittaker's examples show that he means 'off-off-Broadway,' and that he does not distinguish between the two New York movements.

2 Interview, 12 Nov. 1986

3 The physical participation of young audiences is most closely identified with the work of British educator Brian Way, who has had an enormous effect on creative dramatics and children's theatre in this country. See, for instance, Joyce Doolittle, *A Mirror of Our Dreams* (Vancouver: Talonbooks 1979), 88–9, 98–117; and Joyce Doolittle, 'A Canadian Perspective,' *CTR* 10 (Spring 1976), 8–11.

4 Respectively, Ron Evans, 'Theatre for kids,' *Tele*, 24 Oct. 1966; and George Anthony, 'Oedipus Rex a la Mod,' *Tele*, 28 Oct. 1966

5 Don Rubin, 'At best, The Beard is actually good fun,' *TStar*, 22 Feb. 1969

6 Cohen, 'The Beard withdrawn over Futz publicity,' *TStar*, 13 Mar. 1969

7 Cohen, 'Revised Dionysus more provoking than provocative,' *TStar*, 2 Nov. 1970. Cohen adds that this opinion, originally expressed in 'Dionysus in '69 has its regulars' (*TStar*, 25 Mar. 1970), 'elicited a lengthy, petulant letter to the editor (unpublished) from Schechner.'

8 Whittaker, 'Dionysus to close after 7-month run,' *GM*, 30 Apr. 1970

9 Quoted by DuBarry Campau, in 'The author likes Dionysus '69,' *Tele*, 28 Feb. 1970

10 According to Daniel Stoffman, 'A theatre's problem: So successful that grants are hard to get,' *TStar*, 14 Nov. 1970. The quotation which follows is from the same source.

11 Quoted by Cohen, in 'Dionysus has its regulars.' See also Whittaker, 'Studio Lab Theatre: a stepchild when they hand out the grants?' *GM*, 23 Jan. 1971.

12 Whittaker, 'Lack of sense of style marks The Brothers' opening,' *GM*, 30 Jan. 1971. True Davidson, a well-known figure in municipal politics, was mayor of East York.

13 Whittaker, 'Dr. Knock has endearing touches, but its satire lacks direction,' *GM*, 27 Dec. 1972

14 According to Frank Rasky, 'Global Village Theatre finds a new life,' *TStar*, 9 Oct. 1975

15 Quoted by Randy Brown, in 'Pianist's day "surrounded by beauty,"' *TStar*, 3 Feb. 1985. Biographical material on the Swerdlows is taken from personal interviews, and from files on the Global Village Theatre, MTL

16 Quoted by Merle Shain, in 'Stony broke but Global Village goes on,' *Tele*, 1 Aug. 1969

17 Respectively, Ralph Hicklin, 'Blue SA left me equally angry and unhappy,' *Tele*, 19 June 1969; and Don Rubin, 'Blue ballet makes for a blue evening,' *TStar*, 19 June 1969

18 Merle Shain, 'The art of female impersonating,' *Tele*, 24 July 1969. *Facad* was devised and directed by Michael Oscars, who later became an important talent agent in Toronto.

19 Quoted in 'Dateline Entertainment: Money crisis may close Global Village,' *TStar*, 25 Oct. 1969. See also Shain, 'Stony broke.'

20 Respectively, Lanny Salsberg, 'What's new,' *TStar*, 20 Feb. 1970; and Cohen, 'The Charlottetown Festival puzzle,' *TStar*, 5 Feb. 1970

21 Cohen, 'Notes brought on by fit of remorse,' *TStar*, 6 Mar. 1970

22 Cohen, 'Musical Justine Global Village hit,' *TStar*, 1 June 1970

23 Respectively, Don Rubin, 'Heart's a Wonder and Spring Thaw shows lost $60,000,' *TStar*, 19 Apr. 1971; and Howie Bateman, letter to the editor, *TStar*, 26 Apr. 1971, p. 7

24 Quoted by Jeniva Berger, in 'Despite hard knocks, Swerdlow shows he's got staying power,' *Canadian Jewish News*, 8 Dec. 1972

25 Whittaker, 'Swerdlow's Rats: a self-indulgent musical about a musical,' *GM*, 27 Nov. 1972

26 Sandra Souchotte, 'Global Village Revisited,' *Scene Changes* 2, no. 11 (Dec. 1974), 14

27 Kareda, 'There's something pathetic about Cosmic Jack musical,' *TStar*, 6 Mar. 1975
28 Quoted by Brown, in 'Pianist's day.' The quotations which follow are from the same source.
29 According to David McCaughna, 'Louis Capson's Creation 2,' *Scene Changes* 3, no. 5 (May 1975), 10
30 Quoted by Linda Bohnen, in 'Sermons on life in form of drama,' *GM*, 12 July 1969. See also Merle Shain, 'They want you to be involved,' *Tele*, 23 Aug. 1969.
31 Undated pamphlet entitled 'Creation 2,' apparently produced in the spring or summer of 1971, in the file 'Creation 2 – Publicity,' MTL
32 Kareda, 'Acting remarkable in a bold powerful play,' *TStar*, 5 Jan. 1972
33 Elie Lalancette, 'Harsh view of separation reflects misunderstanding,' *Montreal Star*, 10 Aug. 1972
34 Quoted by Gina Mallet, in 'Rebel director takes a gamble,' *TStar*, 22 Sept. 1976
35 Respectively, John Fraser, 'Ego-drenched insult to Richard III drags Creation 2 to all-time low,' *GM*, 16 June 1977; and Forster Freed, letter to the editor, *GM*, 21 June 1977, p. 6
36 Kareda, 'Acting remarkable'
37 Kareda, 'Midway Priest: Quite depressing,' *TStar*, 10 Nov. 1972
38 Whittaker, 'Inventive work excludes audience,' *GM*, 11 May 1973

CHAPTER 8 The Second Wave

1 Greg Leach, 'The "second wave" rides Canadian theatre crest,' *That's Showbusiness*, 7 Apr. 1976
2 Whittaker, 'Masque of Wilde much improved with third production,' *GM*, 29 Oct. 1971; see also Whittaker, 'New young group at St. Lawrence,' *GM*, 13 Oct. 1971. A casting curiosity is that this production featured Liza Creighton and Lyn Griffin, who appeared later that season in *Leaving Home* at Tarragon.
3 Finances were so tight, according to Herbert Whittaker in a friendly report ('Fully planned season a luxury for company,' *GM*, 14 Nov. 1974) that New Theatre had to sell its switchboard. But this story Stanley denies absolutely in private correspondence with the author, saying that this company never owned a switchboard.
4 Whittaker, 'Actors capture essence of Storey's haunting Home,' *GM*, 6 Nov. 1974. See also Kareda, '4 actors quit New Theatre play,' *TStar*, 8 Oct. 1974.
5 Respectively, Kareda, 'Young People's Theatre to play London in July,'

TStar, 26 Mar. 1975; and Kareda, 'New Theatre makes mileage,' *TStar*, 7 Apr. 1975. For a description of the rehearsal process, see Whittaker, 'Probing actors run risk of thin ice,' *GM*, 7 Apr. 1975.

6 To be found in the file 'New Theatre – Publicity', MTL

7 Arnold Edinborough, 'New Theatre leads way in public-private financing,' *Financial Post*, 23 April 1977

8 Gina Mallet, 'Too much too soon just raises yawns,' *TStar*, 28 Apr. 1977

9 According to Bryan Johnson, 'Whelan meets the challenge of taking his own advice,' *GM*, 11 Nov. 1978. Biographical details are also taken from a brochure entitled 'Open Circle Theatre Community Workshops,' in the file 'Open Circle Theatre – Publicity,' MTL

10 Whittaker, 'Good Lord: children emote too,' *GM*, 3 Apr. 1973

11 Kareda, 'No Way, Jose just too tame,' *TStar*, 6 Apr. 1973

12 This information is contained in a brief sent to Alderman Ying Hope, 26 June 1973, in the file 'Open Circle – Publicity,' MTL.

13 Quoted by Whittaker, in 'Good Lord.' Indeed, the title of their next production was even changed to *The Island Show* in later publicity releases.

14 David McCaughna, 'Company with everything but money,' *Toronto Citizen*, 29 Mar. 1974

15 Kareda, 'One small theatre's survival a hopeful sign for others with dreams,' *TStar*, 9 Oct. 1974

16 John Fraser, 'Play with a cause a test of theatre's courage,' *GM*, 28 Feb. 1976

17 Michael Macina, 'Horovitz in Toronto,' *Toronto Theatre Review* 1, no. 2 (Apr. 1977), 3

18 See Bryan Johnson, 'High-toned adland hype is selling theatre tickets,' *GM*, 8 Oct. 1977; and Ray Conlogue, 'Little theatres try to get out of wilderness,' *GM*, 15 Aug 1977.

19 Quoted by Ray Conlogue, in 'Tucker gets the sparkle back,' *GM*, 7 Mar. 1980

20 See Ray Conlogue, 'The show can't go on: Open Circle closes,' *GM*, 26 Mar. 1982

21 Gina Mallet, 'Open Circle Theatre cancels new show,' *TStar*, 26 Mar. 1982

22 Gina Mallet, 'Phoenix "Butler" all enthusiasm,' *TStar*, 6 Aug. 1976

23 Interview, 1 Dec. 1985

24 Foster continued to operate Menagerie Players until the following summer, when he sold it to a university student for $3000. See Whittaker, 'Amateur groups showing lots of life,' *GM*, 2 Sept. 1975.

25 Monique Sand, 'Phoenix Theatre rises from ashes with brilliant production of "Butley,"' *Scene Changes* 3, no. 5 (May 1975), 8

26 Quoted by Gina Mallet, in 'Theatre thrives on guts and gumption,' *TStar*, 9 Mar. 1977

27 'Backstage,' GM, 14 May 1977
28 Gina Mallet, 'Phoenix recaptures the Restoration,' TStar, 17 Nov. 1978
29 According to Jamie Portman, 'Audiences divided over play,' Citizen [Ottawa], 24 Oct. 1979
30 Conlogue's review appeared on 29 Sept. 1979, McKenzie Porter's in the Sun on 1 Oct. 1979, and the advertisement on 5 Oct. 1979. Harley recalls that the Globe and Mail's editorial staff demanded a number of revisions before they finally agreed to print the advertisement.
31 Quoted by Stephen Godfrey, in 'Curtain comes down on ailing Phoenix: Money problems, poor attendance forced shutdown,' GM, 4 Aug. 1983
32 Quoted by Gina Mallet, in 'Man who keeps the Phoenix flying,' TStar, 30 Apr. 1983
33 Quoted by Mallet, in 'Man who keeps the Phoenix flying'
34 Ray Conlogue, 'Company known for independence of artistic director,' GM, 4 Aug. 1983

CHAPTER 9 NDWT

1 Kareda, 'The Donnellys travel on with a new acting group,' TStar, 16 Apr. 1975
2 I am indebted here to Martin Kinch, who gave me copies of several programs from this period.
3 These and other details are taken from Mary Brown's article 'Experiment in Canadian Theatre,' Canadian Literature 31 (Winter 1967). This is the most thorough extant description of Summer Theatre 66.
4 Cohen, 'Keith Turnbull's theatre experiment,' TStar, 8 July 1966. See also Jack Cunningham, 'Author-audience talks at summer festival,' Montreal Star, 6 Aug. 1966.
5 Cohen, 'There are some pluses in Winnipeg situation,' TStar, 20 Feb. 1969. See also 'Good plays a rarity in Canada, says director,' Winnipeg Free Press, 1 Nov. 1968.
6 Quoted in 'Turnbull fired he says,' Tribune [Winnipeg], 22 Apr. 1972, p. 2. Turnbull later described his distaste for boards of directors, acquired during his years at MTC, in Whittaker, 'Director sees danger in boards,' GM, 1 May 1973.
7 Keith Turnbull, 'Reaney and I,' Newsletter [Neptune Theatre] 1 (Dec. 1972), 2, in the file 'Neptune Theatre – Publicity,' MTL
8 Quoted by Keith Turnbull, audiotape, 1986. A copy of this tape, which Mr Turnbull made in response to my preliminary draft of this chapter, is deposited with the NDWT collection, University of Guelph Theatre Archives.
9 Whittaker, 'More about those legendary Donnellys,' GM, 18 Nov. 1974

10 Kareda, 'The Donnelly trilogy comes to a rousing close,' *TStar*, 31 Mar. 1975
11 James Reaney, *14 Barrels from Sea to Sea* (Erin, Ontario: Press Porcepic 1977), 173
12 Quoted by Margaret Daly, in 'Director stages grand finale for Donnelly plays,' *TStar*, 8 Dec. 1975
13 In the file 'NDWT – Publicity,' MTL
14 *Annual Report of the NDWT Company, 1976–1977*, in the file 'NDWT – Publicity,' MTL
15 Patricia Ludwick, 'Souvenirs of a Northern Ontario Tour,' *Northward Journal* 13 (1979), 83–5
16 'NDWT closes down,' *TStar*, 7 Feb. 1982
17 Kareda, 'The Donnelly trilogy comes to a rousing close'

CHAPTER 10 Making Myths

1 Quoted in Wallace and Zimmerman, eds., *The Work*, 344
2 Quoted by Robert Wallace, in 'Paul Thompson at Theatre Passe-Muraille: Bits and Pieces,' *Open Letter* 2nd ser., no. 7 (Winter 1974), 70
3 Robert Wallace, Introd., *The Work*, 14
4 Gass, 'Changing Realities,' 133. Incidentally, while this article is a very important retrospective on Toronto's alternative theatre, it makes two points which are apparently untrue: that the prevalent term for these theatres was *Alternate*, and that the term was coined by Tom Hendry.
5 Gina Mallet, quoted by Annette Snowdon and Mary Kelly, in 'Critics: The Last Word,' *Scene Changes* 8, no. 1 (Mar. 1980), 8
6 Quoted in 'The Star criticized on drama reviews,' *TStar*, 25 June 1976
7 Gina Mallet, 'A look back at eight years on the aisle,' *TStar*, 7 July 1984
8 Fraser, 'The revolution's over'
9 Respectively, Gass, 'Changing Realities,' and Tom Hendry, 'Theatre: How Now Bureaucratic Cow,' *Toronto Life*, Dec. 1978
10 Ronald Bryden, 'Toronto Theatre: Mademoiselle est partie,' *Canadian Forum* 58, no. 683 (Aug. 1978), 7
11 Kinch, 'Long Haul,' 6
12 Quoted in Wallace and Zimmerman, eds., *The Work*, 344–5

Selected Bibliography

My primary source of information has been the Performing Arts Files of the Theatre Department (subsequently the Arts Department) in the Metropolitan Toronto Library. A list of other important archival collections is given in the Preface, along with a list of people interviewed during the course of my research for this work. Besides the daily newspapers cited, the following periodicals have proven invaluable: *Canadian Theatre Review, Performing Arts in Canada, Scene Changes, The Stage in Canada, That's Showbusiness,* and *Toronto Theatre Review.*

There have not been many books published in this field. However, the following list contains important background material to the period, as well as a few overview articles about Toronto's alternative theatres. For anyone planning a closer study, a more extensive bibliography may be found in my PHD thesis, copies of which are deposited at the Metropolitan Toronto Library, the University of Toronto, and several other universities in Canada.

Adelman, Howard. *The Beds of Academe.* Toronto: James Lewis and Samuel 1969
— and Dennis Lee, eds. *The University Game.* Toronto: Anansi 1968
Anthony, Geraldine, ed. *Stage Voices.* Toronto: Doubleday 1978
Arnott, Brian. 'The Passe-Muraille Alternative.' In *The Human Elements.* Ed. David Helwig. [Ottawa:] Oberon Press 1978
Benson, Eugene, and L.W. Conolly, eds. *The Oxford Companion to Canadian Theatre.* Toronto: Oxford University Press 1989
Brake, Mike. *The Sociology of Youth Culture and Youth Subcultures.* London: Routledge and Kegan Paul 1980
Brissenden, Connie. 'Canadian Plays Produced Professionally in Toronto during the 1960's.' MA thesis, University of Alberta, 1971

Bryden, Ronald. 'Toronto Theatre: Mademoiselle est partie.' *Canadian Forum* 58, no. 683 (Aug. 1978), 6–11
– and Boyd Neil, eds. *Whittaker's Theatre*. Greenbank, Ont.: The Whittaker Project 1985
Chambers, Colin. *Other Spaces*. London: Eyre Methuen 1980
Cohen, Nathan. 'A look at theatre in Toronto: The pace-setters fall behind.' *Toronto Star*, 5 Dec. 1970
Conlogue, Ray. 'Little theatres try to get out of wilderness.' *Globe and Mail*, 15 Aug. 1977
Edmonstone, Wayne. *Nathan Cohen: The Making of a Critic*. Toronto: Lester and Orpen, 1977
Filewod, Alan Douglas. *Collective Encounters: Documentary Theatre in English Canada*. Toronto: University of Toronto Press 1987
Fraser, John. 'The revolution's over in underground theatre.' *Globe and Mail*, 27 Sept. 1975
Gass, Ken. Introduction. *The Factory Lab Anthology*. Vancouver: Talonbooks 1974
– 'Toronto's Alternates: Changing Realities.' *Canadian Theatre Review* 21 (Winter 1979), 127–34
Gray, John. Introduction. *Billy Bishop Goes to War*. Vancouver: Talonbooks 1981
– Introduction and Prefaces. *Local Boy Makes Good: Three Musicals by John Gray*. Vancouver: Talonbooks 1987
Hendry, Tom. 'The Natives Are Restless.' *Performing Arts in Canada* 8, no. 4 (Winter 1971), 30–1
– 'The Canadian Theatre's Sudden Explosion.' *Saturday Night* 87, no. 1 (Jan. 1972), 23–8
Johns, Ted, and Paul Thompson. Introduction. *The Farm Show*. Toronto: Coach House 1976
– 'The Trial of Baby Blue.' *Canadian Theatre Review* 13 (Winter 1977), 7–17
Johnston, Denis W. 'Playwrights and Collectives at Theatre Passe Muraille: An Historical Review.' *Canadian Drama* 15, no. 1 (1989), 63–74
Kareda, Urjo. Introduction. *Leaving Home*. By David French. Toronto: New Press 1972
– 'Alternative theatre offers hope for the future.' *Toronto Star*, 16 Sept. 1972
– 'Canada's new playwrights have found a home at home.' *New York Times*, 24 Nov. 1974
Kinch, Martin. 'Canadian Theatre: In for the Long Haul.' *This Magazine* 10, nos. 5–6 (Nov.–Dec. 1976), 3–8
Lane, William. Introduction. *Me?* By Martin Kinch. Toronto: Coach House [1975]

Lee, Betty. 'Can these directors come up with an answer?' *Globe Magazine* [*Globe and Mail*], 21 Feb. 1970, pp. 14–15

Ludwick, Patricia. 'Souvenirs of a Northern Ontario Tour.' *Northward Journal* 13 (1979), 83–7

Mann, W.E., ed. *The Underside of Toronto*. Toronto: McClelland and Stewart 1970

[Moore, Mavor, ed.] *The Awkward Stage: The Ontario Theatre Study Report*. Toronto: Methuen 1969

Ondaatje, Michael, dir. *The Clinton Special*. Mongrel Films 1974

Palmer, John. 'Canadian Playwright Crisis: The Twelfth Hour.' *Performing Arts in Canada* 8, no.3 (Fall 1971), 6–8

Poland, Albert, and Bruce Mailman, eds. *The Off Off Broadway Book*. Indianapolis: Bobbs-Merrill 1972

Popkin, Henry. 'Canadian theater is enjoying a "naissance."' *New York Times*, 15 Jan. 1978

Reaney, James. *14 Barrels from Sea to Sea*. Erin, Ont.: Press Porcepic 1977

– et al. 'Wacousta Workshop.' In James Reaney, *Wacousta!* Toronto: Press Porcepic 1979, 107–59

Rubin, Don. 'Experimental theatre.' *Star Week* [*Toronto Star*], 25 Sept. 1971, pp. 2–6

– 'Creeping toward a Culture: The Theatre in English Canada since 1945.' *Canadian Theatre Review* 1 (Winter 1974), 6–21

– 'Sleepy Tunes in Toronto.' *Canadian Theatre Review* 20 (Fall 1978), 93–5

– 'The Toronto Movement.' *Canadian Theatre Review* 38 (Fall 1983), 8–17

Salutin, Rick. Preface to '1837: The Farmers' Revolt.' In *1837: William Lyon Mackenzie and the Canadian Revolution*. Toronto: James Lorimer 1976

Shank, Theodore. *American Alternative Theatre*. New York: Grove 1982

Souchottte, Sandra. 'Toronto's Baby Building Boom.' *Canadian Theatre Review* 21 (Winter 1979), 35–46

Usmiani, Renate. *Second Stage: The Alternative Theatre Movement in Canada*. Vancouver: University of British Columbia Press 1983

Wallace, Robert. 'Growing Pains: Toronto Theatre in the 1970's.' *Canadian Literature* 85 (Summer 1980), 71–85

– and Cynthia Zimmerman, eds. *The Work: Conversations with English-Canadian Playwrights*. Toronto: Coach House 1982

Whittaker, Herbert. 'The Theatre.' In *Culture of Contemporary Canada*. Ed. Julian Park. Ithaca: Cornell University Press 1957

– 'The Alternate Theatre in Toronto.' *The Stage in Canada* 7, no. 1 (Sept. 1972), 6–9

Picture Credits
and Sources

TWP archives, courtesy Dr Neil Carson: TWP's original production of
Hey, Rube! (1961); Ludvik Dittrich: Dermer and Weiss in *Memories for My Brother*
(1969); Lionel Douglas: Jim Garrard; Lionel Douglas, courtesy of the Arts
Department, Metropolitan Library: *Doukhobors* (1971); Harry McLorinan / *Globe
and Mail*, courtesy of the Arts Department, Metropolitan Toronto Library:
interior of the original Theatre Passe Muraille at Trinity Square; Arts Depart-
ment, Metropolitan Toronto Library: *Dionysus in 69* at the Studio Lab (1969–70),
Anglin and Thompson in *Out to Breakfast* (1971), Paul Thompson in front of
Theatre Passe Muraille, Factory Theatre Lab over the Lonsdale Garage on
Dupont Street, *Creeps* at the Tarragon Theatre (1971), Swerdlow, MacDonald,
and the company of *Rats*; Hugh Travers: *Hair* at the Royal Alex (1970); Erik
Christensen / *Globe and Mail*: New Directors Group; Michel Lambeth: John
Palmer directing *Me?* (1973), Hendry and Vallières (1973); Michel Lambeth,
courtesy Canadian Stage Company: Mancuso, Webster, and Brymer in *Clear
Light* (1973); Robert Barnett: James Reaney's Donnelly trilogy at Tarragon
Theatre, Glassco directing Henshaw and Hamilton in *Bonjour Là Bonjour* (1975);
Robert Barnett, courtesy Tarragon Archives, University of Guelph: Richard
Monette in *Hosanna* (1974)

Index

productions at Passe Muraille 66,
70, 112–14, 119–38; on Toronto
Free 172
Thomson, R. H. 224, 234
Three Musketeers, The (Raby) 241
Three Sisters, The (Chekhov) 241
Tipe, David 151, 159
To Covet Honour (McEnaney) 83
Tom Paine (Foster) 30, 31; at Rochdale College 37–8, 54, 57; at
Trinity Square 63–4, 67, 111,
177, 202
Toman, Adolf 221, 222
Tooth of Crime, The (Shepard) 222
Toronto, City of 12, 16, 70, 257
Toronto Actors' Studio 232
Toronto Arts Foundation 12, 15–
16, 98
Toronto Arts Productions (TAP) 16,
58, 154, 159, 169, 177, 178,
196. *See also* Canadian Stage Company, CentreStage, St Lawrence
Centre, Toronto Arts Foundation
Toronto Centre for the Arts 232
Toronto Dance Theatre 23, 98, 207
Toronto Drama Bench 98
Toronto Free Theatre 170–96; after 1975 194–6, 249, 257;
founding of 4, 27, 62, 90, 170–3,
176–82, 242: goals of 170–3,
176–7, 186, 195–6; influence
of 27, 172–3, 250; name of
171–2, 179, 221; and other alternative theatres 98, 99, 170,
225, 249; policy of free admission 91, 171, 180, 181, 184,
186, 191; productions 1972–75
182–93, 258; style 63, 155,
172–3; theatre on Berkeley

Street 180, 184, 194–5. *See also
Clear Light*; Hendry, Tom; Jaffe,
Shain; Kinch, Martin; Palmer,
John
Toronto Globe and Mail 25, 58, 69,
161, 233, 234, 253; Fraser
at 194, 216, 229, 253; Whittaker
at 23–4, 193, 253
Toronto Islands 71, 227, 229
Toronto Pixie Caper (Theatre Passe
Muraille) 128
Toronto Star 42, 45, 62, 72, 163;
Cohen at 24–5, 90, 151; Kareda at 25, 90, 102, 151, 183–4,
253; Mallet at 194, 253–4
Toronto Sun 26, 234
Toronto Telegram 19, 26, 42
Toronto Theatre Festival (1981) 72,
235
Toronto Theatre-Go-Round 221
Toronto Workshop Productions
18–23; influence of 23, 74,
203; and other alternative theatres 23, 40, 138, 169, 199, 228;
people who worked at 38, 116,
226; theatre on Alexander
Street 15, 21, 22, 127, 169; theatre
at Colonnade 20, 222. *See also*
Faulkner, June; *Hey, Rube!*;
Luscombe, George; Winter,
Jack
Touch of God in the Golden Age, A
(Palmer) 90–1, 177, 178
Towards a Poor Theatre
(Grotowski) 30
Town Hall. *See* St Lawrence Centre,
Town Hall in
Transistor (Davis) 239
Transmission (Swerdlow) 209–10